DEPRESSIVE ILLNESS

DEPRESSIVE ILLNESS
Some Research Studies

Edited by

BRIAN DAVIES
BERNARD J. CARROLL
ROBERT M. MOWBRAY

Department of Psychiatry
University of Melbourne
Royal Melbourne Hospital
Melbourne, Victoria

CHARLES C THOMAS · PUBLISHER
Springfield · Illinois · U.S.A.

Published and Distributed Throughout the World by

CHARLES C THOMAS • PUBLISHER

BANNERSTONE HOUSE

301-327 East Lawrence Avenue, Springfield, Illinois, U.S.A.

NATCHEZ PLANTATION HOUSE

735 North Atlantic Boulevard, Fort Lauderdale, Florida, U.S.A.

© 1972, by CHARLES C THOMAS • PUBLISHER

ISBN 0-398-02268-2

Library of Congress Catalog Card Number: 70-187650

With THOMAS BOOKS *careful attention is given to all details of
manufacturing and design. It is the Publisher's desire to present books
that are satisfactory as to their physical qualities and artistic possibilities
and appropriate for their particular use.* THOMAS BOOKS *will be true
to those laws of quality that assure a good name and good will.*

Printed in the United States of America

C-1

CONTRIBUTORS

TIMOTHY G. BLASHKI, M.A.N.Z.C.P.

Research Fellow
University Department of Psychiatry
Royal Melbourne Hospital
Victoria, Australia

BERNARD J. CARROLL, Ph.D., D.P.M., M.A.N.Z.C.P.

Senior Research Fellow
National Health and Medical Research Council of Australia
University Department of Psychiatry
Royal Melbourne Hospital
Victoria, Australia

BRIAN DAVIES, M.D., F.R.C.P., F.R.A.C.P., F.A.N.Z.C.P., D.P.M., D.C.H.

Cato Professor of Psychiatry
University of Melbourne
Royal Melbourne Hospital
Victoria, Australia

MARGARET F. McLEOD, Ph.D.

Former Research Biochemist
University Department of Psychiatry
Royal Melbourne Hospital
Victoria, Australia

WILLIAM R. McLEOD, M.D., M.A.N.Z.C.P., D.P.M.

Associate Professor
Department of Psychiatry
University of Auckland
Auckland, New Zealand
Former Consultant Psychiatrist
Mental Health Authority
Victoria, Australia

v

ROBERT M. MOWBRAY, Ph.D., F.B.Ps.S., F.A.Ps.S.

Professor of Clinical Psychology
Memorial University
St. John's
Newfoundland, Canada
Former Reader in Medical Psychology
Department of Psychiatry
University of Melbourne
Victoria, Australia

PREFACE

THIS monograph describes clinical investigations into depressive illnesses. All have been carried out by the authors as members of the University of Melbourne's Department of Psychiatry. The studies include biochemical, endocrine and therapeutic studies on severely depressed patients in hospital and clinical and therapeutic studies on depressed patients in general practice. In addition there is an important study by Professor R. M. Mowbray that presents a factor analysis of the Hamilton Depression Rating Scale, on data from severely ill hospital patients and mildly ill general practice patients.

The major part of the monograph details studies of the hypothalamic-pituitary-adrenal axis that have been carried out by Dr. B. J. Carroll, who is the major contributor to the monograph. Reversible abnormalities in the feedback control of the adrenal cortex have been found in some depressed patients as shown by their response to dexamethasone. The clinical associations of this phenomenon are detailed and its implications discussed.

Studies of the 5-hydroxy-indoleacetic acid concentrations in the cerebrospinal fluid are described by Dr. W. McLeod and they suggest that some severely depressed patients show abnormalities. The possible implications of this finding are discussed.

Two therapeutic trials are described, one a sequential trial of electroconvulsive therapy and l-tryptophan in severely depressed patients, and one a controlled trial of amitriptylline in general practice. In both instances special emphasis is placed on the methodology of the trials.

While some of the results obtained and presented in this monograph have been published elsewhere, presentation here in more detail along with other related studies (done very often on the same patients) seems worthwhile on two counts. First, the preparation of the monograph has enabled us to put our own results into perspective and to define further research goals and needs. Second, we hope it will encourage replication of our studies.

Clinically orientated psychiatric research is at the stage when centers produce interesting results that sometimes fail to be replicated in another center. Chapters 8, 9, 10 and 14 replicate reported studies done elsewhere. In all instances, methodological improvements were made. Chapter 9 deals with the supposed antidepressant effects of l-tryptophan but the original findings were not confirmed. Final conclusions about indoleamine concentration, and radioactive sodium entry in the cerebrospinal fluid (Chaps. 8 and 10) in depression seem premature. Unfortunately the conclusions from the original reports have been widely quoted in the psychiatric literature as if they were already "facts" about which theories could and have been built.

The main studies in this monograph by Dr. B. J. Carroll, on the hypothalamic-pituitary-adrenal axis have been described in some detail so that replication can be made elsewhere, but again improved methods of testing the hypothalamic-pituitary-adrenal axis are now possible and should be incorporated in the new work. Only when a rigorous methodology is used and results can be replicated, can we accept that we have facts in this field.

This monograph aims to describe clinical research studies in depression in such a way that replication can occur at other centers, so that some agreement can be reached about what are the facts in biological studies of depression.

BRIAN DAVIES

ACKNOWLEDGMENTS

WE are grateful to the Residents, Sisters and Nurses in the Psychiatric Ward of the Royal Melbourne Hospital and the Parkville Psychiatric Unit for their continuous help with these clinical studies.

We would like to thank our Laboratory Technicians, especially Elizabeth Horton and Barbara Heath for their help with the investigations. Sylvia Fraser, Ann Jeffery and Elisabeth Cant deserve special mention for typing the several drafts of the manuscript.

Finally we would like to thank our patients who have been seen regularly for many years. Without their cooperation these clinical studies would not have been possible.

CONTENTS

DEPRESSIVE ILLNESS

Section I

Introduction and Patients Studied

Chapter 1

AN INTRODUCTION TO BIOLOGICAL RESEARCH STUDIES OF DEPRESSION AND MANIA

BRIAN DAVIES

RESEARCH studies on depressed and manic patients now form a significant part of the content of present-day psychiatric journals and conferences. This chapter presents an account, for the general reader, of how biological research in this field has developed. Complex problems have been deliberately simplified in order to provide an overview of the field, and at the end of the chapter, references are given to more detailed review articles.

Although it is difficult to define precisely, "mood" is a useful descriptive term, which refers to a certain feeling tone. Under usual conditions this feeling tone is consistent and stable, but changes in mood may occur and be experienced as "the blues" or conversely as feeling particularly well and active. These minor changes in mood, which last for a few hours or for a few days, are usually, but not always, associated with personal problems or with environmental changes. In women, menstruation is often accompanied by such minor mood changes. When the changes in mood persist and are more marked, certain symptoms can be observed to accompany the mood change. A persistently lowered or depressed mood is the most common form of mood disorder. Early *depressive symptoms* seem "physical," such as sleep disturbances, tiredness, loss of appetite and of weight, but mental symptoms, feelings of guilt, inability to concentrate, loss of interest and morbid worrying thoughts soon develop. Such depressive symptoms are a common *secondary* feature of many physical and psychiatric illnesses, and their relief in these conditions may be of great benefit to the patient.

With *primary* mood disorders, the fundamental feature is the mood change, and there are no other associated illnesses.

5

This form of illness has been recognized throughout the history of medicine. The early Greek physicians described it as melancholia, attributing its origins to an accumulation of black bile. *It is these primary depressive disorders that are the focus of the research studies to be described.*

There is a very wide range in the *severity* of such depressive symptoms. Most patients have mild symptoms which are usually of short duration and are often associated with some special problem in the patient's life circumstances. These symptoms are so frequent that they have been called the "common cold" of psychiatry! Certainly patients with mild depressive symptoms form a large part of the family doctor's daily practice. Most of these patients respond well to the doctor's care and interest. If tablets are given, then improvement in some 65 per cent of patients can be found with inert tablets alone.

Psychiatrists see the less common patients with severe or chronic depressive symptoms. Such patients often feel that life is not worth living and they may have made suicidal attempts. Severe symptoms can last for weeks, months or even one or two years, but usually a complete remission will occur.

In addition to *spontaneous remission* it has been recognized for centuries that the natural history of mood disorders involves *recurrence* of illness. Some patients tend to get recurring episodes of depression throughout their life. In other patients depressive symptoms may be followed by a persistently elevated mood—*mania* when patients are overactive, talkative and euphoric. Their sleep is disturbed, and sexual interests and behavior may increase. Less commonly, some patients show their mood disorder as recurrent attacks of manic symptoms, which again remit spontaneously, usually over the course of some months.

Psychiatrists are not in agreement on how to label these illnesses of mood; one review showed that thirty-eight classificatory systems of depression were currently in use! However, comparisons of signs and symptoms, the natural history, responses to treatment and more recent metabolic studies suggest that these illnesses of mood are probably a heterogeneous group of conditions. The depressive or manic syndrome can be likened to the heart failure or renal failure syndromes of general medicine, where similar clinical presentations may arise from different fundamental etiological factors.

It is often useful for clinical management to decide if the patient's depressive illness is *endogenous,* i.e. arises out of some unknown constitutional background and cannot be related to current life problems; or *reactive,* where the patient's present symptoms can be understood in terms of a particular personality's response to particular life problems. Such "reactive" symptoms usually respond to environmental changes. Some psychiatrists emphasize the value of such a dichotomy while others do not find it useful.

Recently in research studies particular attention has been paid to *unipolar* mood disorders, i.e. patients who have attacks of *only* depression or mania and *bipolar* mood disorders, where patients have histories of attacks of both depressed and elevated mood. This whole problem of types of depression is discussed fully in Chapter 11.

The growth of biological research into depression and mania is closely linked with the discovery of effective physical methods of treatment. The most effective treatment for severe depression, *convulsive treatment,* was discovered in 1934 by Von Meduna. At first these convulsions were induced chemically, but in 1938 Cerletti and Bini produced them electrically. Electroconvulsive therapy (ECT) produces striking and dramatic relief of symptoms in most severely depressed patients. This discovery stimulated a good deal of research work in the 1940s, but no fundamental hypothesis about the mode of action of convulsive treatment was derived. Even now the mode of action of ECT has not been clearly shown, because ways of studying the biological effects of this treatment in the living brain of a depressed patient are not available. Thus, although it is an effective treatment, ECT has not led to new ways of studying the nature of mood disorder.

Historically the discovery of the antimanic properties of the *lithium* ion by Cade in Melbourne in 1949 should have been the start of present-day research, yet only in recent years has the fundamental significance of this finding been appreciated. It was, in fact, the description of depression occurring in patients being treated with *reserpine* for hypertension in the early 1950's that gave the impetus to present-day biologically based research into mood disorders. Some 10 to 20 per cent of patients treated with reserpine develop depressive symptoms and some suicides were reported. These observations were the prelude to the present-day approach to the biological basis of mood disorders. Their importance lay in the fact that pharmacologists were able to successfully investigate the mode of action of reserpine.

In 1957 Carlsson and his co-workers showed that reserpine depletes all body cells of certain monoamines—namely the *catecholamines:* noradrenaline (NA) and dopamine (DA); and *indoleamine* 5 hydroxytryptamine (5 HT), serotonin. The behavioral changes observed in reserpinized animals became used as an animal model of depression. Although pharmacologists differ in evaluating the evidence about the relative importance of *specific* catecholamine or serotonin depletion, the relationship between changes in brain monoamines and depression became a useful heuristic hypothesis. At the same time methodological advances began to provide a more complete picture of the occurrence, distribution, synthesis, storage, functional role and degradative pathways of these amines in the brain.

Studies by histochemical fluorescence have shown that DA, NA and 5 HT neurons exist in the central nervous system. These monoamines are stored in granules within certain nerve cells, are released at the synapses in an active form by nervous stimulation, and are then inactivated by enzymes. They occur in different parts of the brain in different amounts. DA is found in large amounts in the basal ganglia while NA and 5 HT are present in high concentrations in the hypothalamus and limbic systems.

Another important clinical observation was made in 1951, when eighty-two patients with chronic tuberculosis were being treated with a new antibiotic—*iproniazid* (Marsalid®). Dramatic improvements occurred, but were also found in patients with advanced cancer, who were given the drug. The effects of this drug on the mental state were obviously important, and in 1956, Crane described his observations on the effects of iproniazid—the first antidepressant drug. It was known that iproniazid was an inhibitor of the enzyme *monoamine oxidase,* which is concerned with the breakdown of both catechol and indoleamines, and since this time, other monoamine oxidase inhibitors have been developed for use as antidepressant drugs.

Imipramine (Tofranil®) was originally introduced as a tranquilizing drug, but in 1957 Kuhn showed that this iminodibenzyl derivative was not a tranquilizer but an antidepressant, though it is not a monoamine oxidase inhibitor. Today this, and related tricyclic compounds, are the drugs most frequently prescribed for depression.

In practice it has been found that clinical improvement does not begin for some 10 to 21 days after starting these tricyclic compounds. This is of considerable practical and theoretical interest. Recent animal studies have shown that there is a gradual alteration in the turnover of brain norepinephrine during three-week administration of imipramine. When thyroid hormone is given with imipramine, clinical antidepressant effects occur more rapidly than with imipramine alone. In animals the noradrenalin turnover changes occur more rapidly. These pharmacological clues may be important in future research.

Therefore, in 1957 there was one drug (reserpine) that could cause depression in some patients. Two drugs, iproniazid (a monoamine oxidase inhibitor) and imipramine, that could relieve depression in some patients, and a simple substance (lithium) that had a specific effect in most manic patients. *The original clinical observations on these four drugs were unexpected, serendipitous and not predictable, but they provided the important clues for research into mood disorders.*

It is not possible to detail the vast volume of research into the mode of action of these compounds. Papers have ranged widely from fundamental studies of the biochemistry of brain functioning and the development of new laboratory techniques, to studies on the clinical use of these drugs. Here special attention has to be paid to the large number of patients who respond to nondrug factors, i.e. the interaction between doctor and patient and his environment. Because of this, the use of double-blind studies with comparisons of active and inert medications and reliable measures of change are an essential part of present-day clinical psychopharmacology.

In 1959 Jacobsen first defined what has become known as the

catecholamine hypothesis of mood disorders. Schildkraut clearly states the hypothesis:

> That some, if not all, depressions are associated with an absolute or relative deficiency of catecholamines, particularly noradrenaline, at functionally important adrenergic receptor sites in the brain. Elation, conversely, may be associated with an excess of such amines."

This hypothesis has guided many research studies on depression and mania, especially in the United States, though it suggests a bipolarity of depression and mania that is not proven. The results of animal experiments defining the metabolic pathways of brain monoamines have been especially important in providing basic information which could then be applied in clinical investigations.

Many of these studies originally concentrated on complex urinary analyses for catechol metabolites, in an attempt to find abnormalities that could be related to the catecholamine hypothesis. Unfortunately such urinary metabolites, in the main, reflect peripheral catechol metabolism and do not serve as a guide to brain metabolism, since brain noradrenaline cannot pass the brain-blood barrier. However, one particular metabolite, 3-methoxy-4-hydroxy-phenlyglycol (MHPG) is derived from brain noradrenaline metabolism, and a lowered excretion of this substance has been reported in depressed patients.

One way of testing the catecholamine hypothesis would be to experimentally raise the levels of catechols in the brain and thus relieve depression or to lower the levels in mania with chemical blocking agents and produce improvement. The amino acid *l-dopa* crosses the blood-brain barrier and increases the content of brain NA and DA. The use of this substance has now been shown to be a major advance in the treatment of Parkinson's disease, where low DA levels are found in the extrapyramidal system. In their studies on depressed patients, Bunney and Goodwin at the National Institute of Mental Health, have shown that l-dopa is an antidepressant for some patients who show retardation but that it has no such action in other depressed patients who show agitation. In some of these experiments they combined l-dopa and a decarboxylase inhibitor to prevent breakdown of the monoamine in the periphery. The same group have also tested the catecholamine hypothesis experimentally by lowering the levels of brain catechols in manic patients. They found that an inhibitor of catecholamine synthesis, alpha-methyl-para-tyrosine, was therapeutically effective in five of seven manic patients and produced increasing depression in three depressed patients.

Such *complex metabolic studies* have a methodology that has become refined over the years. They depend upon relating metabolic findings to changes in clinical state. The metabolic findings must in the first place be unrelated to diet, drugs and activity, and behavioral ratings must be reliable and valid. These principles, that can be defined in a sentence, take many years of work to perfect in clinical practice in the longitudinal study of disturbed patients. The replication of results obtained by these studies in one center are still difficult yet are a definite need in this field, e.g. the results from NIMH summarized above depend upon an analysis of a particular rating scale completed daily by trained skilled nurses.

European workers have tended to focus more interest on disturbances of indoleamine metabolism in affective disorders. Measurements of the levels of the 5 HT metabolite, 5 hydroxy-indoleacetic acid (5 HIAA) in the cerebrospinal fluid of depressed and manic patients led to the claim that lowered CSF 5 HIAA was specific to depression, but conflicting results have been reported. More recently, attention has been focused on 5 HIAA levels in CSF after the patient has received probenecid. This substance inhibits the transport of 5 HIAA from brain to blood and the rate of rise of 5 HIAA in CSF then provides an index of 5 HT turnover rate. Recent studies suggest that some depressed patients show differences in CSF 5 HIAA levels after probenecid blocking.

Biochemical studies of *suicide victims* have received attention, and the few studies reported have found a low 5 HT and 5 HIAA concentration in suicide brain tissues compared with controls who died a sudden but natural death. The problems of assays and the effects of previously taken drugs on brain monoamine levels are important ones that are not clearly resolved yet.

A precursor of 5 HT, l-tryptophan, has been used in depressed patients, but there is no convincing evidence that it has antidepressant qualities. Parachlorphenylalanine, an inhibitor of 5 HT synthesis, used in the treatment of the carcinoid syndrome, has produced severe psychiatric symptoms that include sleep disturbance and depression in some of the few patients so treated.

The evidence from these studies is suggestive (but perhaps not conclusive to the professional skeptic) that in some severely depressed and manic patients, disturbances in cerebral monoamines are found. The monoamine hypothesis has had a great heuristic value in stimulating and guiding research. It is not a final statement. It should be appreciated that fundamental to the catecholamine hypothesis is the notion that NA is a cerebral excitant. In fact experimental physiology has shown that NA (and DA) are inhibitors of cortical neurones, so that the notion that NA produces a state of cerebral arousal is still speculative. In different parts of the brain 5 HT neuron stimulation produces different effects and again it cannot be said that such stimulation produces arousal.

Other evidence suggests that these hypotheses are too simple. Firstly, amphetamine is a vigorous stimulant of central NA activity, but is not of use clinically as an antidepressant. Secondly, the actual ability of the drug to inhibit monoamine oxidase (MAO) is not related to its clinical antidepressant action. Finally the lack of response of some depressed patients to antidepressants despite (presumably) biochemical brain changes having occurred, and the subsequent successful therapeutic effects of a few ECT are still unexplained by these hypotheses. The relationship of another psychiatric syndrome, schizophrenia, to changed metabolism of cerebral monoamines is another problem that has been the subject of much research and speculation.

These studies that have been reviewed have been concerned with showing a direct relationship between brain monoamines and mood change. Other research areas have developed and interesting findings have been reported.

The first concerns disturbances in *water and electrolytes* in mood disorders. The studies have been many, and not all are in agreement. Some point to changes in intracellular sodium in both depression and mania. Such changes in mineral metabolism have been linked with the so-called premenstrual syndrome and also suggest a possible mode of action of lithium. However, the need in this field is replication of original observations with a closer scrutiny of methodology and control procedures. More and more research recently has been devoted to lithium and how it works in mania. Its possible modes of action include effects on electrolytes, endocrines and cerebral monoamines. Schou and his colleagues in Denmark have claimed that lithium given continuously prevents recurrences of depressive and manic attacks. Such continuous treatment needs strict control, but appears, at this stage, to be an important advance in treatment, since recurrences of depression and mania are a real problem. Its mode of action in this situation is not clear.

Since the early part of the century there has been speculation about the *endocrine basis* for some psychiatric disorders. Research in this field has concentrated on the pituitary adrenal system and mood disorders. The clinical observations that depression and suicide are prominent features of Cushing's syndrome, and the mood changes produced by cortisone and ACTH administration, give a clinical basis for the many studies in this area. Since this field is to be reviewed in a succeeding chapter, only the conclusion need be given here that some severely depressed patients do show abnormal results when subjected to a number of tests of hypothalamic pituitary adrenal function. Such changes seem restricted to psychiatric patients with depression. The most convincing evidence of this is the raised levels of free cortisol in the CSF of some depressed patients, associated, in the same patient, with abnormal tests of hypothalamic function.

Depressive symptoms are frequent in the premenstrual period, after childbirth and at menopause. In addition, the development of such symptoms in some 10 per cent of women on the contraceptive pill have shown that some important relationship exists between ovarian hormones and disorders of mood. The effects of such hormones on the adrenal glands, brain steroids and brain monoamines are important present-day research studies.

Abnormalities in *enzyme systems,* perhaps concerned with

monoamine synthesis and breakdown have been suggested as causal factors in mood disorders. To date there is little evidence to support this hypothesis. More recently attention has been focused on adenosine 3' 5' cyclic monophosphate (cyclic AMP). This substance is present in cells throughout the body and acts as a substrate for many enzyme and hormonal actions. Changes in urinary excretion of this compound in depression and mania have been reported, that have led to more basic work on the factors that regulate its excretion by the kidneys.

The problems of assessing subtle biochemical changes in the living human brain are central to this whole story. It is perhaps surprising to find that studies of *sleep* and *dreaming* have yielded one method of studying brain metabolism. The studies on sleep have shown that there are two major phases of sleep: rapid eye movement sleep (REM) and nonrapid eye movement sleep (non-REM). Animal research has provided evidence that catecholamines are associated with REM and 5 HT with non-REM sleep. In man 5 HT seems to be involved with REM sleep. Studies of sleep in psychiatric patients are now a current interest in research in this field. The effects of psychotropic drugs on NA and 5 HT systems in the brain can be studied by analysis of sleep recordings.

CONCLUSION

The newcomer to this field will not be able to appreciate the impetus given to studies of depression by the chance drug findings described earlier. The complex problems inherent in clinical psychiatric studies have led to a sophistication of methods and techniques that study, on the one hand, a patient's feelings and behavior, and on the other, several physiological variables. It is true to say that today, findings reported from one center cannot always be repeated elsewhere and it is still difficult to be able to define operationally a patient sample of "depression" so that other centers can study what appear to be similar patients. It is realized soo, that patients so studied are usually severely ill patients who somehow get into research units and who are not representative of "depression" as it occurs in the community. Consequently, generalizations from such samples have to be drawn with caution. Despite all these drawbacks and problems, these recent research studies of depression and mania have been of great importance. In particular they have produced, in many countries, teams of biologically orientated psychiatrists and co-workers who attempt to define what they are doing so that replication elsewhere is possible. Psychiatry has taken a long time to get to such a stage, and only now are we at its beginning.

SUGGESTED READINGS

General Review of Mania and Depression

Winokur, G., Clayton, P.J. and Reich, T.: *Manic Depressive Illness.* St. Louis, C.V. Mosby Co., 1969.

Drugs and Mood Disorders

Efron, D.H. and Kety, S.S.: Anti-depressant drugs of the non-monoamine oxidase inhibitor type. Proceedings of a Workshop, National Institute of Mental Health, 1966.

Pletscher, A.: Pharmacology of monoamine oxidase inhibitors. In Marks, J. and Pare, C.M.B. (Eds.) : *Scientific Basis of Drug Therapy in Psychiatry.* Oxford, Pergamon Press, 1965.

Schildkraut, J.J.: *Neuropsychopharmacology and the Affective Disorders.* Boston, Little, Brown and Co., 1969.

Electrolytes and Mood Disorders

Gibbons, J.L.: Electrolytes and depressive illness. *Postgrad Med,* 39:19, 1963.

Endocrines and Mood Disorders

Gibbons, J.L.: Endocrine changes in depressive illness. *Proc Roy Soc Med,* 58:519, 1965.

Michael, R.P. and Gibbons, J.L.: Inter-relationships between the endocrine system and neuropsychiatry. *Int Rev Neurobiol,* 5:243, 1963.

Monoamines and Mood Disorders

Bunney, W.E. and Davis, J.M.: Norepinephrine in depressive reactions. *Arch Gen Psychiat,* 13:483, 1965.

Praag, H.M. van: Indoleamines and the central nervous system. *Psychiat Neurol Neurochir,* 73:9, 1970.

Schildkraut, J.J.: The catecholamine hypothesis of affective disorders: a review of supporting evidence. *Amer J Psychiat,* 122:509, 1965.

Schildkraut, J.J. and Kety, S.S.: Biogenic amines and emotion. *Science,* 156:21, 1967.

General Review Articles of Research Studies

Coppen, A.: The biochemistry of affective disorders. *Brit J Psychiat,* 113: 1237, 1967.

Davies, B.: Recent studies of severe depressive illnesses. *Med J Aust,* 1:487-491, 557-565, 1969.

Dewhurst, W.G.: Cerebral amine functions in health and disease. In Shepherd, M. and Davis, D.L. (Eds.) : *Studies in Psychiatry.* London, Oxford Medical Publication, 1968.

Chapter 2

PATIENTS AND METHODS OF STUDY

BRIAN DAVIES

IN clinical research in psychiatry it is important to define the
patient population and the selection of patients actually
studied. There is evidence that age, sex and social class of the
patient can influence phenomenology and responses to treatment.

The patients studied in the investigations that are described
in the following chapters were admitted under the care of the
University of Melbourne's Department of Psychiatry. There are
two clinical facilities of the department that need to be described separately.

Within the Psychiatric Ward of the *Royal Melbourne Hospital* (660 bed general teaching hospital) are 14 beds where patients are admitted under the care of the author. Patients are
public patients and are all admitted informally. They are mainly skilled, semi-skilled or unskilled workers or their wives. Patients are admitted over the age of sixteen and are usually referred either from the Casualty Department, from the outpatient clinics or directly from a general practitioner or psychiatrist.

Parkville Psychiatric Unit (P.P.U.) is a psychiatric unit for
informal inpatients and day patients and is a joint venture of
the Victorian State Psychiatric Services (Mental Health Authority) and the University of Melbourne. It is about two miles
from the Royal Melbourne Hospital. Twelve of the thirty-two
beds were used by patients in some of the studies reported in
this book. Patients admitted to this unit are from the same social classes as at the general hospital but are usually less severely
ill. Admissions to this unit come from outpatient clinics, general practitioners or psychiatrists or from the Royal Melbourne
Hospital.

At both units there is undergraduate and postgraduate training and there is a low nurse/patient ratio. As time went by, many colleagues began referring depressed patients to the units, because of our known research interests.

SELECTION OF PATIENTS

Only patients with a *primary* depressive illness were selected for the clinical studies described. Most had been ill for between one and six months. Such patients had a depressed mood and showed features of agitation, retardation, self reproach and feelings of guilt, inability to concentrate, loss of interest, difficulty in sleeping, loss of appetite and weight and suicidal thoughts. Somatic symptoms were prominent in some patients. A few had had previous manic episodes.

After the usual detailed history-taking (from patients and relatives) and physical examination a provisional diagnosis was made at the teaching round between five and seven days after admission. *Consecutive patients whose symptoms persisted for this time were considered for the research studies.* No patients with schizophrenia, or organic brain syndromes, or alcoholism with secondary depressive symptoms were included in the studies. There was no upper age limit if patients had clear-cut depressive disorders.

No attempt was made to separate these depressive disorders any further but in the usual terms, patients at the general hospital would be classified as mainly endogenous and severe while, at the other unit the majority were reactive and mixed depressive disorders. Those in the general hospital had a mean age of about 60 years, while those at the P.P.U. were aged about 40. At any one time between two or six patients in each unit would be depressed patients being studied by the methods described. In the same wards other nondepressed patients with other psychiatric syndromes were used as controls for some of the studies.

All patients admitted to both units were withdrawn from medication on admission. In the early studies sodium amylobarbitone (200 mg) was allowed as a hypnotic and as required, in smaller dosage during the day to deal with agitation. Later it was possible to manage most patients without drugs until specific anti-depressive treatment was started. At the general hospital this was usually electroconvulsive treatment, since most patients were severely ill. At the Parkville Unit, many of the moderately depressed patients were treated with anti-depressants, usually imipramine or amitriptyline. No dietary controls were enforced at either unit.

Patients at both units were under the care of the author. Some of the investigations were done only at the Royal Melbourne Hospital (e.g. the radioactive sodium transfer into CSF, and the tests of hypothalamic functioning). Other studies (the tryptophan trial and the 5 HIAA in the CSF study) were done in both units.

The Hamilton Rating Scale was completed by one or other of the authors on all patients admitted to the studies. The Taylor Anxiety Scale and Zung Depression Scale were also used routinely.

After discharge from the units, patients were looked after as outpatients by the respective authors.

In summary, patients studied were consecutive middle and lower class patients, with no upper age limit, with primary depressive symptoms admitted as service commitments to two teaching units, all patients being informally admitted. Details are given of the selection and initial management of patients studied.

Section II

The Hypothalamic-Pituitary-Adrenal
Axis in Depression

Chapter 3

THE HYPOTHALAMIC-PITUITARY-ADRENAL AXIS: FUNCTIONS, CONTROL MECHANISMS AND METHODS OF STUDY

Bernard J. Carroll

INTRODUCTION

IN this chapter a brief, orienting account is given of the functional organization of the hypothalamic-pituitary-adrenal cortical (HPA) axis, to provide a background for the work to be described later. The major emphases made in this review concern the following:

1. The *types of control* which the brain exerts on the axis.
2. The role of brain *transmitter agents* in each of these mechanisms.
3. The advantage of *dynamic procedures*—stimulation and suppression tests—over basal measures in the evaluation of HPA activity.
4. The importance of *free cortisol* measurements and their advantage over the traditional laboratory procedures used in psychoendocrine studies.

HYPOTHALAMUS

The HPA axis is the object of intensive psychoendocrine research for a number of theoretical and practical reasons. Among the most important are the *neural connections and functional roles* of the hypothalamus itself.

Through its connections the hypothalamus can be seen as the "nodal point" of several limbic system-midbrain circuits (Nauta, 1963; Livingston and Escobar, 1971) with important relays to the pyriform cortex, amygdala, hippocampus, septal region, cingulate gyrus, entorhinal area, thalamus and midbrain. The

---

Note: Bibliographic references are included at end of Chapter 6.

internal organization of the hypothalamic nuclei is discussed by
Raisman (1966); the connections between the lateral hypothalamus (where most of the external relays are made) and the medial "executive" hypothalamic nuclei are not well understood.

Apart from its endocrine importance two major functions of
the hypothalamus are known, which are pertinent to psychoendocrine studies. These are as follows: a) the regulation of
autonomic activity and b) the integration of appetitive and affective behavior. The *autonomic* functions are well known and
accounts are available in standard works (Hess, 1954; Ingram,
1960). Included in this category are effects of the hypothalamus
on blood pressure, heart rate, temperature regulation, bowel and
bladder control.

Behavioral phenomena dependent in part on hypothalamic
control include affective behavior and instinctive activities of an
appetitive type (eating, drinking, sexual function).

The most prominent affective response mediated by the hypothalamus is that of aggression. *Sham rage* may be induced in
animals by stimulation of the posterior hypothalamus. The syndrome is readily provoked in decorticate cats and can be abolished by hypothalamotomy (see Ingram, 1960 and Kaada, 1967
for detailed references). Fear responses and sexual excitement
may also be seen in these "hypothalamic" animals.

Bilateral destruction of the posterior hypothalamus is followed by complete *loss of emotional responsiveness* in both cats
and monkeys. Their behavior is then characterized by gross inactivity, stolidity, diminished vocalization, expressionless faces
and a tendency to somnolence or catalepsy (Ingram *et al.*, 1936;
Ranson, 1939). Some of these features occur in the retarded
form of depression and in some schizophrenic patients.

The role of the hypothalamus in the *control of pituitary
function* is well established, despite some unresolved details
(see Harris, 1955; Harris and Donovan, 1966; Martini and Ganong, 1966-67). The experimental techniques and strategies
which have established the reality of hypothalamic neurosecre-
tion, the hypothalamohypophyseal vascular portal system and
hypothalamic releasing factors may be found in these reviews.

Anterior pituitary function is controlled by specific hypothalamic releasing factors, which are short polypeptides of mo-

lecular weight 1200 to 2500, like the posterior pituitary hormones. These "hypophyseotrophic principles" are released into the pituitary portal vessels, through which they reach the anterior pituitary, where they stimulate (or, in some cases, inhibit) the release and possibly the synthesis of the various pituitary trophic hormones.

The pituitary hormones, in their turn, act on peripheral organs (e.g. thyroid, adrenal cortex, ovary) to regulate hormone release from these distant sites. Feedback mechanisms, of both a negative and positive type, maintain the integrated functions of the hypothalamic–hypophyseal–end-organ systems (Szentagothai *et al.,* 1968). *Feedback receptors* which respond to alterations in end-organ hormone production have been identified both in the hypothalamus and in extrahypothalamic brain structures. In general, however, the anterior pituitary does not itself contain feedback receptors.

CENTRAL NERVOUS SYSTEM REGULATION OF ACTH RELEASE

Indirect Negative Feedback System

The elements of the feedback system which regulates ACTH and cortisol secretion are shown in Figure 3-1. The system is designated *indirect* because of the role played by the hypothala-

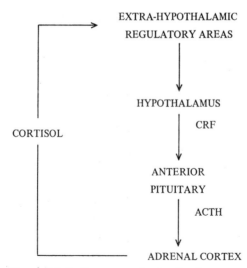

Figure 3-1. Indirect negative feedback system.

mus, i.e. it does not operate simply between the anterior pituitary and adrenal cortex. It is a *negative* feedback system because information signals received at the hypothalamic level result in altered production of corticotropin releasing factor (CRF), adrenocorticotropic hormone (ACTH) and cortisol such that the system remains stable. Thus, falling levels of cortisol in the circulation result in increased secretion of CRF, followed by ACTH secretion and finally of cortisol from the adrenal cortex, to restore the plasma cortisol levels. Similarly, high levels of plasma cortisol result in decreased adrenocortical stimulation by a reduction in CRF and ACTH release. Synthetic glucocorticoids can substitute for endogenous cortisol in the feedback system (see Yates *et al.*, 1969).

No consistent evidence supports the concept of a direct negative feedback effect of glucocorticoids at the anterior pituitary level, despite some claims to this effect (Rose and Nelson, 1956; de Wied, 1964). Most workers have established that direct implantations of cortisol or of synthetic glucocorticoids such as dexamethasone (9 alpha-fluoro-16 alpha-methyl prednisolone) into the pituitary do not affect ACTH secretion. Implants into the hypothalamus, especially the median eminence region, do inhibit ACTH release under basal and stress conditions (see Mangili *et al.*, 1966 for detailed references), although a dissociation between inhibition of basal secretion and inhibition of stress responses commonly occurs.

Hypothalamic Receptor Areas

Apart from the steroid implant studies which implicate the anteromedial hypothalamus and the median eminence, *direct microelectrode confirmation* of steroid-sensitive hypothalamic sites has now been obtained.

Micro-iontophoresis of dexamethasone inhibited the firing rates of single neurones in the periventricular grey area of the hypothalamus, and also in the periaqueductal region of the midbrain (Ruf and Steiner, 1967). Adrenalectomy changed the pattern of firing and increased the spontaneous discharge rate of anterior hypothalamic neurones (Dafny and Feldman, 1970). The same authors observed that cortisol itself increased the firing rate of anterior-tuberal hypothalamic neurons; following sensory stimulation the discharge rates increased in control rats but decreased in cortisol-treated animals (Feldman and Dafny, 1970).

Extra-Hypothalamic Receptor Areas

A number of brain regions, which connect with the hypothalamus, have been shown to contain glucocorticoid receptor areas and to modify HPA function.

Injections and implants of cortisol into the *reticular formation of the midbrain* reduce the corticosteroid production of the adrenal gland in both cats and rats (Enzroczi *et al.*, 1961) while midbrain lesions can interfere with HPA feedback responses (Szentagothai, 1958; Moll, 1959; Martini *et al.*, 1960). The effects of cortisol implants in the midbrain on adrenal steroid production vary according to the time of day. The diurnal variation of plasma steroid levels is abolished (Slusher, 1966), an observation which implicates the midbrain in the control of the adrenal circadian rhythm. Neurones in the periaqueductal region of the midbrain alter their firing rates in response to microelectrophoretic applications of dexamethasone (Ruf and Steiner, 1967).

Several areas of the *limbic system* have also been identified as glucocorticoid receptor regions. Cortisone implants in the *amygdala* of the rat inhibit corticosterone secretion under basal conditions and also in response to stress (Zimmermann and Critchlow, 1969). *Hippocampal* implants, on the other hand, cause an increased adrenal response to stress (Knigge, 1966; McHugh and Smith, 1966). Cortisol implants in the hippocampus also obliterate the diurnal rhythm of plasma corticosterone levels in rats (Slusher, 1966). Depth electrode recordings from the amygdaloid nucleus show reduced activity following parenteral corticosteroid administration (Kawakami *et al.*, 1966). A similar effect was observed in the midbrain reticular formation and the anterior hypothalamus; in the dorsal hippocampus EEG activation was seen.

Stress-induced secretion of ACTH has been blocked by steroid implants in the *septal region* and in the *anterior thalamus* by Dallman and Yates (1968) who regard these sites as important feedback modulators.

PROPERTIES OF STEROID RECEPTORS IN BRAIN

Experiments with isotopically labeled corticosterone in rats have shown that the hormone (which is the major glucocorticoid in this species) quickly enters all parts of the brain. In most regions a rapid clearance and metabolism of the hormone follows, so that after two hours less than 10 per cent of the original amount remains. In the hypothalamus and limbic areas, however, *selective retention* of corticosterone occurs, and the rate of metabolism is less than in the rest of the brain (Eik-Nes and Brizzee, 1965; McEwen *et al.*, 1968; Zarrow *et al.*, 1968). The septum and hippocampus in particular retain corticosterone for long periods. In the hippocampus McEwen and associates (1970) demonstrated that the labeled hormone was bound chiefly by the neuronal nuclei. Smaller but significant amounts were bound in the nuclei of the preoptic-hypothalamic area, amygdala and cerebral cortex. Nuclear binding of cortisol has also been reported by Fontana *et al.* (1970).

The *chemical nature* of brain glucocorticoid receptors has not been determined but they appear to be *acidic nuclear proteins* (McEwen *et al.*, 1970). The corresponding receptors for estradiol have been characterized as macromolecules, at least in part protein and containing sulfhydryl groups, similar to the estradiol receptors of the uterus (Kahwanago *et al.*, 1969; Eisenfeld, 1969).

"SHORT" FEEDBACK SYSTEM FOR ACTH

In addition to the commonly recognized indirect negative feedback system which involves both ACTH and cortisol, a "short" feedback control system has been identified. In this case the pituitary production of ACTH modulates hypothalamic CRF secretion. Detailed references to the work which underlies this concept will not be given; they may be found in the review of Mess and Martini (1968). The reality of this negative feedback action of ACTH at the hypothalamic level is firmly established and the *receptors* for the short feedback effect of ACTH are associated with several of the cortisol feedback sites—median eminence, amygdala, hippocampus. At these common sites

ACTH and cortisol tend to have complementary actions; for example, in the amygdala, midbrain and hippocampus rising ACTH concentrations cause opposite electrophysiological responses to those caused by rising levels of cortisol, and vice versa. This arrangement emphasizes the importance of the extra-hypothalamic areas for HPA regulation and demonstrates the complexity of the integrating mechanisms for the fine control of ACTH release.

At the present time the clinical significance of this short feedback system is quite unexplored.

POSITIVE FEEDBACK

There is *little experimental evidence* as yet to support the concept of a positive feedback effect of cortisol on ACTH release (or of ACTH on CRF release). Steiner *et al.* (1969) reported that, whereas dexamethasone inhibited and ACTH activated most neuronal units studied in the hypothalamus and midbrain, some neurones were activated by both agents. This finding would be consistent with a positive glucocorticoid feedback effect.

Some authors have *speculated* that such a positive feedback action might occur in a situation such as clinical depressive illness, when the normal CNS response to cortisol is prevented by an abnormality of brain and liver indoleamine metabolism (see e.g. Lapin and Oxenkrug, 1969).

A number of clinical observations support the possibility that positive feedback between circulating glucocorticoids and ACTH release may sometimes occur.

The first such report was from James *et al.* (1965) whose procedure does not appear to have been used by subsequent workers. Using an infusion of dexamethasone (1 mg per hour, intravenously) they found that six of twelve patients with diencephalic Cushing's disease* responded with a significant elevation

---

* Cushing's disease refers to the syndrome of hypercortisolism caused by a primary hypothalamic dysfunction, with adrenal hyperplasia (with or without a pituitary basophil adenoma). Cushing's syndrome is the term appropriate for hypercortisolism from other causes. See James *et al.* (1968a).

of plasma cortisol levels. In all later investigations only the extended dexamethasone suppression regimens of Liddle (1960) have been employed.

Thus, Brooks *et al.* (1966) described a patient with Cushing's disease (adrenocortical hyperplasia) who responded to dexamethasone with an anomalous increase of cortisol metabolites excreted in the urine. A simultaneous increment of plasma ACTH levels could not be demonstrated with the available biological assay procedure. After operation, *in vitro* testing showed that dexamethasone did not directly stimulate steroid production by the excised adrenal tissue.

Similar findings were reported by Linn *et al.* (1967) in a patient with Cushing's disease. The response of ACTH to dexamethasone was not studied in this patient until after bilateral adrenalectomy and pituitary irradiation had been performed. At that time dexamethasone had no effect, but withdrawal of her maintenance cortisol therapy was followed by an increase of plasma ACTH activity.

A paradoxical response to dexamethasone, again in a patient with Cushing's disease, was observed by French *et al.* (1969). In this case a rise in plasma ACTH activity (by bio-assay) was confirmed during the period that urinary 17-hydroxycorticosteroid (17-OHCS), 17-ketogenic steroid (17-KGS) and 17-ketosteroid (17-KS) excretions rose following dexamethasone administration. *In vitro* testing again showed that dexamethasone was not directly stimulating the adrenal cortex. An effect of dexamethasone on adrenal steroid metabolism was excluded by chromatography of urine extracts before and during administration of the drug. The authors concluded that the adrenocortical response to dexamethasone was mediated by ACTH. A pituitary basophil adenoma was present in their patient; the woman studied by Linn *et al.* (1967) had an enlarged pituitary fossa.

Clinically demonstrable pituitary or adrenocortical disease is *not*, however, *essential* for this paradoxical dexamethasone response phenomenon. Two patients studied by Rose *et al.* (1969) showed a rise in urinary 17-OHCS excretion when given 8 mg of dexamethasone daily, as compared with their normal suppression of 17-OHCS excretion while receiving a dose of 2 mg daily. Their 17-OHCS excretions during treatment with the larger dose were not as high as their basal 17-OHCS excretion values; they were, however, greater than the low-dose excretion values by a factor of 4 and 2 respectively. In the second patient this phenomenon was observed on two occasions. Neither patient had abnormal adrenocortical function, as judged by the diurnal rhythm of plasma cortisol and of urinary 17-OHCS and 17-KS, responses to ACTH and to metyrapone or to rapid intravenous dexamethasone; radiographic studies of their adrenal glands were normal. The authors noted that both patients were aggressive, active and apprehensive, with "definite elements of depression," and postulated that the abnormal results could be explained by reference to their subjects' "psychic hyperkinesis."

These observations are consistent with the concept of a positive glucocorticoid feedback effect in man, under conditions where the baseline level of HPA activity is already high. Such a possibility is not only provocative but potentially very important. Further detailed studies of this question can be expected when sensitive radio-immunoassay procedures for plasma ACTH levels become generally available.

EXTRA-HYPOTHALAMIC REGULATORY AREAS

When the hypophysiotrophic area (medial basal hypothalamus) is isolated from all its neural connections in the rat, plasma corticosterone is maintained at a steady, high level, which shows no diurnal variations (Halasz *et al.*, 1967). Areas outside the hypothalamus are required for the integration of HPA activity in response to physiological demands. *The usual influence exerted by the brain on CRF release is inhibitory*, and discrete brain areas have been identified which, when stimulated, inhibit HPA activity. It has further been suggested (see Egdahl, 1968) that the brain might produce an *inhibitory hormone*, opposite in action to CRF, which acts at a pituitary level, since total brain removal of dogs results in sustained adrenocortical hypersection.

In general, the specific brain regions which, when stimulated or lesioned, modify HPA activity are those in which feedback receptors have also been demonstrated (see Mangili, Motta and Martini, 1966; Mess and Martini, 1967, for references to the experimental work).

Amygdala and Hippocampus

Stimulation of the amygdala usually results in increased HPA activity, while hippocampal stimulation is followed by a decrease of adrenocortical secretion, not only in animals but also in man (Mandell *et al.*, 1963; Rubin *et al.*, 1966). Amygdaloid lesions are also associated with impairment of the HPA response to stress. *Functional localization within the amygdala* itself was revealed by Slusher and Hyde (1961) who found that anteromesial amygdaloid stimulation caused HPA activation, while similar stimuli, when applied to the basolateral amygdala had the opposite effect.

The early studies which reported HPA activation after stimulation of the amygdala were conducted over *short periods of time.* It had been assumed that chronic activation of the amygdala would result in chronic elevation of adrenocortical activity. Recently Salcman *et al.* (1970) examined the plasma corticosteroid responses of dogs to amygdaloid stimulation over the course of two and a half to five hours. The *initial rise* in plasma corticosteroid levels was *not maintained* beyond one to two hours although the adrenals were still capable of responding to ACTH, and other, e.g. pupillary effects of amygdaloid stimulation were still present. These results cast some doubt on the "chronic overstimulation of neuronal pools" model as an appropriate concept for the study of neuroendocrine disorders such as Cushing's disease.

Findings such as these illustrate the difficulties involved in attempting to correlate regional neuropharmacological effects with *sustained* alterations of function in the integrated mechanisms which control ACTH release (cf. Lapin and Oxenkrug, 1969).

Midbrain and Pons

The reticular formation (ascending reticular activating system) of the brain stem is established as a center for the tonic inhibition of ACTH release; it is required for the normal HPA response to some, but not all stresses and may be involved in the diurnal variation of HPA activity (see Mangili *et al.*, 1966; Taylor, 1969 for detailed references). Here again, however, lesion studies have revealed that the acute effects do not necessarily persist for long periods (Gibbs, 1969).

TYPES OF C.N.S. CONTROL

From the studies outlined above, three types of CNS control over ACTH release have been recognized.

Negative Feedback

Under conditions which are not stressful, negative feedback can be demonstrated. To account for the increased adrenocortical activity caused by stress it was postulated that afferent stimuli could produce a variable "resetting" of the reference input to the feedback control loop (Yates and Urquhart, 1962). A "discrepancy would then appear between the input signals and the feedback signals, which would be interpreted by the control system as an error signal that resulted in CRF secretion." Improved versions of this "reset hypothesis" were later developed to take account of the experimental findings that pretreatment with cortisol (or one of its equivalents) did not always prevent the HPA activation caused by stress (Dallman and Yates, 1968; Yates *et al.*, 1969).

Recent careful studies in man have now shown that even under basal conditions *the HPA axis does not operate continuously with minute-to-minute feedback control.* Rather, episodic secretion of cortisol occurs, with intervening periods of total adrenocortical quiescence (Hellman *et al.*, 1970). Secretion of cortisol occurred for a total period of only about six hours in the day and over half the daily cortisol production was achieved in the early morning hours during sleep. The plasma cortisol levels at which adrenal secretion "switched on" were variable, and to a lesser extent so were the levels at which "switch off" occurred. For a period of four hours the plasma cortisol level of one subject fell continuously, from about $17\mu g/100$ ml to $2\mu g/100$ mg. with a subsequent rapid restoration to $15\mu g/100$ ml.

This information, which could be obtained only by very frequent sampling and monitoring of the specific activity of plasma cortisol, effectively disposes of the idea that a smooth and constant regulation occurs.

Thus, while negative feedback can be demonstrated under basal conditions by the suppression of HPA activity following glucocorticoid administration (in pharmacological amounts) its importance for the ordinary regulation of plasma cortisol levels must now be reconsidered. The physiological negative feedback system appears to be less responsive to decreases of plasma cortisol levels than it is to increases of the "load" which must be regulated (see Shuster and Williams, 1961; James *et al.*, 1968b).

Response to Stress

Many kinds of noxious stimuli, which may be grouped under the general category of stressors, cause HPA activation. The nonspecific nature of most of the stimuli suggests that afferent collaterals to the brain stem *reticular formation,* rather than direct lemniscal pathways, are important in mediating their common effect (Taylor, 1969). The *limbic areas* involved in HPA regulation are also activated by pain and distress, including emotional stimuli, and act as integrative centers for the adrenocortical response.

Psychological stress is well recognized as a potent stimulus to HPA activation and the range of situations which can provoke a response is very wide; indeed Hamburg (1962) concluded that almost any environmental change which produces an emotional change can increase adrenocortical activity. In general, the adrenocortical response occurs when individuals perceive the *threat of personal injury* (physical or psychological), and constitutes part of the general adaptation reaction (Selye, 1950).

Anticipation of noxious stimulation can cause HPA activation, as shown by the responses of monkeys to conditioned fear and conditioned avoidance procedures (Mason, 1968). Conditioned *suppression* of stress responses has also been observed in rats when feeding was introduced after daily injections (Komaromi and Donhoffer, 1963) but little work has appeared which deals with HPA suppression in man. Hypnosis has been reported to achieve this effect in some subjects (Persky *et al.*, 1959; Sachar *et al.*, 1965; Sachar *et al.*, 1966).

During *prolonged exposure* of animals to stress, *adaptation* can occur (Smookler and Buckley, 1969; Komaromi and Donhoffer, 1963) and a similar habituation is seen in man when control or mastery of the stressful situation is achieved (Rubin *et al.*, 1969).

Other nonspecific variables which modify HPA function include ecological factors, especially population density, social rank in animal colonies, role factors, genetic strain differences, climate, activity cycles and body weight. Detailed references to the vast literature dealing with both animal and human studies may be found in the monograph of Mason (1968) who, in reviewing this subject advanced the following conclusions:

1. Adrenocortical activation is not related to a specific affective state but reflects an undifferentiated state of emotional arousal or involvement, especially in anticipation of an event which is perceived as stressful or threatening.

2. The elements of novelty, uncertainty, unpredictability and frustration of coping attempts are potent stimuli to HPA activation.

3. The quality of the emotional response, the type and effectiveness of psychological defenses against anxiety and the interaction between these defenses and the reality of the situation being defended against are important variables.

4. Significant individual differences occur in the response to a given situation. The multiple determinants of these differences have yet to be clarified.

5. The factors which determine HPA activation in psychopathological states, where emotional disorganization and behavioral breakdown are seen, are essentially the same factors as operate in normal persons under stress.

Until recently the idea that the stress response of psychological disturbance could be resistant to suppression by glucocorticoids was considered unrealistic (James, 1968). The work to be presented later demonstrates that such an effect can be observed in patients with a psychiatric illness.

Diurnal Variation

The third controlling influence which the CNS exerts is concerned with the diurnal variation of HPA activity. The level of HPA function varies in a cyclic fashion over the daily period of twenty-four hours. Other terms applied to this phenomenon are circadian rhythm and nyctohemeral rhythm.

Levels of plasma cortisol in man are usually lowest in the middle of the night, reach a peak at about 6:00 to 8:00 AM and decline gradually during the rest of the day (Migeon *et al.*, 1956). A parallel variation in the excretion of corticosteroid metabolites, first described by Pincus (1943), follows the plasma rhythm by about two hours (Doe *et al.*, 1956; Loras *et al.*, 1970). The excretion pattern of free cortisol in urine is very close to that of 17-OHCS (Vagnucci *et al.*, 1965; Loras *et al.*, 1969), and the rhythm of free cortisol levels in lumbar cerebrospinal fluid also lags behind the plasma cortisol rhythm by about two hours (Uete *et al.*, 1970).

In the many early studies of the diurnal variation of plasma cortisol levels, the blood samples were obtained at infrequent intervals throughout the day, usually every three or four hours. Reference has already been made to the study by Hellman's group which showed that the diurnal plasma cortisol curve is in reality quite uneven. Nevertheless, the bulk of the total daily cortisol secretion occurred early in the morning, when the plasma level was approaching its diurnal peak.

This recent work confirms the earlier studies of Perkoff *et al.* (1959) who excluded change of the rate of removal of cortisol from plasma and change of adrenocortical sensitivity to ACTH as the causes of the rhythm in plasma cortisol levels. They suggested that a *circadian rhythm of ACTH release* from the pituitary was responsible for the plasma cortisol rhythm. Direct estimations of plasma ACTH levels both by biological assay (Ney *et al.*, 1963) and by radio-immunoassay (Berson and Yalow, 1968) have shown that the conclusion of Perkoff's group was correct. The plasma ACTH rhythm is absent in Cushing's disease and during treatment with glucocorticoids. In adrenal hypofunction, however, as in Addison's disease or after adrenalectomy for Cushing's disease, the plasma ACTH rhythm is observed, despite the fact that morning levels are enormously elevated (Retiene *et al.,* 1965; Besser and Landon, 1968).

As predicted, a diurnal variation of hypothalamic CRF content has likewise been shown to underlie the ACTH rhythm (Nelson and Brodish, 1969; Retiene and Schulz, 1970) and this rhythm persists after adrenalectomy (Hiroshige and Sakakura, 1971).

The neural mediation of the diurnal rhythm of HPA activity has thus been established. It is not a fixed, innate rhythm, however, and like some other human circadian rhythms (Mills, 1966) *can be altered* by environmental changes, such as reversal of the daily cycle of activity, i.e. of sleep and wakefulness (Perkoff *et al.,* 1959). The period of the rhythm can be shortened or lengthened experimentally in man to as little as twelve hours or as much as thirty-three hours (Orth *et al.,* 1967). In this respect the HPA rhythm differs from some animal circadian rhythms which may assume a "free running" twenty-four-hour period following a gross disturbance of external circadian signals (Halberg, 1960). Subsequently, Orth and Island (1969) were able to show that the stimulus of light was a more important synchronizing signal than was activity under experimental conditions. In the total absence of light, however, social cues (activity) are effective organizers of the rhythm (Migeon *et al.,* 1956; Aschoff *et al.,* 1971).

In the light of these recent studies the suggestion of Weitzman *et al.* (1966) that the early morning surge of cortisol secretion was related to REM sleep episodes must be reconsidered. It is clear from their subsequent work (Hellman *et al.,* 1970) that there is no episode—for episode relationship between REM periods and cortisol secretion.

The *neural mechanisms* which mediate the circadian rhythm *can be blocked* by centrally-acting drugs which do not, however, interfere with the response of the HPA axis to stress (Krieger *et al.,* 1968). To be effective, the drugs must be given within a critical period before the circadian rise in plasma cortisol is expected.

A *similar diurnal variation in the suppressibility* of the axis by glucocorticoids has also been established (Nichols *et al.*, 1965). Dexamethasone in a dose of 0.5 mg caused prolonged HPA suppression for twenty-four hours when given at midnight, but only partial and temporary suppression was seen following the same dose at 8:00 AM or 4:00 PM. Ceresa *et al.* (1969) obtained similar results with the use of dexamethasone infusions. Doses of 30μg per hour were effective in the early morning period but not between 8:00 AM and midnight. During the day and evening only pharmacological doses (200μg/hr.) were able to lower the rate of urinary 17-OHCS excretion. The authors used the expression "once-a-day neurally stimulated ACTH secretion" to describe the steroid-sensitive mechanism which causes the diurnal rise in HPA activity. *This mechanism is the object of study by the midnight dose dexamethasone suppression tests, and should be distinguished from the basal ACTH secretion mechanisms which operate through the day and evening.*

This diurnal responsiveness of the HPA axis to suppression in the early morning hours is accompanied by a *similar diurnal variation* in the *stimulation* produced by standard procedures such as metyrapone (Jubiz *et al.*, 1970), pyrogen (Takebe *et al.*, 1966) and vasopressin (Clayton *et al.*, 1963). All three are most effective in man in the period preceding the major diurnal release of ACTH, i.e. between midnight and 4:00 AM.

NEUROTRANSMITTERS AND ACTH RELEASE

The control which extra-hypothalamic steroid-sensitive brain areas exert on the release of CRF and ACTH can be mediated only through synaptic connections with neurones in the hypophysiotrophic region of the hypothalamus. Modification of these control mechanisms is possible, therefore, by endogenous or experimental disturbances of synaptic neurotransmitter function. In view of the contemporary importance of the neurotransmitter (monoamine) theory of affective illness it becomes important to consider the relationship between HPA regulation and transmitter functions. It is only in recent years that adequate information about this subject has been obtained, and our understanding of it is still quite limited.

The *anatomy* of cholinergic and monoaminergic synaptic

pathways in the hypothalamus has been extensively studied (Fuxe, 1965; Shute and Lewis, 1966). Because there is no discrete localization of the hypothalamic control of ACTH release, however (D'Angelo *et al.*, 1964), the contribution of anatomical and histochemical studies has been disappointing; more information has come from neurochemical and pharmacological investigations.

Drug effects on ACTH release are well recognized but poorly understood. Much confusion has arisen because many drugs are able to both stimulate and inhibit the release of ACTH. In some cases (e.g. morphine, reserpine, chlorpromazine) an initial stimulatory response is followed by inhibition of basal and stress-induced output to ACTH. The very large number of studies on the effects of all kinds of drugs carried out to the mid-1960's have been reviewed by Gold and Ganong (1967), and by Gaunt *et al.* (1965).

In this discussion the neuropharmacological studies will be considered with reference to particular aspects of HPA function. Drugs which act at the level of the adrenal cortex will not be included (see Gaunt *et al.*, 1965). The effects of reserpine and chlorpromazine will not be discussed, because of their widespread central and peripheral actions. More reliable conclusions are possible from studies with drugs which have more specific actions on amine mechanisms.

Circadian Rhythm

The anticholinergic drug *atropine* blocks the circadian rise in plasma 17-OHCS levels in a dose-dependent manner when it is administered to cats two hours before the rise is expected. Injection of the adrenergic blocking agent *dibenzyline* does not block the circadian rise, while short-acting *barbiturates* (sodium thiamylal) have an effect similar to that of atropine (Krieger and Krieger, 1967a). Preliminary studies in man, however, reveal no lowering of plasma cortisol levels following a midnight dose of atropine (Carroll, unpublished observations).

Alteration of brain *serotonergic* mechanisms in various ways was also found to inhibit the circadian rise of plasma 17-OHCS levels in cats (Krieger and Rizzo, 1969). The serotonin (5 HT) antagonists cinanserin and cyproheptadine had this effect; so did para-chlorophenylalanine (PCPA), which inhibits the synthesis of serotonin. Unexpectedly, a monoamine oxidase (MAO) inhibitor (Monase, which in the cat is thought to elevate brain serotonin levels without affecting those of noradrenalin) had a similar effect to the other drugs. Parachloroamphetamine, which inhibits both serotonin synthesis (tryptophan hydroxylase) and monoamine oxidase and which selectively lowers brain serotonin levels, also blocked the circadian rise of plasma 17-OHCS levels. Inhibition of noradrenalin synthesis by alpha-methyl-para-tyrosine (AMPT) or depletion of both serotonin and noradrenalin by reserpine, had no effect. In addition, none of the agents which were effective modified the responses to ACTH, vasopressin, insulin hypoglycemia or pyrogen. Neither did any of the effective drugs alter the baseline plasma 17-OHCS levels (with the exception of a transient elevation observed in some animals following the monoamine oxidase inhibitor).

It appears from these studies that *in the cat the diurnal relaxation of inhibition of ACTH release (i.e. the circadian increase) operates through cholinergic and serotonergic synaptic mechanisms.*

The place of *noradrenergic transmission* in producing the circadian increase of HPA activity seems to be *less important.* In rats, inhibition of catecholamine synthesis by AMPT resulted in large increases of plasma corticosterone levels (measured nine hours after AMPT injection) regardless of the time at which the drug was given, and the diurnal rhythm was disturbed. Peak plasma corticosterone levels occurred at 4:00 AM whereas control rats had their maximum levels at 8:00 PM (Scapagnini et al., 1970). In these experiments the soluble methyl ester of AMPT was used. Suspensions of insoluble AMPT were used in cats by Krieger and Rizzo (1969) and in rats by Carr and Moore (1968); the doses given by these workers were also lower than those used by Scapagnini. When AMPT was administered in this way both cats and rats responded with elevations of plasma corticoid levels but a return to baseline values was seen within four hours, and no effect on the diurnal rise of cat plasma 17-OHCS levels was observed.

The results suggest that the control of plasma corticoid levels, in the period remote from the "once-a-day" surge of ACTH release, may be mediated by noradrenergic or dopaminergic synaptic mechanisms. The absence of effect of alpha-adrenergic receptor blocking drugs (dibenzyline and phenoxybenzamine) on either baseline levels or on the circadian rise has already been mentioned (Krieger and Krieger, 1967; Krieger *et al.*, 1968). By contrast, the beta-adrenergic receptor blocking drug *propranolol* caused an acute and *prolonged elevation of plasma 17-OHCS levels* in cats, so that any effect on circadian periodicity was obscured (Krieger and Rizzo, 1969). This effect of propranolol in cats thus resembles that of AMPT methyl ester in rats (Scapagnini *et al.*, 1970) and strengthens the possibility that, *throughout most of the day, noradrenergic mechanisms control baseline plasma corticoid levels*. Specific dopaminergic receptor blocking drugs such as pimozide and fluspirilene have not been investigated for their effects of circadian plasma corticoid levels.

Human studies of diurnal plasma cortisol levels after centrally-acting drug administration have not been extensive. Drugs which selectively alter serotonergic mechanisms appear not to have been studied at all.

Single doses of dexamphetamine (5 mg) were shown to prevent the normal fall in plasma cortisol levels which occurs at 6:00 PM. An increased rate of fall of the plasma cortisol levels was seen after chlordiazepoxide (20 mg) and the two drugs in combination antagonized each other (Butler, Besser and Steinberg, 1968). Larger doses of oral dexamphetamine or intravenous methylamphetamine have been found, in acute experiments, to elevate plasma cortisol levels. The effect is dose-dependent and is greater in the evening and at night than in the morning. These changes in normal volunteers were associated with evidence of mild central stimulation (Besser *et al.*, 1969). The authors suggested that in spite of the central stimulation, the effect on plasma cortisol levels might represent a specific action on adrenergic mechanisms in the midbrain and hypothalamus. Further studies of this question are obviously required.

Using *prolonged treatment* for two weeks Krieger and Krieger (1967a) could not demonstrate any alteration of the circadian pattern of plasma 17-OHCS levels in normal subjects, with reserpine (0.25 mg b.d.), chlorpromazine (25 mg t.i.d.), chlordiazepoxide (10 mg q.i.d.), meprobamate (400 mg t.i.d.) or diphenylhydantoin (100 mg t.i.d. for eight weeks). In this study, however, the last dose of the drugs was given at 9:00 PM, which is distant from the "critical period" in man for blocking the diurnal rise in plasma cortisol (midnight to 4:00 AM). Nevertheless it is clear from the data that none of the drugs significantly lowered plasma 17-OHCS levels during the day or evening either.

To summarize from the studies with more specific drugs: the "once-a-day" rise in plasma corticoid levels seems to be mediated by a combination of cholinergic and serotonergic synaptic mechanisms. During the remainder of the day noradrenergic transmission processes appear to exert an inhibitory effect on the release of ACTH.

Response to Stress: Adrenergic Mechanisms

Activation of the HPA axis occurs in response to many stressful stimuli. A coincident increase in the turnover rate of brain noradrenalin (NA) is seen as well during various stresses, e.g. immobilization (Corrodi *et al.*, 1968), enforced activity to the point of exhaustion (Gordon *et al.*, 1966), electric shocks to the feet (Thierry *et al.*, 1968; Bliss *et al.*, 1968) multi-sensory stress with flashing lights, noise and oscillation (Smookler and Buckley, 1969) and sham rage (Fuxe and Gunne, 1964; Reis and Fuxe, 1968). A similar association of ACTH release and increased NA turnover is seen after adrenalectomy in rats (Javoy *et al.*, 1968; Fuxe *et al.*, 1970) and both can be diminished by injection of hydrocortisone. In hypophysectomized rats, however, the NA turnover rate is reduced, despite the fact that increased CRF release is then taking place (Fuxe *et al.*, 1970).

The exact relationship between these coincident stress responses is not entirely clear, and the release of ACTH does not necessarily depend upon an increased NA turnover rate.

In fact, *raising brain NA levels will inhibit the ACTH response to stress*. Van Loon, Scapagnini *et al.* (1971) obtained such an effect with the injection of NA into the third cerebral ventricle of dogs anesthetized with pentobarbitone. The same group has shown that dopamine, dopa, tyramine (which releases NA from nerve endings), and alpha-ethyltryptamine could also inhibit stress-induced ACTH release when they were injected into the third ventricle (van Loon *et al.*, 1969). The systemic administration of drugs which both release NA and stimulate NA receptors (amphetamine and methylamphetamine) inhibited the steroid response to stress (Lorenzen *et al.*, 1965). In conscious man, by contrast to the anesthetized dog, methylamphetamine stimulates ACTH release and raises the plasma levels of ACTH and of cortisol (Besser *et al.*, 1969).

The inhibitory effect of dopa was obtained after its intravenous injection as well, and was not blocked by phenoxybenzamine. Previous treatment with the MAO inhibitor pargyline potentiated the inhibitory effect of DOPA; after treatment of the dogs with AMPT, however higher doses of dopa were necessary to cause inhibition of ACTH release (van Loon and Ganong, 1969).

These studies from Ganong's group indicate that the *release of ACTH after stress is probably not caused by the increase of NA turnover* which occurs at the same time.

Supporting evidence comes from experiments in which depletion of brain catecholamines failed to block the stress-induced release of ACTH. Carr and Moore (1968) depleted rat brain catecholamine stores with reserpine, then gave AMPT as well to prevent synthesis of dopamine and NA. The rats showed normal plasma corticoid increases, even after the mild stress of entering a new environment, as well as after other procedures (ether, histamine, formaline, restraint). Similarly, AMPT did not affect the ACTH responses of cats to vasopressin, insulin hypoglycemia or pyrogen (Krieger and Rizzo, 1969).

Longitudinal studies of the ACTH and NA turnover responses to prolonged stress have shown that *adaptation of both parameters* occurs at about the same time (four weeks) although other stress effects such as neurogenic hypertension may persist in spite of these neuroendocrine and neurochemical adaptations (Smookler and Buckley, 1969).

Attempts to correlate NA turnover and ACTH responses to

stress in man have been limited by the indirect nature of esti-mates of central adrenergic function. Since the demonstration by Maas and Landis (1966) that the best index of brain NA turnover may be provided by the urinary excretion of the neutral glycol catechol metabolite, 3-methoxy-4-hydroxy-phenylglycol (MHPG), only one study of stress responses has been reported. The urinary and plasma cortisol and the urinary MHPG re-sponses of jet fighter pilots and their flight officers increased in a generally parallel manner during three stress situations. The cortisol values were well below maximal stress levels and were obviously influenced by the diurnal variation factor. As a result, some apparent dissociation between the MHPG and cortisol re-sponses was seen (Miller *et al.*, 1970; Rubin *et al.*, 1970).

On balance, the evidence favors the interpretation that *the release of ACTH by stress is subject to an adrenergic inhibitory influence, which may be activated simultaneously by the stress.* Noradrenergic processes do not appear to cause the HPA activa-tion.

Response to Stress: Serotonergic Mechanisms

While an acceleration of NA turnover is to be seen after many kinds of stress, a similar change of serotonin (5 HT) turnover has been less frequently reported. During immobiliza-tion of rats the steady-state levels of brain 5 HT were reduced, but so was the level of 5-hydroxyindoleacetic acid (5 HIAA, the principal 5 HT metabolite) and the turnover rate of 5 HT was unchanged (Corrodi *et al.*, 1968; Curzon and Green, 1968). Not all workers agree, however, that immobilization stress does not affect the brain 5 HT turnover rate: significant increases have been reported in the turnover rate (Nistico and Preziosi, 1969) and brain levels (de Schaepdryver *et al.*, 1969) of 5 HT of re-strained rats. Increased 5 HT turnover has also been observed after other types of stress such as electric shocks to the feet (Bliss *et al.*, 1968; Thierry *et al.*, 1968).

An explanation of the fall in brain 5 HT and 5 HIAA levels which they observed with immobilization stress has been pro-posed by Green and Curzon (1968). Hydrocortisone injections produced similar acute falls in the brain levels of 5 HT and 5 HIAA, but within twelve hours a return to normal values had occurred. The decreases, which were maximal at 6 to 7 hours, were preceded by an increase of liver tryptophan pyrrolase activity, and could be prevented by previous treatment with inhibitors of tryptophan pyrrolase, such as allopurinol or yohimbine. The initial hypothesis elaborated by these workers was that increased utilization of dietary tryptophan along the pyrrolase-kynurenine pathway could result in diminished availability of tryptophan for 5 HT synthesis in the brain (Curzon, 1969a and b) although the plasma tryptophan level was lowered for only a few hours (Curzon and Green, 1969). Subsequently they demonstrated that kynurenine, 3-hydroxykynurenine and 3-hydroxyanthranilic acid, formed as a result of the increased pyrrolase activity, were all able to compete with tryptophan for uptake into the brain, thereby causing a fall in brain 5 HT levels (Green and Curzon, 1970).

The process responsible for the return of normal brain 5 HT levels following the initial fall which immobilization stress or hydrocortisone injections produced was identified by Azmitia and McEwen (1969). They showed that the activity of brain tryptophan hydroxylase which in the rat has a rapid, steroid-dependent turnover rate, decreased following adrenalectomy and increased after corticosterone injections and during various stresses. Later, this effect of corticosterone was localized to the brainstem (midbrain, pons and medulla); in the telediencephalon corticosterone had no effect on the conversion index of ^{3}H-tryptophan to ^{3}H-serotonin of adrenalectomized rats. (Azmitia, Algeri and Costa, 1970).

This effect of corticosterone on brain tryptophan hydroxylase activity may be an important adaptive mechanism which permits increased 5 HT turnover during prolonged stress; it is possible that without such an increase of 5 HT turnover behavioral coping with the stress could be impaired.

In general however, *it does not appear that serotonergic mechanisms are essential for the acute release of ACTH in stressed animals.* Thus, in the study of Krieger and Rizzo (1969) Monase, parachloramphetamine, cinanserin and cyproheptadine failed to affect the plasma 17-OHCS responses to lysine vasopressin, insulin hypoglycemia or pyrogen. Similar results were reported by Dixit and Buckley (1969) and de Schaepdryver *et al.* (1969) while elevation of brain 5 HT levels by tryptophan or 5-hydroxytryptophan did not affect HPA stress responses in dogs (Lorenzen *et al.*, 1965). These pharmacological studies confirm that the brain mechanisms which release CRF and ACTH in response to stress are different from those which produce the circadian increase of HPA activity.

Response to Stress: Cholinergic Mechanisms

Parenteral injections of atropine to cats did not affect the plasma 17-OHCS responses caused by lysine-vasopressin, pyrogen or insulin hypoglycemia (Krieger, *et al.*, 1968). However stress responses to surgery, ether and arginine vasopressin have been inhibited by intrahypothalamic implantation of atropine in rats (Hedge and Smelik, 1968). On the other hand parenteral administration of atropine does not affect the plasma cortisol responses of cats or humans to lysine-vasopressin (Krieger *et al.*, 1968; Carroll *et al.*, 1969).

Localized Injections of Neurotransmitters

Another approach to the relationship between central transmitter mechanisms and HPA function consists of the microinjection or microimplantation of transmitter agents into the hypophysiotrophic area or extra-hypothalamic regulatory centers.

Hypothalamus

In the median eminence all the transmitters tested have produced ACTH and corticosteroid release. In conscious cats, carbachol, noradrenaline, gamma-aminobutyric acid (GABA) and serotonin have this effect (Krieger and Krieger, 1964; 1970a). Only carbachol occasionally produced a coincident behavioral response (sham rage) and dissociation between the behavioral and endocrine changes was commonly seen. Very similar results were reported by Endroczi *et al.* (1963), using somewhat different techniques. Injection of liquid carbachol or eserine into the anterolateral hypothalamus of the cat caused an inhibition of ACTH release, in spite of marked sham rage responses. In the median eminence carbachol caused adrenal activation. Adrenergic agents (noradrenalin, adrenalin and ephedrine) stimulated adrenal venous 17-OHCS levels, although the animals remained quiet. The adrenergic drugs were able to overcome the inhibition caused by carbachol or eserine.

Studies in the rat indicate that in this species acetylcholine, when applied to single neurones by microiontophoresis, increases the firing rates of most of the units examined over a wide area of the hypothalamus. Noradrenalin, however, inhibits these neurones, an effect which is similar to that of dexamethasone, so that the functional response would be one of HPA activation by acetylcholine and inhibition by NA (Steiner *et al.*, 1969).

In guinea pigs Naumenko (1968) obtained results in substantial agreement with those reported by the Kriegers in cats: NA, carbachol and 5 HT all caused HPA activation when injected into various regions of the hypothalamus.

Krieger and Krieger (1970a) in discussing their results suggested that the responses of the hypothalamic neurones which secrete CRF may depend on the integration of the effects of two or more different transmitters. The fact that all four transmitters tested caused HPA activation could be interpreted to mean that different populations of CRF-secreting neurones are present, each with its own specific activating transmitter. It has also been suggested (de Robertis, 1967) that the postsynaptic membrane may have multiple receptor sites for multiple neurochemical synaptic transmitters.

The responses of the terminal CRF-secreting neurones to transmitter implantations in the median eminence could *not* be inhibited by prior systemic administration of dexamethasone (Krieger and Krieger, 1970b). The same doses of dexamethasone did abolish the plasma 11-OHCS response to hypoglycemia, and the effect of carbachol was specifically blocked by atropine.

The steriod-sensitive elements of the CNS appear, therefore, to be above the level of the median eminence. The CRF-secreting neurones then act as a "final common pathway" which integrates stimulatory and inhibitory information coming from limbic and midbrain regions. These findings with the use of transmitter agents are not easy to reconcile with the steroid implantation studies, which suggest that hypothalamic and median eminence implants can block CRF and ACTH release.

Extra-Hypothalamic Areas

Whereas, in the median eminence, implantations of carbachol, NA, GABA and 5 HT all caused HPA activation, the responses of extra-hypothalamic areas to these transmitters were not uniform (Krieger and Krieger, 1970a).

Considering for the present purpose only NA and 5 HT, some areas responded to both amines, while in other regions a dissociation of responses was observed. No definite inhibitory effects were reported for any of the areas studied.

Noradrenalin was effective in the mammillary body, hippocampus, lateral amygdala and dorsal septal region. In the study of Endroczi *et al.* (1963) NA increased adrenal venous 17-OHCS output after its injection into the ventral midbrain tegmentum.

Serotonin, in the Kriegers' study of cats, increased plasma 17-OHCS levels when implanted into the dorsal septal region only. In particular, no effect was observed after 5 HT application to either the lateral regions of the amygdaloid complex or to the hippocampus. In guinea pigs serotonin injections into the caudal ventral hippocampus, septal region, rostral midbrain reticular formation and rostral ventral midbrain tegmentum elevated plasma 17-OHCS levels. Similar injections into the caudal dorsal hippocampus, however, caused a lowering of plasma 17-OHCS values. Once again injections into the amygdala resulted in little change: a slight tendency to decrease plasma 17-OHCS levels was observed (Naumenko, 1969). These recent findings that 5 HT does not affect the amygdala provide some experimental contradiction of the hypothesis of Lapin and Oxenkrug (1969) who had speculated that functional brain 5 HT deficiency would cause HPA activation in man by means of amygdaloid activation.

Steiner and his colleagues (1969) used the approach of attempting to identify steroid-sensitive neurones by micro-iontophoresis of dexamethasone, and then studying the effects of ACh and NA applications on the same neurones. They located steroid-responsive neurones in the hypothalamus and midbrain, but not in the hippocampus or thalamus. In the midbrain, as in the hypothalamus, NA had a similar effect to dexamethasone: inhibition of unit firing rates was observed, which suggests that the functional response would be inhibition of ACTH release.

It is apparent from the studies mentioned here that both NA and 5 HT (to say nothing of ACh and GABA) are of functional importance both in the hypothalamic and extra-hypothalamic regulation of HPA activity. At the present time inhibition of ACTH release by local applications of transmitter agents seems to be an uncommon finding; the stimulatory effects of NA in particular are difficult to reconcile with the pharmacological studies previously reviewed, which suggest that noradrenergic mechanisms inhibit both diurnal plasma steroid levels and the responses to stress.

A particular need in this area is a detailed investigation, in man, of the effects of drugs specifically altering NA and 5 HT mechanisms on the various parameters of HPA function, i.e. diurnal variation, response to stress and inhibition.

EVALUATION OF HYPOTHALAMIC-PITUITARY-ADRENAL FUNCTION

The methods used to assess the level of HPA activity until recently have relied upon the level of cortisol in plasma and the urinary excretion products of cortisol. Direct assay of *plasma ACTH* activity by radio-immunoassay procedures is now a realistic possibility and will improve the detection of changes in the hypothalamic-pituitary part of the axis (see Berson and Yalow, 1968; Greenwood, 1968; Lefkowitz *et al.,* 1970).

PLASMA CORTISOL

A large number of routine methods for measuring plasma cortisol are available, based on three principles. *Colorimetric* techniques employing the phenylhydrazine reaction detect 17-hydroxycorticosteroids (17-OHCS) with a dihydroxyacetone side-chain and are still widely used, especially in the United States. The use of *fluorometric* methods has expanded greatly in the last decade. Their chief advantages over the color methods are increased sensitivity and reduced interference by drugs. At the present time the procedure of choice for the routine handling of large numbers of samples is that of *radiostereoassay* (competitive protein binding radioassay; saturation analysis; displacement analysis) developed by Murphy (1967). The sensitivity and specificity of this method is very good and the values obtained are closer to those of true plasma cortisol than those given by either of the two previous methods. Drug interference is minimal and in addition the procedure can be readily adapted to measure cortisol in urine and tissue extracts, where interfering fluorescence can be a very difficult problem.

All of these routine methods lack specificity in varying degree but they are quite adequate for the detection of *change* in the plasma cortisol level, e.g. diurnal variation, stimulation and suppression.

Significance of Plasma Cortisol Levels

Whatever method is used, measurement of the cortisol level in plasma gives information about the functional activity of the HPA axis at only one point in time. For that reason little can be inferred from studies in which samples are obtained only once or twice a day, unless grossly abnormal levels are found: in psychoendocrine investigations most of the values seen will be within the normal range and not much real significance can be assigned to moderate differences between patient groups, whatever the statistical significance might be.

In the first place the plasma level of cortisol (or of any other hormone) is a function of two factors: a) the rate at which cortisol is being introduced into the circulation (*cortisol secretion* rate, CSR) and b) the rate at which cortisol is being removed from blood—defined by Tait (1963) and Tait and Burstein (1964) as the *metabolic clearance rate* (MCR). The MCR is the volume of plasma irreversibly cleared of hormone in unit time. The plasma cortisol level is then obtained from the expression:

$$\frac{\text{Plasma Cortisol}}{(\mu g/100 \text{ ml})} = \frac{\text{C.S.R. (mg/24 hrs.)}}{\text{M.C.R. (liters/24 hrs.)}}$$

For an average CSR of 18 mg/day and an average MCR of 180 liters/day the average plasma cortisol concentration will be 10μg/100 ml.

From the expression given it is obvious that the plasma level can be raised either by increasing the CSR or by decreasing the MCR. In following plasma cortisol changes over relatively short time intervals it is generally assumed that the MCR remains constant, so that the parameter actually measured reflects changes in the rate of secretion of cortisol from the adrenal cortex. For most practical purposes this assumption is acceptable.

Situations do arise, however, where this assumption underlying the measurement of plasma cortisol can be misleading, especially when individual results are referred to normative data. In patients with liver disease or severe malnutrition, for example, the MCR is greatly reduced and high plasma cortisol levels are found, although the CSR is in fact not elevated (Peterson, 1959; Alleyne and Young, 1967). Conversely, in thyrotoxicosis the MCR and rate of cortisol turnover is greatly accelerated, with above normal cortisol secretion rates and no significance change in the plasma level of cortisol (Peterson, 1959).

A further consideration which is of critical importance to psychoendocrine research is that *the total plasma cortisol level,* as measured by the usual techniques, *does not necessarily reflect the exposure of tissues to the active hormone.*

Over 90 per cent of the total plasma cortisol is bound to a specific high-affinity protein, which is an alpha globulin called *transcortin* (Slaunwhite *et al.,* 1959) or *corticosteroid-binding globulin* (CBG) (Daughaday, 1958). The bulk of the total plasma cortisol, bound to CBG, is not physiologically active, so that less than 10 per cent of what is customarily measured is responsible for the biological effects of circulating cortisol (Slaunwhite *et al.,* 1962). Thus, in normal subjects, unbound plasma cortisol levels of 1.27 and 0.36μg/100 ml were found at 9:00 AM and 9:00 PM, when the total cortisol (17-OHCS) levels were 16.5 and 6.3μg/100 ml respectively (Doe *et al.,* 1969).

Although its affinity for cortisol is high the *capacity* of plasma CBG is limited so that saturation normally occurs when the total plasma cortisol level reaches 15 to 20μg/100 ml. Above this saturation level the relative amount of unbound cortisol in plasma increases sharply, and in a disproportionate manner to the increments of total plasma cortisol (Sandberg *et al.,* 1960; de Moor *et al.,* 1962; Murray, 1967; Hamanaka *et al.,* 1970).

The two last mentioned authors also obtained some evidence to suggest that during the stresses of surgery and critical illnesses, the cortisol binding capacity of plasma was decreased, so that unbound cortisol levels were more than doubled, often without a change in total plasma cortisol concentration.

There is no doubt that the *unbound plasma cortisol level is the most relevant parameter for psychoendocrine research* if the effects of glucocorticoids on CNS function are being investigated. Methods are available for its measurement in plasma, parotid fluid, cerebrospinal fluid and urine without undue difficulty (Burke, 1969c; Katz and Shannon, 1969; Murphy *et al.*, 1967; Murphy, 1968). Up to the present time virtually no psychoendocrine units have concerned themselves with this question, and have relied on less specific and less informative measures such as plasma and urinary 17-OHCS.

URINARY MEASURES OF HPA FUNCTION

Estimations of the urinary excretion of cortisol or of its metabolites are of great importance for three reasons: a) over 90 per cent of administered cortisol can be accounted for in terms of urinary excretion products within twenty-four hours (Flood *et al.*, 1961; Fukushima *et al.*, 1960); b) urinary collections are simple and more practical than blood sampling for many patients; c) urinary measures provide an index of HPA activity over time, a dimension which is not achieved by sporadic blood sampling.

Urinary 17-Hydroxycorticosteroids

In the United States the Porter-Silber method for 17-OHCS estimation is the most widely used. Steroids with the 17, 21-dihydroxy 20-keto configuration are determined, chiefly cortisol, cortisone, their dihydro and tetrahydro derivatives, 11-desoxycortisol and 5-tetrahydrocortisol (Kurland, 1964; James and Landon, 1968). These metabolites account for *at most 50 per cent* of the total cortisol pool. Interference by drugs applies to the urinary determinations even more than to the plasma estimations.

Urinary 17-Ketogenic Steroids

As much as 80 per cent of the cortisol metabolites can be accounted for by measuring 17-ketogenic (oxogenic) steroids (17-

KGS) in urine by methods based on that of Appleby and No-rymberski (Appleby *et al.*, 1955; Appleby and Norymberski, 1955; Few, 1961; M.R.C. Committee on Clinical Endocrinology, 1963, 1969; James and Caie, 1964). The ketogenic steroids include the Porter-Silber chromogens, together with cortol, cortolone, pregnanetriol and pregnenetriol. A large number of drugs are known to interfere with the determinations (M.R.C. Committee on Clinical Endocrinology, 1969).

Urinary 17-Ketosteroids

Preformed 17-ketosteroids (17 KS) account for a further 10 per cent of the total amount of cortisol metabolized. Of the 17 KS appearing in the urine of male patients, two-thirds is of adrenal origin and one-third is derived from testicular androgens. Androsterone, dehydroepiandrosterone, etiocholanolone and isoandrosterone are the principal compounds measured (Norymberski *et al.*, 1953). Suppression of testicular, but not of adrenal androgen production has been reported in monkeys during avoidance conditioning sessions (Mason *et al.*, 1968) and in man after surgical stress (Tanaka *et al.*, 1970).

Urinary Free Cortisol Excretion

The estimation of 17-OHCS or 17 KGS excretion in urine provides an approximate index of corticosteroid production over time. What is measured by these procedures reflects both the level of adrenocortical activity and the efficiency of hepatic metabolism of the daily steroid output. As was discussed in the case of plasma estimations, however, the *functional significance* of changes in urinary 17 OHCS or 17 KGS may be rather different from what the figures suggest. This statement applies particularly in the area of mild to moderate elevations of adrenocortical function with which most psychoendocrine studies of HPA activity are concerned.

In general it has not been appreciated that the laboratory procedures for measuring 17 OHCS and 17 KGS were first developed as screening tests of adrenocortical activity in patients with definite endocrine disease, and that they were validated chiefly by reference to clinical judgments, not by comparison with accurate measures of adrenal function. They were not intended for use in the evaluation of relatively minor or subtle differences between or within individuals and their limitations are most obvious in the diagnosis of doubtful cases of hyper-cortisolism.

For a number of years there has been good evidence that, in and slightly above the range of normal activity, 17 KGS and 17 OHCS bear no significant relationship to the cortisol secretion rate (Cope and Black, 1959; Rosner *et al.*, 1963; Cope and Pearson, 1965). Yet until very recently these measures (usually the less informative 17 OHCS) have been the only urinary parameters considered by psychoendocrine investigators.

A much more sensitive indication of adrenocortical stimulation is provided by the amount of *free cortisol* excreted in the urine. The particular advantage of *this parameter* is that it *reflects, better than any other, the effective level of circulating plasma cortisol over time* (West, 1957; Greaves and West, 1960; Rosner *et al.*, 1963; Schedl *et al.*, 1959; Beisel *et al.*, 1964). Only the unbound fraction of plasma cortisol is filtered at the glomerulus and clearance studies have shown that about 90 per cent of the filtered load is reabsorbed by the renal tubules (Schedl *et al.*, 1959). *Excreted cortisol increases in direct proportion to the plasma unbound cortisol level* and no renal tubular maximum for cortisol reabsorption was demonstrated by Beisel *et al.* (1964), even at total plasma cortisol levels as high as $120\mu g/100$ ml in normal subjects. Cortisol thus appears to be reabsorbed by passive diffusion, principally in the distal tubule, which is also the site at which it acts to promote sodium reabsorption (Scurry and Shear, 1969). In several series increasing age has been found not to affect the urinary free cortisol (UFC) excretion, but only subjects with normal renal function have been studied. Renal disease might be expected to alter the UFC but systematic data are lacking. Significant reductions of the glomerular filtration rate (caused by sodium depletion) did not affect the UFC excretions of two patients whose baseline renal function was normal (Schedl *et al.*, 1959). In addition no evidence for increased cortisol excretion with forced increases of the urine flow rate was observed. In a study of critically ill patients Espiner (1966) obtained data which suggest that the effect of im-

TABLE 3-I

URINARY-FREE CORTISOL (UFC) EXCRETION BY NORMAL SUBJECTS
(Arithmetic Means Only)

Authors	Method	No. Subjects	UFC (μg/24 hrs.) Mean and Range	Comment
Beardwell, 1968	CPB	24	41.9 (0-145)	
Murphy, 1968	CPB	23	48 (0-108)	
Meikle, 1969	CPB	9	82 (50-123)	
Meikle, 1969	CPB	9	42 (28-75)	After P.Cy.
Burke and Roulet, 1970	CPB	33	39 (0-98)	
Hsu and Bledsoe, 1970	CPB	54	33 (16-71)	
de Moor, 1962	F	139	191 —	
Mattingly and Tyler, 1967	F	59M	229 (108-396)	
Mattingly and Tyler, 1967	F	50F	174 (78-311)	
Gantt, 1964	F	17	86.8 (31-150)	
Vagnucci, 1965	D.I.	12	47.1 (23-81)	
Rosner, Cos, 1963	G.F.Cy.; P-S	38	71.4 (0.181)	
Harris and Crane, 1964	P.Cy.; P-S	21	9.6 (4-20)	Uncorrected
Cope and Black, 1959	P.Cy.; Color	70	43 (0-110)	Uncorrected
Streeten et al., 1969	P.Cy.; Color	21	19.7 (6-51)	Uncorrected
Ross, 1960	P.Cy.; Color	58	15.4 (3-48)	Uncorrected
Schteingart et al., 1963	P.Cy.; Color	14	20.4 (5-50)	Uncorrected
Espiner, 1966	P.Cy.; Color	13	74 (35-98)	

CPB: Competitive protein binding; F: fluorometric; D.I.: double isotope derivative; G.F.Cy.: glass fiber chromatography; P-S: Porter-Silber; P.Cy.: paper chromatography; Color: other colorimetric quantitation procedures.

paired renal function is likely to be in the direction of lowering the UFC excretion.

The range of daily UFC excretion in normals is given in Table 3-I. The distribution is approximately log-normal, with most values being found in the lower half of the normal range, a characteristic which is shared by the plasma unbound cortisol level (Burke, 1969c). In absolute terms the UFC represents less than 1 per cent of the total daily cortisol production and binding to CBG is obviously an important mechanism for conservation of the hormone.

Comparison of Urine Free Cortisol with Other Measures

Because normal subjects may excrete very low amounts the UFC is most valuable in the detection of adrenal hyperactivity.

For the confident assessment of adrenal hypofunction other measures such as THE and THF are preferred (Cope and Black, 1959). The general conclusions which can be taken from the studies cited above are the following: urinary cortisol excretion is more than twice as sensitive as 17 KGS or 17-OHCS for demonstrating hyperfunction and for detecting inhibition of such hyperfunction, e.g. by synthetic steroids. The UFC is not affected by body weight so that it is not raised in obesity, whereas other measures, including the cortisol secretion rate, are often grossly elevated. In the differentiation of Cushing's disease from obesity and from normality, a clear and impressive separation is given by the UFC while considerable overlap of values of 17 KGS, 17 OHCS and CSR occurs in the same groups. The same comment applies to the assessment of responses to ACTH and to suppression by synthetic steroids. In hyperthyroid states where increased cortisol secretion rates and 17 OHCS excretions are found the UFC is normal, reflecting the essentially euadrenal status of such patients, who do not have raised plasma free cortisol levels despite the rapid turnover rate. With increasing rates of cortisol production the UFC increases exponentially, whereas 17 OHCS and 17 KGS increase only in a linear manner. Standardization of UFC to creatinine excretion is not necessary, since UFC is independent of body mass; for the effective separation of normal and elevated 17 OHCS, 17 KGS and CSR estimations reference to creatinine excretion is a distinct advantage.

Simultaneous measurement of *both free and conjugated cortisol in urine* has been performed by some workers. In this case both the free cortisol and cortisol which has been conjugated as glucuronide or sulfate in the liver is measured. Pinsker *et al.* (1968) found that measurement of both gave a better separation of normal patients from those with Cushing's disease, especially when the free cortisol level was only minimally raised. The *total* urinary cortisol was found by Clark *et al.* (1970) to correlate +0.90 with the Porter-Silber chromogen (17 OHCS) excretion in 153 samples. By contrast the correlation between 17 OHCS and free cortisol alone was less powerful: r = +0.30 in 38 samples (calculated from the data of Rosner *et al.*, 1963). From the data of Harris and Crane (1964) the correlation between 17 KGS and urine-free cortisol was +0.52 in 17 samples. In another study Miller, *et al.* (1970), found greater proportionate increases of 17 OHCS than of total cortisol excretion when the total plasma cortisol levels were low; when the plasma levels approached stress values the total urine cortisol increased to a much greater extent than the 17 OHCS excretion. Because the conjugated urine cortisol excretion, like the conjugated metabolites measured as 17 OHCS, reflects hepatic activity rather than free cortisol availability to tissues it would seem that *urinary free cortisol is more informative* than the total urinary cortisol excretion.

Conditions other than Cushing's syndrome in which the UFC is elevated include pregnancy (Murphy, 1968; Burke and Roulet, 1970) acute medical illnesses (Murphy, 1968; Espiner, 1966) and estrogen treatment (Burke, 1969c). Metabolism of cortisol by extrahepatic tissues, in disease states, also appears to influence the UFC excretion. Thus, Bailey *et al.* (1967) found that patients with active rheumatoid arthritis excreted increased amounts of cortisol, 20-dihydrocortisol and 6-β-hydroxycortisol, compared with normal subjects or patients with inactive disease. When patients with connective tissue diseases were maintained on a fixed dose of 100 mg cortisol daily, the UFC excretion of those with active disease ($37\mu g$) was found to be lower than that of control subjects ($190\mu g$) or of patients in remission ($169\mu g$). In an individual patient a rise in UFC coincident with clinical remission of systemic lupus erythematosus was observed (Popert *et al.*, 1964), *while the daily cortisol dosage was held constant*. The development of signs of hypercortisolism followed the rise in UFC excretion. These findings illustrate the difficulty of inferring free cortisol activity from estimations of the cortisol production rate. Cope and Black (1959) noted a poor correlation between production rate and UFC excretion. When the UFC was expressed logarithmically a better relationship with cortisol production rate was obtained, but confident prediction of one value from knowledge of the other was clearly not possible (Meikle *et al.*, 1969).

For the diagnosis of functional adrenocortical hyperactivity, with consequences at the tissue level, Streeton *et al.* (1969) concluded that the measurement of plasma unbound cortisol at periods during the day may well become the most important criterion. Since the urinary-free cortisol excretion increases linearly with the plasma unbound cortisol level, the UFC is the most directly relevant urinary parameter available; it probably is more informative than the cortisol secretion rate.

It should be noted that the UFC indicates functional glucocorticoid excess but does not necessarily reflect adrenal stimulation which fails to produce significant elevations of the plasma unbound cortisol level. For the estimation of these minor changes measurement of urinary 17 OHCS and of total plasma 17 OHCS is more informative (Miller *et al.*, 1970).

There are few observations concerning the effect of psychological factors on the UFC excretion. Espiner (1966) recorded grossly elevated values in patients awaiting elective surgery. Five of eleven values were above the normal range, some being well into the range found in Cushing's disease. There were no clinically obvious distinguishing features to suggest that these subjects were experiencing more severe HPA activation than those with normal UFC excretion. In a small study of depressed women Ferguson *et al.* (1964) found significant elevations of the UFC before treatment, with more normal values after recovery.

CLINICAL EVALUATION OF HPA CONTROL MECHANISMS

A number of *dynamic tests* have been developed which are designed to assess the integrity of the CNS mechanisms involved in the feedback control, circadian rhythm, suppression and stimulation of the axis. Most of these procedures were introduced and standardized only within the last ten or fifteen years and our understanding of their uses and limitations has reached a reasonable level of confidence only within the last five years. Like the earlier tests, they were developed for use in the diagnosis and management of endocrine diseases, and their application to psychoendocrine studies is very recent.

DIURNAL RHYTHM

While it is exceptional to find grossly elevated plasma cortisol levels in Cushing's syndrome if samples are taken only in the morning, a more complete separation from normal values is obtained when afternoon and evening values are measured. The usual circadian fall does not occur in such patients and the values often remain at around morning levels throughout the day (Doe *et al.*, 1960; Ekman *et al.*, 1961; Ernest, 1966; McHardy-Young *et al.*, 1967). The finding of sustained high levels during the night indicates that the exposure of tissues to unbound cortisol over time is increased and this is reflected by the urinary-free cortisol excretion. Whereas at 8:00 AM the normal range of plasma cortisol levels is a wide one (about 8 to 25μg/100 ml), at midnight values below 7μg/100 ml are the rule (Mattingly, 1965; Ross *et al.*, 1966). The common practice of sampling only in the morning and late afternoon is not really adequate for assessment of the diurnal rhythm in an individual patient: the absence of an afternoon fall needs to be confirmed by estimating the levels later during the night (10:00 PM or midnight).

Some authors (Butler and Besser, 1968) seem to regard the finding of high night-time plasma cortisol levels as diagnostic of a disturbed diurnal rhythm, without regard to the *relative change* from 8:00 AM to midnight. In the depressed patients whom they studied a clear diurnal rhythm was present, despite the fact that the cortisol levels were elevated throughout the twenty-four-hour period. There is no general agreement on the amount of relative or absolute change in plasma cortisol levels which characterizes the normal circadian rhythm so that the confidence limits for judging an abnormal rhythm are not established. It is also known that some normal subjects, as well as patients with obesity or myxoedema may have a barely detectable rhythm, usually in association with low plasma cortisol levels throughout the day (Martin *et al.*, 1963; Wynn, 1968).

In psychoendocrine studies examination of the plasma cortisol diurnal rhythm has proved useful in distinguishing affective psychotics from patients in other diagnostic categories (Conroy *et al.*, 1968; Fullerton *et al.*, 1968). Frequent sampling is essential, however, if one is not to be misled by elevations due to intercurrent stressful events.

ACTH STIMULATION TESTS

Since many of the HPA stimulation tests rely on the demonstration of an increase in plasma cortisol levels it may at times be important to confirm that the adrenal cortex itself is capable of responding to ACTH. Otherwise an impaired response, e.g. to hypoglycemia or to pyrogen cannot be interpreted to necessarily indicate dysfunction of the hypothalamic-pituitary portion of the axis.

There is no standard way of carrying out short ACTH stimulation tests. In most units a supraphysiological amount of ACTH is infused over four to six hours and the plasma cortisol or urinary 17-OHCS response is measured (Eik-Naes *et al.*, 1954; Christy *et al.*, 1955). Both the rise in plasma cortisol levels and the maximum level reached are considered in evaluating the response (Greig, 1968).

More standardized procedures, with the use of physiological degrees of stimulation, have been introduced since synthetic β 1-24 corticotropin (tetracoside, Synacthen) became generally available (Landon *et al.*, 1964; Greig *et al.*, 1968; Wynn, 1968). In particular, criteria for the *threshold* adrenocortical sensitivity to Synacthen have been established (Landon *et al.*, 1967a; Wynn, 1968).

A brisk or excessive rise of plasma cortisol levels in response to ACTH may be found in subjects with Cushing's disease, and in those with ectopic ACTH-producing tumors, but not in patients with adrenocortical tumors (which are usually not responsive to ACTH) (James and Landon, 1968). The urinary-free cortisol response to ACTH in Cushing's disease is also excessive and may be prolonged for one or two days after the test is given (Ross, 1960; Harris and Crane, 1964). In these studies supramaximal stimulation was used, and the exaggerated responses may reflect simply the increased amount of functioning adrenocortical tissue which is present. Whether the sensitivity of the adrenal cortex to normal amounts of ACTH is increased in such patients remains to be determined by studies with Synacthen. In psychoendocrine studies it would also be useful to establish the threshold adrenocortical sensitivity of patients with evidence of HPA activation.

METYRAPONE TEST

This procedure was introduced by Liddle *et al.* (1959) as a measure of the *feedback control* of ACTH release. Metyrapone

(SU-4885, Ciba) is a drug which can block the adrenal cortical enzyme 11-β-hydroxylase, required in the final step of cortisol biosynthesis. The principle of the test is that falling levels of cortisol will stimulate ACTH release, which in turn will lead to a great increase in the production of 11-desoxycortisol. This steroid may then be measured in plasma or its metabolites determined as 17-OHCS and 17 KGS in the urine. In fact the ACTH response in normal subjects is sufficient to maintain cortisol production, together with a large increase of 11-desoxycortisol output (Cope *et al.*, 1966; Vermuelen *et al.*, 1967), since complete enzyme inhibition is seldom achieved.

The interpretation and problems associated with the usual metyrapone tests extending over twenty-four or forty-eight hours are discussed by James and Landon (1968), Sprunt, Browning *et al.* (1968) and Metcalf and Beaven (1968). Drugs known to interfere with the test include chlorpromazine, amitriptyline, chlordiazepoxide (Metcalf and Beaven, 1968) and estrogens (Sprunt, Rutherford *et al.*, 1968).

The validity of the feedback control concept of the metyrapone test can be questioned in the light of more recent work. Jubiz, Matsukura *et al.* (1970) measured simultaneously plasma levels of metyrapone, ACTH, cortisol and 11-desoxycortisol during both oral and intravenous administration of the drug, together with urinary 17-OHCS measurements. The *ACTH response occurred mainly at the time of the normal circadian rise,* while definite but less marked elevations were seen at other times in the day, when the responses were related to the degree of 11-β-hydroxylase inhibition. In the early morning period cortisol infusions abolished the ACTH and 11-desoxycortisol increases only if the plasma cortisol level exceeded 7.5μg/100 ml. During the day, however, much smaller infusions of cortisol (with plasma cortisol levels around 4μg/100 ml) prevented the ACTH and 11-desoxycortisol responses.

Clearly what is customarily measured as an increase of twenty-four urinary 17-OHCS or 17 KGS excretion during the extended metyrapone tests gives information about the "once-a-day phase" of HPA activity even more than it does about the feedback control mechanism.

As a result of these studies Jubiz, Meikle, West and Tyler (1970) introduced a *single-dose metyrapone test* in which 2 to 3 gm are given at midnight. Measurement of plasma 11-desoxycortisol eight hours later separated normal subjects from those with pituitary insufficiency. The midnight to midnight excretion of 17-OHCS also gave a complete separation between these groups. When used in this way the metyrapone test measures some aspect of the circadian control mechanism. At present the precise mechanism of the early morning stimulation of ACTH release by metyrapone is not clear: in metyrapone-treated subjects the absolute levels of plasma cortisol between midnight and 4:00 AM were not significantly lower than those which are commonly seen in normal subjects (mean $3.3\mu g/100$ ml) (Mattingly, 1965).

The extended metyrapone tests have been of most use in the diagnosis of hypofunction of the HPA axis, although Metcalf and Beaven (1968) and others have noted that exaggerated responses may be seen in Cushing's syndrome. At this stage the single-dose metyrapone test has not been applied to patients with adrenal hyperfunction, in either an endocrine or psychoendocrine setting.

PYROGEN TEST

This acute stimulating test was developed from the observations that injections of purified bacterial polysaccharide pyrogens caused HPA activation as well as fever (Bliss, Migeon *et al.*, 1954a) and that the endocrine response was abolished in hypophysectomized animals (Wexler *et al.*, 1957). The febrile response is generally held to be not essential for the HPA activation. A temporal dissociation between the two responses is commonly seen (Jenkins, 1968) and prevention of the fever by aspirin does not diminish the rise in plasma cortisol (Jenkins, 1968; Carroll *et al.*, 1969). Fever alone is not sufficient to cause the adrenal response: etiocholanolone produces a greater and more prolonged febrile response than does pyrogen, as well as more severe constitutional symptoms, yet no change in plasma cortisol levels is seen (Kimball *et al.*, 1968). The HPA response to pyrogen shows a diurnal variation, with the maximal increases occurring during the early morning (Takebe *et al.*,

1966). The normal range of responses from a number of studies with various pyrogen preparations is remarkably uniform (Jenkins, 1968; Carroll *et al.,* 1969).

The exact *site and mode of action* of pyrogen is not yet established, although it certainly depends on pituitary ACTH release (Takebe *et al.,* 1966). Patients with pituitary disease and with Cushing's disease have been described who responded to lysine vasopressin (LVP) but not to pyrogen, a finding which is difficult to reconcile with a direct pituitary site of action (James, Landon *et al.,* 1968a; Carroll *et al.,* 1969). The response to pyrogen can be blocked by dexamethasone (2 to 4 mg) (Jenkins, 1968; Moses and Miller, 1969) which again indicates a suprahypophyseal site of action, although lower doses (0.25 mg) of dexamethasone are sufficient to block the response to LVP (Jenkins, 1968).

The potential importance of the pyrogen test for the study of HPA control in psychiatric patients lies in the finding that in diencephalic Cushing's disease responses to this test as well as to hypoglycemia and to dexamethasone tend to be impaired simultaneously (James, Landon *et al.,* 1968a). It is possible, therefore, that these tests could distinguish patients with reactive or secondary HPA activation from others who may have developed an autonomous overactivity of the axis.

LYSINE VASOPRESSIN TEST

The posterior pituitary hormone pitressin (vasopressin) was found to stimulate ACTH release in rats, even in the presence of hypothalamic lesions which impaired their responses to nonspecific stresses (McCann and Brobeck, 1954), and vasopressin was thought for a time to be the functional corticotropin releasing factor (see Mess and Martini, 1968). Later, vasopressin and synthetic lysine-8-vasopressin were shown to elevate plasma 17-OHCS levels in man (McDonald and Weise, 1956; McDonald *et al.,* 1956). From these early observations a number of groups have developed standardized test procedures using intravenous or intramuscular injections or intravenous infusions of synthetic lysine-vasopressin (LVP) (see James and Landon, 1968; deWied *et al.,* 1968). Similar results have been reported in normal subjects by several groups using comparable techniques and the criteria for normal responses have been established (Carroll *et al.,* 1969).

Lysine vasopressin causes a prompt increase in plasma cortisol levels which is maximal at 30 to 60 minutes after intravenous injection of the drug and which is preceded by pituitary ACTH release (Gwinup *et al.,* 1967). Peripheral symptoms such as vasoconstriction, abdominal cramps, defecation, uterine cramps and occasionally ischemic cardiac pain occur, especially when intravenous injections are used, and have been thought by some workers to be at least partly responsible for the HPA activation. However, there is no close correlation between these effects and the rise in plasma cortisol; in addition the cortisol response is not affected when the peripheral symptoms are blocked by the prior administration of atropine (Carroll *et al.,* 1969). As with pyrogen, the response to LVP varies throughout the twenty-four-hour cycle, with maximum responses being found at night (Clayton *et al.,* 1963).

Initially it was thought that LVP acted directly on the anterior pituitary in a similar manner to CRF (Clayton *et al.,* 1963; Gwinup, 1965) and its use was suggested as a way of distinguishing pituitary from hypothalamic disorders (Landon *et al.,* 1965). It is more likely that LVP acts at a hypothalamic level, since its effect is blocked by acute administration of dexamethasone, even in low doses (Gwinup, 1965; James *et al.,* 1968b; Jenkins, 1968; Takebe *et al.,* 1968), as well as by morphine and chlorpromazine (Gwinup, 1965; de Wied *et al.,* 1968). De Wied's group has also obtained more direct evidence from hypothalamic lesion studies to indicate that LVP acts at a suprahypophyseal level, thus confirming the conclusion of Hedge *et al.* (1966), who implanted vasopressin directly into the median eminence and anterior pituitary.

At present the LVP test finds its chief use in the investigation of suspected hypofunction of the HPA axis and for this reason it may not be applied widely in psychoendocrine studies. Normal responses to the test have been reported in four patients with anorexia nervosa (Tucci *et al.,* 1968). Other endocrine and metabolic sequelae to LVP administration, such as growth hormone release and lowering of plasma nonesterified fatty acid levels appear to be more variable than the cortisol response and may be more closely related to the occurrence of side effects (Greenwood and Landon, 1966; Gagliardino *et al.*, 1967; Czarny *et al.*, 1968; Brostoff *et al.*, 1968; Librik and Clayton, 1963; Karp *et al.*, 1968).

INSULIN HYPOGLYCEMIA

The induction of hypoglycemia by insulin has been known for a long time to result in an increase of adrenocortical activity (Vogt, 1947, 1951; Gershberg and Long, 1948; Bliss, Migeon *et al.*, 1954 a and b; Staehelin *et al.*, 1955; Amatruda *et al.*, 1960). The mechanism of the corticosteroid (and growth hormone) responses to the lowering of blood sugar is not known in detail, although it does require intact hypothalamic and pituitary function (Landon *et al.*, 1966) and it does not result from a change in cortisol clearance (Landon *et al.*, 1963). The occurrence of symptoms of neuroglycopenia is believed by some (Marks *et al.*, 1967) to be an important factor in determining the adrenal response, while others place more emphasis on the rate and degree of fall in the blood glucose concentration, and describe the subjective effects as "not unduly unpleasant" (Greenwood *et al.*, 1966).

With increasing experience and the use of intravenous injections of crystalline insulin the test has become standardized in its application to patients and to normal subjects, with the result that the criteria for an adequate degree of hypoglycemia and for a normal plasma cortisol response have been established (Landon *et al.*, 1963; Greenwood *et al.*, 1966; Landon *et al.*, 1966; Bethge *et al.*, 1967a; Carroll *et al.*, 1969; Moses and Miller, 1969). Varying amounts of insulin may be required, depending on the clinical circumstances. Provided that the blood glucose level falls below 45 mg/100 ml for at least ten minutes the responses of normal subjects are characterized by a brisk rise of plasma cortisol, beginning after thirty minutes from the start of the test and reaching a peak at sixty to ninety minutes. A rise in plasma ACTH levels precedes the cortisol response (Berson and Yalow, 1968). Data from a number of series of control subjects are available in the papers referred to above. Increasing doses of insulin cause greater plasma cortisol increments together with a prolongation of the period of effective hypoglycemia. Most groups have found that a *minimum sugar level of 45 mg/ 100 ml* is needed, although others have obtained good responses with minimum blood sugars as high as 60 to 65 mg/100 ml (Arner *et al.*, 1962).

Obese patients may have attenuated responses, which can be improved by the use of larger doses of insulin (James *et al.*, 1968a; Wynn, 1968). *Absent responses* are the rule when HPA suppression has occurred during *prolonged corticosteroid therapy* (Jasani *et al.*, 1967) and may persist for months after treatment is stopped (Livanou *et al.*, 1967) but good adrenocortical responses to natural stresses such as infections may nevertheless occur (Wynn, 1968). *Acute pretreatment* with dexamethasone, however, usually does not affect the increments of plasma cortisol, although larger doses of insulin may be required (James, *et al.*, 1968b; Moses and Miller, 1969). Pretreatment with 1 mg dexamethasone six-hourly for twenty-four hours will suppress the ACTH response to hypoglycemia (Berson and Yalow, 1968).

In Cushing's syndrome absent responses to hypoglycemia have been reported (Bethge *et al.*, 1969). In Cushing's disease the plasma cortisol levels are usually not affected by insulin hypoglycemia, even when severe symptoms are produced, and in this condition there appears to be a fundamental defect in the control of ACTH secretion (Bethge *et al.*, 1966; Bethge, Irmscher *et al.*, 1967; James *et al.*, 1968; Bethge *et al.*, 1969). This appears now, however, to be not an invariable finding in Cushing's disease (Brooks *et al.*, 1966; Jacobs and Nabarro, 1969) but is more consistent than is an impaired response to pyrogen (Landon *et al.*, 1968).

The insulin hypoglycemia test may be of considerable use, therefore, in evaluating the central control mechanisms of patients with increased HPA activity in association with stress or with psychopathological states.

DEXAMETHASONE SUPPRESSION TEST

The final test of HPA control relies on the use of synthetic corticosteroids to attempt suppression of HPA activity and, like the metyrapone test, was introduced by Liddle (1960). In its original form varying doses of dexamethasone were given orally at six-hourly intervals for forty-eight hours and the response was determined by measurement of plasma and urinary steroids. Discrimination between normal subjects and those with Cushing's syndrome, and between the various causes of the syndrome was possible. This test is superior to basal plasma or urinary measures, which do not reliably separate normal subjects from those with HPA disease. Infusions of dexamethasone phosphate may also be used to distinguish normals from those with Cushing's syndrome (James *et al.,* 1965; James *et al.,* 1968b).

A diurnal variation in the response to both orally and intravenously administered dexamethasone was then demonstrated (Nichols *et al.,* 1965; Ceresa *et al.,* 1969): as with the LVP, metyrapone and pyrogen tests a maximal response was obtained in the period preceding the circadian rise of plasma cortisol.

Following this discovery, Nugent *et al.* (1965) introduced a single-dose (midnight) dexamethasone suppression test, the endpoint of which was the plasma cortisol level the following morning. Several groups have documented their experience with this procedure and the criteria for normal responses are reasonably established (see Chap. 5). With the single-dose test no distinction is possible at present between Cushing's syndrome and Cushing's disease.

It must be appreciated that infusions of dexamethasone during the daytime give a measure of negative feedback control, since they reflect the cessation of cortisol secretion in response to the addition of the synthetic steroid to the glucocorticoid pool. The midnight doses, however, test the regulation of the diurnal variation mechanisms (the "once-a-day phase" of HPA activity—Ceresa *et al.,* 1969). The studies reviewed earlier clearly indicate that separate mechanisms are involved in the early morning from those which operate in the daytime.

After a midnight dose of dexamethasone the plasma cortisol levels at 8:00 to 9:00 AM are distributed in an approximately log-normal manner, in contrast to the normal distribution of basal plasma cortisol levels (Nugent *et al.,* 1965; McHardy-Young *et al.,* 1967; Asfeldt, 1969; Connolly *et al.,* 1968) and for this reason logarithmic conversion is appropriate before statistical comparisons are carried out (Gaddum, 1945; Heath, 1967).

Further discussion of the factors which can influence responses to dexamethasone is presented in Chapter 5. The paradoxical association, in Cushing's disease, of impaired HPA suppression by dexamethasone, and impaired stimulation by hypoglycemia has not been satisfactorily explained, especially since responses to metyrapone are normal or exaggerated in this condition.

The suppression procedures provide a very useful way of evaluating the nature of HPA activation in psychoendocrine studies and are now beginning to be employed in several centers.

Chapter 4

PLASMA CORTISOL LEVELS IN DEPRESSION

Bernard J. Carroll

INTRODUCTION

SEVERAL groups of investigators have reported finding elevated plasma levels of cortisol in depressed patients and their findings have been reviewed by Coppen (1967) and by Gibbons (1968 a and b).

The general conclusions have been that an increase in plasma cortisol is a common but by no means universal finding in severe depression. The procedure of hospital admission is considered by some authors to be largely responsible for the increase (Brooksbank and Coppen, 1967; Sachar, 1967b). Others have not found such a "first-sampling effect" and ascribe the increase to emotional disturbance associated with the illness itself (Gibbons and McHugh, 1962; Hullin *et al.*, 1967). Some authors have suggested that the increase in adrenocortical activity might play a causal role in the development of the illness (Clower and Migeon, 1967) while others consider this improbable (Coppen, 1967).

In all studies the reported increases in plasma cortisol have been modest, with most values falling in the upper limit of the normally accepted range. Large increases beyond the normal range are not commonly observed.

The judgment of an increase in plasma cortisol levels in the depressed state rests on a comparison of pre-treatment and post-treatment levels and also on a comparison with the values found in control subjects. A fall in plasma levels has been consistently reported following all forms of effective antidepressant treatment. Estimates of the amount of increase seen in the untreated phase vary widely, however, and range between 2 per cent and

Note: Bibliographic references are included at end of Chapter 6.

Depressive Illness

TABLE 4-I

PLASMA CORTISOL LEVELS IN DEPRESSIVE ILLNESS BEFORE AND
AFTER TREATMENT (Mean values, μg/100 ml)

Authors	N	Time	Before Treatment	After Treatment	Ratio Before/After
Gibbons and					
McHugh, 1962 ...	17	9:00 AM	20.8	10.8	1.93
Gibbons, 1964	8	9:00 AM	17.6	10.6	1.66
Anderson and					
Dawson, 1965	17	9:00 AM	33.5	27.4	1.22
Bridges and					
Jones, 1966	13	9:00 AM	23.2	18.4	1.26
		9:30 PM	15.2	14.8	1.02
McClure, 1966b	5	7:00 AM	36.2	18.4	1.97
		10:00 PM	18	7.2	2.49
Brooksbank and					
Coppen, 1967	29	9:00 AM	22.1	17.9	1.23
		9:00 PM	11.9	8.6	1.38
Hullin *et al.*, 1967 ..	6	9:00 AM	30.5	25.0	1.22
Sachar, 1967c	10	8:00 AM	19.6	16.7	1.17
Present Series	40	8:30 AM	23.9	16.6	1.44
		4:30 PM	16.7	8.4	1.99

Note: To allow comparison between the results of workers using different methods for "plasma cortisol" estimation a before/after treatment ratio has been calculated.

150 per cent above post-treatment values. Table 4-I summarizes these reports. Sachar has pointed out (1967b) that some of the discrepancy may be explained by a "first-sampling effect" before the patients had settled into the hospital environment. The overwhelming impression obtained from the literature, however, is that this possibility is overrated as a sufficient explanation. The careful studies of Gibbons (1964) and McClure (1966a) cannot be criticized on this count. Other possible reasons for the differing results reported are differences between the types of patients studied and differences in the accepted degree of recovery following treatment.

Reports of failure to find significant changes in adrenocortical function which could be related primarily to the depressive state originate mainly from centers in the United States (Bunney *et al.*, 1965a; Sachar 1967c). Physical methods of treatment are used less commonly in these centers than in Australia or in Britain and the emphasis is on intense personal interaction

TABLE 4-II

PLASMA CORTISOL LEVELS IN DEPRESSED (D) AND CONTROL (C) PATIENTS

Author	Number D	Number C	Plasma D	Cortisol C	Time	Method	D/C Ratio	Nature of Controls
Board et al., 1956	21	5	19.2	18.1	AM	P	1.06	Acute schizophrenics
Board et al., 1957	33	24	19.5	12.3	AM	P	1.56	Normal subjects
Anderson and Dawson, 1965	19 (1)	28	33.9	20.8	AM	P	1.63	Chronic schizophrenics
	15 (2)	28	23.5	20.8	AM	P	1.13	Depressions in (1) admission, (2) research ward
Lingjaerde, 1964	8	50	27.1	17.4	AM	P	1.56	Normal subjects
	8	62	27.1	22.7	AM	P	1.19	Schizophrenics
	8	7	27.1	20.7	AM	P	1.31	Manics
Doig et al., 1966	10	9	10.0	6.4	2400 hrs	F	1.56	Medical and surgical patients
			22.1	11.0	3:00 AM	F	2.01	
			22.2	15.9	6:00 AM	F	1.40	
Bridges and Jones, 1966	13	13	23.2	22.7	AM	F	1.02	Convalescent surgical patients
			15.2	18.6	9:30 PM	F	0.82	
McClure 1966a	7	7	39.4	17.6	7:00 AM	M	2.24	Normal subjects
			19.3	5.4	10:00 PM	M	3.57	
Hullin et al., 1966	6	6	30.5	13.2	AM	F	2.31	Normal subjects
			19.8	9.1	4:00 AM	F	2.18	
Knapp et al., 1967	6	7	21.4	19.6	8:00 AM	F	1.09	Normal subjects
			13.0	14.4	4:00 PM	F	0.09	Normal subjects
Present Series, 1969	40	20	23.9	21.7	8:30 AM	F	1.10	Nondepressed psychiatric patients
			16.7	13.7	4:30 PM	F	1.22	

P = methods based on Porter-Silber reaction (17-OHCS)   Normal range 6-25µg/100 ml
M = protein binding method of Murphy et al., 1963   Normal range 4-20µg/100 ml
F = fluorometric methods   Normal range 5-24µg/100 ml

between nursing staff and patient. As described by Sachar (1967c) ". . . nursing personnel encouraged patients to discuss life problems at every opportunity; it was therefore more difficult for patients to maintain denial of relevant psychological issues both before and after recovery, and this milieu factor may have influenced adrenal cortical responses." Such an atmosphere may be persistently threatening to some patients and may prevent part of the expected fall in adrenocortical activity from occurring; it might also be expected to exaggerate the "first-sampling effect."

There is even less agreement in the literature on the second point of comparison, that of depressives with control subjects (Table 4-II). Some authors report depression/control ratios of less than one while others find ratios up to 3.6. Variations in the type of control patients chosen are sufficient to account for these differences. The studies of Board *et al.* (1956) and of Lingjaerde (1964) satisfy most completely the requirements for an adequate control group. These authors report only modest elevations of plasma cortisol levels in depression, the values being 6 per cent to 19 per cent higher than those found in schizophrenia.

The present study was designed partly as an essential preliminary to work to be reported later and also to reexamine some of the areas of disagreement outlined above.

1. Plasma cortisol levels before and after treatment were measured in a group of forty depressed patients; a suitable control group has also been studied.

2. The "admission to hospital" stress effect has been investigated and the effect of a stressful situation during treatment has been examined.

3. The relationship between plasma cortisol levels and important clinical features has also been investigated.

SUBJECTS AND METHODS

Forty depressed patients were studied. They were chosen according to the criteria detailed in Chapter 2 as were a group of twenty control subjects in the same wards.

The mean age of the forty depressives was sixty years (range

40 to 82) while that of the control subjects was thirty-seven years (range 20 to 65).

The control subjects were studied only on admission; tests were not repeated on them before discharge because they had received a variety of drugs during treatment which are known to interfere with the release of adrenocorticotrophic hormone (ACTH) and to lower plasma cortisol levels in some circumstances (Butler, Besser and Steinberg, 1968; Gold and Ganong, 1967).

Blood was collected by venepuncture at 0830-0900 hours and at 1630-1700 hours for diurnal plasma cortisol estimations. The plasma was separated, frozen quickly and stored until the estimations were done.

The first sampling was performed at least four days after admission. In most cases the resting period before first sampling was one week. The data of Mason *et al.* (1965) and of Sachar (1967c) indicate that values obtained after the fifth to seventh day of hospitalization are stable, compared with the fluctuating levels seen earlier in the first week.

Where more than one estimation was performed on any patient before or after treatment the mean value is recorded. In some depressed patients testing was carried out at intervals during treatment. All were studied after treatment shortly before discharge. The post-treatment sampling was delayed for at least one week after the last electroconvulsive treatment (ECT).

TABLE 4-III

DIURNAL PLASMA CORTISOL LEVELS IN FORTY DEPRESSED PATIENTS ON ADMISSION AND AFTER TREATMENT AND IN TWENTY CONTROL SUBJECTS ON ADMISSION (Means ± S.D.)

	0830 hrs. Plasma Cortisol ($\mu g/100\ ml$)	1630 hrs. Plasma Cortisol ($\mu g/100\ ml$)
Depressives on Admission	23.9	16.7
(n = 40)	(±8.8)	(±6.8)
Depressives after Treatment	16.6	8.4
(n = 40)	(±6.0)	(±4.0)
Control Patients on Admission	21.7	13.7
(n = 20)	(±6.2)	(±6.0)

Antidepressant drugs (imipramine or amitriptyline) were continued during the pre-discharge study period in those few patients who were treated with these agents.

Plasma cortisol was measured as total 11-hydroxycorticosteroids (11OHCS) by the method of Mattingly (1962). Barbiturates and imipramine were shown not to interfere with the procedure.

RESULTS

The diurnal plasma cortisol levels found in the patients are shown in Table 4-III.

A significant fall in both morning and afternoon levels was seen in the depressives following treatment. The before-after treatment ratios were 1.44 (AM) and 1.99 (PM).

The diurnal values in the forty depressives on admission did not differ significantly from the values found in the twenty control patients. After treatment, however, the depressives had plasma cortisol levels significantly lower than those seen in the control patients on admission.

These comparisons are summarized in Table 4-IV.

TABLE 4-IV

COMPARISONS OF PLASMA CORTISOL LEVELS

Comparison	N	t	p
AM Depression before treatment	40		
versus		4.3	0.001
AM Depression after treatment	40		
PM Depression before treatment	40		
versus		6.6	0.001
PM Depression after treatment	40		
AM Depression before treatment	40		
versus		1.02	0.3
AM Controls	20		
PM Depression before treatment	40		
versus		1.65	0.1
PM Controls	20		
AM Depression after treatment	40		
versus		−3.05	0.01
AM Controls	20		
PM Depression after treatment	40		
versus		−4.09	0.001
PM Controls	20		

TABLE 4-V

MORNING PLASMA CORTISOL LEVELS IN TWENTY DEPRESSED
PATIENTS DURING PERIOD IN HOSPITAL (Mean Values)

	Week after Admission					
	1	2	3	4	5	6
Mean Plasma Cortisol (μg/100 ml)	21.6	22.7	16.9	21.4	18.2	16.8
Number of Estimations	37	27	15	10	13	16

ADMISSION TO HOSPITAL EFFECT ON MORNING PLASMA CORTISOL LEVELS

Ten depressed patients had morning plasma cortisol levels measured during both the first and second weeks after admission. Nineteen values were obtained in the first week and thirteen in the second. Specific treatment was not commenced in these subjects until after the second week.

The mean value found in week 1 was 20.7μg/100 ml and 24.0μg/100 ml in week 2. In only one patient was a lower value obtained during the second week.

A similar trend is seen in Table 4-V in which the values obtained in the first twenty patients of the series are summarized. As the numbers indicate, each patient is not represented in each weekly cohort.

In this group of severely depressed patients no evidence has been obtained to suggest that morning plasma cortisol levels are significantly elevated during the first week in the hospital, as a response to the stress of admission.

EFFECT OF AWAITING ELECTROCONVULSIVE TREATMENT ON MORNING PLASMA CORTISOL LEVELS

Fifteen patients were studied on twenty-three occasions. Blood was collected at 0830 hours on mornings when ECT was to be given and also on the immediately preceding mornings. At the time of testing the patients were not markedly improved and had already received two or three treatments. They were required to fast from 2200 hours on the night preceding ECT and they received 0.6 mg atropine sulphate intramuscularly at 0730 hours on the ECT days. Neither of these procedures ma-

TABLE 4-VI

PLASMA CORTISOL LEVELS ON ECT AND NON-ECT
MORNINGS (n = 23 in Fifteen Patients)

	ECT Day	Non-ECT Day
Mean Plasma Cortisol (μg/100 ml)	20.7	19.3
S.D.	6.1	6.4

terially affects the diurnal fall in plasma cortisol occurring at this time of day (Lingjaerde, 1964; Krieger *et al.*, 1968). However the patients were aware for at least ten hours in advance, that they were to receive ECT the following morning.

Friedman (1957) has documented the frequency and nature of the fear and anxiety associated with ECT. To varying degrees the patients feared the treatment as punishment, feared their own helplessness and feared what the treatment might do to their minds.

The patients frequently expressed feelings of apprehension about their treatments. Their attitudes were not systematically probed on the ECT mornings so as not to provoke a stress response by discussion of the topic. It was assumed that if fear of ECT was to produce any effect on plasma cortisol levels then it would be an obvious effect and that attempts to quantify the level of anxiety on the mornings in question would be unnecessary.

The results of this investigation are given in Table 4-VI.

No significant difference is seen between the two values. On eleven of the twenty-three occasions the value obtained on the non-ECT day was the greater.

Expectation of ECT thus had no obvious effect on the morning plasma cortisol levels.

RELATION OF PLASMA CORTISOL LEVELS TO CLINICAL FEATURES

The plasma cortisol levels found are summarized according to age groups in Table 4-VII.

The mean afternoon level seen in the 41- to 50-year cohort is lower than that in the 61- to 70-year group (t = 2.02, p <0.05). *No other significant effect of age is seen.*

TABLE 4-VII

RELATION OF AGE TO PLASMA CORTISOL LEVELS
(Means ± S.D., μg/100 ml)

	Age (Years)			
	41-50	*51-60*	*61-70*	*71-80+*
Number of Patients	5	20	7	8
AM Plasma Cortisol	21.4	26.3	21.5	21.1
	±13.1	±8.5	±8.4	±6.3
PM Plasma Cortisol	11.9	17.1	19.6	16.1
	±6.6	±6.5	±6.4	±7.5

The nineteen males had diurnal plasma cortisol levels (μg/100 ml) of 23.2 ± 8.7 (AM) and 15.6 ± 6.7 (PM). The corresponding values for the twenty-one females were 24.6 ± 9.1 and 17.6 ± 6.9. *These levels do not differ significantly.*

Previous History of Depressive Illness

Twenty-seven patients had been previously admitted for depressive illness. None had suffered with previous manic episodes. The diurnal plasma cortisol levels of those with a positive past history were 23.1 ± 9.1 (AM) and 17.7 ± 6.9 (PM), compared with 25.2 ± 8.3 and 14.5 ± 6.2 for the thirteen subjects with a negative past history. *These differences are not significant.*

Diurnal Mood Variation

Twenty-four subjects experienced diurnal variation in mood of the classical type associated with depression; i.e. mood was lowest and depressive affect and symptoms were most severe in the mornings, with some improvement occurring later in the day.

These patients had mean plasma cortisol levels of 22.9 (AM) and 15.7 (PM) μg/100 ml. The corresponding values for the remaining sixteen subjects were 25.2 and 18.1 μg/100 ml.

These differences are not significant. *Contrary to what might have been expected the morning levels tended to be lower in those with a classical diurnal mood rhythm.*

Retardation

Twenty-seven patients were considered to show significant psychomotor retardation on admission. Their mean plasma cortisol

levels were 23.8 (AM) and 15.6 (PM) μg/100 ml compared with
23.7 and 18.9μg/100 ml for the thirteen patients without retardation.

*These differences are not significant although some earlier re-
ports have suggested that the values tend to be higher in retarded depressives (Board et al., 1957).*

Agitation

Thirty-two patients displayed agitation as a feature of their
illness. In some it was mild and inconstant while in others a diurnal variation was obvious in this symptom, in company with
the variation in mood. Eight subjects were considered definitely
not to be agitated at any time. These eight had mean plasma
cortisol levels of 21.6 (AM) and 16.1 (PM) μg/100 ml compared
with 24.3 and 16.8μg/100 ml for the agitated patients. *These
values do not differ significantly.*

Sleep Disturbance

The patients were questioned regarding initial, middle and
delayed sleep disturbance as suggested by Hamilton (1960).
Twenty-eight had *initial sleep disturbance* while twelve did not.
Those with such disturbed sleep had mean diurnal plasma cortisol levels of 23.2 (AM) and 16.3 (PM) μg/100 ml compared
with 25.3 and 17.6μg/100 ml in those who experienced no early
sleeping difficulty. *These values do not differ significantly.*

Only two patients did not have middle or terminal insomnia.
Their plasma cortisol levels were not remarkable.

Suicide Attempt in Present Illness

Bunney and Fawcett (1965) have suggested that adrenocortical activity tends to be higher in patients who attempt suicide
when depressed than in those who do not. Eight of the forty patients in this series had attempted suicide by various means.
Five took a barbiturate overdosage, two gassed themselves (car-
bon monoxide) and one shot himself. This last man was tested
before his suicide attempt. The others were admitted to hospital
as a result of their action and were not tested until at least one
week after complete physical recovery. At this time most were
not actively suicidal.

The mean plasma cortisol levels in these patients were not different from the group mean. The values were 22.1 (AM) and 16.6 (PM) μg/100 ml.

The levels of the man studied shortly before his suicide attempt were among the highest seen in the whole group 35.0 (AM) and 23.7 (PM) μg/100 ml.

Weight Loss

Twenty-eight patients were noted to have lost at least seven pounds (3.2 kg) weight during the period of illness before admission. *These subjects had significantly higher morning plasma cortisol levels* than did the twelve without such loss of weight. The mean values obtained were 26.0 $\pm$ 9.1 compared with 18.6 $\pm$ 8.2μg/100 ml (t = 2.63, p <0.01).

The afternoon levels were also higher in the wasted group but the difference did not reach statistical significance. The mean PM values were 17.5 compared with 14.9μg/100 ml (t = 1.1).

Duration of Illness before Admission

The duration of significant symptoms of the illness before admission was recorded in all patients. The information was obtained from relatives whenever possible as well as from the patients themselves. Inevitably in some instances only an approximate time of onset could be determined. The results of this enquiry are given in Table 4-VIII, in which the frequency of significant weight loss in each group is also recorded.

TABLE 4-VIII

PLASMA CORTISOL LEVELS IN RELATION TO DURATION OF ILLNESS
BEFORE ADMISSION (Mean Values, μg/100 ml)

Duration (Weeks)	N	Weight Loss 7 lb. N	AM *Plasma Cortisol*	PM *Plasma Cortisol*
0-4	8	7	27.6	18.0
4-8	11	10	23.9	17.5
8-12	4	1	12.4	13.4
12-16	5	2	20.8	13.0
16-20	8	5	25.1	17.2
20	4	3	21.9	15.0

The lower plasma levels seen in the 8 to 16-week groups may be related to the decreased incidence of weight loss in these subjects. No other reason for this trend seems obvious.

Method of Treatment

All but six of the patients were treated with electroconvulsive therapy (ECT). Two patients were treated with a modified bilateral prefrontal leukotomy. Only four were treated with antidepressant drugs alone.

The plasma cortisol levels of the two patients treated by leukotomy were 7.8 (AM), 19.0 (PM) and 29.3 (AM), 15.1 (PM) μg/100 ml. No useful comment can be made about these values.

The four subjects treated with an iminodibenzyl antidepressant drug (imipramine) had plasma cortisol levels somewhat lower than the group mean figures. The mean values in these four patients were 19.5 (AM) and 11.9 (PM) μg/100 ml. Once again, the numbers are too small to allow realistic comments. *The trend observed here suggests that overall severity of the depression may be related to the plasma cortisol levels,* since in general milder cases are treated with antidepressants alone.

Severity of Illness

The relation between severity of depression and the plasma cortisol levels was examined in twenty-four patients. They comprised sixteen of the forty patients previously discussed as well as eight similar patients whose plasma cortisol levels were studied on admission only. Clinical rating was carried out by the Zung Self-Rating Depression Scale and the Hamilton Depression Scale, as described in Chapter 2. The greatest severity of ill-

TABLE 4-IX

MEAN HAMILTON AND ZUNG RATING SCORES AND PLASMA
CORTISOL LEVELS (μg/100 ml) (n = 24)

	Hamilton Score	Zung Score	AM Cortisol	PM Cortisol
Mean	29.5	51.9	23.6	15.4
S.A.	7.8	12.1	7.4	7.0

TABLE 4-X

HAMILTON RATINGS AND DIURNAL PLASMA CORTISOL LEVELS
(μg/100 ml) (n = 24)

Hamilton Score	N	AM Cortisol Mean	AM Cortisol S.D.	PM Cortisol Mean	PM Cortisol S.D.
10-19	3	16.0	—	7.7	—
20-29	9	23.8	4.5	15.1	7.6
30-40	12	25.3	8.9	17.5	5.8

ness would be indicated by the maximum possible Zung score of 80 and the maximum Hamilton rating of 52. The mean rating scores and plasma cortisol levels are shown in Table 4-IX.

Tables 4-X and 4-XI demonstrate the relations between increasing rating scores and the plasma cortisol levels.

These figures indicate a positive relationship between severity and plasma cortisol levels in the patients who are least depressed. In the more severely ill subjects, however, the diurnal plasma cortisol levels do not continue to rise pari passu with the rating scores.

To further examine the relationship between the plasma cortisol levels and the ratings of severity, product-moment (Pearson) and rank order (Spearmann) correlation coefficients were calculated (Table 4-XII).

The patient's self-rating score on the Zung Scale bears a relationship to the diurnal plasma cortisol levels, while the objective index of severity, the Hamilton score, does not. This conclusion applies to both Pearson and Spearmann coefficients. The

TABLE 4-XI

ZUNG RATINGS AND DIURNAL PLASMA CORTISOL LEVELS
(μg/100 ml) (n = 24)

Zung Score	N	AM Cortisol Mean	AM Cortisol S.D.	PM Cortisol Mean	PM Cortisol S.D.
30-39	5	17.1	3.4	10.3	5.3
40-49	5	20.4	5.9	11.8	4.0
50-59	6	29.7	6.4	18.8	5.8
60-69+	8	25.0	7.3	18.3	8.0

differences between the two coefficients are due to a large number of ties on ranking the scores.

The degree of correlation between the Hamilton and Zung scores warranted further investigation, so it was decided to examine the relationships between the components of each scale.

Zung (1965) claims that his scale measures three aspects of depressive illness, namely depressive affect (2 items), physiological aspects (8 items) and psychological aspects (10 items).

Hamilton (1960) has isolated four factors from scores on his rating scale. Factor 1 is a measure of depressive affect. Factor 2 of somatic features and Factor 3 of anxiety-agitation. Factor 4 could not be identified. The following principal items from the first three factors were chosen: depressed mood, guilt, suicide and retardation from Factor 1; initial, middle and delayed insomnia, gastrointestinal somatic symptoms and weight loss from Factor 2; and agitation, somatic anxiety and psychic anxiety from Factor 3. The correlation matrix between these items is shown in Table 4-XIII.

Several important relationships are apparent from the matrix. The *physiological component* of the Zung scale relates well to the total Hamilton Score ($r = 0.500$, $p < .01$) and also to the physiological Hamilton factor (Factor 2) ($r = 0.569$, $p < 0.01$). Hamilton Factor 2 relates well to the Total Zung Score ($r = 0.490$, $p < 0.01$). These relationships are considerably better than the total Hamilton-total Zung relationship ($r = 0.398$, $p < 0.05$).

The *depressive component* of the Zung scale does not relate to the total Hamilton score, nor to any of the Hamilton factors.

TABLE 4-XII

CORRELATION COEFFICIENTS (n = 24)

	Product-Moment	p	Rank Order	p
Hamilton-Zung	0.3979	0.05	0.2668	
AM-PM Cortisol	0.7768	0.001	0.7685	0.001
Hamilton-AM Cortisol	0.3313	—	0.1820	—
Hamilton-PM Cortisol	0.3723	—	0.3422	—
Zung-AM Cortisol	0.4838	0.01	0.4603	0.02
Zung-PM Cortisol	0.4932	0.01	0.4774	0.02

TABLE 4-XIII

CORRELATION MATRIX OF RATING SCORES AND FACTORS
(Product-moment, n = 24)

	Zung Total	*Zung Depression*	*Zung Physiological*	*Zung Psychological*	*Hamilton Total*	*Hamilton 1*	*Hamilton 2 and 3*
Zung Total							
Zung Depression	.559						
Zung Physiological	.853	.176					
Zung Psychological	.960	.529	.739				
Hamilton Total	.398	.025	.500	.320			
Hamilton 1	.260	.119	.419	.223	.512		
Hamilton 2	.490	.112	.569	.390	.865	.363	
Hamilton 3	.077	.015	.095	.039	.769	.116	.495

Hamilton Factor 1 (depressive affect) relates only to the physiological Zung component ($r = 0.419$, $p < 0.05$).

The psychological Zung component relates only to the Hamilton Factor 2 (physiological) ($r = 0.390$, $p < 0.05$). Hamilton Factor 3 (psychological) relates to none of the Zung components, nor to the total Zung score.

It is obvious that *the two scales give a common reflection of physiological depressive features* but that there is no good cross-reliability between their assessments of psychological features or of depressive affect.

The influence of each of the components of the two rating scales on the diurnal plasma cortisol levels is shown in Table 4-XIV.

Only the physiological Zung component bears strong relationship to the plasma levels.

The psychological components of both scales do not influence the plasma cortisol values. The same conclusion applies to the depressive component of the Zung scale.

Hamilton Factors 1 and 2 are related to the PM plasma cortisol levels. The weakness of the relationships between Hamilton Factor 2 (physiological) and the cortisol levels may be account-

TABLE 4-XIV

CORRELATION COEFFICIENTS OF RATING SCALE FACTORS AND
DIURNAL PLASMA CORTISOL LEVELS (Product-moment, n = 24)

	r	p
Zung Depression-AM	0.1346	—
Zung Depression-PM	0.0627	—
Zung Physiological-AM	0.7112	0.001
Zung Physiological-PM	0.6592	0.001
Zung Psychological-AM	0.3078	—
Zung Psychological-PM	0.3599	—
Hamilton 1-AM	0.1483	—
Hamilton 1-PM	0.4073	0.05
Hamilton 2-AM	0.3780	—
Hamilton 2-PM	0.3949	0.05
Hamilton 3-AM	0.1025	—
Hamilton 3-PM	0.1471	—

ed for by the fact that twelve of the twenty-four subjects were rated 9 or 10 out of a possible score of 10 for this factor.

The results indicate that the plasma cortisol levels in the depressed patients are related to physiological factors rather than to psychological anxiety features.

Anxiety Rating Scale

The results presented do not suggest that anxiety, as reflected by the factors of the *depression* rating scales, is related to diurnal plasma cortisol levels. This question was reexamined using the Taylor Manifest Anxiety Scale (TMAS) (Taylor, 1953). This is a self-rating scale which is widely used to assess the state of anxious arousal of groups of patients.

Nineteen patients completed this scale. The mean diurnal plasma cortisol levels in this group were 22.5μg/100 ml (AM) and 14.1μg/100 ml (PM). The correlations (product-moment) between the TMAS scores and the plasma cortisol levels were found not to be significant—$r = 0.1654$ (AM) and $r = 0.1858$ (PM).

The results obtained thus confirm the conclusions derived from the depression rating scale factors.

SUMMARY

A review is presented of evidence from previous studies of plasma cortisol levels in depression. Most authors agree that a modest increase in the levels does occur. The significance of this elevation is very much in dispute. Some workers regard it as the result of nonspecific arousal factors connected with entering the hospital; others remain unimpressed by this explanation. Comparisons of the levels found in depressives with those of other inpatients are influenced by the nature of the control groups.

Results are presented of a study involving forty depressed inpatients. Attention was paid to the control issues previously mentioned. A control group of twenty psychiatric inpatients was also studied.

A significant fall of diurnal plasma cortisol levels was found in the depressives after treatment.

However, the admission levels of the control patients (patients with psychiatric syndromes other than depression) were no different from those of the depressives.

No significant effect of admission to the hospital on diurnal plasma cortisol levels was found.

Intercurrent anxiety preceding ECT had no effect on morning levels of plasma cortisol.

The following clinical features were found *not* to influence diurnal plasma cortisol levels in any significant way: age, sex, previous history of depression, diurnal mood variation, retardation, agitation, sleep disturbance and suicide attempt before admission.

Weight loss was positively related to the diurnal levels of plasma cortisol.

Severity of illness was related to the cortisol levels in the less ill subjects but the levels in very ill subjects were not higher than in those rated moderately to severely ill.

Diurnal plasma cortisol levels were related to self-ratings of depression (Zung Scale) but not to objective ratings (Hamilton Scale). Only the physiological component of the Zung Scale (but not the depression or anxiety components) influenced the diurnal plasma cortisol levels.

Scores on the Taylor Manifest Anxiety Scale were not related to the diurnal plasma cortisol levels.

CONCLUSIONS

Diurnal plasma cortisol levels in depressed inpatients were significantly elevated before treatment, when compared with post-treatment values.

The plasma cortisol levels were not significantly different from those of a control group of psychiatric inpatients.

Analysis of clinical features and rating scales indicated that, within the group of depressives, biological factors rather than "felt anxiety" were responsible for the high plasma cortisol levels.

Chapter 5

CONTROL OF PLASMA CORTISOL LEVELS IN DEPRESSION: STUDIES WITH THE DEXAMETHASONE SUPPRESSION TEST

BERNARD J. CARROLL

PART I: INTRODUCTION

THE study of diurnal plasma cortisol levels described in Chapter 4 revealed no important differences between the depressives and the control group of patients before treatment. Within the group of depressives, biological factors, rather than anxiety, appeared to be related to the plasma cortisol levels observed before treatment was given.

Measurement of plasma cortisol at two points in the day gives only limited information about adrenal cortical function, and tells us little about the daily production rate of cortisol. More detailed studies are needed to evaluate the dynamic control of the hypothalamo-pituitary-adrenal (HPA) axis. The parameters of HPA function which may be most relevant to central nervous system (CNS) activity in depressed patients are those of suppression and stimulation of the axis.

In this chapter are described the effects of exogenous glucocorticoid on the plasma cortisol levels of depressed and control patients.

CHOICE OF PROCEDURE

The original dexamethasone (9-alpha-fluoro-16-alpha-methyl prednisolone) suppression test of Liddle (1960) was considered for this study. It involves the administration of 0.5 or 2.0 mg of dexamethasone at 6-hourly intervals for forty-eight hours. Plasma cortisol (or 17-OHCS) and urinary 17-OHCS (or cortisol) are measured over this period. Two accurate twenty-four-hour

---

Note: Bibliographic references are included at end of Chapter 6.

urine collections are required, which makes the procedure time consuming and susceptible of systematic errors by the nursing staff.

In view of the number of investigations to be carried out on some patients, and their need for treatment to be not greatly delayed, a simple overnight dexamethasone suppression test was used. Nichols *et al.* (1965) had shown that the suppressive effect of dexamethasone on cortisol production varied greatly according to the time of administration. Temporary suppression occurred at 8:00 AM and 4:00 PM, whereas the same dose (0.5 mg) given at midnight produced almost complete suppression for twenty-four hours in normal volunteers. The same authors then introduced an overnight dexamethasone suppression test, using a single dose of 1 mg at 11:00 PM or midnight. The level of plasma 17-OHCS the following morning (8:00-9:00 AM) reliably distinguished subjects with Cushing's syndrome from other patients, in contrast to the basal 8:00 AM plasma 17-OHCS levels of the same groups which had shown considerable overlap. A post-dexamethasone (post-DEX) level of $<11\mu g/100$ ml of plasma 17-OHCS was recorded for subjects without Cushing's syndrome. An exception to this general finding was noted in the case of five acutely ill subjects (unspecified illnesses) whose post-DEX plasma 17-OHCS levels were $>20\mu g/100$ ml, i.e. within the Cushingoid range. Three of these patients died within two days of the suppression test being performed (Nugent *et al.*, 1965).

Further studies with the 1 mg midnight dexamethasone suppression test indicated that the normal response was reflected by a plasma 17-OHCS level of $<5\mu g/100$ ml (Pavlatos *et al.*, 1965; Tucci *et al.*, 1967). Other categories of patients who responded poorly to the test were those receiving estrogens (Nugent *et al.*, 1965) and subjects with hirsutism and obesity (Pavlatos *et al.*, 1965).

At the time this study commenced (June, 1967) an overnight suppression test using *2 mg* of dexamethasone was described (McHardy-Young *et al.*, 1967). Sixteen normal and seventeen obese subjects all suppressed plasma 11-OHCS (fluorometric method) to $<7\mu g/100$ ml. A further fifteen patients with miscellaneous diseases suppressed to $<10\mu g/100$ ml (in all but 2 of this last group the values were $<7\mu g/100$ ml).

Considering this report together with the previous findings of incomplete suppression by acutely ill patients to a 1 mg dose, *the procedure of McHardy-Young et al. (1967) was chosen for this study, i.e. 2 mg midnight dexamethasone suppression test.*

Since this study was carried out other authors have provided additional information concerning the factors influencing the test. These findings will be reviewed in the discussion of the results of the present study.

TEST PROCEDURE

Blood was taken for plasma cortisol at 8:30 AM and 4:30 PM. At midnight a 2 mg dose of dexamethasone was given orally. A further blood specimen was collected for plasma cortisol at 8:30 AM the next morning. In some cases when the test was repeated, at least forty-eight hours elapsed between such tests. Dexamethasone does not interfere with the determination of plasma 11-OHCS.

PATIENTS STUDIED

Thirty-three depressed patients, from the group of forty described in Chapter 4, were examined. The same control group of twenty patients was also studied. The depressives were studied before and after treatment, while the control subjects were tested only on admission. As in the study of diurnal plasma cortisol levels, no drugs except amylobarbitone were allowed, and patients were not tested until 1 week after admission.

CALCULATIONS

In Chapter 3 it was pointed out that several groups have found the post-dexamethasone (Post-DEX) plasma cortisol levels to be asymmetrically distributed. The possible range of values is closed at the lower end (by zero) and the median values lie close to the lower limit. As Gaddum (1945), Heath (1967) and Asfeldt (1969) have shown, the distribution more closely approaches a normal (Gaussian) pattern after log-transformation of the original values, a procedure which must often be applied to biological parameters.

This is the correct statistical method of handling the data, before means, standard errors, product-moment correlations or t values are computed.

The geometric mean of the sample is then given by the antilogarithm of the mean logarithm. The range of 1 standard deviation about the mean logarithm is given by (mean log − S.D. mean log) and (mean log + S.D. mean log). Conversion of these values to antilogarithms then gives the empirical S.D. range about the geometric mean value. To use the example given by Heath (1967), when the mean logarithm is 0.30 (S.D. 0.30) the mean value is 2, with a standard deviation range of 1-4.

This procedure is essential for data which do have a log-normal distribution, but becomes less important when the arithmetic S.D. is less than 15 per cent of the arithmetic mean. From Table 5-I it can be seen that the arithmetic S.D. greatly exceeds this percentage in the case of post-DEX plasma cortisol levels, so that in a large sample a significant proportion of impossible negative values would be expected.

An illustration of these points is contained in the following figures. Figure 5-1 is a frequency distribution graph of post-DEX plasma cortisol levels in 108 patients without depression. A skew toward zero is seen, with tailing of the higher values, and the *median value is 3.4.* Using untransformed figures the arithmetic *mean is 4.3* (S.D. 2.9) with a standard deviation range from 1.4 to 7.2.

A better approximation to a normal distribution is seen in Figure 5-2, where the same data are displayed after log-transformation. The mean log is 0.53, which now corresponds to the peak of the distribution graph. The S.D. of the mean log is 0.32. From these results the *geometric mean is 3.4* (identical with the median value) and the S.D. range is from 1.6 to 7.1.

In the following chapters all tables and computed values dealing with post-DEX plasma cortisol levels are based on calculations using log-transformed data.

RESULTS

A large number of the depressives did not suppress their plasma cortisol levels normally in response to dexamethasone. In

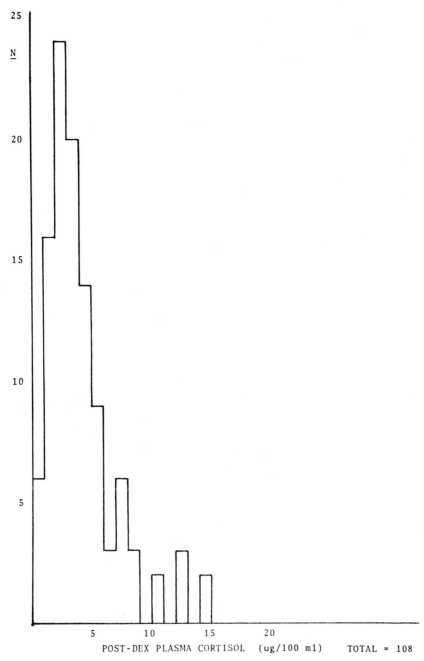

Figure 5-1. Post-DEX plasma cortisol levels in 108 patients without depression.

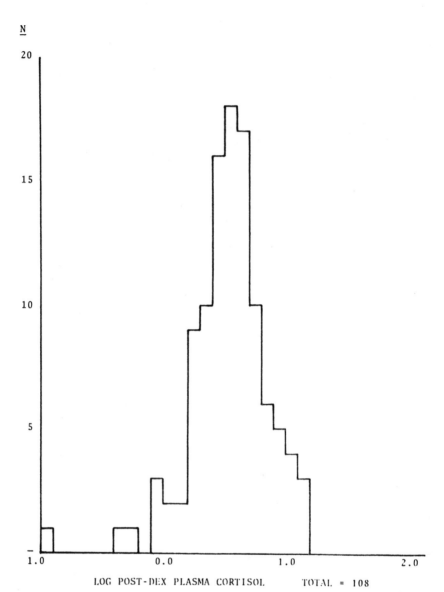

Figure 5-2. Log transformation of Figure 5-1.

many cases the levels of cortisol were within the range that other workers regard as diagnostic of Cushing's disease. In contrast, the results obtained in the control group were similar to those reported for normal subjects. In Figure 5-3 the frequency distribution of 250 post-DEX plasma cortisol results is shown. This number includes the 108 nondepressed patients of Figure 5-2, together with 142 depressed subjects studied by the author. A clear bimodal distribution is seen, from which it is apparent that some of the depressives constitute a separate population with respect to this parameter.

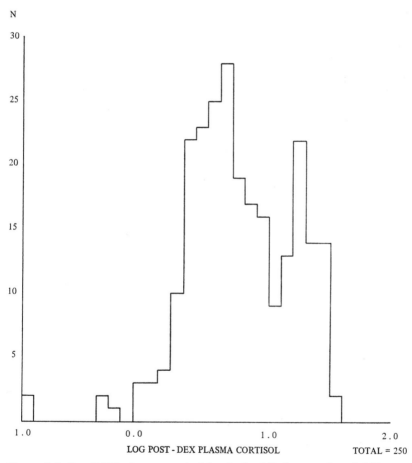

Figure 5-3. Post-DEX plasma cortisol levels in 142 depressed and 108 nondepressed patients (log transformed).

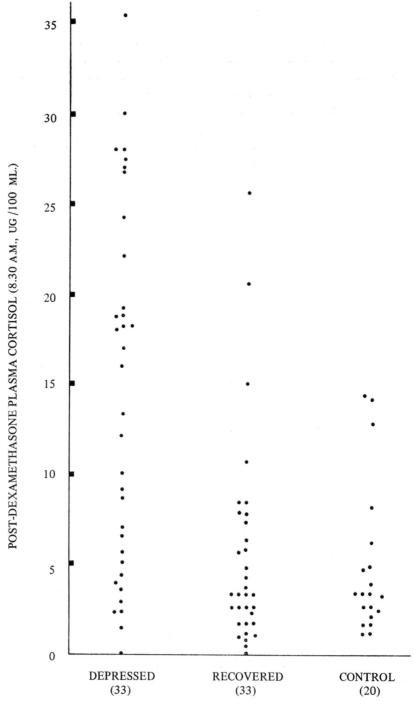

Figure 5-4. Post-DEX plasma cortisol levels of 33 depressed patients after treatment.

The mean post-DEX level in the thirty-three depressed patients discussed in this chapter was 11.0 (S.D. 4.6-26.8) μg/100 ml, with a range from 1.5 to 35.4μg/100 ml. The twenty psychiatric inpatients in the control group had a mean post-DEX plasma cortisol level of 3.8 (S.D. 1.8-8.0) μg/100 ml and a range from 1.4 to 14.5μg/100 ml. After treatment the depressives responded in a more normal manner to dexamethasone: the mean post-DEX plasma cortisol level was then 3.4 (S.D. 1.1-10.2) μg/100 ml with a range from 0.1 to 25.8μg/100 ml. These results are set out in Table 5-I and in Figure 5-4. The table contains for comparison the predexamethasone diurnal cortisol levels of these thirty-three subjects, and of the original group of forty subjects, as well as those of the control group. The diurnal values of the thirty-three patients tested with dexamethasone were not notably different from those of the original forty patients. In Table 5-I both the arithmetic and geometric means and standard deviations are given. *In later tables only the geometric values are considered,* although computations using both original and log-transformed data gave similar results.

The depressed and control groups did not differ with respect

TABLE 5-I

PLASMA CORTISOL LEVELS (μg/100 ml, means ± S.D.) OF DEPRESSED, RECOVERED DEPRESSED AND CONTROL PATIENTS BEFORE AND AFTER DEXAMETHASONE

	Pre-Dexamethasone		
	N	*8:30* AM	*4:30* PM
Depressed	33	23.8 (±8.6)	16.1 (±6.8)
Recovered	33	15.2 (±7.1)	8.8 (±4.2)
Control	20	21.7 (±6.2)	13.7 (±6.0)
Chapter 4 Group			
Depressed	40	23.9 (±8.8)	16.7 (±6.8)
Recovered	40	16.5 (±6.0)	8.4 (±4.0)

	Post-Dexamethasone		
		Arithmetic Mean and S.D. *8:30* AM	*Geometric Mean and S.D. Range* *8:30* AM
Depressed	33	14.9 (±9.8)	11.0 (4.6-26.8)
Recovered	33	5.3 (±5.8)	3.4 (1.1-10.2)
Control	20	5.0 (±4.2)	3.8 (1.8-8.0)

TABLE 5-II

COMPARISONS OF PLASMA CORTISOL LEVELS BEFORE AND AFTER
DEXAMETHASONE IN DEPRESSED, RECOVERED DEPRESSED AND
CONTROL PATIENTS

	N	t	p
Before Dexamethasone			
AM Depressed	33		
versus		0.95	N.S.
AM Control	20		
PM Depressed	33		
versus		1.30	N.S.
PM Control	20		
AM Depressed	33		
versus (paired t)		4.10	0.001
AM Recovered	33		
PM Depressed	33		
versus (paired t)		5.02	0.001
PM Recovered	33		
AM Recovered	33		
versus		−3.38	0.01
AM Control	20		
PM Recovered	33		
versus		−3.49	0.001
PM Control	20		
After Dexamethasone			
Depressed	33		
versus		4.47	0.001
Control	20		
Depressed	33		
versus (paired t)		5.19	0.001
Recovered	33		
Recovered	33		
versus		−0.45	N.S.
Control	20		

to their pre-DEX plasma cortisol levels. The post-DEX levels of
the two groups, however, were significantly different (Table
5-II). On recovery the post-DEX values were not different from
those of the control group on admission.

RELATION OF SUPPRESSION TO CLINICAL FEATURES

Age and Sex

No effect of age on suppression was apparent (Table 5-III).
There are no significant differences between any of the cohorts.

TABLE 5-III

AGES AND POST-DEXAMETHASONE PLASMA CORTISOL LEVELS
(Means, S.D. Range; μg/100 ml)

Age (years)	41-50	51-60	61-70	71-80+
N	4	16	5	8
Post-DEX	7.1	14.5	9.6	8.6
Cortisol	(1.5-34.2)	(7.0-30.1)	(3.9-23.9)	(4.0-18.1)

Males and females suppressed to a similar extent. The mean postdexamethasone plasma cortisol level of the 19 males was 11.2 (S.D. 4.9-25.7) μg/100 ml, compared with a value of 10.7 (S.D. 4.1-27.8) for the fourteen females.

Other nonsignificant clinical features were past history of depression, diurnal mood variation, initial insomnia, delayed insomnia, retardation and suicide attempt (Table 5-IV). Of the six patients who made a suicide attempt this action led to their admission in five cases. The man mentioned in Chapter 4, who attempted suicide shortly after these tests, had the highest postdexamethasone plasma cortisol level of the entire series (35.5 μg/100 ml).

Agitation

Six patients were considered not to have been agitated. They suppressed normally, while many of the agitated group did not.

TABLE 5-IV

CLINICAL FEATURES AND POST-DEXAMETHASONE PLASMA
CORTISOL LEVELS
(Means, S.D. Range; μg/100 ml)

		N	*Post-DEX Cortisol*
Past History	Yes	21	9.7 (3.7-25.3)
	No	12	13.7 (6.5-28.8)
Diurnal Variation	Yes	23	12.1 (5.0-29.0)
	No	10	8.9 (3.6-22.3)
Initial Insomnia	Yes	22	10.6 (4.2-26.5)
	No	11	11.8 (5.1-27.1)
Delayed Insomnia	No	2	2.9, 13.3*
Suicide Attempt	Yes	6	7.7 (3.0-20.0)
Retardation	Yes	24	10.5 (4.0-27.3)
	No	9	12.3 (5.9-25.8)

* Individual values.

The mean postdexamethasone plasma cortisol levels were as follows: agitated 13.3 (S.D. 5.8-30.5); nonagitated 4.6 (S.D. 2.7-7.8μg/100 ml (t = 2.92; p <0.01).

This difference between agitated and nonagitated patients contrasts with the lack of difference between the basal plasma cortisol levels of those patients.

Weight Loss

Subjects with more than 7 lb (3.2 kg) weight loss before admission were shown in Chapter 4 to have significantly higher morning plasma cortisol levels than those without such loss of weight. *A similar association was seen between weight loss and impaired suppression by dexamethasone.* Twenty-two patients in this group had lost >7 lb weight; their mean postdexamethasone plasma cortisol level was 14.1 (S.D. 6.1-32.4) μg/100 ml. The value for the remaining eleven patients was 6.7 (S.D. 2.9-15.4) μg/100 ml (t = 2.46; p <0.02).

Method of Treatment

Three patients of this group received tricyclic antidepressant drugs. Their postdexamethasone plasma cortisol levels tended to be normal; individual values were 13.3; 2.2 and 5.1μg/100 ml. No definitive comment can be made about this small number.

Duration of Illness Before Admission

Some effect of duration of illness on diurnal plasma cortisol levels was seen in Chapter 4. A similar effect emerged when the postdexamethasone levels were examined (Table 5-V).

TABLE 5-V

POST-DEXAMETHASONE PLASMA CORTISOL LEVELS IN RELATION TO
DURATION OF ILLNESS
(Means, S.D. Range; μg/100 ml)

Duration (weeks)	N	Weight Loss >7 lb N	Post-DEX Cortisol
0- 4	6	5	19.3 (11.4-32.8)
4- 8	7	7	11.5 (3.7-35.7)
8-12	3	1	4.8 (2.1-11.0)
12-16	5	2	5.5 (2.9-10.4)
16-20	8	5	12.0 (6.0-24.0)
>20	4	2	12.9 (5.0-33.6)

As in Table 4-VIII the incidence of weight loss in these cohorts has been included. The values of the 8 to 16-week groups are significantly lower than those of the remaining cohorts. The parallel with weight loss is not so striking here as it was when the basal plasma cortisol levels were examined.

CORRELATIONS BETWEEN PRE-DEXAMETHASONE AND POST-DEXAMETHASONE PLASMA CORTISOL LEVELS

In Figure 5-4 it was shown that many of the depressed patients did not suppress their plasma cortisol levels below the normally accepted figure of about 7 to $10\mu g/100$ ml. The basal cortisol levels of these patients were not significantly different from those of the control group, yet the controls did suppress normally. Likewise, the recovered depressives mostly suppressed normally, and their basal values were lower than those found before treatment.

Correlation coefficients (Pearson product-moment) were calculated to examine the interaction between the three cortisol levels in each group (Table 5-VI).

In the control group which responded normally, no significant correlations emerged between any of the cortisol levels, while all correlations were strongly positive in the depressed group before treatment. After treatment less powerful correlations were found.

These findings suggest that the postdexamethasone cortisol level in the depressives was a function of the high AM and PM levels before the suppression test. After treatment the AM basal level still appeared to influence the postdexamethasone level. In

TABLE 5-VI

PRODUCT-MOMENT CORRELATIONS BETWEEN PRE-DEXAMETHASONE (AM AND PM) AND POST-DEXAMETHASONE (DEX) PLASMA CORTISOL LEVELS

	N	Depressed 33	Recovered 33	Control 20
AM-DEX .... r		0.67[1]	0.59[1]	0.28
PM-DEX .... r		0.61[1]	0.39[3]	0.05
AM-PM .... r		0.65[1]	0.44[2]	0.15

Note: (1) $p < 0.001$; (2) $p < 0.01$; (3) $p < 0.05$.

TABLE 5-VII

PARTIAL CORRELATIONS BETWEEN DIURNAL AND
POST-DEXAMETHASONE PLASMA CORTISOL LEVELS

	N	Depressed 33	Recovered 33	Control 20
AM-DEX/PM .... r		0.45[1]	0.50[1]	0.27
PM-DEX/AM .... r		0.31	0.18	0.01

Note: (1) p < 0.01; (2) p < 0.02.

the control patients, however, suppression by dexamethasone was not influenced by the basal levels of plasma cortisol (with a larger number of control subjects a positive AM-DEX correlation may have emerged).

Because of the significant AM-PM correlations the *partial correlations* between AM-DEX and PM-DEX were calculated. This procedure yields correlations between two of the variables when the effect of the third variable on each is held constant. Table 5-VII summarizes these results.

From the table it appears that the AM plasma cortisol level has the major effect on the post-dexamethasone level.

These results indicate a real difference between the depressives and the control patients. They suggest that the degree of suppression by dexamethasone is related to the basal morning cortisol levels. In the control group who suppressed normally, however, the degree of suppression below the upper limit of the normal range is not influenced by the basal cortisol levels.

Interpretation of the correlations involving the post-dexamethasone cortisol levels is *complicated by methodological issues.* The fluorometric method used measures fluorescence of substances other than cortisol in plasma (James *et al.,* 1967; Nielsen and Asfeldt, 1967; Purves and Sirett, 1969). Interference from substances not of adrenal origin may produce background fluorescence equivalent to as much as $8\mu g/100$ ml of cortisol. This *nonspecific fluorescence varies between individuals* and is usually of the order of $3\text{-}5\mu g/100$ ml. For this reason correlations involving plasma levels below about $5\mu g/100$ ml may be less informative than correlations involving higher plasma levels. The number of postdexamethasone values below $5\mu g/100$ ml in the three groups were seven of thirty-three depressed, twenty-one of thirty-three recovered and fifteen of twenty control subjects.

DEXAMETHASONE SUPPRESSION AND SEVERITY OF ILLNESS

The relationship between severity of depression and post-dexamethasone plasma cortisol levels was examined in the subgroup of twenty-four patients detailed in Chapter 4. The mean rating scores and plasma cortisol levels are given in Table 5-VIII.

The diurnal cortisol levels of this subgroup were similar to those of the larger group of thirty-three patients (see Table 5-I). The relations between increasing rating scores and the postdexamethasone cortisol levels are illustrated in the following two tables (Tables 5-IX and 5-X).

TABLE 5-VIII

HAMILTON AND ZUNG RATING SCORES AND PLASMA
CORTISOL LEVELS (μg/100 ml) (n = 24)

	Hamilton Scores	Zung Score	Plasma Cortisol		
			AM	PM	Post-DEX
Mean	29.5	51.9	23.6	15.4	12.3
S.D.	7.8	12.1	7.4	7.0	5.1–29.5

TABLE 5-IX

HAMILTON RATINGS AND POST-DEXAMETHASONE PLASMA
CORTISOL LEVELS (μg/100 ml)

Hamilton Score	N	Post-DEX Plasma Cortisol	
		Mean	S.D. Range
10-19	3	3.2	—
20-29	9	13.0	6.8–24.7
30-40	12	16.5	8.6–31.4

TABLE 5-X

ZUNG RATINGS AND POST-DEXAMETHASONE PLASMA
CORTISOL LEVELS (μg/100 ml)

Zung Score	N	Post-DEX Plasma Cortisol	
		Mean	S.D. Range
30-39	5	6.6	1.7–26.4
40-49	5	12.0	7.5–19.2
50-59	6	16.8	9.3–30.2
60-69+	8	14.6	7.0–30.7

TABLE 5-XI

CORRELATION COEFFICIENTS (n = 24)

Comparison	Product-Moment	P	Rank Order	P
Hamilton—AM	0.33	—	0.18	—
Hamilton—PM	0.37	—	0.34	—
Hamilton—DEX	0.58	0.01	0.41	0.05
Zung—AM	0.48	0.01	0.46	0.02
Zung—PM	0.49	0.01	0.48	0.02
Zung—DEX	0.35	—	0.27	—

As was the case for the diurnal plasma cortisol levels (Tables 4-X and 4-XI) these figures indicate that in the more severely ill patients the levels of postdexamethasone plasma cortisol do not continue to rise in parallel with the rating scores.

The relationship between response to dexamethasone and severity was further examined by calculating product-moment and rank order correlation coefficients (Table 5-XI).

A striking difference between the two scales in their correlations with the cortisol levels is seen. The Hamilton Scores relate

TABLE 5-XII

CORRELATION COEFFICIENTS OF RATING SCALE FACTORS AND
PLASMA CORTISOL LEVELS (Product-moment; n = 24)

Comparison	r	p
Hamilton 1—AM	0.15	—
Hamilton 1—PM	0.41	0.05
Hamilton 1—DEX	0.40	0.05
Hamilton 2—AM	0.38	—
Hamilton 2—PM	0.39	0.05
Hamilton 2—DEX	0.70	0.001
Hamilton 3—AM	0.10	—
Hamilton 3—PM	0.15	—
Hamilton 3—DEX	0.26	—
Zung Depression—AM	0.13	—
Zung Depression—PM	0.06	—
Zung Depression—DEX	−0.003	—
Zung Physiological—AM	0.71	0.001
Zung Physiological—PM	0.66	0.001
Zung Physiological—DEX	0.58	0.01
Zung Psychological—AM	0.31	—
Zung Psychological—PM	0.36	—
Zung Psychological—DEX	0.20	—

only to the postdexamethasone levels, while the Zung scores relate only to the diurnal levels.

In Chapter 4 the components of the two scales were examined; it was concluded that they both reflect physiological features of depression but that they did not reliably duplicate each other in respect of psychological and affective aspects of the illness. The influence of each of the components of the two scales on the response to dexamethasone was examined (Table 5-XII).

From this table it appears that the postdexamethasone plasma cortisol levels relate chiefly to the second Hamilton factor (insomnia, gut symptoms and weight loss) and to the physiological component of the Zung scale (insomnia, gut symptoms, weight loss, diurnal variation, libido, tachycardia and fatigue).

In particular no significant correlations were found between psychological anxiety features and poor response to dexamethasone.

ANXIETY RATING SCALE

In agreement with the findings from the depression scale components, no correlation was found between postdexamethasone plasma cortisol levels and scores on the Taylor Manifest Anxiety Scale ($r = 0.10$, $n = 19$). Seven patients with Taylor scores <30 points had a mean level of $7.8\mu g/100$ ml; the twelve patients with scores >30 points had a mean level of $10.4\mu g/100$ ml postdexamethasone.

SUMMARY OF DEXAMETHASONE SUPPRESSION RESULTS

Before treatment the depressed patients had significantly higher postdexamethasone plasma cortisol levels than after treatment. The values found after treatment were similar to those of the control group on admission and were close to those reported for normal subjects by other workers. The 2 mg midnight dexamethasone suppression test thus discriminated the depressives from the recovered depressives *and from the control patients.* In contrast the diurnal plasma cortisol levels did not distinguish depressed from control patients.

Factors significantly associated with nonsuppression by dexamethasone were agitation, weight loss and duration of illness.

In the depressed group high postdexamethasone cortisol levels were related to high predexamethasone diurnal levels.

Failure to suppress after dexamethasone correlated strongly with physiological features but not with anxiety symptoms.

DISCUSSION OF DEXAMETHASONE SUPPRESSION RESULTS

The results of this study support the original hypothesis that the dynamics of HPA function in depression may be abnormal. *The suppression test distinguished clearly between the depressed and control patients who could not be distinguished simply on the basis of their diurnal plasma cortisol levels.* In seventeen of thirty-three cases the responses of the depressives were grossly abnormal and, but for the absence of other features, would have been diagnostic of Cushing's syndrome (postdexamethasone plasma cortisol $>15\mu g/100$ ml). Six other patients showed partial suppression to a level of between 7 and $15\mu g/100$ ml, and only ten of the thirty-three suppressed normally. After treatment only three responses were clearly abnormal, six were partially suppressed and twenty-four were suppressed normally.

The site of action of dexamethasone in suppressing HPA function is at the level of the hypothalamus and other limbic regulatory areas. The evidence for this statement has been discussed in Chapter 3. Failure of normal suppression by the depressed patients may have several possible causes. Impaired absorption of orally administered dexamethasone, inadequate penetration of dexamethasone to the hypothalamus, insensitivity of the steroid-responsive neurones to the drug or an abnormal drive from cortical and other limbic areas on the "final common pathway" for CRF release in the median eminence are some of the mechanisms which must be considered.

Steroid malabsorption is not likely to account for these findings. Dexamethasone is a freely diffusible molecule with a solubility comparable to that of cortisol itself (Stecher, 1960). Cortisol is rapidly absorbed from the stomach and small bowel (Peterson *et al.*, 1955; Schedl, 1965) and high blood levels after oral administration are reached faster than after cortisol is given by the intramuscular route. In addition, studies of cortisol and corticosterone secretion rates in depressives using oral ^{14}C-steroids provide no evidence for steroid malabsorption in the depressed state (Gibbons 1964, 1966; Sachar *et al.*, 1971).

Transport of dexamethasone to the hypothalamus is principally as the free steroid, since very little is bound to corticosteroid-binding globulin (Keller *et al.*, 1969).

Entry of dexamethasone into the central nervous system is a process which has not received close study. Cortisol and corticosterone enter animal brains very rapidly and appear in higher concentrations in the hypothalamus and limbic areas than in other brain regions (see Chapter 3). Progesterone, pregnanedione, pregnanolone and testosterone also rapidly enter the brain in rats (Arai *et al.*, 1967; Raisinghani *et al.*, 1968; Green *et al.*, 1970). Some competition between steroids for brain absorption has been described by Bidder (1968), who found that high doses of intracarotid estradiol impaired the brain entry of progesterone. Variations in regional distribution and rate of estradiol uptake by brain have been described in relation to age and estrous cycles in rats (Woolley *et al.*, 1969; Kato *et al.*, 1969; Kato, 1970). It has not been possible to estimate the rate of dexamethasone entry into the hypothalamus in the patients studied; however the possibility that this process was impaired does not seem likely. Saturation of the transport and retention mechanisms for corticosterone and hydrocortisone in brain can be demonstrated with high doses (3 mg) in rats; high endogenous tissue levels prevent the uptake of exogenous steroid (McEwen *et al.*, 1968). There is no experimental evidence concerning interaction between dexamethasone uptake and high tissue cortisol levels. The total endogenous brain tissue cortisol levels of suicides is not higher than those of nonsuicides (Carroll, unpublished); prevention of hypothalamic dexamethasone uptake by high endogenous brain cortisol levels in the depressives does not therefore seem to be a serious possibility.

Abnormally rapid metabolism of dexamethasone by the depressed patients must also be considered as a factor leading to nonsuppression. Dexamethasone has a long plasma half-life (200 minutes) when compared with cortisol (110 minutes) and prednisone (60 minutes) (Rabhan, 1968). Metabolism of dexamethasone occurs in the liver and the activity of the liver microsomal enzymes can be increased by corticosteroids themselves

and by drugs such as diphenylhydantoin (Dilantin) and phenobarbitone (Dwyer *et al.*, 1967; Jubiz *et al.*, 1970; Conney *et al.*,
1965). Phenobarbitone has been shown to shorten the half-life
of exogenous cortisol in humans (Morselli *et al.*, 1970) and a
similar effect of diphenylhydantoin on the rates of metabolism
of both dexamethasone and metyrapone has been reported in
animals and human subjects (Jubiz, Meikle *et al.*, 1970a; Jubiz,
Levinson *et al.*, 1970).

Interference by diphenylhydantoin in the various forms of
the dexamethasone suppression test has now been convincingly
demonstrated (Werk *et al.*, 1969; Asfeldt and Buhl, 1969). High
doses (4 mg at midnight) were needed to suppress plasma cortisol levels in epileptic patients receiving long-term diphenylhydantoin therapy.

The ability of barbiturates to affect steroid metabolism was not
known at the time this study was carried out. Amylobarbitone was
used for sedation and as a hypnotic because barbiturates consistently depress ACTH release (Gaunt *et al.*, 1965), so that their
presence in this situation would be expected to work against the
finding of nonsuppression by dexamethasone. In the light of our
present knowledge, however, the amylobarbitone may have been
responsible for some of the nonsuppression observed.

*Several lines of evidence suggest that interference by amylo-
barbitone in the metabolism of dexamethasone can not completely account for the results obtained.*

In the first place, individual patients who suppressed normally were receiving equal amounts of amylobarbitone to those
who were resistant to dexamethasone suppression. Similar amounts
of amylobarbitone were also used in the control group.

Secondly, after treatment the depressives were still receiving
amylobarbitone at night and sometimes during the day, yet they
then showed a normal response to dexamethasone.

Thirdly, since a preliminary report of these findings was published (Carroll *et al.*, 1968) other workers have reported similar
results in depressed patients not receiving barbiturates. Butler
and Besser (1968) used an extended dexamethasone dosage regimen and found that three depressed patients failed to suppress
normally; two of their subjects received doses as high as 8 mg

daily. Both had a normal plasma cortisol half-life (99 and 100 minutes, normal range 90-130 minutes). Platman and Fieve (1968) studied five patients with the 1 mg midnight test. Three cases of nonsuppression were found on admission and all showed normal responses after treatment. Bunney and Fawcett (1967) mention (without providing details) that some patients they had studied with agitated psychotic depressions failed to suppress normally after dexamethasone.

Another detailed investigation by Stokes (1972) has clarified this issue of the possible interference by barbiturates in the overnight suppression test. He found no significant difference between the plasma 17-OHCS levels of unmedicated and sedated groups of depressives, either predexamethasone or postdexamethasone, using 1 mg, 2 mg and 8 mg at midnight. The sedated group received short-acting barbiturates up to 350 mg daily. Twenty-three of thirty-two observations showed levels $>10\mu g/100$ ml after 1 mg; six of eleven tests with 2 mg gave values $>5\mu g/100$ ml and after 8 mg fourteen of nineteen results were $>5\mu g/100$ ml, with ten of these being $>10\mu g/100$ ml. These results are similar to those of the present study. The same author found that medicated patients responded less well than unmedicated patients to 2 mg and 4 mg extended suppression tests of the Liddle type. Inspection of the data shows that individual nonmedicated patients had abnormal responses to these tests (4 of 13 after 2 mg and 3 of 7 after 4 mg dexamethasone given over forty-eight hours).

The fourth line of evidence which supports the conclusion that barbiturates are not the sole cause of nonsuppression comes from experience in further studies since barbiturates were replaced by benzodiazepines or chloral hydrate or placebo. This change was instituted after the work described in this chapter was completed. Depressed patients continue to be identified who are nonsuppressors. Detailed studies are required to confirm the effects of these new drugs on steroid metabolism, since present evidence is conflicting. Butler *et al.* (1968) described a marked fall of plasma cortisol levels after acute chlordiazepoxide administration in man. However, Superstine and Sulman (1966) reported an increased 17-ketosteroid excretion and increased ad-

renal weights after chronic administration of both chlordiazepoxide and diazepam in mice; Marc and Morselli (1969)
found that diazepam caused sustained elevations of plasma corticosterone levels in the rat, while Jori *et al.* (1969) have found
that chronic administration of diazepam can induce liver microsomal enzyme activity. No studies of the effects of nitrazepam
appear to have been reported.

If it can be assumed that absorption, metabolism, transport
and brain entry of dexamethasone were not responsible for the
results obtained in the depressed patients, other possibilities may
be considered.

The steroid-responsive neurones are located away from the
"final common pathway" in the median eminence for CRF release. The factors affecting the response of such neurones to
dexamethasone are not fully understood. It has usually been assumed that they will respond to equipotent doses of the various
natural and synthetic glucocorticoids. An important observation
of Rayyis and Bethune (1969) suggests that this assumption
may not always be valid. They studied patients with Cushing's
disease of diencephalic origin and measured circulating ACTH
levels by radio-immunoassay. No suppression of ACTH was
found after doses of dexamethasone as high as 32 mg per day.
Intravenous hydrocortisone injections, however, caused a prompt
fall in circulating ACTH levels. They ventured the suggestion
that the receptor mechanism for dexamethasone may have been
disturbed, but that hydrocortisone was still "recognized." The
nature of this change in glucocorticoid receptors and the questions of its presence and possibly reversible nature in depressed
patients can at present only be subjects for speculation.

The final possible cause of nonsuppression which must be
logically considered is that other diencephalic and limbic areas
exerted an abnormal drive on the median eminence and thus
were able to override the inhibitory effect of dexamethasone on
CRF release. Rubin and Mandell (1966) have expressed this
hypothesis clearly in the following terms, "it may be that 'functional' depressive states are concomitants of a suprahypophyseal
brain dysfunction which is also responsible for hyperstimula-
tion of the anterior pituitary."

This hypothesis argues for a special relationship between depression and HPA activation which is different from the increase in adrenocortical activity caused by psychological "stress" experienced in other psychopathological states. The results of the dexamethasone suppression test in depressed and control patients support this hypothesis. Areas of the brain which are concerned with both mood and HPA regulation include the amygdala, hippocampus, ventral diencephalon and rostral midbrain tegmentum. Amygdaloid stimulation increases plasma 17-OHCS levels (Rubin *et al.,* 1966) and the amygdala in particular is not responsive to dexamethasone implantation (Zimmerman and Critchlow, 1969).

Depression is commonly accompanied by anxiety which is clinically similar to that seen in other psychiatric disorders (Ross, 1937). In the present study, however, anxiety bore no relationship to the results obtained, whereas the physiological features of the presenting illnesses were significantly related to impaired HPA suppression. Several authors have argued that there is no special relationship between depression and HPA activity and that any HPA activation which is present results from nonspecific anxiety and arousal factors, and particularly from failing defenses against the attendant anxiety (Bunney *et al.,* 1965a and b; Sachar *et al.,* 1968). The results of this study, measuring the dynamic control of HPA function, clearly discriminate the depressives from other patients with anxiety, and the abnormality of overnight suppression seems to be a physiological feature of the illness rather than caused, as an epiphenomenon, by psychogenic factors. This question is examined in more detail in a later section.

RELATION TO OTHER CLINICAL FEATURES

The finding that *age* had no influence on plasma cortisol levels predexamethasone or postdexamethasone is in agreement with other reports. Urinary 17-OHCS excretion is known to decrease in elderly subjects, especially women, both in absolute levels and relative to creatinine excretion (Grad *et al.,* 1967). A marked fall in aldosterone secretion and metabolic clearance rates also occurs in the elderly (Flood *et al.,* 1967). A normal nycthemeral rhythm of plasma 17-OHCS levels in such patients was noted by Silverberg *et al.* (1968). A trend to high morning and midnight plasma cortisol levels has been noted in the largest group of elderly patients studied, although overnight dexamethasone suppression, and responses to synacthen, ACTH and hypoglycemia were normal (Green and Friedman, 1968).

The interaction between *weight loss* and both the diurnal and postdexamethasone plasma cortisol levels has been noted. Another observation which agrees with the present findings is that of Board *et al.* (1957), who found that ten depressives with poor nutritional status had significantly higher plasma 17-OHCS levels at 9:00 AM (mean $20.8\mu g/100$ ml) compared with seven others considered to be well nourished ($15.5\mu g/100$ ml).

None of the patients in the present study was grossly malnourished, to the extent that HPA function might be affected by this factor alone. Body weight changes following treatment were not great, usually of the order of 2 to 3 kg, which is similar to that found by other investigators (Coppen and Shaw, 1963). *Severe malnutrition* is known to be associated with gross abnormalities of HPA function. Children with marked protein-calorie deficiency have high plasma cortisol levels, which fall after recovery. The half-life of exogenous cortisol is greatly prolonged and only partial suppression by dexamethasone may occur. Impaired cortisol catabolism by the liver is responsible for these effects (Alleyne and Young, 1967). In children with kwashiorkor the percentage of cortisol not bound to plasma proteins is also greatly increased (Leonard and MacWilliam, 1964). A similar failure of cortisol catabolism and impaired dexamethasone suppression is seen in right ventricular failure (Connolly and Wills, 1969) and in moribund patients (Nugent *et al.*, 1965; Beisel and Rapoport, 1969). Enforced fasting of obese adolescent subjects is attended by a significant fall in cortisol secretion rates and urinary 17-OHCS levels (Garces *et al.*, 1968). In patients with Cushing's syndrome, however, the cortisol secretion rate does not fall during starvation (Vingerhoeds *et al.*, 1970). Animal studies have shown that starvation can lead to increased median eminence levels of CRF, and raised plasma corticosterone levels, with an increased adrenal weight relative to total body weight (Chowers *et al.*, 1969).

Other studies have clearly shown that severely depressed patients do not have cortisol catabolism impairment which is characteristic of severe malnutrition (Butler and Besser, 1968; Carpenter and Bunney, 1971). High metabolic clearance rates and production rates of cortisol were found, which would not be consistent with gross malnutrition.

Duration of illness was also found to have some relationship to both diurnal and postdexamethasone plasma cortisol levels. Relatively low (normal) levels were recorded in the groups with a duration from eight to sixteen weeks before admission. It is possible that patients with a history of sixteen weeks or longer actually required admission because of an acute worsening of a mild chronic depressed state. The true interaction between duration and cortisol levels may then consist of high levels in the acute phase, with the appearance of normal values as the condition becomes established. Further detailed studies will be needed to clarify this question. Animal data concerning the response to continued stress is of some relevance to this problem. Smookler and Buckley (1969) report that HPA activation and increased brain noradrenalin turnover occurs in rats under stress, together with the development of neurogenic hypertension. As the exposure to stress continues beyond four weeks, however, the HPA and noradrenalin changes disappear, although the hypertension persists. These findings suggest an interesting parallel with depression and HPA activation.

RATING SCALES OF BEHAVIOR

The diurnal plasma cortisol levels were found to relate to the Zung Self-Rating Depression Scale scores but not to scores on the Hamilton Rating Scale for Depression. This situation was reversed in the case of the postdexamethasone plasma cortisol levels. In both instances the physiological component of each scale was responsible for the degree of correlation observed. Scores on the Taylor Manifest Anxiety Scale (TMAS) did not correlate with any of the plasma cortisol levels.

One of the earliest and best studies of HPA function in depression (Board *et al.*, 1957) found no correlation between severity of depression (global clinical rating) and 9:00 AM 17-

OHCS levels, although a trend was found for severely ill patients to have higher levels. Other nonsignificant factors were distress, disintegration of ego defenses against anxiety, psychomotor agitation, crying, negative attitudes to hospital and expressions of loss of status. Retardation and inhibition of crying did correlate with the plasma 17-OHCS levels.

Bunney *et al.* (1965a) did find high positive correlations between both depression and anxiety ratings and urinary 17-OHCS excretion levels in seventeen patients studied longitudinally. However, this applied only to serial data from individual patients; pooling of the results from all patients caused a loss of the correlations found in the individual subjects. This was ascribed to the presence of a subgroup of depressives with high behavioral ratings and low urinary 17-OHCS levels. The rating scale used in this study was that of Bunney and Hamburg (1963) which records anxiety and depression (as well as other items) on a 15-point scale. Psychotic behavior was also related to the 17-OHCS excretion values, but the factors of activity, anger and somatic complaints were not.

Similar findings were reported in another good Scandinavian study (Stenback *et al.*, 1966). Urinary total 17-OHCS excretion was measured in twenty-eight patients and ratings were obtained on the Beck Depression Inventory (Beck *et al.*, 1961) and the Taylor M.A.S. No overall correlation was found between the steroid results and the rating scale scores. Patients with high 17-OHCS excretion (>10 mg/24 hrs.) had similar Beck and Taylor scores to those with low excretion. The high excretors, however, were found to have much greater changes in rating scale scores after treatment, and the authors commented that these seemed to be biologically determined depressives "in an indefinable way."

Apprehension is well known to cause elevated plasma cortisol levels (Davis *et al.*, 1962), yet two studies have failed to find any correlation between anxiety scale ratings and the steroid response in normal subjects. Bursten and Russ (1965), in fact, found a negative relationship between TMAS scores and plasma cortisol levels in ten surgical patients before or after their oper-

ations. A rating of preoperative discomfort-involvement correlated positively with preoperative plasma levels but negatively
with the change in steroid levels during the first forty-five minutes of surgery (all elective hernia repair). Bridges and Jones
(1967) studied thirty-two medical students before and after an
oral examination. The rise in plasma cortisol levels bore no relationship to TMAS scores, neuroticism or extraversion scores on
the Eysenck Personality Inventory (Eysenck, 1956) or to a somatic measure of androgyny.

It seems therefore that either a) the rating scales used do not
validly measure anxiety; b) individuals respond to anxiety with
their own characteristic degree of HPA activation but that
inter-individual comparisons introduce too much variance to
render such comparisons meaningful; or c) that anxiety as measured is not a powerful factor leading to HPA activation in depressed subjects. The present study tends to support this last interpretation. In particular, the clinical assessment of psychological and somatic anxiety as part of the Hamilton rating is not
open to the methodological criticisms that might be applied to
the various self-rating scales (Carroll *et al.*, 1971).

In this connection the absence of effect of apprehension
(awaiting ECT) provides supporting evidence. The same finding was reported by Persky *et al.* (1956) in anxious patients. A
contrived stressful interview led to no increase in plasma or urinary steroid levels above the "basal" values (which were 60 to
70 per cent above control figures). Bliss *et al.* (1956) also studied patients awaiting ECT. Mean values of plasma 17-OHCS of
22 ± 8 and $19 \pm 4\mu g/100$ ml were found on non-ECT and ECT
days respectively. These results are very close to those reported
in this study.

The sum of this evidence strongly suggests that anxiety is not
the major factor in HPA activation in depressed patients. The
results of the studies reported here indicate that physiological
factors are chiefly responsible. Another school of thought main-
tains that breakdown of psychological defenses against anxiety
is the major cause of HPA activation. This claim will be examined in a later section.

PART 2: FURTHER STUDIES OF
HPA SUPPRESSION

Following the early results with overnight suppression tests, a number of related investigations were carried out to assess the significance of these findings. The further studies examine certain procedural variables, clinical features and other parameters of HPA function as they relate to the responses of the patients to the dexamethasone suppression test.

The investigations are presented in a logical sequence in this section.

TIMING OF DEXAMETHASONE ADMINISTRATION

A midnight dose of dexamethasone was chosen because in normal subjects HPA function is suppressed most completely when the drug is given at this time (Nichols *et al.*, 1965). In normal individuals the diurnal variation in responsiveness to dexamethasone coincides inversely with the rhythm of plasma cortisol levels. As was indicated in Chapter 3, the mechanisms which control the early morning peak of cortisol production seem to differ from those which regulate HPA function during the rest of the day.

An *abnormal diurnal rhythm* of plasma cortisol levels has been reported in many studies of depressed patients. Doig *et al.* (1966) found that in seven of ten depressives the peak plasma cortisol level occurred at 3:00 AM rather than at the normal time of 6:00 to 8:00 AM. On recovery, five of six subjects they were able to reexamine showed a shift in peak values to 6:00 AM. Mc-Clure (1966, 1966a) found that cortisol levels at 10:00 PM were more elevated than those at 7:00 AM or noon in seven depressives, compared with normal control subjects. Knapp *et al.* (1967) found levels at 4:00 AM to be clearly outside normal limits in six patients with depression whose blood was sampled at four-hourly intervals. At the other five times during the twenty-four-hour cycle the mean values of the depressives were within one standard deviation of the normal mean. Butler and Besser (1968) described grossly-elevated midnight plasma cortisol levels in the three patients they examined. Brooksbank and Coppen

(1967) found that levels at 9:00 PM bore a closer relationship to depression ratings than did morning levels (8:00 AM). Conroy *et al.* (1968) found that six manic depressed patients (in the depressed phase) had a diurnal rhythm quite different from schizophrenics or other psychotic subjects. Using a four-hourly sampling schedule they showed that the normal evening fall in plasma cortisol levels did not occur and that values at 10:00 PM and 2:00 AM were the most abnormal. A similar finding is that of Fullerton *et al.* (1968) who collected plasma and fractional urine samples at three-hourly intervals. The lowest plasma and urinary 17-OHCS levels in twenty-one depressives occurred three hours earlier than in control subjects, the nadir being reached at 11:00 PM compared with 2:00 AM. At around midnight plasma cortisol levels were (presumably) rising.

In view of these results the possibility was considered that a *midnight dexamethasone dose may have been too late* to prevent the "once-a-day neurally stimulated ACTH secretion phase" (Ceresa *et al.*, 1969) in the depressed subjects. The major part of the total daily cortisol production occurs during the early morning hours (Hellman *et al.*, 1970) and Ceresa *et al.* (1969) have shown that there is a critical early morning period for blocking this secretion phase with dexamethasone in low doses (30μg/hr.). Only massive doses (200μg/hr.) given outside the critical period lowered the prevailing cortisol levels at other times of the day. This study may explain why Gibbons and Fahy (1966) found no difference between depressed and control subjects using a 2 mg intramuscular dose of dexamethasone at 2:00 PM.

It was decided, therefore, to examine the effect of dexamethasone given at 9:00 PM in suppressing plasma cortisol levels. The data of McHardy-Young *et al.* (1967) showed that the cortisol levels of normal and obese subjects remained in most cases below 5μg/100 ml up to 8:00 PM the next night after a 2 mg dose of dexamethasone given at midnight. The time of 9:00 PM was chosen for this further study therefore to attempt to eliminate any possible artifact of an abnormal diurnal rhythm in causing the results obtained in the depressives. A 9:00 PM dose would be theoretically early enough to block the advanced peak of cortisol secretion, which the diurnal variation studies had shown to be a possibility.

Method

The test was administered as previously described. A midnight timing was used first and two or three days later a 9:00 PM dose of 2 mg dexamethasone was given. This sequence was performed fifteen times in fourteen patients. One patient (No. 5) was studied in two separate admissions.

Results

The findings are given in Table 5-XIII. In only one case (patient 1) was normal suppression observed at 9:00 PM but not at midnight. In nine of fifteen cases the suppression was less complete after the 9:00 PM dose, especially those who suppressed normally with the midnight dose. In the remaining five cases (patients 5 (a), 10, 11, 12 and 14) suppression at 9:00 PM was marginally better than at midnight.

TABLE 5-XIII

EFFECT OF DOSE TIMING ON RESPONSE TO DEXAMETHASONE
8:30 AM Plasma 11-OHCS (μg-100 ml) after 2 mg

	Midnight	9:00 PM
Patient 1	15.0	5.5
Patient 2	9.4	12.2
Patient 3	5.8	12.0
Patient 4	17.2	22.2
Patient 5 (a)	27.2	21.0
Patient 5 (b)	15.4	23.0
Patient 6	17.6	24.6
Patient 7	1.5	7.0
Patient 8	2.3	7.2
Patient 9	18.3	18.8
Patient 10	27.5	21.5
Patient 11	35.4	34.6
Patient 12	19.2	14.6
Patient 13	2.3	27.4
Patient 14	27.2	19.2
Arithmetic Mean	16.1	18.1
S.D.	10.4	8.2
Geometric Mean	11.4	16.0
S.D. Range	4.2-31.4	9.3-27.6

Comment

These results do not support the possibility that nonsuppression in the depressives is related to an abnormal circadian rhythm of HPA function. Rather, they confirm that a real abnormality of HPA sensitivity to exogenous glucocorticoids exists.

PLASMA CORTISOL HALF-LIFE AND DEXAMETHASONE SUPPRESSION

The possible interference by barbiturates in causing nonsuppression has already been discussed. The drug effect could be mediated through liver microsomal enzyme induction, with accelerated clearance of dexamethasone from plasma. The finding of Butler and Besser (1968) that their patients had normal cortisol half-lives was noted yet did not suppress normally after dexamethasone.

This small study was carried out to examine plasma cortisol half-lives in both the depressed and recovered phases, and to relate these results to the responses to dexamethasone.

Method

The half-life of cortisol in plasma was measured by the technique of Peterson *et al.* (1955). A loading dose of 200 mg hydrocortisone as the hemisuccinate salt in water was injected intravenously and the rate of disappearance estimated by measuring plasma levels over a period of 2 to 2½ hours. Because of the high concentrations obtained, a 1 in 10 dilution of plasma was used in the fluorometric method previously described (Mattingly, 1962). Peterson has demonstrated that this technique, with pharmacological doses of unlabeled hydrocortisone, yields the same result as procedures which employ tracer doses of ^{14}C-hydrocortisone.

Patients

Three patients were studied, both before and after treatment. In one case the cortisol half-life was measured at 10:00 AM while the other two subjects were tested at 11:00 PM so as to obtain clearance rates at the time that dexamethasone was received.

All patients received the 2 mg midnight dexamethasone suppression test within forty-eight hours of the half-life studies.

Calculations

Cortisol disappears from plasma in an exponential manner; a linear expression can be stated as:

$$y = a + b x$$

where
- $y = \log_{10}$ (plasma cortisol concentration)
- $x =$ time in minutes
- $b =$ slope of linear regression of y on x
- $a =$ intercept on y axis

From the equation the half-life of cortisol may be calculated as follows:

$$y = a + b x \text{ when plasma cortisol level is } 2Z$$
$$y' = a + bx' \text{ when plasma cortisol level is } Z$$

$$\text{Then } y - y' = b (x - x')$$
$$\text{But } y - y' = \log_{10} \frac{2Z}{Z}$$
$$= \log_{10} 2$$
$$\text{Thus } \log_{10} 2 = b (x - x')$$
$$\text{So } (x - x') = \frac{\log_{10} 2}{b}$$
$$= \frac{0.3010}{b}$$

And $(x - x') =$ half-life of plasma cortisol (i.e. time for level to fall from 2Z to Z).
So cortisol half-life $(t\frac{1}{2}) = 0.3010/b$

Results

Patient 1: Before treatment the plasma cortisol half-life at 10:00 AM was 100.3 minutes, with the constants a and b being 2.62 and −0.0030 respectively. The post-DEX plasma cortisol level was 26.8μg/100 ml.

After treatment the cortisol half-life at 10:00 AM was 81.4 minutes (a = 2.65, b = −0.0037), and the post-DEX plasma cortisol was 1.2μg/100 ml.

Patient 2: Before treatment a cortisol half-life of 66.9 minutes was found at 11:00 PM compared with 60.2 minutes found at the same time of night after treatment (a = 2.61 and 2.65; b = −0.0045 and −0.0050 before and after treatment respectively). The corresponding post-DEX plasma cortisol levels were 17.8 and 2.2µg/100 ml.

Patient 3: At 11:00 PM before treatment the cortisol half-life was 71.7 minutes, compared with 70.2 minutes after treatment at 11:00 PM (a = 2.73 and 2.79; b = −0.0042 and −0.0043). The post-DEX plasma cortisol levels corresponding to these results were 7.3 and 5.7µg/100 ml.

Comment

In each case the cortisol half-life was longer before treatment than it was after recovery. Patients 1 and 2 demonstrate the change from nonsuppression to normal suppression that occurs with treatment. The rate of cortisol clearance from plasma appears not to be related to the suppressive response to dexamethasone.

The cortisol half-life values found were generally shorter than those of 90 to 120 minutes reported by Peterson *et al.* (1955) but they agree with those found by Hellman *et al.* (1970) for normal subjects. These authors found that the half-life varies throughout the day from 45 to 95 minutes.

The results of this study argue strongly against nonsuppression being a "barbiturate artifact." The rate of steroid disappearance from plasma in nonsuppressors does not tend to be faster than in patients who suppress normally. It has been shown that when diphenylhydantoin is given to humans in doses which alter the metabolism of dexamethasone (and thereby cause impaired suppression by dexamethasone) the cortisol half-life in plasma is significantly shortened (Choi *et al.*, 1971). In each of the three patients reported here the half-life was slightly longer at the time of nonsuppression than it was after treatment.

CORRELATIONS WITH URINARY PARAMETERS OF HPA FUNCTION

The results with the dexamethasone suppression test indicate: a) many depressives do not suppress plasma cortisol levels normally after a midnight dose of dexamethasone, and b) the same patients tend to have higher diurnal plasma cortisol levels than those who suppress normally.

This study was carried out to answer two questions relating to the interpretation of the suppression test results:

1. Does nonsuppression imply excessive HPA function throughout the day, or simply reflect a disturbance of *control* of the "once-a-day" phase of HPA activity?
2. Does the high postdexamethasone plasma cortisol level in nonsuppressors reflect continuing HPA activity from midnight to 8:30 AM, or is it rather an early "escape" phenomenon from temporary suppression?

Methods

As a measure of HPA function throughout the day the twenty-four-hour urinary excretion of free cortisol was estimated. This parameter was chosen in preference to urinary 17-OHCS or 17-KGS for the reasons already outlined (Chap. 3). It is a more sensitive index of adrenal hyperfunction than the other measures, and reflects the tissue exposure to free, unbound, physiologically active cortisol over time.

The radiostereoassay of Murphy (1968) was used to assay urinary free cortisol. The coefficient of variation (mean/S.D.) of thirty-seven samples assayed in quadruplicate (148 estimations) was 11.5 per cent.

Protocol

A twenty-four-hour urine sample was collected from 10:00 PM to 10:00 PM. A twelve-hour urine sample was then taken from 10:00 PM to 10:00 AM the following morning. At midnight in the second period of collection 2 mg dexamethasone phosphate was given orally. Blood was collected for plasma cortisol estimation at 8:30 AM on each morning (for the standard fluorometric assay). The twelve-hour urine sample included urine passed in the two hours before dexamethasone was given. For practical reasons this was unavoidable at the time.

Patients

Twenty-nine consecutive admissions were studied. All had some depressive symptomatology, although in fifteen cases the primary diagnosis was personality disorder or anxiety neurosis. These fifteen were similar to the control group patients studied in the previous sections. Fourteen patients were primarily depressed, by the criteria previously described.

Results

The group mean results are presented in Table 5-XIV.

The arithmetic mean twenty-four-hour urinary free cortisol excretion was 154μg. The normal range for this parameter by the method used is 0 to 108μg, with an arithmetic mean value of 48μg per day (Murphy, 1968). The plasma cortisol (11-OHCS) levels of this group were similar to those of the groups studied in previous sections (Tables 4-III and 5-I).

The correlations between the variables studied are contained in Table 5-XV. For these calculations log-transformed values of the urinary and post-DEX plasma data have been used, for the reasons previously stated.

From the table it can be seen that the twenty-four-hour (pre-DEX) urinary free cortisol excretion is related to both the pre-DEX and post-DEX plasma cortisol levels as well as to the post-DEX urinary free cortisol excretion. The post-DEX urinary

TABLE 5-XIV

URINARY AND PLASMA CORTISOL LEVELS BEFORE AND
AFTER DEXAMETHASONE (Twenty-nine Patients)

| | Urinary Free Cortisol (μg) | | Plasma 11-OHCS (μg/100 ml) 8:30 AM | |
| | | Post-DEX | | |
	24 hr.	12 hr.	Pre-DEX	Post-DEX
Arithmetic Mean ± S.D.	154 ± 116	33 ± 41	20.2 ± 6.9	10.7 ± 8.7
Geometric Mean	120	13.4	—	7.6
S.D. Range	34-309	3-66	—	3.2-18.2
Range of Values	5-465	2-165	11.2-36.0	1.7-32.2

TABLE 5-XV

CORRELATIONS BETWEEN URINARY AND PLASMA
CORTISOL LEVELS (Product-moment, n = 29)

	r	p
Pre-DEX Plasma-Post-DEX Plasma	0.57	0.001
Pre-DEX Plasma-Pre-DEX Urine	0.49	0.01
Pre-DEX Plasma-Post-DEX Urine	0.61	0.001
Post-DEX Plasma-Pre-DEX Urine	0.39	0.05
Post-DEX Plasma-Post-DEX Urine	0.65	0.001
Pre-DEX Urine-Post-DEX Urine	0.59	0.001

free cortisol is closely related to the post-DEX plasma cortisol levels. Individual post-DEX urine and post-DEX plasma results are plotted in Figure 5-5. In the figure a small number of cases can be seen whose post-DEX plasma levels are high (>7μg/100 ml) but whose twelve-hour free cortisol excretion is low (<25μg). These may represent individuals who suppressed and then "escaped" abnormally early from the dexamethasone effect; in that way they could have high plasma levels at 8:30 AM with low free cortisol excretion over the preceding hours.

In general, however, the relationship between post-DEX plasma cortisol and post-DEX urinary free cortisol excretion is very good. The nonsuppressors do have high free cortisol excretion after dexamethasone.

The relationship between the urinary and plasma indices was examined further by dividing the twenty-nine patients into suppressors and nonsuppressors, according to their post-DEX plasma cortisol levels. Suppression was defined as normal when the post-DEX plasma cortisol was below 7μg/100 ml. Sixteen patients were suppressors by this criterion, while thirteen were not. Table 5-XVI compares the results in each subgroup.

The subgroup of thirteen nonsuppressors included ten of the

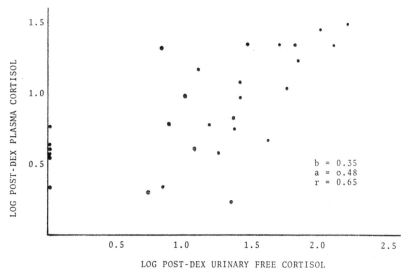

Figure 5-5. Post-DEX cortisol in plasma and urine. (n = 29)

TABLE 5-XVI

COMPARISON OF RESULTS OF SUPPRESSORS AND NONSUPPRESSORS

	Suppressors (16)	Nonsuppressors* (13)	t	p
Plasma Cortisol (μg/100 ml)				
Pre-DEX (± S.D.)	17.1 (± 3.8)	24.0 (± 8.1)	3.08	0.01
Post-DEX	3.8 (2.6-5.9)	17.4 (11.6-26.1)	9.7	0.001
Urinary Free Cortisol (μg)				
24-Hour Pre-DEX	71.4 (16-250)	158.5 (76-333)	2.04	0.05[1]
12-Hour Post-DEX	5.5 (1.3-23.6)	40.4 (15-109)	4.2	0.001

(1) one-tail.
* Nonsuppressors defined as subjects with post-DEX plasma cortisol > 7μg/100 ml. Geometric means and S.D. ranges given for urinary and post-DEX plasma results.

fourteen patients with a primary depressive illness and three of the fifteen control patients.

The results in Table 5-XVI complement the information gained from the correlation coefficients. The group of nonsuppressors had significantly higher twenty-four-hour and twelve-hour urinary free cortisol excretions than did the suppressors.

This study answers the two questions raised:

1. Nonsuppression is associated with excessive HPA function throughout the day. The mean twenty-four-hour urinary free cortisol excretion in the nonsuppressors (159μg) was much greater than normal values. The disturbance is not simply one of control of the "once-a-day" phase of HPA activity.

2. Nonsuppression as determined by 8:30 AM post-dexamethasone plasma cortisol levels does not represent simply an early "escape" from temporary HPA suppression. Rather, it reflects continuing HPA activity from midnight to 8:30 AM.

CORRELATION WITH FREE CORTISOL LEVELS IN CEREBROSPINAL FLUID

The study of urinary free cortisol excretion showed that nonsuppressors have high twenty-four-hour HPA activity as judged by this parameter. The urinary free cortisol excretion provides the best index of tissue exposure to physiologically active cortisol levels (i.e. the fraction not bound to corticosteroid-binding globulin).

Before any speculation is possible about the role of this increased HPA activity in causing or maintaining the depressed state, it must first be shown that the exposure of the central nervous system (CNS) to free cortisol is increased. Such an increase is strongly suggested by the urinary free cortisol results, but requires further demonstration. One way of confirming this possibility is to measure the level of cortisol in the cerebrospinal fluid (CSF) of the patients.

Cortisol is present in CSF in much lower concentrations than in blood (Baron and Abelson, 1954; Sandberg *et al.*, 1954; Abelson *et al.*, 1955). Cortisol in CSF is assumed to represent the freely diffusible steroid and the level is approximately that of the unbound fraction of the total cortisol concentration of plasma (Murphy *et al.*, 1967). The level in lumbar CSF shows a diurnal rhythm which lags about two hours behind that of the total plasma level (Uete *et al.*, 1970). Other hormones found in CSF in low concentrations include progesterone (Lurie and Weiss, 1967), estradiol (Kumar and Thomas, 1968) thyroxine (Hansen and Siersbaek-Nielsen, 1969) and insulin (Margolis and Altszular, 1967). A rapid exchange of cortisol between plasma and CSF was demonstrated by Murphy *et al.* (1967).

Method

Preliminary work with a fluorometric method for the assay of CSF cortisol proved unsatisfactory although Uete *et al.* (1970) obtained reproducible results with a similar procedure. The levels were too low to allow accurate measurement of cortisol in the small samples available. The cortisol values in CSF by fluorometry (Uete *et al.*, 1970) are considerably higher than those obtained by radiostereoassay (Table 5-XVIII).

The more sensitive ultramicro radiostereoassay of Murphy (1967) was developed for this purpose and was found to be more suitable. This method is similar to the assay used for urinary free cortisol but employs dog plasma instead of human plasma. The range of sensitivity is 0 to 4 ng of cortisol, while that for the urinary estimations was 0 to 40 ng. A working volume of 0.1 ml of CSF is required, so that duplicate or quadruplicate aliquots of the one sample can be assayed. In this study all samples were assayed in quadruplicate. The coefficient of variation was 14 per cent.

Patients and Protocol

Seven depressed patients were studied. Lumbar puncture was performed with the patient in the lateral position at least one week after admission, and again following treatment with ECT. The mean interval between samplings was forty-two days, and the second lumbar puncture was delayed at least one week after the last ECT. The procedures were carried out at the same time of day in individual subjects and between 11:30 AM and 3:00 PM for the group as a hole. This was to allow for diurnal variation in the CSF cortisol level. Blood was collected immediately after the lumbar puncture for fluorometric estimation of total plasma cortisol.

The patients also received the midnight dexamethasone suppression test within forty-eight hours of each lumbar puncture.

Results

The total plasma cortisol levels showed the usual rise to 30 to 40 per cent in the depressed phase, compared with recovery val-

TABLE 5-XVII

CORTISOL LEVELS (μg/100 ml) IN CSF AND PLASMA IN
DEPRESSED (D) AND RECOVERED (R) PHASES

Patient	CSF		Plasma		Post-Dexamethasone Plasma	
	D	R	D	R	D	R
1	1.30	0.67	8.9	6.0	6.6	1.8
2	1.75	0.65	23.8	7.5	18.8	0.1
3	3.40	1.00	25.0	32.2	23.1	1.1
4	1.60	1.20	21.2	13.7	27.2	3.9
5	0.70	0.45	10.0	9.1	19.2	4.5
6	2.50	1.40	16.5	20.3	23.4	25.0
7	2.40	1.45	26.2	7.4	19.2	2.7
Mean	1.76*	0.90*	18.8	13.7	18.2*	2.2*
S.D.	1.05	0.57	±7.1	±9.5	11.4	0.4
	to	to			to	to
	2.93	1.40			29.1	11.7
Paired γ	5.5		1.37		3.39	
p	0.01		N.S.		0.01	

* Geometric means.

ues. In contrast, the CSF cortisol levels were raised by a factor of 100 per cent at the same time (Table 5-XVII). In the depressed phase the mean CSF cortisol level was $1.76\mu g/100$ ml compared with $0.90\mu g/100$ ml after treatment. In every case the CSF cortisol level fell with recovery, while the plasma levels were variable in this respect. The elevation in CSF cortisol levels was significant ($p < 0.01$).

The CSF/plasma ratio was 10.6 per cent in the depressed phase, compared with 9.0 per cent on recovery.

In six of the seven patients the response to dexamethasone was better after treatment than it had been on admission.

The levels in CSF and plasma showed some correlation ($r = 0.59$, $n = 14$, $p < 0.05$). A good correlation was present also between the CSF levels and the post-dexamethasone plasma levels ($r = 0.60$, $n = 14$, $p < 0.01$).

Log-transformation of the CSF cortisol values has been performed for all computations, since this parameter is virtually identical with the plasma unbound cortisol level, which is known to be log-normally distributed (Burke, 1969c). In Table 5-XVII the geometric means and S.D. range are given. The corresponding arithmetic values were $1.95 \pm 0.89\mu g/100$ ml (depressed and $0.97 \pm 0.39\mu g/100$ ml (recovered). These values are used in Table 5-XVIII for comparison with the arithmetic means which other groups have published.

Comment

In this group of patients nonsuppression was associated with high CSF cortisol levels.

Comparative data for CSF cortisol levels are shown in Table 5-XVIII. The results of Murphy's (1967) series are the most appropriate for comparison. The values reported by Uete *et al.*, (1970) using a fluorometric method, are considerably higher than those found with the radiostereoassay.

By comparison with Murphy's data the CSF cortisol levels in the depressed phase were significantly elevated in the patients studied and the values found on recovery may also be higher than normal. Even when compared with the normal data from Uete's series the values in depression are clearly elevated.

TABLE 5-XVIII

CSF CORTISOL LEVELS IN VARIOUS CONDITONS

(μg/100 ml; Means (Arithmetic) Only)

Author	Condition	N	CSF	Plasma	CSF/Plasma Ratio %
Uete *et al.*,	Normal	26	1.26	15.8	8.0
1970	Epilepsy and schizophrenia	7	1.37	14.5	9.4
	Brain tumor	12	0.96	16.6	9.0
	Meningitis	19	3.54	36.4	9.6
	Late pregnancy	5	3.2	41.0	6.6
Murphy *et al.*,	Normal	12	0.32	—	—
1967	Epilepsy	30	0.41	—	—
	Miscellaneous chronic	23	0.40	—	—
	Febrile	7	1.63	—	—
	Chronic neurological	7	0.58	8.9	6.8
	Estrogen-treated	4	1.34	25.4	5.8
Present series	Depression	7	1.95	18.8	10.6
	Recovered depression	7	0.97	13.7	9.0

Another standard of comparison for these results comes from studies of unbound cortisol levels in plasma. In a recent study (Doe *et al.*, 1969) non-protein-bound cortisol values of 1.27 and 0.36μg/100 ml at 9:00 AM and 9:00 PM respectively were found in normal subjects. Somewhat lower values were reported by Burke (1969b) who used a gel filtration method rather than equilibrium dialysis. He found unbound plasma cortisol concentrations of 0.68μg/100 ml in thirty-six normal males at 9:00 AM and 0.66μg/100 ml in thirty-one females. The corresponding total plasma cortisol levels were 10.8 and 12.0μg/100 ml (also by radiostereoassay).

Cortisol levels in parotid fluid are similar to those in CSF; Katz and Shannon (1969) reported a value of 1.03μg/100 ml in normal parotid fluid (both cortisone and hydrocortisone were present). The parotid fluid content was shown to correlate closely with plasma dialyzable (unbound) hydrocortisone levels.

By all of these standards the CSF cortisol levels in the depressed patients were substantially elevated. In fact they were higher than the levels in estrogen-treated patients reported by Murphy *et al.* (1967). The mean CSF cortisol level of 1.95μg/100 ml in the depressed patients is higher than the unbound plasma cortisol levels of 1.02μg/100 ml in women on oral contraceptives and 1.84μg/100 ml in estrogen-treated males; in Cushing's syndrome the unbound plasma cortisol level is much higher (4.03μg/100 ml) (Burke, 1969b).

The significance of CSF cortisol levels with respect to CNS function is not known. Kumar and Thomas (1968) have suggested that *paraventricular receptors* for estradiol may be present in the rhesus monkey, and that such receptors detect the hormone in CSF as part of the hypothalamic regulation of gonadotropin release. A number of corticosteroid-responsive neurones are located in the periventricular grey matter of the third ventricle and it is possible that such neurones are sensitive to CSF cortisol levels (Ruf and Steiner, 1967). Recent electron-microscopic studies of the lining of the third ventricle indicate that active transport occurs at the ependymal surface and that a functional relationship exists between cerebrospinal fluid and the blood of the pituitary portal vessels. Among other substances, ^{3}H-cortisol is rapidly transferred from CSF to the anterior pituitary gland (Knigge and Scott, 1970).

The findings of this small study require replication. In addition control patients with similar plasma cortisol levels to the depressives should also be studied in the same manner. For ethical reasons this was not done in the pilot study reported here.

RESPONSES TO DEXAMETHASONE DURING TREATMENT WITH ECT

The occurrence of a change from nonsuppression before treatment to a normal response to dexamethasone after treatment has been described. In five patients the midnight dexamethasone test was given at intervals during a course of treatment with ECT so that the *timing of this change in response* could be determined. In the beginning of this chapter it was shown that reproducible results were obtained when the test was given two times before treatment commenced.

Results

Patient 1

On admission the post-dexamethasone (post-DEX) cortisol level was 15.0μg/100 ml. After three weeks she was still not suppressing normally (14.4μg/100 ml). Her clinical course was fluctuating and after six weeks the post-DEX cortisol level was 26.8μg/100 ml. Six days later, when her condition was greatly improved following more treatments, she suppressed to a normal value of 3.4μg/100 ml and shortly before discharge, after another six days, to a level of 7.2μg/100 ml. This patient was very agitated and anxious and was receiving amylobarbitone (200 mg) three times daily throughout her entire stay in the hospital.

Patient 2

This agitated, depressed lady had a post-DEX level of 27.2μg/100 ml on admission. Three weeks later she was clinically little improved and the value was 34.5μg/100 ml. On discharge after a further two weeks she suppressed to the normal level of 3.9μg/100 ml.

Patient 3

Her admission post-DEX cortisol level was 18.0μg/100 ml. Five days later the value was 20.6μg/100 ml and after a further eight days was 15.2μg/100 ml. On recovery seven days later a more normal level of 7.4μg/100 ml was found.

Patient 4

At the time of admission this man suppressed to a level of 6.6μg/100 ml. After sixteen days the value was 6.3μg/100 ml with substantial clinical improvement. After another nine days he was ready for discharge and the value then was 1.8μg/100 ml.

Patient 5

This man developed a sudden illness. On first testing, seven days after the onset, his post-DEX cortisol level was 9.2μg/100 ml. Two weeks later his condition was much improved but the value was still abnormal at 9.7μg/100 ml. After a further eight days he was ready for discharge and then suppressed to the level of 5.7μg/100 ml.

Comment

Abnormal test responses persisted in all of these patients well beyond the first week of admission to the hospital. A change in response to dexamethasone was not seen until after substantial clinical improvement had occurred. This was seen particularly in the cases of patients 3, 4 and 5, in whom the major presenting symptoms of agitation and anxiety had been controlled soon after admission.

These findings clearly exclude the "admission to hospital" factor as the cause of nonsuppression. The delay in return of normal test responses until after major clinical improvement does suggest that nonsuppression may be a function of the underlying depressive process.

PATIENTS WITH ABNORMAL RESPONSES TO DEXAMETHASONE AFTER TREATMENT

Seven patients have been seen during the four years of these studies who continued to show an abnormal response to the 2 mg midnight dexamethasone suppression test at the time of their discharge from the hospital. A definitely abnormal response was defined as a post-DEX 8:30 AM plasma cortisol level greater than $10\mu g/100$ ml.

All of these patients continued to have definite physiological symptoms of depression. Six stated that they still had some depression of mood and active outpatient (O.P.) treatment was required in five cases, to prevent early readmission. These patients were considered ready for discharge by consensus of the ward staff and research psychiatrist; in most cases an early recurrence of symptoms was not anticipated. Brief descriptions of these patients are given below.

Patient 1

A fifty-eight-year-old man admitted after a suicide attempt (drug overdose). One week after admission his post-DEX cortisol level was $35.4\mu g/100$ ml. After four ECTs had been given, he persuaded the ward staff to allow weekend leave; he then made another serious attempt to kill himself by shooting and stabbing his chest and abdomen. Three days later, after surgery, his post-DEX cortisol level was $18.7\mu g/100$ ml. He improved slowly but incompletely with a total of fourteen ECTs and made a further improvement with imipramine over another four weeks. At the time of discharge he was moderately active, occupied with ward tasks, but lacking animation. His facial expression was immobile and he had brief episodes of agitation and tremor. The post-DEX plasma cortisol then was $15.1\mu g/100$ ml.

After discharge he took three months to return to work. Mild agitation and tremor continued and middle insomnia was a persistent problem. He stated that he did not feel depressed but complained of lack of energy and drive, and his facial appearance was that of a moderately retarded depressive. His agitation settled when thioridazine was given and he continued to take imipramine. After two months he became more activated, did not appear depressed and finally returned to work, stating that his only problem was the sleep disturbance. Five months after discharge thioridazine was stopped and imipramine was stopped six months later. No relapse occurred.

Patient 2

A sixty-three-year-old woman admitted in a suicidal condition from a surgical ward where she was being investigated for the complaint of constipation. She had been treated for depression one year earlier. On admission her post-DEX cortisol level was $16.0\mu g/100$ ml. She improved with twelve ECTs and had three satisfactory trial leave periods. On discharge she was still complaining of middle and late insomnia, was generally inactive and apathetic and had frequent hypochondriacal complaints. However she had lost her depressed mood, suicidal ideas and delusions of cancer and of heart disease, and she was no longer agitated. Before discharge her post-DEX plasma cortisol was $20.7\mu g/100$ ml.

At O.P. review she said she felt moderately depressed, with absence of energy and interests, poor appetite and marked sleep disturbance. She developed increasing hypochondriacal ideas and hostile thoughts about a family member. She was treated with thioridazine, despite which her condition slowly worsened, so that readmission was necessary eight months after discharge.

Patient 3

A fifty-eight-year-old woman admitted for the fifth time after failed O.P. treatment of her symptoms. Her post-DEX plasma cortisol after admission was $27.5\mu g/100$ ml. A course of twelve ECTs was given following which her anxiety lessened, she had no panic attacks, agitation was not present, her mood was more cheerful, and she had no suicidal thoughts. Her recovery was not considered good in that she remained hesitant, apathetic, apprehensive and uncertain about her future ability to cope with life. On discharge her post-DEX plasma cortisol was $25.8\mu g/100$ ml. At review ten days later she said she did not feel depressed, was managing better than she had expected to, and her only complaint was severe sleep disturbance. Three weeks later she developed a recurrence of her depressed mood, was anxious, weeping often and having more disturbed sleep. Weekly ECT as an outpatient was ordered but the patient did not agree to have it. With drug treatment she continued to be depressed for another six months and she then suicided by drug overdosage.

Patient 4

A fifty-two-year-old man admitted with a three-month history of depressed mood, tension, guilt feelings, loss of interests, suicidal ideas and sleep disturbance. On admission his post-DEX plasma cortisol was 23.4μg/100 ml. He was treated with ten ECTs and was then very much improved, although he remained withdrawn and had little spontaneous activity. His post-DEX plasma cortisol then was 25.0μg/100 ml. At O.P. review ten days later he had failed to return to work, admitted to occasional brief periods of depressed mood, was anxious, agitated and complained of severe middle and late insomnia. Amitriptyline was given and over the next four weeks these symptoms subsided, apart from the persistent sleep disturbance. The drug was stopped after three months and on review four months later there was no sign of recurrence.

Patient 5

An isolated fifty-three-year-old man who had intermittent depressive symptoms for two years, with a marked increase for four months before admission. He was retarded, apathetic, hostile, with a diurnal variation, middle insomnia, weight loss and anorexia. His post-DEX plasma cortisol was 5.6μg/100 ml (within the normal range). After a long course of fourteen ECTs, he was not greatly improved, being apathetic, withdrawn, anxious about his future working ability and still sleeping badly. His prognosis on discharge was considered poor and his post-DEX plasma cortisol level was abnormal at 10.8μg/100 ml. He failed to obtain employment and became more depressed, despite support from the psychiatric social worker. Two weeks after leaving the hospital he was readmitted for further treatment.

Patient 6

A seventy-two-year-old woman, with no previous depressive episodes. Over three months she developed early awakening, anorexia, weight loss, social withdrawal, tension and loss of energy. Shortly before admission she attempted suicide. Before treatment her post-DEX plasma cortisol level was 22.9μg/100 ml. After six ECTs she was much better; she admitted to no symptoms, her behavior was normally active but her appearance was one of depression, with apparent tension at times. Her post-DEX plasma cortisol then was 20.7μg/100 ml. As an outpatient she continued to appear tense and seemed anxious to deny any depressed feelings, but did admit to severe middle and late insomnia. Four months later she had a mild recurrence of depressive symptoms following the deaths of two friends but did not require admission to hospital.

Patient 7

A forty-nine-year-old woman admitted for the fourth time, with severe anxiety, panic attacks, agitation, weeping, depressed mood, suicidal ideas (and a suicide attempt), weight loss and severe sleep disturbance. She failed to respond to a three-week trial of 1-tryptophan and her post-DEX plasma cortisol at that time was 17.0µg/100 ml. A course of thirteen ECTs was then given, with considerable improvement. She had a number of successful trial leave periods and was considered ready for discharge, although she continued to have anxiety symptoms and was sometimes noted to be tearful and miserable. Her post-DEX plasma cortisol level then was 17.0µg/100 ml. On review after two weeks her condition was worse and weekly O.P. treatments with ECT were required.

Comment

In these patients whose response to dexamethasone was abnormal on discharge definite features of depression continued to be a problem. On practical clinical grounds they were considered well enough to go home, although in some their treatment had clearly not been fully effective, so that early relapse might have been anticipated on clinical grounds alone. In other cases, however, a good prognosis was expected when they left the hospital.

Since early relapse following ECT is a common finding, only a properly designed prospective study could give reliable information about the association described here between nonsuppression and recurrence of symptoms. The test may be useful in the detection of patients at risk of early relapse following treatment. In patients who do not suppress normally on admission the test may also provide an index of improvement complementary to the usual clinical indices. These are two practical issues which clearly require planned investigation.

RESPONSES TO DEXAMETHASONE IN RECURRENT ILLNESSES

Eight patients have been seen who had an abnormal response to dexamethasone and who also received the test during a later admission. When the clinical presentation remained similar, the response to dexamethasone was comparable in the later admissions. A change in the degree of suppression was observed in two patients whose clinical features also changed from one admission to the next. These patients are briefly described below.

Patient 1

First Admission: A fifty-two-year-old man who became ill over a period of two months, and who had three previous admissions for psychotic

depression. He presented with extreme withdrawal, psychomotor retardation, agitation, inability to work, weight loss, sleep disturbance
and guilty thoughts but no active affective arousal. His post-DEX
plasma cortisol was 23.1μg/100 ml, which fell to 1.1μg/100 ml after
treatment with ECT.

Second Admission: Four months later he was free of symptoms until
he awoke one night at 1.00 AM feeling restless, agitated, perplexed
and lacking in energy and drive. He was readmitted one week after
the onset of these symptoms because he was unable to work and his
post-DEX plasma cortisol then was 9.2μg/100 ml.

Patient 2

First Admission: A seventy-four-year-old woman who seven years
earlier had ECT for severe depression. Over six weeks she had developed agitation, guilty and worthless thoughts, ideas of reference,
suicidal ideas, sleep disturbance and loss of appetite. Her post-DEX
plasma cortisol was 30.0μg/100 ml and fell to 8.0μg/100 ml after
ECT. As an outpatient she continued to have sleep disturbance and
morning agitation despite drug treatment.

Second Admission: One year later she was readmitted with a very
similar depressive illness which again developed over the course of
six weeks. Her post-DEX cortisol level then was 17.6μg/100 ml.

Patient 3

First Admission: A seventy-two-year-old woman who had one depressive illness over thirty years earlier. In two months she became
severely retarded with agitation, lost her usual interests, developed
guilt feelings, ideas of reference (that people were laughing at her
forlorn appearance), and marked sleep disturbance. She attempted
suicide before admission. Her post-DEX plasma cortisol was 27.2μg/
100 ml and the value was 3.9 after treatment with ECT.

Second Admission: Seven months later she experienced a similar illness and her post-DEX cortisol value then was 15.4μg/100 ml.

Patient 4

First Admission: A sixty-eight-year-old man with a six-month illness
who presented with morbid ruminations, panic attacks, suicidal behavior, a conviction of impending destruction, loss of self-regard,
hypochondriacal delusions (of cancer and other incurable illnesses)
together with weight loss, anorexia and severe sleep disturbance. His
post-DEX plasma cortisol was 18.3μg/100 ml and fell to 3.3μg/100 ml
after treatment with ECT.

Second Admission: Two months after discharge his symptoms recurred in a less severe form and his post-DEX plasma cortisol then was 10.3μg/100 ml.

Patient 5

First Admission: A sixty-year-old woman admitted for the first time with an illness of one month's duration. She was severely ill, with extreme agitation, was almost mute with her retardation of speech, had extreme guilt feelings, fluctuating delusions (of rotting away, of infecting other patients) and had severe sleep disturbance, anorexia and loss of weight. When tested nine days after admission her post-DEX plasma cortisol was 26.8μg/100 ml and it fell to 3.4μg/100 ml after a course of ECT.

Second Admission: Eleven months later she developed a similar but less severe illness following her husband's death. Her post-DEX plasma cortisol was 18.8μg/100 ml and fell to 0.1μg/100 ml after treatment with ECT.

Third Admission: Eight months after discharge she had to be admitted for similar recurrent symptoms and the post-DEX plasma cortisol then was 26.8μg/100 ml.

Fourth Admission: For two years she remained well, taking lithium carbonate. Over a period of six weeks she then became severely agitated, restless and confused, tremulous, lacking in energy and experienced threatening auditory hallucinations on one occasion. She was found in a dirty condition at home, having soiled her clothing and locked the house because of a fluid delusion that she had been robbed.

An initial diagnosis of recurrent agitated depression was made but it was quickly apparent that she now had thyrotoxicosis. This was supported by ^{131}I uptake studies, a protein-bound iodine (PBI) level of 10.8μg/100 ml and a serum free thyroxine level of 17.5μg/100 ml. (At her first admission ^{131}I uptake studies were normal and her PBI was 4.7μg/100 ml.) Lithium toxicity was excluded by the finding of a serum lithium level of 0.8 mEq/l.

Despite the fluctuating psychotic features of her presentation she suppressed normally, with a post-DEX plasma cortisol level of 4.7μg/100 ml. She responded to treatment with propranolol and carbimazole and did not require ECT. After four weeks in the hospital she was discharged and has remained well for a further three months, without the need for antidepressant treatment.

Patient 6

First Admission: A seventy-five-year-old woman who had had three previous episodes of depression. On admission two months after the onset of recurrent symptoms she was tearful, self-recriminatory, retarded with periods of agitation, lacking interests and complaining of fatigue. Anorexia, weight loss and severe sleep disturbance were also present. Her post-DEX cortisol value was 20.4µg/100 ml.

Second Admission: Eight months later she suffered a further recurrence and her post-DEX plasma cortisol was 29.0µg/100 ml.

Patient 7

First Admission: A fifty-two-year-old woman, with three previous admissions for psychotic depression, whose mother had committed suicide. She was severely agitated, restless, tremulous, anxious, full of guilty statements and unable to carry on at home. She had severe sleep disturbance and had lost appetite and weight. Her post-DEX plasma cortisol was 28.0µg/100 ml and fell to 7.9µg/100 ml after ECT.

Second Admission: While taking lithium carbonate she had mild mood swings and persistent sleep disturbance but remained generally well for three years. She then developed another similar illness and needed to be readmitted. Her post-DEX plasma cortisol then was 16.2µg/100 ml.

Patient 8

First Admission: A sixty-year-old woman with a strong family history of depression (three siblings had suicided and two others had recurrent depression). She became ill for the first time with a sudden personality change extending over two months. She was depressed in mood, indecisive, anxious, tremulous, had guilty ruminations, loss of interests, severe retardation, agitation and marked sleep disturbance. Her post-DEX plasma cortisol was 20.6µg/100 and fell to 7.4µg/100 ml after ECT.

Second Admission: Fifteen months later she became ill again, with a similar presentation. She had suicidal thoughts, severe guilt feelings, fears of "going crazy," hypochondriacal delusions of genital disease, ideas of reference, retardation, agitation and physiological symptoms of depression. Her post-DEX plasma cortisol was 14.6µg/100 ml.

Third Admission: Five months later she was readmitted but no psychotic features were present. She complained of lonely and rejected feelings, had self-pitying ideas rather than guilty thoughts and readily expressed anger. She behaved in a hostile, dependent and manipulative manner towards the hospital staff and had frequent somatic complaints but no anorexia or weight loss, she was not retarded in her speech and her mood was fluctuating. These symptoms had failed to respond to amitriptyline before admission and they did not improve very much with ECT in the hospital. Her post-DEX plasma cortisol this time was 4.2μg/100 ml.

Fourth Admission: A month after discharge she was admitted again, in much the same condition. ECT was not given; with supportive therapy and continued amitriptyline a slow resolution of some of her hostile and dependent feelings was achieved. Her post-DEX plasma cortisol at this admission was 4.7μg/100 ml.

Comment

In general these patients showed consistent abnormalities of suppression at each admission. The finding of normal suppression in patient 5 when she was psychotic but not depressed suggests that a poor response to dexamethasone is related to the affective disturbance rather than to nonspecific psychological distress. In the case of patient 8 the differences in the clinical presentation between the first two and the last two admissions were striking, although the general term "depressed" was applicable each time. In terms of the traditional distinction, the suppression abnormality seems to be associated with the "endogenous" features of retardation, loss of self-regard, guilt, agitation and physiological symptoms, rather than with the hostile, self-pitying "reactive" constellation of symptoms.

RELATION TO INTEGRITY OF PSYCHOLOGICAL DEFENSES

Reference has been made to the finding that the suppression test results correlated best with physiological rather than psychological symptoms. It was concluded that, amongst the depressed patients studied, nonsuppression could not be ascribed simply to "emotional distress."

Several groups of workers, chiefly in the United States, have made important contributions to identifying the *psychological variables associated with HPA activation under stress conditions.*

It is almost axiomatic that HPA activation follows exposure to anxiety-provoking situations. *In normal subjects* the early studies of Wolff *et al.* (1964) showed that the major determinant of high urinary 17-OHCS excretion was the *breakdown of psychological defenses.* The parents of dying leukemic children showed maximum 17-OHCS elevations at times when denial and control of the situation were no longer possible, i.e. when hope was finally abandoned and the affects of sadness and grief were aroused.

This affective arousal, with an active sense of loss, together with felt anxiety, absence of denial and insight into the severity of the situation have been grouped under the heading "failing psychological defense strength." The term signifies the breakdown of psychological mechanisms which reduce the awareness of illness or awareness of threat of injury and loss (Rubin and Mandell, 1966; Katz *et al.*, 1970).

In depressed patients some groups have reported that the same factors correlate best with HPA activation. Bunney, *et al.* (1965a) found positive correlations, within individual patients, between both depression and anxiety ratings and urinary 17-OHCS excretion. Pooling of the results from all 17 patients resulted in a loss of the correlations seen within individuals. This was ascribed to the presence of a subgroup of the depressed patients with high ratings for depression but low 17-OHCS excretion. Such individuals displayed extensive denial of their illness, while the high excretors of 17-OHCS were described as being much more involved in the struggle with their illness and with distressing thoughts. Severe psychotic depressive crises, in particular, were associated with large increases in urinary 17-OHCS excretion. Such crises were characterized by an intense awareness and struggle and the appearance of ego-alien material such as depressive delusions (Bunney *et al.*, 1965b).

This line of inquiry has been carried furthest by Sachar and his colleagues in a series of psychoendocrine studies. A number of critical distinctions have been emphasized by Sachar, especially between anxiety and agitation; between affective arousal and depressive gloom or misery; between struggle with a painful loss and warding-off of confrontation with loss and conflict (mourning versus melancholia); between alerting anxiety and the ruminative worries of depressives; between acute psychotic disorganization and organized psychotic equilibrium (Sachar, 1967b). Major corticosteroid changes were described during psychotherapy of depressions when confrontation with the precipitating psychological loss was achieved (Sachar *et al.*, 1967;

1968). Similar changes in urinary 17-OHCS excretion occurred during the course of schizophrenic illnesses in association with acute psychotic turmoil and breakdown of ego defenses. The magnitude of steroid changes in the schizophrenics was, if anything, more marked than in the depressives (Sachar *et al.*, 1963; Sachar *et al.*, 1970).

In the most recent paper from this group (Sachar *et al.*, 1971) the cortisol production rate was measured in sixteen depressed patients before and after treatment (by ECT in thirteen cases). A rating scale based on that of Hamilton (1960) was used to allow correlation of the steroid and clinical changes in the patients. Change in cortisol production rate after treatment was found to correlate with change in scores of items from the three clinical dimensions of sad affect, anxiety and acute psychotic disorganization. Change in other clinical features did not correlate with the steroid changes. The significant items, called "core" items by Sachar, are listed in Table 5-XIX.

TABLE 5-XIX

"CORE" ITEMS INDICATING PSYCHOLOGICAL DEFENSE BREAKDOWN*

1. *Sad affect:* Conscious and expressed feelings of sadness, expressed verbally or by posture, crying etc.; grief, sorrow. Is the feeling like previous experiences of grief? Are they coming to mind now?
2. *Anxiety, psychic:* A subjective sensation of dread, and apprehension, often unfocussed. Startles easily. Feels something dreadful is going to happen. Distinguish from ruminative worries of depression.
3. *Anxiety, somatic:* Sweating, tremor, palpitations, tightness in chest, hyperventilation, tension headache, tightness or "butterfles" in abdomen, diarrhea, abdominal cramps, urinary frequency, dysphagia, dizzy and giddy feelings, tinnitus, paresthesiae.
4. *Ideas of reference:* Uncertain suspiciousness that other people talk about the patient, regard him with hostility, avoid him, wish him ill.
5. *Feelings of bodily disintegration:* Falling apart, going to pieces (literally), boiling inside, blowing up.
6. *Feelings of depersonalisation and unreality:* "Not me"; unreal, numb sensations; turned to stone; dead inside.
7. *Feelings of loss of control:* Fear of going crazy; fears he will give way to unacceptable (ego-alien) sexual, homicidal or suicidal impulses; thoughts cannot be controlled.
8. *Fluid delusions:* Distinguish from pervasive, organized delusions which are resistant to testing. Fleeting ideas, able to be tested, e.g. of being robbed, of infecting other patients; of bizarre organic disorders, e.g. bowels rotting, worms in head, syphilis, etc.

* Sachar, Hellman *et al.*, 1971.

From these items a psychiatric "core" score was summed for correlations with the cortisol secretion rates. *Change* in "core" score and *change* in secretion rate correlated +0.89 (rank order, p <0.001). Rank order correlation of the before-treatment cortisol production alone with before-treatment "core" scores was +0.71 (p <0.01). The cortisol production was expressed with reference to creatinine excretion.

The authors of this elegant study concluded that adrenal activation was related "not to the depressive illness per se, but rather to more universal ego phenomena such as . . . neurotic 'signal' anxiety or psychotic 'disintegrative' anxiety." They stated that it was "more than likely that those depressed patients who fail to show suppression of plasma cortisol in response to dexamethasone are the patients with high levels of emotional arousal and elevated cortisol (production) rates."

Following a personal discussion with Sachar about this question a further study was carried out using the same rating scale. The dexamethasone suppression test was performed at the time of the clinical rating.

Protocol

In this study both plasma and urinary measures of HPA function and response to dexamethasone were measured. Two twenty-four-hour urine collections, each commencing at midnight, were obtained. At the end of the first collection a 2 mg dose of dexamethasone was given orally. Blood was collected for plasma cortisol at 8:30 AM on each of the two days, i.e. before and after dexamethasone. The study was performed one week after admission. Chloral hydrate, diazepam and nitrazepam were the only drugs permitted.

Patients

Twenty-one depressed and ten schizophrenic patients have been studied so far. The experimental design was to compare the results obtained before treatment only in the two diagnostic groups. The earlier studies of depressed and control patients showed that nonsuppression by dexamethasone was not found in control patients, although these were selected for a range of clinical "distress" similar to that seen in the depressed group. In view of Sachar's reports, it was felt that schizophrenics would constitute the most appropriate control group for this investigation, despite the difference in age of the two groups.

The patients were rated by the Sachar scale and also by the Hamilton rating scale for depression. Strictly speaking, of course, the Hamilton scale is not applicable to subjects without a primary clinical diagnosis of depression.

Biochemical Methods

Urinary free cortisol excretion was measured in the two twenty-four-hour urine specimens. *The radiostereoassay previously described was used for this purpose. Plasma cortisol in this study was also measured by radiostereoassay (Murphy, 1967), not by the previous fluorometric method.* Quadruplicate aliquots of each sample were assayed routinely.

Results

Five of the twenty-one depressed patients had post-dexamethasone plasma cortisol levels greater than $7\mu g/100$ ml. All ten schizophrenics suppressed below this level.

Before dexamethasone the mean 8:30 AM plasma cortisol lev-

TABLE 5-XX

COMPARISONS OF DEPRESSED AND SCHIZOPHRENIC PATIENTS

	Depressed (21)	Schizophrenic (10)	t	p
Age (yrs.)	57.8	28.5	4.8	0.001
	(±15.4)	(±16.9)		
"Core" Item Score	22.7	27.9	−1.6	—
	(±8.8)	(±7.8)		
Hamilton Score	30.4	25.4	2.3	0.05
	(±5.4)	(6.0)		
Pre-DEX AM	17.8	14.6	1.2	—
Plasma Cortisol	(±7.5)	(±5.8)		
Post-DEX AM	5.0	3.1	1.8	0.05[2]
Plasma Cortisol	(2.5-10.4)	(1.6-6.0)		
Pre-DEX UFC[1]	104	39	3.2	0.01
	(52-206)	(14-107)		
Post-DEX UFC	49	9.7	4.0	0.001
	(15-158)	(4.5-21)		

(1) UFC: Urinary free cortisol (24 hrs.) ; (2) one-tail.
(Means ± S.D. and S.D. ranges given where appropriate)

el of the depressives was similar to that of the schizophrenic patients. After dexamethasone the mean value of the depressives
was 1.6 times that of the schizophrenics; t = 1.84, p <0.05 (one
tail) (Table 5-XX).

The twenty-four-hour urinary free cortisol excretions both before and after dexamethasone were significantly elevated in the
depressed group (Table 5-XX). The basal mean value of the depressives ($104\mu g$) was near the upper limit of the normal range
(Murphy, 1968) while all the individual values of the schizophrenics were within the normal range of 0 to $108\mu g$ and their
mean value ($39\mu g$; arithmetic mean $52.9\mu g$) compares well with
normal arithmetic mean of $48\mu g$. By contrast, in thirteen of the
twenty-one depressives the basal UFC excretion exceeded the upper limit of the normal range.

The depressed patients were much older than the schizophrenics. Within the group of depressives *no effect of age* was found
on the urinary free cortisol excretion, before or after dexamethasone (Table 5-XXI).

After dexamethasone the urinary free cortisol excretion of the
depressives was increased five-fold over that of the schizophrenics
and the mean value of the depressive ($49\mu g$) was equivalent to
the normal basal mean. Individual results are shown in Figure
5-6.

As measured by the rating scale, however, the schizophrenics
showed evidence of slightly greater breakdown of psychological
defenses than did the depressives.

Within the two groups correlations (product-moment) were
calculated between the urinary results and the rating scale scores

TABLE 5-XXI

AGE AND URINARY FREE CORTISOL EXCRETION
(Means: $\mu g/24$ hrs.)

| Age | N | Urinary Free Cortisol | |
		Before Dexamethasone	After Dexamethasone
40-50	7	92	53
51-60	4	109	28
61-70	3	139	98
71-80	6	112	52

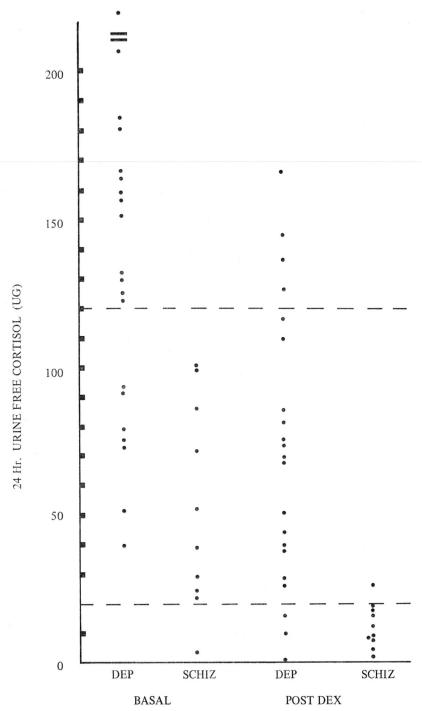

Figure 5-6. Post-DEX urinary free cortisol in depressed and schizophrenic patients. Broken lines indicate range of normal basal values.

TABLE 5-XXII

CORRELATION COEFFICIENTS (Product-moment)

Comparison	Depressives (21)	Schizophrenics (10)
Pre-DEX Urine Cortisol		
"Core" Items	+0.06	−0.20
Hamilton Score	+0.23	−0.03
Hamilton Physiological	+0.38	−0.61[1]
Sachar Physiological	+0.43[1]	−0.26
Post-DEX Urine Cortisol		
"Core" Items	+0.30	−0.46
Hamilton Score	+0.26	−0.23
Hamilton Physiological	+0.45[1]	−0.53
Sachar Physiological	+0.36	−0.44

(1) $p < 0.05$.

(Table 5-XXII). The "core" score was obtained as described above. Physiological components of the Hamilton scale were as detailed in Chapter 4, i.e. middle and delayed insomnia, weight loss and gut symptoms. The same items were extracted from the Sachar scale (items 3, 4, 9, 10 and 34) to give a score for physiological features. The physiological scores of the Hamilton and Sachar scales correlated +0.84 in the whole group of thirty-one subjects.

Comment

These are extremely interesting results. They do not support Sachar's thesis and they throw some light on the importance of physiological symptoms in relation to nonsuppression after dexamethasone.

The basal and postdexamethasone urinary results clearly distinguish the two groups of patients. After dexamethasone there is little overlap between the individual values. The differences between the plasma cortisol levels are less significant: the superiority of the urinary free cortisol excretion over the plasma cortisol level as an index of adrenal hyperfunction is confirmed by these results.

In the depressed group each of the rating scale scores correlates positively with both the urinary free cortisol excretions. The total Hamilton Score and the physiological component of the Hamilton Scale are showing the most powerful correlations at this stage of the study (which is still continuing).

All of the correlations in the schizophrenic group are negative.

The negative correlations between the urinary cortisols and the physiological symptoms in this group are especially notable. It would seem that it is not the simple presence of these physiological features in an individual which determines an impaired response to dexamethasone. Rather, from the data presented, there are grounds for concluding that the correlation seen *in the depressed group* between physiological symptoms and urinary cortisol signifies a common determinant of the two parameters. That is to say, both nonsuppression and physiological symptoms seem to result from the underlying depressive process.

The scores obtained by the schizophrenic patients on the Hamilton Rating Scale for depression also call for comment. The scale was not constructed as a diagnostic instrument (Hamilton, 1960) but as a means of objectively scoring elements of primary depressive illness in patients already diagnosed on clinical grounds as suffering from that condition.

A number of authors have drawn attention to the presence of depressive symptomatology in patients with a primary diganosis of schizophrenia (Bleuler, 1950; Sachar *et al.,* 1963; Bowers and Astrachan, 1967; Steinberg *et al.,* 1967). While Sachar and Steinberg both emphasize the appearance of depressive features during recovery from the acute psychotic phase of schizophrenia, others have identified these symptoms throughout the course of the illness; during recovery they are more easily recognized (Shanfield *et al.,* 1970).

The mean Hamilton Score of the schizophrenic group (25.4) would, in depressives, indicate severe illness requiring ECT. The results of this study provide a psychoendocrine distinction between primary depressive behavior and secondary depressive symptomatology, and complement the same distinction which can be made on clinical grounds (Bleuler, 1950), in terms of response to treatment (Bowers and Astrachan, 1967) and in terms of factor analysis of the Hamilton Scale (Michaux *et al.,* 1969).

MANIC PATIENTS

Mania is rarely seen in the Royal Melbourne Hospital. Only three cases were encountered between 1967 and 1970. All had nor-

TABLE 5-XXIII

PLASMA CORTISOL LEVELS OF THREE MANIC PATIENTS (µg/100 ml)

Patient	8:30 AM	4:30 PM	8:30 AM Post-Dexamethasone
1	24.9	24.0	4.9
2	17.6	11.0	5.0
3	13.3	13.9	5.6

mal plasma cortisol levels and suppressed normally in response to dexamethasone (Table 5-XXIII).

From this small group it appears that mania is not associated with nonsuppression by dexamethasone. Only one of these patients (No. 3) had a history of depressive episodes but none occurred during the course of this study.

SUMMARY OF PART II

Further studies were performed to answer questions relating to the phenomenon of resistance to dexamethasone in depressed patients.

1. When given at 9:00 PM, dexamethasone did not cause greater HPA suppression than when a midnight dose was used. These results exclude an advanced diurnal rhythm as the cause of nonsuppression.

2. The half-life of cortisol in plasma showed, in three patients, no change upon clinical recovery. Change in response to dexamethasone was not associated with change in plasma cortisol half-life. These results confirm that nonsuppression is not related to abnormally rapid steroid metabolism, such as could be caused by barbiturate drugs.

3. The urinary excretion of free cortisol was measured concurrently with plasma cortisol estimations before and after dexamethasone. In general, high plasma levels were associated with high free cortisol excretion. The results confirmed that nonsuppressors have a high level of HPA function throughout the day, and that their abnormality is not simply one of *control* of the "once-a-day" phase of HPA activity. The results also show that the 8:30 AM plasma cortisol level in general provides a good index

of HPA function during the period from midnight to 8:30 AM. The high plasma cortisol levels at 8:30 AM do not indicate an early "escape" from temporary HPA suppression.

4. The free cortisol levels in cerebrospinal fluid (CSF) were significantly elevated in all of seven patients studied before and after treatment. The difference in CSF levels was greater than the difference in total plasma cortisol levels. The unbound cortisol levels in CSF in the depressed phase were intermediate between the plasma unbound cortisol levels of estrogen-treated subjects and those of patients with Cushing's syndrome.

5. During the course of treatment, change in response to dexamethasone did not occur until *major* clinical improvement had occurred. Relief of the presenting agitation and anxiety was not sufficient to reverse the abnormal response to dexamethasone.

6. Patients who, in spite of apparent clinical improvement, did not suppress normally at the time of discharge had persistent symptoms, tended to suffer early relapses and to require active outpatient treatment.

7. Patients who had more than one admission for depressive illness showed a return of resistance to dexamethasone at each admission.

8. A detailed study was made of the extent of breakdown of psychological defenses in a group of depressives and a control group of schizophrenic patients. In both groups the plasma cortisol and urinary free cortisol excretion was measured before and after dexamethasone.

The depressives had significantly greater free cortisol excretion before and after dexamethasone. The plasma cortisol levels of the two groups were similar before dexamethasone; after dexamethasone the depressives had a mean plasma cortisol level 1.6 times that of the schizophrenics.

Both groups had comparable degrees of breakdown of psychological defenses.

Within the group of depressives defense breakdown items did not correlate significantly with the urinary cortisol excretions. The Hamilton Depression Rating Scale scores and physiological items from that scale showed more powerful correlations with the urinary cortisol excretion.

From this study it was concluded that nonsuppression is related to the underlying depressive process rather than to the less specific features of breakdown of psychological defenses. The results also provide a psychoendocrine distinction between primary depressive behavior and the secondary depressive symptomatology which could be seen in the schizophrenic patients.

9. In the three manic patients who could be studied normal responses to the midnight dexamethasone suppression test were obtained.

Chapter 6

STUDIES WITH HYPOTHALAMIC-PITUITARY-ADRENAL STIMULATION TESTS IN DEPRESSION

BERNARD J. CARROLL

RESPONSES TO HPA STIMULATION PROCEDURES

THE importance of acute stimulation tests of the HPA axis was discussed in Chapter 3. The procedures which depend on suprahypophyseal pathways for the mediation of their effect may be capable of detecting dysfunction of the neural mechanisms which regulate ACTH release.

Four such tests have been applied to the study of HPA regulation in this investigation of depressed patients.

RESPONSE TO ADRENOCORTICOTROPIC HORMONE (ACTH)

The plasma cortisol response to an infusion of ACTH was measured, before and after treatment, in five patients. It appeared important early in the course of these investigations to confirm that the adrenocortical responses of depressed patients to ACTH were normal, since the other tests to be described rely on the plasma cortisol response as an index of hypothalamic-pituitary stimulation.

Method

An intravenous infusion of ACTH in 500 ml of normal saline was maintained over a period of six hours. Porcine ACTH (Commonwealth Serum Laboratories, Melbourne) was used in a dose of 40 International Units (IU). The patients remained in bed during the infusion and blood was collected for plasma cortisol (11-OHCS) estimation at 0 and 6 hours.

Results

In all five patients similar increments of plasma cortisol were obtained, both before and after treatment. Individual and group data are given in Table 6-I.

149

TABLE 6-I

RESPONSES TO I.V. INFUSION OF 40 I.U. PORCINE ACTH OVER
SIX HOURS (Plasma Cortisol μg/100 ml)

Patient	0 Hours		6 Hours		Increment	
	D	R	D	R	D	R
1	20	12.4	77.5	55.6	57.5	43.2
2	22.9	19.7	67	58	44.1	38.3
3	13.3	8.2	57.6	62.8	44.3	54.6
4	17.5	12.7	75	95	57.5	82.3
5	17	13	66	62	49	49
Mean	18.1	13.2	68.6	66.7	50.5	53.5

D: depressed, before treatment.
R: recovered, after treatment.

Comment

No consistent trend was noted for the responses to be exaggerated before treatment. These results confirm that adrenocortical responses to supramaximal stimulation by ACTH are not different before and after treatment for depression. The responses are also similar to those observed in normal subjects studied by the same technique in the Royal Melbourne Hospital. Responses of depressives to ACTH have been studied by one other group who also reported no difference between the post-ACTH plasma cortisol levels of fourteen depressives and eight control subjects (Carpenter and Bunney, 1971).

In a long-term study of rhesus monkeys, Sassenrath (1970) has shown that the urinary 17-OHCS responses to a short-acting ACTH preparation vary according to the position of the animals in the dominance hierarchy. The greatest responses were obtained in the lowest ranking animals. The responses could be predictably altered by inducing changes in the hierarchy which either increased or reduced the amount of social stress.

In man Persky (1957) has found that anxious patients with high daily plasma and urinary 17-OHCS levels also have exaggerated urinary 17-OHCS responses to ACTH, although the elevations produced in plasma 17-OHCS were less remarkable.

Since the plasma cortisol levels produced by these large infusions of ACTH are much higher than those found in response to stimulated ACTH release, complementary studies with threshold and physiological doses of synthetic ACTH (synacthen) would be desirable.

RESPONSE TO LYSINE VASOPRESSIN

Six patients received lysine vasopressin (LVP) before and after treatment of their depression. The mode of action of LVP in stimulating ACTH release was discussed in Chapter 3. Most of the evidence points to a neural site of primary action, the mechanism of which is not understood.

Method

LVP monomer (Sandoz) was given in a dose of 5 units as a rapid intravenous injection between 8:30 and 10:00 AM. The patients had eaten breakfast at 7:30 AM and had remained in bed. Atropine was not given to minimize gastrointestinal side effects. Blood was collected for plasma cortisol at 0, 1 and 2 hours.

Results

In five of the six patients the plasma cortisol response to LVP before treatment was comparable to that obtained on recovery (Table 6-II). Severe side effects occurred in all cases, with marked

TABLE 6-II

RESPONSES TO I.V. INJECTION OF 5 I.U. LYSINE VASOPRESSIN
(Plasma Cortisol, μg/100 ml)

Patient		0 Hours	1 Hour	2 Hours	Increment
1	D	20.6	20.6	—	0
	R	12.9	28.0	—	15.1
2	D	22.4	32.2	21.0	9.8
	R	13.2	24.2	15.8	11.0
3	D	11.7	42.5	19.6	30.8
	R	7.9	49.5	31.3	41.6
4	D	34.6	45.2	29.0	10.6
	R	9.4	28.4	16.4	19.0
5	D	6.1	28.2	17.2	22.1
	R	18.8	26.1	18.8	7.3
6	D	25.3	43.0	35.4	17.7
	R	10.8	27.2	14.0	16.4

D: depressed.
R: recovered.

cutaneous pallor and a bowel movement took place within five
minutes of the injection.

Before treatment the mean plasma cortisol increment caused
by LVP was 15.2µg/100 ml and after treatment the corresponding value was 18.4µg/100 ml.

The criteria established in the Royal Melbourne Hospital for
a normal response to this type of LVP test are that the plasma
cortisol increment should exceed 5µg/100 ml and that the maximum plasma cortisol level should exceed 21µg/100 ml (Carroll
et al., 1969). By these criteria all the responses obtained were positive, except for that of patient 1, while she was depressed. She
had also not suppressed her plasma cortisol level normally (post-
DEX value 18.3µg/100 ml) before treatment, although a normal
result (1.0µg/100 ml) was obtained after recovery.

Of the six patients detailed in Table 6-II only two (subjects
1 and 2) also had dexamethasone suppression tests carried out,
since these LVP tests were performed early in the course of the
project (1967). Subject 2 who responded to LVP had a post-DEX
plasma cortisol level of 7.0µg/100 ml (i.e. normal suppression).

In the light of the findings with subject 1, seven other patients
were given both LVP and dexamethasone tests before treatment
of their depression. The results of this study are given in Table
6-III. Included in Table 6-III are the results of the tests on subjects 1 and 2 from Table 6-II.

TABLE 6-III

RESPONSES TO LVP AND DEXAMETHASONE TESTS (Nine Depressed
Patients Before Treatment; Plasma Cortisol, µg/100 ml)

Patient	Post LVP Maximum	Post LVP Increment	Post-Dexamethasone 8:30 AM
1	20.6	0	18.3
2	32.2	9.8	7.0
3	31.2	14.7	3.0
4	20.4	6.4	8.4
5	13.9	0	0.9
6	30.5	12.9	4.2
7	38.2	18.0	26.8
8	58	34	30
9	25.2	0	16.0

From this table it is apparent that two additional patients (5 + 9) failed to respond to LVP. However, their responses to dexamethasone were not concordant: one suppressed normally while the other clearly did not. On the other hand, in two other patients (7 + 8) the responses to dexamethasone were abnormal but good increments of plasma cortisol followed LVP injection.

There was no consistent relationship, therefore, between poor response to LVP and poor response to dexamethasone.

Comment

In general the responses of these patients to LVP were normal, with only three of thirteen subjects having an impaired response before treatment. Only one other group has studied the response to LVP in depressed patients. Jakobson *et al.* (1969) examined sixteen depressives before treatment. They did not publish detailed plasma cortisol data but judged their responses according to the ratio of maximal/initial level. Their criterion of a normal response was that the maximal plasma cortisol level, post LVP, should be twice the initial value. A maximal/initial ratio of 3 or more was considered excessive. By these standards only one subject had a normal response, while three responses were exaggerated and the remaining twelve were "moderate." The real significance of this data is impossible to evaluate because of the method of presentation. Reference to Table 6-II, however, shows that several positive responses would be considered "moderate" by Jakobson's criteria.

Summary of LVP Responses

Thirteen depressed patients received LVP before treatment. In three cases a definitely impaired response was obtained. No clear association was found between impaired responses to LVP and impaired responses to the midnight dexamethasone suppression text.

Six patients received LVP before and after treatment. In general the responses obtained on the two occasions were comparable.

Dangerous side effects following LVP administration intravenously were not observed in these patients.

RESPONSE TO PYROGEN

In eight patients the HPA response to pyrogen was tested before and after treatment. Like LVP, pyrogen is thought to act above the level of the pituitary to cause the release of ACTH and elevate plasma cortisol levels. Impaired responses to pyrogen have been described not only in association with destructive lesions of the hypothalamus or pituitary but also in patients with Cushing's disease. A high incidence of impaired pyrogen response in such patients is another indication of the disturbance of HPA control mechanisms found in this disease (Chap. 3).

Method

The patients remained in bed and, between 8:30 and 10:00 AM, were given an intravenous injection of $1\mu g$ of Salmonella polysaccharide pyrogen (Pyrexal, Wander). Soluble aspirin 0.6 to 0.9 gm was always given orally at the time of injection and if required for discomfort thereafter. Blood was collected for plasma cortisol (11-OHCS) at 0 and 3 hours.

Results

The criteria for a normal response to this pyrogen used in the manner described in the Royal Melbourne Hospital are that the plasma cortisol level should rise by at least $8\mu g/100$ ml, with the level at three hours being greater than $22\mu g/100$ ml. By these criteria most of the responses obtained were normal.

Patient 2 had a response which was marginally impaired while

TABLE 6-IV

RESPONSES TO PYROGEN (Plasma Cortisol, $\mu g/100$ ml)

Patient	0 Hours		3 Hours		Increment	
	D	R	D	R	D	R
1	45	13.8	57	40.9	12	27.1
2	26.3	11.7	34.2	28.2	7.9	16.5
3	25.0	16.1	54.0	36.1	29.0	20.0
4	24.8	32.6	63.3	61.5	38.5	28.9
5	25.4	9.2	54.6	39.2	29.2	30.0
6	24.1	8.2	32.4	26.0	8.3	17.8
7	10.3	20.6	37.9	24.6	27.6	4.0
8	51.2	21.2	51.2	32.8	0	11.6

she was depressed. She had also failed to respond to dexamethasone (post-DEX level 26.8) although her response to LVP was normal (subject 7-Table 6-III).

In patient 7 the response to pyrogen after treatment was impaired. This woman had received a modified prefrontal leukotomy and the question arose whether this procedure had affected the response. However, patient 1 was also treated by leukotomy and her response to pyrogen was normal after the operation.

Patient 8 did not show a rise in plasma cortisol after pyrogen. Her basal level was so high, however, that a response would be difficult to demonstrate. The same patient had a normal response to LVP and was not tested with dexamethasone.

Comment

In general it does not appear that the depressed state is associated with significant alterations in the response to pyrogen.

RESPONSE TO INSULIN HYPOGLYCEMIA

The mechanism of the adrenocortical response to hypoglycemia was outlined in Chapter 3, where it was pointed out that this procedure had revealed an unsuspected defect of HPA response in patients with Cushing's disease. In that condition of excessive hypothalamus-induced ACTH secretion, the ACTH, growth hormone (GH) and cortisol responses to hypoglycemia are usually defective or absent. In view of the results already obtained which showed that some depressed patients have HPA abnormalities similar to those seen in Cushing's disease, it was obviously important to investigate their responses of hypoglycemia.

Subjects and Methods

Sixteen depressed patients from the main group of forty (Chap. 4) received the insulin tolerance test (ITT) both before and after treatment. Their ages ranged from forty-two to seventy-seven, with a mean of sixty-one years. All were treated with electric convulsion therapy (ECT) and none received antidepressant drugs concurrently. Amylobarbitone was given as required for sedation, except on the morning of the tests.

The patients fasted from 10:00 PM overnight and remained in

bed until the test was completed. An indwelling venous cannula was inserted fifteen minutes before the injection of insulin. Crystalline insulin (Commonwealth Serum Laboratories) was given intravenously in a dose of 0.1 units per kilogram of body weight at 8:30 AM. Samples were taken through the cannula for blood sugar at fifteen-minute intervals and for plasma cortisol and GH at thirty-minute periods over sixty or ninety minutes.

The author remained with the patients throughout the procedure and glucose was always available for intravenous injection if severe symptoms developed.

The criteria for evaluating responses to the ITT are discussed in detail elsewhere (Carroll *et al.*, 1969). A positive response when the blood sugar falls below 45 mg/100 ml, is defined as a rise in plasma cortisol of greater than 5μg/100 ml together with a maximum level of at least 25μg/100 ml. If only one of these criteria is satisfied the response is regarded as impaired. Failure to satisfy either criterion constitutes a negative response. A normal GH response consists of a rise in plasma GH levels to at least 7 ng/ml during the test.

Thirteen of the sixteen patients also received the midnight dexamethasone suppression test, with an interval of at least forty-eight hours between this test and the ITT.

Plasma cortisol was measured by the author with a fluorometric method (Mattingly, 1962) and blood sugar by a ferro-ferricy-

TABLE 6-V

CHANGES IN BLOOD SUGAR, PLASMA CORTISOL AND PLASMA GROWTH HORMONE DURING INSULIN TOLERANCE TEST IN SIXTEEN DEPRESSED PATIENTS ON ADMISSION AND AFTER RECOVERY

	Depressed		Recovered	
	Mean + S.E.	Range	Mean + S.E.	Range
Fasting blood sugar (mg/100 ml)	85 ± 2.3	72-100	78 ± 3.3[2]	50-100
Minimum blood sugar	37 ± 3	18-64	28 ± 2.5[2]	12-50
Fall in blood sugar	48 ± 2.3	26-60	50 ± 3.5	26-68
Fasting plasma cortisol (μg/100 ml) ..	19.4 ± 1.9	5.8-31.6	16.8 ± 1.7	8.5-30.4
Rise in plasma cortisol	9.3 ± 1.6	2.5-23.2	15.9 ± 1.55[1]	5.1-23.2
Maximum growth hormone (ng/ml) *	19 ± 5.1	0-53	17.1 ± 2.8	0-32
Rise in growth hormone*	18.4 ± 4.5	0-46.6	16.1 ± 2.7	0-32

(1) p <0.01; (2) p <0.05 paired t test.
* Fourteen patients.

TABLE 6-VI

INDIVIDUAL DATA FOR MINIMUM BLOOD SUGAR, PLASMA CORTISOL
RISE, PLASMA GROWTH HORMONE RISE AND POST-DEXAMETHASONE
8:30 AM. PLASMA CORTISOL LEVELS IN DEPRESSED (D)
AND RECOVERED (R) PHASES

Subject	Minimum Blood Sugar (mg/100 ml)		Plasma Cortisol Rise (μg/100 ml)		Plasma G.H. Rise (ng/ml)		Post-DEX Plasma Cortisol (μg/100 ml)	
	D	R	D	R	D	R	D	R
1	28	12	15.4	19.6	1.0	15.6	18.3	1.0
2	20	12	2.7	20.8	0	2.0	26.8	3.4
3	64	50	5.6	9.5	21.6	2.4	20.8	8.5
4	50	36	7.8	21.5	0	0	30.0	8.6
5	32	32	11.1	18.7	46.6	27.6	17.0	1.8
6	32	24	18.4	21.5	10.0	11.2	18.8	0.5
7	48	26	16.5	17.8	38.0	32.0	16.0	20.7
8	46	32	3.4	5.1	28.0	28.0	27.5	25.8
9	44	44	9.7	6.4	—	—	8.7	5.9
10	18	28	23.2	10.2	41.0	16.0	1.5	2.6
11	32	28	8.4	23.2	7.4	23.0	2.3	2.5
12	24	28	10.3	12.6	25.4	28.2	2.9	3.2
13	30	22	7.2	12.4	6.8	15.0	6.6	1.8
14	44	24	3.4	19.1	30.0	11.4	—	—
15	42	20	2.5	21.0	0	15.4	—	—
16	36	26	3.4	14.6	—	—	—	—

anide method with an auto-analyzer (Technicon) by courtesy of
the Department of Biochemistry, Royal Melbourne Hospital.
Growth hormone was measured by Dr. F. I. R. Martin, endocri-
nologist to the Royal Melbourne Hospital, using a radio-immunoassay procedure (Jacobs, 1969).

Results

The changes in blood sugar, plasma cortisol and plasma growth
hormone following insulin are summarized in Table 6-V.

In Table 6-VI the individual data for minimum blood sugar,
rises in plasma cortisol and GH, and post-dexamethasone 8:30
AM plasma cortisol levels are given.

Cortisol Response

Four negative and three impaired responses to hypoglycemia
were found in the depressed phase. In all these cases the minimum blood glucose level was below 45 mg/100 ml. After treat-

TABLE 6-VII

SUMMARY OF VARIANCE ANALYSIS OF PLASMA CORTISOL
RESPONSES TO HYPOGLYCEMIA

	Sum of Squares
Total	1436 with 31 degrees of freedom
Between Subjects	553 with 15 degrees of freedom
Within Subjects	883 with 16 degrees of freedom
Between Phases	344 with 1 degree of freedom
Residual	330 with 15 degrees of freedom

$F = 15.66$; $p < 0.001$.

ment one response was impaired (x^2 (with Yates correction) = 4.12; not significant).

The mean rise in plasma cortisol on recovery was significantly greater than the mean rise when the patients were depressed—Table 6-V (paired $t = 3.10$, $p < 0.01$). In fourteen of the sixteen cases the rise in cortisol was greater on recovery (X^2 with Yates correction) = 15.1, $p < 0.001$) and an analysis of the variance (Winer, 1962) of the plasma cortisol responses also supports this conclusion ($F = 15.66$, $p < 0.001$). The variation in response *between* subjects does not account for the differences observed *within* subjects between the phases of depression and recovery.

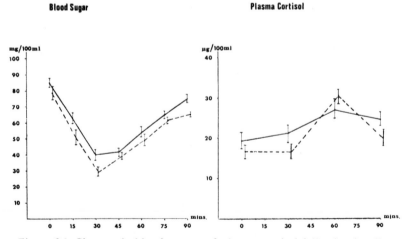

Figure 6-1. Changes in blood sugar and plasma cortisol following insulin.

TABLE 6-VIII

PLASMA CORTISOL RESPONSES TO HYPOGLYCEMIA
(Means and Ranges)

Investigators	Minimum Blood Sugar (mg/100 ml)	Plasma Cortisol Rise (μg/100 ml)	Maximum Plasma Cortisol (μg/100 ml)	Subjects
Present series	37 (20-64)	9.3 (2.5-23.2)	27.4 (14-44)	16 depressed
Present series	28 (12-50)	15.9 (5.1-23.2)	30.7 (18-45)	16 recovered depressives
Greenwood *et al.*, 1966	31 (18-53)	15.4 (>7.7)	28.1 (>21.7)	28 normal
Bethge *et al.*, 1967	<45	13.1 (>6.4)	25.3 (S.D. 4.3)	17 normal

When depressed, the patients had fasting blood sugar levels significantly higher than their levels on recovery—Table 6-V (paired $t = 2.27$, $p < 0.05$). In the depressed phase the minimum blood sugar was higher than after recovery (paired $t = 3.92$, $p < 0.01$). However, the rate of fall of blood sugar and the absolute fall in blood sugar was similar on each occasion (Fig. 6-1).

Four patients did not achieve a degree of hypoglycemia below 45 mg/100 ml. When the results of these patients were omitted from analysis a significant difference in the mean rise in plasma cortisol between the clinical phases in still observed (paired $t = 2.60$, $p < 0.02$, one tailed; 0.05, two tailed).

A significant correlation was found between the minimum blood sugar levels and the plasma cortisol rises in the recovered phase ($r = -0.546$, $p < 0.02$). In the depressed phase, however the correlation was poor ($r = -0.366$, $p > 0.10$).

A comparison of the plasma cortisol responses obtained with those of normal patients from other series is given in Table 6-VIII. In the recovered phase the rises seen were close to those of normal subjects.

RELATION BETWEEN CORTISOL RESPONSE TO HYPOGLYCEMIA AND DEXAMETHASONE SUPPRESSION

Thirteen patients received the midnight 2 mg dexamethasone suppression test before and after treatment. In six cases (Table

TABLE 6-IX

RELATIONSHIP BETWEEN CHANGES IN RESPONSE TO
DEXAMETHASONE AND TO HYPOGLYCEMIA*

N	Post-DEX Plasma Cortisol Change (depressed minus recovered)[1]	Change in Plasma Cortisol Rise During ITT (recovered minus depressed)
6 .... 17.6		8.4
7 .... 0.0		1.3

(1) Calculated from log-transformed values.
* Six patients with reversible resistance to dexamethasone and seven patients with no change in response to dexamethasone; mean values.

6-VI, Nos. 1-6) impaired suppression was found on admission and a normal response was seen after treatment. There was no significant change in the responses of the remaining seven subjects to dexamethasone; two continued to be nonsuppressors after treatment.

The patients whose responses to dexamethasone changed also showed a change in response to hypoglycemia; in the seven patients with similar responses to dexamethasone before and after treatment the plasma cortisol responses to hypoglycemia did not alter significantly (Table 6-IX).

Correlations

In the group of six who showed reversible resistance to dexamethasone the correlation found was a strong one ($r = -0.7020$, $n = 12$, $p < 0.01$). No significant correlation was found for the group who showed no change in their response to dexamethasone ($r = -0.3952$, $n = 14$, p N.S.).

These relationships are displayed in Figure 6-2.

PLASMA GROWTH HORMONE RESPONSE (GH)

Considering only patients whose blood glucose levels fell below 45 mg/100 ml during the ITT, there were four patients out of ten who did not show a normal plasma GH response when depressed (Table 6-VI, Nos. 1, 2, 13, 15).

After treatment one of these patients again did not respond normally (No. 2).

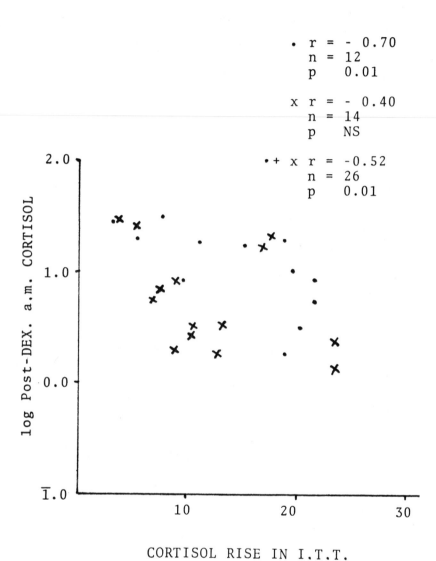

CORTISOL RISE IN I.T.T.

Figure 6-2. Post-DEX plasma cortisol levels and plasma cortisol during insulin tolerance test.

In three of these four cases the plasma cortisol response was also impaired in the depressed phase.

In other patients an impaired GH response was seen but the blood glucose level was not low enough to allow definitive interpretation. Patient 4 (Table 6-VI) had no GH response after treatment even though the blood glucose fell to 36 mg/100 ml.

There was no consistent relationship between poor GH responses and impaired responses to dexamethasone.

Plasma Cortisol Responses

The results of this study show a clear deficiency of adrenocortical response to hypoglycemia in the depressed patients, which has been confirmed by a number of statistical evaluations. After treatment normal responses were obtained.

In addition, an association has been demonstrated between impairment of the responses to both the ITT and the dexamethasone test. This association of change in sensitivity to hypoglycemia with change in sensitivity to dexamethasone suggests that the impaired plasma cortisol responses to hypoglycemia may be due to reversible dysfunction of central HPA control mechanisms. The similarity of these abnormalities in depressives to those seen in Cushing's disease is very suggestive.

Other possible explanations of these findings must be considered but do not appear to be satisfactory.

Inhibition of the ACTH response by barbiturates during the depressed phase is one such possibility. There is good experimental evidence that, in the cat at least, barbiturates alone do not affect the HPA response to hypoglycemia (Krieger, *et al.*, 1968). In addition, the patients received similar amounts of barbiturate on the nights before each of the tests. Nevertheless, this question should be reexamined in drug-free patients.

The other critical factor to consider is the degree of hypoglycemia produced on each occasion. The mean minimum blood sugar (37 mg/100 ml) was well below that regarded as necessary to stimulate an adrenocortical response in normal subjects (45 mg/100 ml) (Greenwood *et al.*, 1966). As described above, the omission from analysis of the results of four patients who did not achieve this degree of hypoglycemia does not affect the finding of a significant change in response with clinical improvement in the case of the remaining twelve subjects.

These twelve patients with adequate hypoglycemia had a mean minimum blood glucose level of 32 mg/100 ml and a mean plasma cortisol rise of 9.6µg/100 ml. By comparison Greenwood *et al.* (1966) used the same dose of insulin in six normal subjects and found a mean blood glucose minimum of 31.5 mg/100 ml, with a mean plasma cortisol rise of 15.0µg/100 ml. They repeated the ITT in four subjects and obtained closely similar plasma cortisol responses on the two occasions.

The association of impaired response to dexamethasone with the impaired ITT responses is the most compelling evidence that these results are more than artifacts related to the factors discussed above.

Further studies with the ITT, using a larger dose of insulin would be useful to examine this association in greater detail.

Growth Hormone Responses

Four out of ten patients with adequate hypoglycemia did not increase the plasma GH levels normally, and in three cases the response was still abnormal after treatment. The range of GH responses seen was very wide, so that the mean plasma GH increment was similar in the two clinical phases. Normal subjects are known to have a marked variability in plasma GH response when the ITT is repeated, although their plasma cortisol responses are much more reproducible (Greenwood *et al.* 1966). Provided that the criteria for a normal response are satisfied it is not clear what significance, if any, can be attached to differences between plasma GH responses.

In a study of the plasma GH responses of depressed patients, before and after treatment with amitriptyline, Mueller *et al.* (1969) found that the mean responses of manic depressives and psychotic depressives were significantly less than those of neurotic depressives. After treatment these differences were not found. Individual data concerning positive and absent responses or the degree of hypoglycemia were not given, however, so that it is difficult to compare these results with the present findings.

Absent GH responses were not clearly related to the finding of an impaired response to dexamethasone. Four patients who had an impaired growth hormone response (three before, one after treatment) received the dexamethasone test as well. In all four an improved response to dexamethasone occurred after treatment. Other patients were noted, however, who had normal GH responses, despite being resistant to suppression by dexamethasone.

SUMMARY OF RESPONSES TO HPA STIMULATION TESTS

Depressed patients were tested with four standard procedures designed to stimulate the HPA axis. The aim was to assess the functioning of the central mechanisms involved in HPA responses.

ACTH produced normal increments of plasma cortisol in five patients before and after treatment. Further studies with low doses of synthetic ACTH are suggested.

Lysine vasopressin produced a normal rise in plasma cortisol in ten of thirteen patients before treatment. Three patients did not respond to LVP. There was no consistent relationship between poor response to LVP and poor response to dexamethasone. No significant change in response to LVP occurred after treatment (six patients).

Eight patients received the pyrogen test before and after treatment. The responses were not remarkably different from normal.

In response to insulin hypoglycemia seven of sixteen patients had an impaired increment of plasma cortisol. A significant improvement in the response was noted after treatment. A strong association was demonstrated between change in response to hypoglycemia and change in response to dexamethasone.

The plasma growth hormone response to hypoglycemia was absent in four of ten patients before treatment and in three of the same patients after treatment. No consistent relationship with the dexamethasone response was found.

Taken together with the results of the dexamethasone suppression tests, these findings confirm that some depressed patients have abnormalities of HPA regulatory mechanisms, similar to the abnormalities seen in Cushing's disease.

GENERAL DISCUSSION AND SUGGESTIONS FOR
FURTHER STUDIES OF HPA FUNCTION

Chapters 4, 5 and 6 report the finding of significant neuro-endocrine disturbances in some depressed patients. Two major conclusions are advanced:

1. Some depressives have defective regulation of their hypo-thalamo-pituitary-adrenal (HPA) control mechanisms.
2. They are also exposed to high amounts of physiologically active hydrocortisone (cortisol).

The evidence for these conclusions comes from the study of total plasma cortisol levels, of free cortisol levels in urine and cerebrospinal fluid, and of the responses of HPA suppression and stimulation procedures. The disturbances were shown to correlate with physiological rather than with nonspecific psychological features of the depressed patients. The control groups had no significant HPA disturbance, despite the presence of severe nonspecific symptoms; also, within the control groups there was no correlation between physiological symptoms and any of the endocrine parameters.

Replication of the Results

The first question to be asked of new findings such as these is, can they be reproduced in other centers? The work reported here was planned independently of other workers. Since publication of an early report (Carroll *et al.*, 1968) we have learned that others were also proceeding along similar lines, and *all reported confirmatory results* (Butler and Besser, 1968; Platman and Fieve, 1968; Stokes, 1966, 1970, 1972). Fawcett and Bunney (1967) mentioned, without giving details, that some depressives did not respond to dexamethasone. In a later study (Carpenter and Bunney, 1971) normal suppression was found in all patients when dexamethasone was given as 2 mg daily for two days, then as 4 mg daily for two days. Another negative report comes from Shopsin and Gershon (1971) who used a 2 mg dose given at 11:00 PM. None of their fourteen patients were seriously ill, none were agitated, nor did any require treatment with ECT. In these two reports the

factors of dosage and of patient selection may be responsible
for the negative findings. Another recent study by Blumenfield
et al. (1970), which like Shopsin and Gershon's was stimulated
by our own first report, has also produced confirmatory evidence:
the subjects were United States Air Force trainees referred because of symptoms of depression and anxiety.

Failure of suppression after dexamethasone was reported by
Bethge *et al.* (1970) in patients with anorexia nervosa; impaired
cortisol responses to hypoglycemia were also found. The effect of
severe weight loss on HPA control mechanisms was discussed in
Chapter 5 and this variable will need to be considered in assessing
results in such patients.

Clinical Prediction of Nonsuppression

The bimodal distribution of post-dexamethasone plasma cortisol levels (Chap. 5) raises the question whether the two groups
can be distinguished by their clinical features. This question was
examined in a study of twenty-five suppressors and twenty-five
nonsuppressors (all inpatients) reported elsewhere (Carroll and
Davies, 1970). No confident prediction of response to dexamethasone is possible simply on the basis of clinical presentation. The
nonsuppressors had significantly greater agitation scores, and fewer adverse childhood experiences; there was also a trend toward
a more frequent past history of depression, a family history of
depression and fewer obsessional features in the nonsuppressors.
These findings taken with the correlations previously noted between nonsuppression and physiological symptoms are suggestive
of the "endogenous" picture of depression. In daily practice,
however, with individual patients the issue is not clear-cut.

Etiological Significance?

Despite the difficulty of clinical prediction it does appear that
the phenomenon of nonsuppression, when it is present, is not
simply a function of current symptomatology, arousal or "ego
disintegration." To the extent that it is not reversed until after
major clinical improvement it does not seem to be an epiphenomenon indicative of distress. To the extent that it may persist in
patients who continue to have physiological symptoms and early

relapse it may be determined by a brain mechanism linked with the underlying depressive process. It may be an epiphenomenon in that sense, but not in the less specific sense.

A third possibility, which is open to further testing, is that a subgroup of depressed patients has been identified in whom non-suppression and high free cortisol exposure do have an etiological significance. To evaluate this possibility a number of strategies suggest themselves. There are also several ways in which these neuroendocrine disturbances could be relevant to the amine theory of depression. Although it could easily be done, no attempt will be made to construct a speculative framework to accommodate these findings and the amine theory. Some practical suggestions for further studies will be presented instead: speculation is premature at this stage.

Further Studies of HPA Regulation

On the practical side a number of clinical investigations are warranted:

Serial testing of HPA suppression during a course of treatment—the aim is to evaluate this parameter as an index of improvement.

Testing of suppression before discharge from hospital—this follows from the first study and may give information to predict early relapse.

Longitudinal studies of suppression in patients with recurrent illnesses—the aim is to identify the time of change in response to dexamethasone in relation to the time of clinical change. The results may be useful in anticipating a recurrence.

Evaluation of the suppression response as an index of suicide potential—Bunney and Fawcett (1965) suggested that urinary 17-OHCS estimations could provide such an index but later experience with this parameter has been disappointing (Bunney *et al.*, 1969; Levy and Hansen, 1969). Krieger (1970) claimed on the basis of his data that the plasma cortisol level was a more reliable indicator of suicide potential than was the urinary 17-OHCS excretion.

The evidence presented indicates that response to dexamethasone is a much more sensitive measure of HPA activation than is any basal parameter. It may then have an advantage over the other measures in predicting suicidal behavior.

To further define the extent and mechanisms of HPA dysfunction in depressed patients a number of cognate studies of HPA control are also suggested.

Responses to threshold and physiological doses of ACTH—at present we have no information about the responsiveness of any group of psychiatric patients to "normal" amounts of ACTH.

Investigation for positive glucocorticoid feedback in patients who are nonsuppressors. The clinical reports suggestive of positive feedback responses to dexamethasone were discussed in Chapter 3. Some of the data of Stokes (1970) and of Blumenfield *et al.* (1970) in psychiatric patients could also be consistent with this idea.

The optimal method for demonstrating this phenomenon is that of James *et al.* (1965) who used intravenous infusions of dexamethasone in patients with Cushing's disease. As an index of the response the measurement of plasma ACTH together with plasma cortisol levels would be an advantage.

The optimal time for the infusions may be around midnight to 4:00 AM since it is the "once-a-day" phase of HPA activity which is being suppressed. Gibbons and Fahy (1966) obtained no evidence of positive feedback when they used intramuscular injections of dexamethasone at 2:00 PM.

The midnight metyrapone test (Jubiz, Meikle, *et al.*, 1970) separates patients with Cushing's disease from normal subjects. Since it is a stimulation test in a sense "opposite" to the midnight dexamethasone test it seems worthwhile applying it to depressed patients. Carpenter and Bunney (1971) obtained normal results with the usual extended metyrapone tests in their depressives.

Studies of drug effects on the response to dexamethasone. The neurohumoral mechanisms involved in HPA regulation were discussed in Chapter 3. The production of resistance to suppression with drugs could be a valuable strategy toward understanding the mechanism of this phenomenon in patients. The reverse maneuver, abolishing nonsuppression by drugs, is another obvious line of investigation. Drugs which selectively alter catecholamine or indoleamine metabolism in the brain should be considered for these studies. The results may allow some relationship to be established between the finding of nonsuppression and the amine theory. Other classes of drugs should also be included.

Study of Effects of Hypercortisolism on Brain Function and Behavior

The association of high free cortisol levels with HPA disturbances in the patients resembles the situation in Cushing's disease, where a high incidence of depression is also found. Glucocorticoids are known to affect brain function and behavior in several ways, apart from their role in the regulation of ACTH release. Some of these effects are worth exploring, to see whether direct evidence can be obtained in the patients of steroid-induced abnormalities.

ELECTROPHYSIOLOGY

Nerve conduction velocity (NCV) is increased in the hypoadrenal state and is rapidly slowed to normal by prednisolone (Henkin *et al.*, 1963). On the other hand prednisolone did not affect the NCV of normal subjects and this parameter is known to be normal in depressed and hypomanic patients (Thies and Kooyman, 1970).

Electroshock threshold (EST), as well as the sensitivity to chemical and audiogenic seizures, is lowered by adrenalectomy (Woodbury and Vernadakis, 1967; Gallagher and Glaser, 1968). Cortisol will lower the EST in rats although corticosterone does not (Woodbury and Vernadakis, 1967) and the diurnal rhythm of audiogenic seizure susceptibility is close to that of the HPA rhythm in rats (Wada and Asakura, 1970). The author is not aware of any studies of seizure thresholds in depressed patients in relation to HPA activity. Quantitation of the stimulus may be easier with inhaled convulsants such as hexafluorodiethylether (Indoklon) than with electrical convulsions.

Sensory thresholds to taste, smell and hearing are lowered by adrenalectomy in man, and these changes are also specifically reversed by glucocorticoids (Henkin and Daly, 1968; Henkin, 1970). Integration of sensory information is impaired, despite the lowering of thresholds for sensation. In *hypercortisolism* increased sensory thresholds for taste, smell, hearing and proprioception are found. Study of these parameters in depressed and control patients, with reference to adrenocortical function may be fruitful.

On *polysynaptic systems* the absence of glucocorticoids is associated with delay of synaptic transmission, despite the increased NCV, so that retardation of the multisynaptic component of *cortical evoked potentials* is seen. Dexamethasone will shorten the latency of the multisynaptic component in both normal and adrenalectomized cats and prednisolone has a similar effect in adrenalectomized patients. In normal subjects hydrocortisone has also been shown to alter the characteristics of visual evoked potentials and to slow the subjects' perception of time (Chambers *et al.*, 1963; Ojemann and Henkin, 1967; Kopell *et al.*, 1970).

These areas may be worthy of study in depressed patients with and without evidence of hypercortisolism, although other factors are known to affect evoked responses. There is evidence that unipolar and bipolar depressives differ in their patterns of visual evoked response (Buchsbaum *et al.*, 1970).

NEUROCHEMISTRY

Tissue Concentrations of Hydrocortisone

One effect of hypercortisolism that could be expected is that the tissue levels of the hormone would be elevated. Direct investigation of this possibility has revealed no difference in the postmortem brain tissue cortisol concentrations of depressed suicides, nondepressed suicides and control subjects (Carroll, 1971, unpublished observations).

Effects on Brain Catecholamines

While there is little evidence that glucocorticoids have a widespread permissive influence on adrenergic mechanisms (Harrison *et al.*, 1968) there are specific areas of steroid-catecholamine interaction that are relevant to the possible behavioral effects of hypercortisolism.

Adrenaline Formation in Brain

One specific effect of cortisol is in the induction of the enzyme phenylethanolamine-N-methyl transferase (PNMT) which catalyzes the formation of *adrenaline* from noradrenaline (Axelrod, 1962). Apart from the well-known presence of this enzyme in the outer zone of the adrenal medulla it is also found in limbic areas of the brain and is inducible in those sites by corticosteroids (Pohorecky and Wurtman, 1968; Pohorecky *et al.*, 1968; Ciaranello *et al.*, 1969). The functional role of adrenaline in the brain is not known, but it can displace noradrenaline from tissue stores and possibly act as a false transmitter (Haining *et al.*, 1969).

This area of PNMT induction might be approached through study of the enzyme activity in suicide brains. The differential estimation of adrenaline and noradrenaline and their respective metabolites metanephrine and normetanephrine in cerebrospinal fluid may also be suggested.

Steroid Effects on Catecholamine Uptake Mechanisms

Using isolated brain synaptosomes Smallberg (1969) was unable to demonstrate an effect of hydrocortisone on the uptake of noradrenaline (NA). An increase of NA uptake by brain slices was reported by Maas and Mednieks (1971) when hydrocortisone was present in pharmacological amounts. The effective concentrations were several orders of magnitude greater than the brain cortisol levels reported by Touchstone *et al.* (1966) and even greater therefore, than the true brain cortisol levels. Iversen and Salt (1970) also found that pharmacological but not physiological amounts of corticosterone and other steroids inhibited catecholamine uptake-2 by the rat heart and suggested that this mechanism might potentiate the peripheral effects of catecholamines during stress.

Ovarian hormones have also been linked with central adrenergic mechanisms by their action of inhibiting the uptake and release of noradrenaline (and serotonin) (Janowsky *et al.*, 1970; Vogel *et al.*, 1970). Following ovariectomy the tissue levels of cortisol are reduced (Schou *et al.*, 1967; Jansen *et al.*, 1970) and the turnover rate of NA in brain is increased (Anton-Tay *et al.*, 1970). An association between depression and ovarian activity (menstrual cycles and after pregnancy) is well known. Despite the *in vitro* studies of ovarian hormone effects on amine mechanisms, in the clinical situation large changes in plasma free cortisol levels are occurring at the same time. In the puerperal period the changes in plasma free cortisol are greater, both in absolute and relative terms, than the changes in plasma free progesterone levels (Rosenthal *et al.*, 1969). *These simultaneous changes in glucocorticoid function need to be taken into account in studies of ovarian hormones and mood.*

Steroid Effects on Indoleamine Metabolism

The effects of glucocorticoids on brain indoleamine metabolism were reviewed in Chapter 3. The important points of interaction are at the level of the two enzymes trytophan hydroxylase (in brain) and trytophan pyrrolase (in liver). The suggestion of Curzon (1969a) that pyrrolase induction by cortisol could significantly alter brain serotonin production and cause depression does not seem likely. If any effect is to be expected it is at the level of tryptophan hydroxylase in brain itself. Impaired activity or a reduced capacity for induction of this enzyme by cortisol during stress could lead to a failure of behavioral coping mechanisms, since the expected rise in serotonin turnover would be prevented.

The other suggestion of Lapin and Oxenkrug (1969) that functional brain serotonin deficiency, especially in the amygdala could result in positive-feedback HPA activation was also discussed in Chapter 3. There is some evidence against this aspect of their general hypothesis but further basic studies are required of the effects of drugs which specifically alter brain serotonin metabolism on the various parameters of HPA function.

One specific clinical approach which is relevant here is the simultaneous study of HPA function (including CSF cortisol levels) and of indices of brain serotonin turnover, such as 5-hydroxyindoleacetic acid levels in cerebrospinal fluid (see Chap. 8).

BEHAVIORAL STUDIES

Whereas depression is seen in man in association with hypercortisolism, the response of animals to high dosage treatment with cortisol is one of *aggression*. Cortisol can both induce and facilitate aggressive behavior in animals (Kostowski *et al.*, 1970). This observation is of some interest for the ethological model of depression and complements Sassenrath's study (1970) of adrenocortical function in relation to position in the dominance hierarchy. Levine *et al.* (1970) have also noted a relationship between dominance, aggression and adrenocortical function in primates.

Another important kind of behavioral study attempts to relate *early experience* to emotionality, with effects on the magnitude of HPA responses to stress later in life, e.g. Ader, 1970; Zarrow *et al.*, 1970. Increased adrenocortical responsiveness is shown by rats which have been stimulated in infancy; the effect is seen in stressful conditions but not in situations which are merely novel. Females also tend to show greater responses than do males. This "organizing" effect of experience on HPA responses may be important for the frequent suggestions that depressed subjects tend to have disturbed family backgrounds (see Slater and Roth, 1969).

CORTICOSTEROID METABOLISM

One way of showing that the high cortisol levels are affecting the brain is to attempt to measure cortisol metabolites produced in extrahepatic tissues. In general these are highly polar compounds and are not measured in the routine urinary 17-OHCS assays. No unique metabolites of cortisol are known to be produced in the brain: tetrahydrocortisol and 20-beta-dihydrocortisol have been isolated from the human brain by Touchstone *et al.* (1966). Measurement of 20-beta-dihydrocortisol and 6-beta-hydroxycortisol was found useful by Bailey *et al.* (1967) as an index of peripheral tissue utilization of cortisol in connective tissue disorders. The only study of these compounds in depressed patients seems to be that of Ferguson *et al.* (1964) who reported high excretion of 6-beta-hydroxycortisol before treatment in depressed women. There are some observations which suggest that the urinary 17-OHCS excretion in neurotic patients is lower than predicted from the plasma 17-OHCS levels (Kusama, 1964) and that this may be explained by the action of ACTH in promoting the uptake of cortisol by extrahepatic tissues (Kusama *et al.*, 1970).

Serial measurement of these polar metabolites might then provide a better index of steroid action on brain than measurement of 17-OHCS, which are derived chiefly from the liver. Bailey *et al.* (1967) mention finding very high 6-beta-hydroxycortisol excretion in one manic patient whom they studied.

Alterations of 17-ketosteroid fractions have also been reported in depression which are similar to those seen in patients with hypothalamic disturbances—increased androsterone/etiocholanolone ratio (Ferguson *et al.*, 1964; Johnsen, 1968) but these do not appear to be consistent findings (Mendels, 1969).

EFFECTS OF ADRENOCORTICOTROPIC HORMONE (ACTH)

Another way, and one of the most important, in which this work might be extended is through the study of plasma ACTH levels as well as cortisol and through investigation of the direct actions of ACTH on the brain. Measurement of this parameter can provide a more direct and sensitive index of hypothalamic-pituitary activity. The importance of ACTH assay does not consist simply in providing a more elegant measure of HPA function.

Extra-adrenal actions of ACTH are now well established, and they include effects on cortisol metabolism (Kusama *et al.*, 1970), on plasma lipid concentrations (Friedman *et al.*, 1967), on amino acid uptake by brain (Jakoubek *et al.*, 1970) and on brain electroshock thresholds (Wasserman *et al.*, 1965). Direct injection of ACTH into the lateral ventricle results in a testosterone-dependent and cyclic-AMP-mediated response of sexual behavior (Bertolini *et al.*, 1969). All of these effects of ACTH are independent of its action on the adrenal cortex. ACTH and cortisol also have independent and sometimes complementary effects on the performance of animals in conditioned learning experiments (Weiss *et al.*, 1970; Nyakas and Endroczi, 1970; Gray, 1971). ACTH is found to increase excitability and fear responses while corticosterone may have the opposite effect in rats (Weiss *et al.*, 1970). A diminution of brain noradrenaline turnover was found as well in rats without ACTH.

A full understanding of the relation between HPA activity and behavior will clearly not be possible until the separate and combined effects of ACTH and cortisol are clarified.

There are few clinical observations relating depression to ACTH. For a period attempts were made to treat depression with ACTH (as well as with steroids) and almost universal failure was reported. Some patients became worse but it is not clear whether this was an effect of ACTH or the spontaneous course of events (see Kobbernagel, 1953 for a summary of these trials). High resting plasma ACTH levels were found in depressed patients by Berson and Yalow (1968), who also measured the plasma ACTH responses to ECT but no systematic study of ACTH in depression has yet appeared.

REFERENCES FOR CHAPTERS 3, 4, 5 AND 6

Abelson, D., Baron, D.N. and Toakley, J.G.: Studies of cerebrospinal fluid following oral administration of cortisone acetate or hydrocortisone. *J Endocrinol,* 12:87-92, 1955.

Ader, R.: The effects of early experience on the adrenocortical response to different magnitudes of stimulation. *Physiol Behav,* 5:837-839, 1970.

Alleyne, G.A.O. and Young, V.H.: Adrenocortical function in children with severe protein-calorie malnutrition. *Clin Sci,* 33: 189-200, 1967.

Amatruda, T.T., Hollingsworth, D.R., D'Esopo, N.D., Upton, V. and Bondry, P.K.: A study of the mechanism of the steroid withdrawal syndrome. Evidence for integrity of the hypothalamic-pituitary-adrenal system. *J Clin Endocrinol,* 30:339-354, 1960.

Anderson, W. McC. and Dawson, J.: The variability of plasma 17-hydroxy-corticosteroid levels in affective illness and schizophrenia. *J Psychosom Res,* 9:237-248, 1965.

Anton-Tay, F., Anton, S.M. and Wurtman, R.J.: Mechanism of changes in brain norepinephrine metabolism after ovariectomy. *Neuroendocrinology,* 6:265-273, 1970.

Appleby, J.I., Gibson, G., Norymberski, J.K. and Stubbs, R.D.: Indirect analysis of corticosteroids. 1. The determination of 17-hydroxycorticosteroids. *Biochem J,* 60:453-460, 1955.

Appleby, J.I. and Norymberski, J.K.: Indirect analysis of corticosteroids. 2. The determination and identification of urinary 17-hydroxy-20-oxo-steroids unsubstituted at C_{21}. *Biochem J,* 60:460-467, 1955.

Arai, Y., Hiroi, M., Mitra, J. and Gorski, R.A.: Influence of intravenous progesterone administration on the cortical electroencephalogram of the female rat. *Neuroendocrinology,* 2:275-282, 1967.

Arner, B., Hedner, P. and Karlefors, T.: Adrenocortical activity during induced hypoglycaemia. An experimental study in man, *Acta Endocrinol,* 40:421-429, 1962.

Aschoff, J., Fatranska, M., Giedke, H., Doerr, P., Stamm, D. and Wisser, H.: Human circadian rhythms in continuous darkness: entrainment by social cues. *Science,* 171:213-215, 1971.

Asfeldt, V.H.: Simplified dexamethasone suppression test. *Acta Endocrinol,* 61:219-231, 1969.

Asfeldt, V.H. and Buhl, J.: Inhibitory effect of diphenylhydantoin on the feedback control of corticotrophin release. *Acta Endocrinol,* 61:551-560, 1969.

Axelrod, J.: Purification and properties of phenylethanolamine-N-methyl transferase. *J Biol Chem,* 237:1657-1660, 1962.

Azmitia, E.C., Algeri, S. and Costa, E.: *In vivo* conversion of ^{3}H-L-tryptophan into ^{3}H-serotonin in brain areas of adrenalectomised rats. *Science,* 169:201-203, 1970.

Azmitia, E.C. and McEwen, B.S.: Corticosterone regulation of tryptophan hydroxylase in midbrain of the rat. *Science,* 166:1274-1276, 1969.

Bailey, E., Greaves, M.S. and West, H.F.: Hydrocortisone metabolism in rheumatoid arthritis. *Lancet,* II:431-434, 1967.

Baron, D.N. and Abelson, D.: Cortisone and hydrocortisone in cerebrospinal fluid. *Nature,* 173:174, 1954.

Beardwell, C.G., Burke, C.W. and Cope, C.L.: Urinary free cortisol measured by competitive protein binding. *J Endocrinol,* 42:79-89, 1968.

Beck, A.T., Ward, C.H., Mendelson, M., Mock, J. and Erbaugh, J.: An inventory for measuring depression. *Arch Gen Psychiatry,* 4:561-571, 1961.

Beisel, W.R., Cos, J.J., Horton, R., Chao, P.Y. and Forsham, P.H.: Physiology of urinary costisol excretion. *J Clin Endocrinol,* 24:887-893, 1964.

Beisel, W.R. and Rapoport, M.I.: Inter-relations between adrenocortical functions and infectious illness. *N Engl J Med,* 280:541-546; 596-604, 1969.

Berson, S.A. and Yalow, R.S.: Radioimmunoassay of ACTH in plasma. *J Clin Invest,* 47:2725-2751, 1968.

Bertolini, A., Vergoni, W., Gessa, G.L. and Ferrari, W.: Induction of sexual excitement by the action of adrenocorticotrophic hormone in brain. *Nature,* 221:667-669, 1969.

Besser, G.M. and Butler, P.W.P.: Cortisol circadian rhythm. *Br Med J,* 2:446-447, 1967.

Besser, G.M., Butler, P.W.P., Landon, J. and Rees, L.: Influence of amphetamines on plasma corticosteroid and growth hormone levels in man. *Br Med J,* 4:528-530, 1969.

Besser, G.M. and Landon, J.: Plasma levels of immuno-reactive corticotrophin in patients with Cushing's syndrome. *Br Med J,* 4:552-554, 1968.

Bethge, H., Bayer, J.M. and Winkelmann, W.: Diagnosis of Cushing's syndrome. The differentiation between adrenocortical hyperplasia and adrenocortical adenoma by means of lysine vasopressin. *Acta Endocrinol,* 60:47-59, 1969.

Bethge, H., Irmscher, K., Solbach, H.G., Winkelmann, W., Zimmermann, H. and Bayer, J.M.: Der Insulinhypoglykamie-Test als Funktionsprufung des Hypothalamus-Hypophysen-Nebennierenrinden-Systems. II. Bei Patienten mit hypothalamischen und hypophysaren Krankheiten und bei Patientinnen mit Anorexia nervosa. *Acta Endocrinol,* 54:681-695, 1967.

Bethge, H., Nagel, A.M., Solbach, H.G., Wiegelmann, W. and Zimmermann, H.: Zentrale Regulationsstorung der Nebennierenrindenfunktion beider Anorexia Nervosa. *Mat Med Nordmark,* 22:204-214, 1970.

Bethge, H., Nahmer, D. and Zimmermann, H.: Der Insulin-hypoglykamie-Test als Funktionsprufung des Hypothalamus-Hypophysen-Nebennieren-rinden-Systems. I. Bei Normalpersonen. *Acta Endocrinol,* 54:668-680, 1967a.

Bethge, H., Winkelmann, W. and Zimmermann, H.: Fehlender Anstieg der Corticosteroide im Plasma wahrend der Insulin-hypoglykamie beim Cushing-Syndrom. *Acta Endocrinol,* 51:166-174, 1966.

Bidder, T.G.: Modification of progesterone translocation into brain. *Endocrinology,* 83:1353-1355, 1968.

Bleuler, E.: *Dementia Praecox.* International Universities Press, New York, 1950.

Bliss, E.L., Ailion, J. and Zwanziger, J.: Metabolism of norepinephrine, serotonin and dopamine in rat brain with stress. *J Pharmacol Exp Ther,* 164:122-134, 1968.

Bliss, E.L., Migeon, C.J., Branch, C.H.H. and Samuels, L.T.: Reaction of the adrenal cortex to emotional stress. *Psychosom Med,* 18:56-76, 1965.

Bliss, E.L., Migeon, C.J., Eik-Nes, K., Sandberg, A.A. and Samuels, L.T.: The effects of insulin, histamine, bacterial pyrogen and the antabuse-alcohol reaction upon the levels of 17-hydroxy-corticosteroids in the peripheral blood of man. *Metabolism,* 3:493-501, 1954a.

Bliss, E.L., Migeon, C.J., Nelson, D.H., Samuels, L.T. and Branch, C.H.H.: Influence of ECT and insulin coma on levels of adrenocortical steroids in peripheral circulation. *Arch Neurol Psychiatry,* 72:352-361, 1954b.

Blumenfield, M., Rose, L.I., Richmond, L.H. and Beering, S.C.: Dexamethasone suppression in basic trainees under stress. *Arch Gen Psychiatry,* 23:299-304, 1970.

Board, F., Persky, H. and Hamburg, D.A.: Psychological stress and endocrine functions: Blood levels of adrenocortical and thyroid hormones in acutely disturbed patients. *Psychosom Med,* 18:324-333, 1956.

Board, F., Wadeson, R. and Persky, H.: Depressive affect and endocrine functions. Blood levels of adrenal cortex and thyroid hormones in patients suffering from depressive reactions. *Arch Neurol Psychiatry,* 78:612-620, 1957.

Bowers, M. and Astrachan, B.: Depression in acute schizophrenic psychosis. *Am J Psychiatry,* 123:976-979, 1967.

Bridges, P.K. and Jones, M.T.: The diurnal rhythm of plasma cortisol concentration in depression. *Br J Psychiatry,* 112:1257-1261, 1966.

Bridges, P.K. and Jones, M.T.: Personality, physique and the adrenocortical response to a psychological stress. *Br J Psychiatry,* 113:601-605, 1967.

Brooks, R.V., Jeffcoate, S.L., London, D.R., Prunty, F.T.G. and Smith, P.M.: Intermittent Cushing's syndrome with anomalous response to dexamethasone. *J Endocrinol,* 36:53-62, 1966.

Brooksbank, B.W.L. and Coppen, A.: Plasma 11-hydroxycorticosteroids in affective disorders. *Br J Psychiatry*, 113:395-404, 1967.

Brostoff, J., James, V.H.T. and Landon, J.: Plasma corticosteroid and growth hormone response to lysine-vasopressin in man. *J Clin Endocrinol*, 28:511-519, 1968.

Buchsbaum, M., Borge, G., Murphy, D.L. and Goodwin, F.K.: Average evoked responses in affective disorders. American Psychiatric Association Meeting, San Francisco, May 11-17, 1970.

Bunney, W.E., Jr. and Fawcett, J.A.: Possibility of a biochemical test for suicide potential: and analysis of endocrine findings prior to three suicides. *Arch Gen Psychiatry*, 13:232-239, 1965.

Bunney, W.E., Fawcett, J.A., Davis, J.M. and Gifford, S.: Further evaluation of urinary 17-hydroxycorticosteroids in suicidal patients. *Arch Gen Psychiatry*, 21:138-150, 1969.

Bunney, W.E. and Hamburg, D.A.: Methods for reliable longitudinal observation of behaviour. *Arch Gen Psychiatry*, 9:114-128, 1963.

Bunney, W.E., Mason, J.W. and Hamburg, D.A.: Correlations between behavioural variables and urinary 17-hydroxycorticosteroids in depressed patients. *Psychosom Med*, 27:299-308, 1965a.

Bunney, W.E., Mason, J.W., Roatch, J.E. and Hamburg, D.A.: A psychoendocrine study of severe psychotic depressive crises. *Am J Psychiatry*, 122:72-80, 1965b.

Burke, C.W.: The effect of oral contraceptives on cortisol metabolism. *J Clin Pathol*, 23: Suppl. *(Assoc Clin Pathol)*, 3:11-18, 1969a.

Burke, C.W.: Accurate measurement of steroid-protein binding by steady-state gel filtration. *Biochim Biophys Acta*, 176:403-413, 1969b.

Burke, C.W.: Biologically active cortisol in plasma of oestrogen-treated and normal subjects. *Br Med J*, 2:798-800, 1969c.

Burke, C.W. and Roulet, F.: Increased exposure of tissues to cortisol in late pregnancy. *Br Med J*, 1:657-659, 1970.

Bursten, B. and Russ, J.J.: Preoperative psychological state and corticosteroid levels of surgical patients. *Psychosom Med*, 27:309-316, 1965.

Butler, P.W.P. and Besser, G.M.: Pituitary-adrenal function in severe depressive illness. *Lancet*, II:1234-1236, 1968.

Butler, P.W.P., Besser, G.M. and Steinberg, H.: Changes in plasma cortisol induced by dexamphetamine and chlordiazepoxide given alone and in combination in man. *J Endocrinol*, 40:391-392, 1968.

Carpenter, W.T. and Bunney, W.E.: Adrenal cortical activity in depressive illness. *Am J Psychiatry*, 128:31-40, 1971.

Carr, L.A. and Moore, K.E.: Effects of reserpine and alpha-methyltyrosine on brain catecholamines and the pituitary-adrenal response to stress. *Neuroendocrinology*, 3:285-302, 1968.

Carroll, B.J.: Corticosteroid levels in brain tissue. In preparation, 1971.

Carroll, B.J.: Unpublished observations, 1971.

Carroll, B.J. and Davies, B.M.: Clinical associations of 11-hydroxycortico-steroid suppression and non-suppression in severe depressive illnesses. *Br Med J*, I:789-791, 1970.

Carroll, B.J., Fielding, J.M. and Blashki, T.G.: Ratings of depression. A comparison of the Zung and Hamilton scales. *Arch Gen Psychiatry*, accepted for publication, 1971.

Carroll, B.J., Martin, F.I.R. and Davies, B.M.: Resistance to suppression by dexamethasone of plasma 11-OHCS levels in severe depressive illnesses. *Br Med J*, III:285-287, 1968.

Carroll, B.J., Pearson, M.J. and Martin, F.I.R.: Evaluation of three acute tests of hypothalamic-pituitary-adrenal function. *Metabolism*, 18:476-483, 1969.

Ceresa, F., Angeli, A., Boccuzzi, G. and Molino, G.: Once-a-day neurally stimulated and basal ACTH secretion phases in man and their response to corticoid inhibition. *J Clin Endocrinol*, 29:1074-1082, 1969.

Chambers, W.F., Freedman, S.L. and Sawyer, C.H.: The effect of adrenal steroids on evoked reticular responses. *Exp Neurol*, 8:458-469, 1963.

Choi, Y., Thrasher, K., Werk, E.E., Sholiton, L.J. and Olinger, C.: Effect of diphenylhydantoin on cortisol kinetics in humans. *J Pharmacol Exp Ther*, 176:27-34, 1971.

Chowers, I., Einat, R. and Feldman, S.: Effects of starvation on levels of corticotrophin releasing factor, corticotrophin and plasma corticosterone in rats. *Acta Endocrinol*, 61:687-694, 1969.

Christy, N.P., Wallace, E.Z. and Jailer, J.W.: The effect of intravenously administered ACTH on plasma 17, 21-dihydroxy-20-ketosteroids in normal individuals and in patients with disorders of the adrenal cortex. *J Clin Invest*, 34:899-906, 1955.

Ciaranello, R.D., Barchas, R.E., Byers, G.S., Stemmle, D.W. and Barchas, J.D.: Enzymatic synthesis of adrenalin in mammalian brain. *Nature*, 221: 368-369, 1969.

Clark, B.R. and Rubin, R.T.: New fluorometric method for the determination of cortisol in serum. *Anal Biochem*, 29:31-39, 1969.

Clark, B.R., Rubin, R.T., Kales, A. and Poland, R.: Comparison of fluorometric method for urinary cortisol with modified Porter-Silber method for 17-OHCS. *Clin Chim Acta*, 27:364, 1970.

Clayton, G.W., Librik, L., Gardner, R.L. and Guillemin, R.: Studies on the circadian rhythm of pituitary adrenocorticotrophic release in man. *J Clin Endocrinol*, 23:975-980, 1963.

Clower, G.C. and Migeon, C.J.: Psychoendocrine aspects of depression and ECT. *Johns Hopkins Med J*, 121:227-233, 1967.

Conney, A.H., Jacobson, M., Schneidman, K. and Zuntzman, R.: Induction of liver microsomal 6-hydroxylase by diphenylhydantoin or phenobarbital: An explanation for the increased excretion of 6-hydroxycortisol in humans treated with these drugs. *Life Sciences*, 4:1091-1098, 1965.

Connolly, C.K., Gore, M.B.R., Stanley, N. and Wills, M.R.: Single-dose dexamethasone suppression in normal subjects and hospital patients. *Br Med J*, 2:665-667, 1968.

Connolly, C.K. and Wills, M.R.: Plasma "cortisol" levels in right and left ventricular failure. *J Clin Pathol*, 22:598-601, 1969.

Conroy, R.T.W.L., Hughes, B.D. and Mills, J.N.: Circadian rhythm of plasma 11-hydroxycorticosteroids in psychiatric disorders. *Br Med J*, 3:405-407, 1968.

Cope, C.L. and Black, E.G.: The reliability of some adrenal function tests. *Br Med J*, II:1117-1122, 1959.

Cope, C.L., Dennis, P.M. and Pearson, J.: Some factors determining the adrenal response to metyrapone (SU 4885). *Clin Sci*, 30:249-257, 1966.

Cope, C.L. and Pearson, J.: Clinical value of the cortisol secretion rate. *J Clin Pathol*, 18:82-87, 1965.

Coppen, A.: The biochemistry of affective disorders. *Br J Psychiatry*, 113:1237-1264, 1967.

Coppen, A. and Shaw, D.M.: Mineral metabolism in melancholia. *Br Med J*, II:1439-1444, 1963.

Corrodi, H., Fuxe, K. and Hokfelt, T.: The effect of immobilisation stress on the activity of central monoamine neurons. *Life Sciences*, 7:107-112, 1968.

Curzon, G.: Tryptophan pyrrolase: A biochemical factor in depressive illness? *Br J Psychiatry*, 115:1367-1374, 1969a.

Curzon, G.: A relationship between brain serotonin and adrenocortical secretion and its possible significance in endogenous depression. *Neuropsychopharmakologie*, 2:234, 1969b.

Curzon, G. and Green, A.R.: Effect of hydrocortisone on rat brain 5-hydroxytryptamine. *Life Sciences*, 7:657-663, 1968.

Curzon, G. and Green, A.R.: Rat liver tryptophan pyrrolase activity and brain 5-hydroxytryptamine. *Biochem J*, 111:15 P, 1969.

Czarny, D., James, V.H.T., Landon, J. and Greenwood, F.C.: Corticosteroid and growth hormone response to synthetic lysine-vasopressin, natural vasopressin, saline solution and venepuncture. *Lancet*, II:126-129, 1968.

Dafny, N. and Feldman, S.: Single cell activity in the hypothalamus in intact and adrenalectomised rats. *Physiol Behav*, 5:873-878, 1970.

Dallman, M.F. and Yates, F.E.: Anatomical and functional mapping of central neural input and feedback pathways of the adrenocortical system. *Mem Soc Endocrinol*, 17:39-72, 1968.

D'Angelo, S.A., Snyder, J. and Grodin, T.M.: Electrical stimulation of the hypothalamus: simultaneous effects on the pituitary-adrenal and thyroid system of the rat. *Endocrinology*, 75:417-427, 1964.

Daughaday, W.H.: Binding of corticosteroids by plasma proteins. IV. The electrophoretic demonstration of corticosteroid binding globulin. *J Clin Invest*, 37:519-523, 1958.

Davis, J., Morill, R., Fawcett, J., Upton, V., Bondy, P.K. and Spiro, H.M.:

Apprehension and elevated serum cortisol levels. *J Psychosom Res,* 6:83-86, 1962.

Dixit, B.N. and Buckley, J.P.: Brain 5-hydroxytryptamine and anterior pituitary activation by stress. *Neuroendocrinology,* 4:32-41, 1969.

Doe, R.P., Dickinson, P., Zinneman, H.H. and Seal, U.S.: Elevated nonprotein-bound cortisol (NPC) in pregnancy, during oestrogen administration and in carcinoma of the prostate. *J Clin Endocrinol,* 29:757-766, 1969.

Doe, R.P., Flink, E.B. and Goodsell, M.G.: Relationship of diurnal variation in 17-hydroxycorticosteroid levels in blood and urine to eosinophils and electrolyte excretion. *J Clin Endocrinol,* 16:196-206, 1956.

Doe, R.P., Vennes, J.A. and Flink, E.B.: Diurnal variation of 17-hydroxycorticosteroids, sodium, potassium, magnesium and creatinine in normal subjects and in cases of treated adrenal insufficiency and Cushing's Syndrome. *J Clin Endocrinol,* 20:253-265, 1960.

Doig, R.J., Mummery, R.V. and Wills, M.R.: Plasma cortisol levels in depression. *Br J Psychiatry,* 112:1263-1267, 1966.

Egdahl, R.H.: Excitation and inhibition of ACTH secretion. *Mem Soc Endocr,* 17:29-37, 1968.

Dwyer, J., Lazarus, L. and Hickie, J.B.: A study of cortisol metabolism in patients with chronic asthma. *Australas Ann Med,* 16:297-303, 1967.

Eik-Nes, K.B. and Brizzee, K.R.: Concentration of tritium in brain tissue of dogs given (1, 2-^{3}H$_2$) cortisol intravenously. *Biochim Biophys Acta,* 97:320-333, 1965.

Eik-Nes, K., Sandberg, A.A., Nelson, D.H., Tyler, F.H. and Samuels, L.T.: Changes in plasma levels of 17-hydroxycorticosteroids during the intravenous administration of ACTH. *J Clin Invest,* 33:1502-1508, 1954.

Eisenfeld, A.J.: Hypothalamic oestradiol-binding macromolecules. *Nature,* 224:1202-1203, 1969.

Ekman, H., Hakansson, B., McCarthy, J.D., Lehmann, J. and Sjogren, B.: Plasma 17-hydroxycorticosteroids in Cushing's syndrome. *J Clin Endocrinol,* 21:684-694, 1961.

Endroczi, E., Lissak, K. and Tekeres, M.: Hormonal feedback regulation of pituitary-adrenocortical activity. *Acta Physiol Acad Sci Hung,* 18:291-299, 1961.

Endroczi, E., Schreiberg, G. and Lissak, K.: The role of central nervous activating and inhibitory structures in the control of pituitary-adrenocortical function. Effects of intracerebral cholinergic and adrenergic stimulation. *Acta Physiol Acad Sci Hung,* 24:211-221, 1963.

Ernest, I.: Steroid excretion and plasma cortisol in 41 cases of Cushing's syndrome. *Acta Endocrinol,* 51:511-525, 1966.

Espiner, E.A.: Urinary cortisol excretion in stress situations and in patients with Cushing's syndrome. *J Endocrinol,* 35:29-44. 1966.

Eysenck, H.J.: The questionnaire measurement of neuroticism and extraversion. *Rev di Psicol,* 50-328-333, 1956.

Feldman, S. and Dafny, N.: Effects of cortisol on unit activity in the hypothalamus of the rat. *Exp Neurol*, 27:375-387, 1970.

Ferguson, H.C., Bartram, A.C.G., Fowlie, H.C., Cathro, D.M., Birchall, K. and Mitchell, F.L.: A preliminary investigation of steroid excretion in depressed patients before and after electroconvulsive therapy. *Acta Endocrinol*, 47:58-68, 1964.

Few, J.D.: A method for the analysis of urinary 17-hydroxycorticosteroids. *J Endocrinol*, 22:31-46, 1961.

Flood, C., Gherondache, C., Pincus, G., Tait, J.F., Tait, S.A.S. and Willoughby, S.: The metabolism and secretion of aldosterone in elderly subjects. *J Clin Invest*, 46:960-966, 1967.

Flood, C., Layne, D.S., Ramcharan, S., Rossipal, E., Tait, J.F. and Tait, S.A.S.: An investigation of the urinary metabolites and secretion rates of aldosterone and cortisol in man and a description of methods for their measurement. *Acta Endocrinol*, 36:237-264, 1961.

Fontana, J.A., Walker, M.D., Casper, A.G.T., Meret, S. and Henkin, R.I.: Sequential subcellular localisation of cortisol in cat brain. *Endocrinology*, 86:1469-1471, 1970.

French, F.S., Jefferys, A.M., Baggett, B., Williams, T.F. and Wyk, J.J. van: Cushing's syndrome with a paradoxical response to dexamethasone. *Am J Med*, 47:619-624, 1969.

Friedman, M.H.: Fear of electroconvulsive therapy. *Arch Neurol Psychiatry*, 78:385-391, 1957.

Friedman, M., Rosenman, R.H., Byers, S.O. and Eppstein, S.: Hypotriglyceridaemic effect of corticotrophin in man. *J Clin Endocrinol Metab*, 27:775-782, 1967.

Fukushima, D.K., Bradlow, H.L., Hellman, L., Zurnoff, B. and Gallagher, T.F.: Metabolic transformation of hydrocortisone-4-C^{14} in normal men. *J Biol Chem*, 235:2246-2252, 1960.

Fullerton, D.T., Wenzel, F.J., Lohrenz, F.N. and Fahs, H.: Circadian rhythm of adrenal cortical activity in depression. *Arch Gen Psychiatry*, 19:674-681, 1968.

Fuxe, K.: Evidence for the existence of monoamine neurons in the central nervous system. IV. The distribution of monoamine nerve terminals in the central nervous system. *Acta Physiol Scand*, 64, S. 247:39-85, 1965.

Fuxe, K., Corrodi, H., Hokfelt, T. and Jonsson, G.: Central monoamine neurons and pituitary-adrenal activity. *Progr Brain Res*, 32:42-56, 1970.

Fuxe, K. and Gunne, L.M.: Depletion of the amine stores in brain catecholamine terminals on amygdaloid stimulation. *Acta Physiol Scand*, 62:493-494, 1964.

Gaddum, J.H.: Log-normal distributions. *Nature*, 156:463-466, 1945.

Gagliardino, J.J., Bailey, J.D. and Martin, J.M.: Effect of vasopressin on serum levels of human growth hormone. *Lancet*, I:1357-1358, 1967.

Gallagher, B.B. and Glaser, G.H.: Seizure threshold, adrenalectomy and sodium-potassium stimulated ATPase in rat brain. *J Neurochem*, 15:525-528, 1968.

Gantt, C.L., Maynard, D.E. and Hamwi, G.G.: Experience with a simple procedure for the determination of plasma and urine free 11-hydroxycorticosteroids. *Metabolism*, 13:1327-1332, 1964.

Gaunt, R., Chart, J.J. and Renzi, A.A.: Inhibitors of adrenal cortical function. *Ergebnisse der Physiologie*, 56:114-172, 1965.

Garces, L.Y., Kenny, F.M., Drash, A. and Taylor, F.H.: Cortisol secretion rate during fasting of obese adolescent subjects. *J Clin Endocrinol*, 28:1843-1847, 1968.

Gershberg, H. and Long, C.N.H.: The activation of the adrenal cortex by insulin hypoglycaemia. *J Clin Endocrinol*, 8:587-588, 1948.

Gibbons, J. L.: Cortisol secretion rate in depressive illness. *Arch Gen Psychiatry*, 10:572-575, 1964.

Gibbons, J.L.: The secretion rate of corticosterone in depressive illness. *J Psychosom Res*, 10:263-266, 1966.

Gibbons, J.L.: The adrenal cortex and psychological distress, in *Endocrinology and Human Behaviour*, Ed. Michael, R.P. Oxford University Press, London pp. 220-236, 1968a.

Gibbons, J.L.: Biochemistry of depressive illness, in Recent Developments in Affective Disorders. *Br J Psychiatry*, Special Publication No. 2, pp. 55-64, 1968b.

Gibbons, J.L. and Fahy, T.J.: Effect of dexamethasone on plasma corticosteroids in depressive illness. *Neuroendocrinology*, 1:358-363, 1966.

Gibbons, J.L. and McHugh, P.R.: Plasma cortisol in depressive illness. *J Psychiatry Res*, 1:162-171, 1962.

Gibbs, F.P.: Area of pons necessary for traumatic stress-induced ACTH release under pentobarbital anaesthesia. *Am J Physiol*, 217:84-88, 1969.

Gold, E.M. and Ganong, W.F.: Effects of drugs on neuroendocrine processes. In: *Neuroendocrinology*, Vol. 2, L. Martini and W.F. Ganong (Eds.), Academic Press, New York, pp. 377-438, 1967.

Gordon, R., Spector, S., Sjoerdsma, A. and Udenfriend, S.: Increased synthesis of norepinephrine and epinephrine in the intact rat during exercise and exposure to cold. *J Pharmacol Exp Ther*, 153:440-447, 1966.

Grad, B., Kral, B.A., Payne, R.C. and Berenson, J.: Plasma and urinary corticoids in young and old persons. *J Gerontol*, 22:66-71, 1967.

Gray, J.A.: Effect of ACTH on extinction of rewarded behaviour is blocked by previous administration of ACTH. *Nature*, 229:52-54, 1971.

Greaves, M.S. and West, H.F.: Relation of free corticosteroids in urine to steroid dosage. *Lancet*, I:368, 1960.

Green, A.R. and Curzon, G.: Decrease of 5-hydroxytryptamine in the brain provoked by hydrocortisone and its prevention by allopurinol. *Nature*, 220:1095-1097, 1968.

Green, A.R. and Curzon, G.: The effect of tryptophan metabolites on brain

5-hydroxytryptamine metabolism. *Biochem Pharmacol*, 19:2061-2068, 1970.

Green, M.F. and Friedman, M.: Hypothalamic-pituitary-adrenal function in the elderly. *Geront Clin*, 10:334-339, 1968.

Green, R., Luttge, W.G. and Whalen, R.E.: Uptake of tritiated testosterone in brain and peripheral tissues of normal and neonatally androgenised female rats. *J Comp Physiol Psychol*, 72:337-340, 1970.

Greenwood, F.C.: Discussion. *Mem Soc Endocrinol*, 17:212, 1968.

Greenwood, F.C. and Landon, J.: Assessment of hypothalamic-pituitary function in endocrine disease. *J Clin Pathol*, 19:284-292, 1966.

Greenwood, F.C., Landon, J. and Stamp, T.C.B.: The plasma sugar, free fatty acid, cortisol, and growth hormone response to insulin. 1. In control subjects. *J Clin Invest*, 45:429-436, 1966.

Greig, W.R.: Discussion in *Mem Soc Endocrinol*, 17:190-191, 1968.

Greig, W.R., Jasani, M.K., Boyle, J.A. and Maxwell, J.D.: Corticotrophin stimulation tests. *Mem Soc Endocrinol*, 17:175-189, 1968.

Gwinup, G.: Studies on the mechanism of vasopressin-induced steroid secretion in man. *Metabolism*, 14:1282-1286, 1965.

Gwinup, G., Steinberg, T., King, C.G. and Vernikos-Danellis, J.: Vasopressin-induced ACTH secretion in man. *J Clin Endocrinol*, 27:927-930, 1967.

Haining, C.G., Heydon, J.L. and Murray, L.R.: Histochemical studies on the depletion of noradrenaline by adrenaline in adrenergic nerves of the rat iris. *J Pharm Pharmacol*, 21:639-647, 1969.

Halasz, B., Slusher, M.A. and Gorski, R.A.: Adrenocorticotrophic hormone secretion in rats after partial or total deafferentation of the medial basal hypothalamus. *Neuroendocrinology*, 2:43-55, 1967.

Halberg, F.: Temporal coordination of physiologic function. *Cold Springs Harbor Symp Quant Biol*, 25:289-308, 1960.

Hamanaka, Y., Manabe, H., Tanaka, H., Monden, Y., Uozumi, T. and Matsumoto, K.: Effects of surgery on plasma levels of cortisol, corticosterone and non-protein-bound cortisol. *Acta Endocrinol*, 64:439-451, 1970.

Hamburg, D.A.: Plasma and urinary corticosteroid levels in naturally occurring psychologic stresses. *Res Publ Assoc Nerv Ment Dis*, 40:406-413, 1962.

Hamilton, M.: A rating scale for depression. *J Neurol Neurosurg Psychiatry*, 23:56-62, 1960.

Hamilton, M.: Development of a rating scale for primary depressive illness. *Br J Soc Clin Psychol*, 6:278-296, 1967.

Hansen, J.M. and Siersbaek-Nielsen, K.: Cerebrospinal fluid thyroxine. *J Clin Endocrinol*, 29:1023-1026, 1969.

Harris, G.W.: *Neural Control of the Pituitary Gland*. Arnold, London, 1955.

Harris, G.W. and Donovan, B.T. (Eds.): *The Pituitary Gland*. Butterworths, London, 1966.

Harris, J.J. and Crane, M.G.: Urinary cortisol excretion as a test of adrenal cortical function. *Metabolism*, 13:45-59, 1964.

Harrison, T.S., Chawla, R.C. and Wojtalik, R.S.: Steroidal influences on catecholamines. *N Engl J Med,* 279:136-142, 1968.

Heath, D.F.: Normal or log-normal: Appropriate distributions, *Nature,* 213:1159-1160, 1967.

Hedge, G.A. and Smelik, P.G.: Corticotrophin release: inhibition by intra-hypothalamic implantation of atropine. *Science,* 159:891-892, 1968.

Hedge, G.A., Yates, M.B., Marcus, R. and Yates, F.E.: Site of action of vasopressin in causing corticotropin release. *Endocrinology,* 79:328-340, 1966.

Hellman, L., Nakada, F., Curti, J., Weitzman, E.D., Kream, J., Roffwarg, H., Ellman, S., Fukushima, D.K. and Gallagher, T.F.: Cortisol is secreted episodically by normal man. *J. Clin Endocrinol,* 30:411-422, 1970.

Henkin, R.I.: The effects of corticosteroids and ACTH on sensory systems. *Progr Brain Res,* 32:270-294, 1970.

Henkin, R.I. and Daly, R.L.: Auditory detection and perception in normal man and in patients with adrenal cortical insufficiency: effect of adrenal cortical steroids. *J Clin Invest,* 47:1269-1280, 1968.

Henkin, R.I., Gill, J.R., Warmolts, J.R., Carr, A.A. and Bartter, F.C.: Steroid-dependent increase of nerve conduction velocity in adrenal insufficiency. *J Clin Invest,* 42:941, 1963.

Hess, W.R.: *Diencephalon. Autonomic and Extrapyramidal Functions.* Grune, New York, 1954.

Hiroshige, T. and Sakakura, M.: Circadian rhythm of corticotropin releasing activity in the hypothalamus of normal and adrenalectomised rats. *Neuroendocrinology,* 7:25-37, 1971.

Hsu, T.H. and Bledsoe, T.: Measurement of urinary free corticoids by competitive protein-binding radioassay in hypoadrenal states. *J Clin Endocrinol,* 30:443-448, 1970.

Hullin, R.P., Bailey, A.D., McDonald, R., Dransfield, G.A. and Milne, H.B.: Variations in 11-hydroxycorticosteroids in depression and manic-depressive psychosis. *Br J Psychiatry,* 113:593-600, 1967.

Ingram, W.R.: Central autonomic mechanisms, in *Handbook of Physiology,* Section 1, Vol. 2, Ed. Field, J. American Physiological Society, Washington, D. C., pp. 951-978, 1960.

Ingram, W.R., Barris, R.W. and Ranson, S.W.: Catalepsy: and experimental study. *Arch Neurol Psychiatry,* 35:1175-1197, 1936.

Iversen, L.L. and Salt, P.J.: Inhibition of catecholamine uptake 2 by steroids in the isolated rat heart. *Br J Pharmacol,* 40:528-530, 1970.

Jacobs, H.S.: Use of activated charcoal in the radioimmunoassay of human growth hormone in plasma. *J Clin Pathol,* 22:710-717, 1969.

Jacobs, H.S. and Nabarro, J.D.N.: Tests of hypothalamic-pituitary-adrenal function in man. *Q J Med,* 38:475-492, 1969.

Jakobson, T., Blumenthal, M., Hagman, H. and Heikkinen, E.: The diurnal variation of urinary and plasma 17-hydroxycorticosteroid (17-OHCS) levels and the plasma 17-OHCS response to lysine-8-vasopressin in depressive patients. *J Psychosom Res*, 13:363-375, 1969.

Jakoubek, B., Semiginovsky, B., Kraus, M. and Erdossova, R.: The alterations of protein metabolism of the brain cortex induced by anticipation stress and ACTH. *Life Sci*, 9:1169-1179, 1970.

James, V.H.T.: In discussion of James, V.H.T., Landon, J. and Fraser, R.: Some observations on the control of adrenocortical secretion in man. *Mem Soc Endocrinol*, 17:157, 1968.

James, V.H.T. and Caie, E.: Determination of urinary 17-hydroxycorticosteroids and their relation to cortisol secretion. *J Clin Endocrinol*, 24:180-186, 1964.

James, V.H.T. and Landon, J.: Control of corticosteroid secretion—current views and methods of assessment, in *Recent Advances in Endocrinology*, 8th ed., Ed. V.H.T. James. Churchill, London, pp. 50-94, 1968.

James, V.H.T., Landon, J. and Fraser, R.: Some observations on the control of adrenocortical secretion in man. *Mem Soc Endocrinol*, 17:141-158, 1968b.

James, V.H.T., Landon, J. and Wynn, V.: Oral and intravenous suppression tests in the diagnosis of Cushing's syndrome. *J Endocrinol*, 33:515-524, 1965.

James, V.H.T., Landon, J., Wynn, V. and Greenwood, F.C.: A fundamental defect of adrenocortical control in Cushing's disease. *J Endocrinol*, 40:15-28, 1968a.

James, V.H.T., Townsend, J. and Fraser, R.: Comparison of fluorimetric and isotopic procedures for the determination of plasma cortisol. *J Endocrinol*, 37:XXVIII, 1967.

Janowsky, D.S. and Davis, J.M.: Progesterone-estrogen effects on uptake and release of norepinephrine by synaptosomes. *Life Sci*, 9:525-531, 1970.

Jansen, J.A., Schon, J. and Singh, H.: Cortisol release, distribution and metabolism in induced oestrogenic deficiency. *Acta Endocrinol*, 65:125-132, 1970.

Jasani, M.K., Boyle, J.A., Greig, W.R., Dalakos, T.G., Browning, M.C.K., Thompson, A. and Buchanan, W.W.: Corticosteroid-induced suppression of the hypothalamo-pituitary-adrenal axis: Observations on patients given oral corticosteroids for rheumatoid arthritis. *Q J Med*, 36:261-276, 1967.

Javoy, F., Glowinski, J. and Kordon, C.: Effects of adrenalectomy on the turnover of norepinephrine in the rat brain. *Eur J Pharmacol*, 4:103-104, 1968.

Jenkins, J. S.: The pituitary-adrenal response to pyrogen. *Mem Soc Endocrinol*, 17:205-212, 1968.

Johnsen, S.G.: Abnormal urinary androsterone/etiocholanolone ratio in hypothalamic disturbances in man. *Acta Endocrinol*, 57:595-614, 1968.

Jori, A., Prestini, P.E. and Pugliatti, C.: Effect of diazepam and chlordiazepoxide on the metabolism of other drugs. *J Pharm Pharmacol*, 21:387-390, 1969.

Jubiz, W., Levinson, R.A., Meikle, A.W., West, C.D. and Tyler, F.H.: Absorption and conjugation of metyrapone during diphenylhydantoin administration: mechanism of the abnormal response to oral metyrapone. *Endocrinology,* 86:328-331, 1970.

Jubiz, W., Matsukura, S., Meikle, A.W., Harada, G., West, C.D. and Tyler, F.H.: Plasma metyrapone, adrenocorticotropic hormone, cortisol and deoxycortisol levels. Sequential changes during oral and intravenous metyrapone administration. *Arch Int Med,* 125:468-471, 1970.

Jubiz, W., Meikle, A.W., Levinson, R.A., Mizutani, S., West, C.D. and Tyler, F.H.: Effect of diphenylhydantoin on metabolism of dexamethasone. *N Engl J Med,* 283:11-14, 1970.

Jubiz, W., Meikle, A.W., West, C.D. and Tyler, F.H.: Single-dose metyrapone test. *Arch Intern Med,* 125:472-474, 1970.

Kaada, B.: Brain mechanisms related to aggressive behaviour, in *Aggression and Defense: Neural Mechanisms and Social Patterns* (Brain Function, Vol. V). UCLA Forum Med Sci No. 7, Univ. of California Press, Los Angeles, 1967, Eds. Clemente, C.D. and Lindsley, D.B., pp. 95-133, 1967.

Kahwanago, I., Heinrichs, W. Lee Roy and Hermann, W. L.: Isolation of oestradiol "receptors" from bovine hypothalamus and anterior pituitary gland. *Nature,* 223:313-314, 1969.

Karp, M., Pertzelan, A., Doron, M., Kowaldo-Silbergeld, A. and Laron, Z.: Changes in blood glucose and plasma insulin, free fatty acids, growth hormone and 11-hydroxycorticosteroids during intramuscular vasopressin tests in children and adolescents. *Acta Endocrinol,* 58:545-557, 1968.

Kato, J.: *In vitro* uptake of tritiated oestradiol by the rat anterior hypothalamus during the oestrous cycle. *Acta Endocrinol,* 63:577-584, 1970.

Kato, J., Inaba, M. and Kobayashi, T.: Variable uptake of tritiated oestradiol by the anterior hypothalamus in the postpubertal female rat. *Acta Endocrinol,* 61:585-591, 1969.

Katz, F.H. and Shannon, I. L.: Parotid fluid cortisol and cortisone. *J Clin Invest,* 48:848-855, 1969.

Katz, J.L., Weiner, H., Gallagher, T.F. and Hellman, L.: Stress, distress and ego defences. Psychoendocrine response to impending breast tumour biopsy. *Arch Gen Psychiatry,* 23:131-142, 1970.

Kawakami, M., Koshino, T. and Hattori, Y.: Changes in the EEG of the hypothalamus and limbic system after administration of ACTH, SU-4885 and ACH in rabbits with special reference to neurohumoral feedback regulation of pituitary-adrenal system. *Jap J Physiol,* 16:551-569, 1966.

Keller, N., Richardson, U.I. and Yates, F.E.: Protein binding and the biological activity of corticosteroids: *In vivo* induction of hepatic and pancreatic alanine aminotransferases in normal and estrogen-treated rats. *Endocrinology,* 84:49-62, 1969.

Kimball, H.R., Lipsett, M.B., Odell, W.D. and Wolff, S.M.: Comparison of the effect of the pyrogens, etiocholanolone and bacterial endotoxin on plasma cortisol and growth hormone in man. *J Clin Endocrinol,* 28:337-342, 1968.

Knapp, M.S., Keane, P.M. and Wright, J.G.: Circadian rhythm of plasma

11-hydroxycorticosteroids in depressive illness, congestive heart failure and Cushing's syndrome. *Br Med J*, 2:27-30, 1967.

Knigge, K.M.: Feedback mechanisms in neural control of adenohypophyseal function: effect of steroids implanted in amygdala and hippocampus. Abstr. II Int. Cong. Hormonal Steroids. Excerpta Medica International Congress Series No. 111, Ed. Romanoff, E.B. and Martini, L., p. 208, Amsterdam, Excerpta Medica Foundation, 1966.

Knigge, K.M. and Scott, D.E.: Structure and function of the median eminence. *Am J Anat*, 129:223-244, 1970.

Kobbernagel, F., Vestergaard, P. and Faurbye, A.: Treatment of psychoses with ACTH. *Acta Endocrinol*, 13:162-172, 1953.

Komaromi, I. and Donhoffer, S.: The effect of habituation and reward on adrenal ascorbic acid depletion in response to the intravenous injection of physiological saline in the rat. *Acta Physiol Acad Sci Hung*, 23:293-295, 1963.

Kopell, B.S., Wittner, W.K., Lunde, D., Warrick, G. and Edwards, D.: Cortisol effects on average evoked potential, alpha rhythm, time estimation and two-flash fusion threshold. *Psychosom Med*, 32:39-49, 1970.

Kostowski, W., Rewerski, W. and Piechocki, T.: Effects of some steroids on aggressive behaviour in mice and rats. *Neuroendocrinology*, 6:311-318, 1970.

Krieger, D.T., Glick, S., Silverberg, A. and Krieger, H.P.: A comparative study of endocrine tests in hypothalamic disease. *J Clin Endocrinol*, 28:1589-1598, 1968a.

Krieger, D.T. and Krieger, H.P.: The effects of intrahypothalamic injection of drugs on ACTH release in the cat, Proc. II Int Congr Endocr, Excerpta Medica Int Congr Series No. 83, Excerpta Medica Foundation, Amsterdam, pp. 640-645, 1964.

Krieger, D.T. and Krieger, H.P.: Circadian pattern of plasma 17-hydroxycorticosteroid: alteration by anticholinergic agents. *Science*, 155:1421-1422, 1967.

Krieger, D.T. and Krieger, H.P.: The effect of short-term administration of CNS-acting drugs on the circadian variation of the plasma 17-OHCS in normal subjects. *Neuroendocrinology*, 2:232-246, 1967a.

Krieger, D.T. and Krieger, H.P.: Chemical stimulation of the brain: effect on adrenal corticoid release. *Am J Physiol*, 218:1632-1641, 1970a.

Krieger, D.T. and Krieger, H.P.: Effect of dexamethasone on pituitary-adrenal activation following intrahypothalamic implantation of "neurotransmitters." *Endocrinology*, 87:179-182, 1970b.

Krieger, D.T. and Rizzo, F.: Serotonin mediation of circadian periodicity of plasma 17-hydroxycorticosteroids. *Am J Physiol*, 217:1703-1707, 1969.

Krieger, D.T., Silverberg, A.I., Rizzo, F. and Krieger, H.P.: Abolition of circadian periodicity of plasma 17-OHCS levels in the cat. *Am J Physiol*, 215:959-967, 1968.

Krieger, G.: Biochemical predictors of suicide, *Dis Nerv Syst,* 31:479-482, 1970.

Kumar, T.C.A. and Thomas, G.H.: Metabolites of ³H-oestradiol-17 β in the cerebrospinal fluid of the Rhesus monkey. *Nature,* 219:628-629, 1968.

Kurland, H.D.: Steroid excretion in depressive disorders. *Arch Gen Psychiatry,* 10:554-560, 1964.

Kusama, M.: Studies on the function of pituitary-adrenocortical and autonomic nervous system in neurosis. *Jap J Med,* 3:277-278, 1964.

Kusama, M., Abe, O., Sakauchi, N., Takatani, O., Mayama, T., Demura, R. and Kumaska, S.: Extra-adrenal action of adrenocorticotropin on cortisol metabolism. *J Clin Endocrinol,* 30:778-785, 1970.

Landon, J., Greenwood, F.C., Stamp, T.C.B. and Wynn, V.: The plasma sugar, free fatty acid, cortisol and growth hormone response to insulin and the comparison of this procedure with other tests of pituitary and adrenal function. II. In patients with hypothalamic or pituitary dysfunction or anorexia nervosa. *J Clin Invest,* 45:437-449, 1966.

Landon, J., James, V.H.T., Cryer, R.J., Wynn, V. and Frankland, A.W.: Adrenocorticotropic effects of a synthetic polypeptide—beta 1-24 corticotropin—in man. *J Clin Endocrinol,* 24:1206-1213, 1964.

Landon, J., James, V.H.T. and Peart, W.S.: Cushing's syndrome associated with a "corticotrophin"-producing bronchial neoplasm. *Acta Endocrinol,* 56:321-332, 1967.

Landon, J., James, V.H.T., Wharton, M.J. and Friedman, M.: Threshold adrenocortical sensitivity in man and its possible application to corticotrophin bioassay. *Lancet,* 2:697-700, 1967.

Landon, J., Wynn, V. and James, V.H.T.: The adrenocortical response to insulin-induced hypoglycaemia. *J Endocrinol,* 27:183-192, 1963.

Lapin, I.P. and Oxenkrug, G.F.: Intensification of the central serotoninergic processes as a possible determinant of the thymoleptic effect. *Lancet,* I:132-136, 1969.

Lefkowitz, R.J., Roth, J. and Pastan, I.: Radioreceptor assay of adrenocorticotropic hormone: New approach to assay of polypeptide hormones in plasma. *Science,* 170:633-635, 1970.

Leonard, P.J. and MacWilliam, K.M.: Cortisol binding in the serum in kwashiorkor. *J Endocrinol,* 29:273-276, 1964.

Levine, M.D., Gordon, T.P., Peterson, R.H. and Rose, R.M.: Urinary 17-OHCS response of high- and low-appressive rhesus monkeys to shock avoidance. *Physiol Behav,* 5:919-924, 1970.

Levy, B. and Hansen, E.: Failure of the steroid test for suicide potential. *Arch Gen Psychiatry,* 20:415-418, 1969.

Librik, L. and Clayton, G.W.: Measurement of plasma nonesterified fatty acid levels following ACTH release in man. *Metabolism,* 12:790-791, 1963.

Liddle, G.W., Estep, H.L., Kendall, J.W., Williams, W.C. and Townes,

A.W.: Clinical application of a new test of pituitary reserve. *J Clin Endocrinol,* 19:875-894, 1959.

Liddle, G.W.: Tests of pituitary adrenal suppressibility in the diagnosis of Cushing's syndrome. *J Clin Endocrinol,* 20:1539-1560, 1960.

Lingjaerde, P.S.: Plasma hydrocortisone in mental diseases. *Br J Psychiatry,* 110:423-432, 1964.

Linn, J.E., Bowdoin, B., Farmer, A. and Meador, D.K.: Observations and comments on failure of dexamethasone suppression. *N Engl J Med,* 277:403-405, 1967.

Livanou, T., Ferriman, D. and James, V.H.T.: Recovery of hypothalamo-pituitary-adrenal function after corticosteroid therapy. *Lancet,* II:856-859, 1967.

Livingston, K.E. and Escobar, A.: Anatomical bias of the limbic system concept. *Arch Neurol,* 24:17-21, 1971.

Loon, G.R. van and Ganong, W.F.: Effect of drugs which alter catecholamine metabolism on the inhibition of stress-induced ACTH secretion produced by l-DOPA. *Physiologist,* 12:381, 1969.

Loon, G.R. van, Hilger, L., Cohen, R. and Ganong, W.F.: Evidence for a hypothalamic adrenergic system that inhibits ACTH secretion in the dog. *Fed Proc,* 28:438, 1969.

Loon, G.R. van, Scapagnini, U., Cohen, R. and Ganong, W.F.: Neuroendocrinology. In press, 1971.

Loras, B., Roux, H. and Philippe, M.H.: Dosage du cortisol plasmatique et urinarie par liaison competitive aux proteines. *Annales d'Endocrinologie (Paris),* 31:383-389, 1970.

Lorenzen, L.C., Wise, B.L. and Ganong, W.F.: ACTH-inhibiting activity of drugs related to alpha-ethyltryptamine. *Fed Proc,* 24:128, 1965.

Lurie, A.O. and Weiss, J.B.: Progesterone in cerebrospinal fluid during human pregnancy. *Nature,* 215:1178, 1967.

Maas, J.W. and Landis, D.H.: A technique for assaying the kinetics of norepinephrine metabolism in the central nervous system *in vivo. Psychosom Med,* 28:247-256, 1966.

Maas, J.W. and Mednieks, M.: Hydrocortisone-mediated increase or norepinephrine uptake by brain slices. *Science,* 171:178-179, 1971.

Mandell, A.J., Chapman, L.F., Rand, R.W. and Walter, R.D.: Plasma corticosteroids: Changes in concentration after stimulation of hippocampus and amygdala. *Science,* 139:1212, 1963.

Mangili, G., Motta, M. and Martini, L.: Control of adenocorticotrophic hormone secretion. In *Neuroendocrinology,* Vol. 1, Ed. Martini, L. and and Ganong, W.F., pp. 297-370, Academic Press, New York, 1966.

Marc, V. and Morselli, P. L.: Effect of diazepam on plasma corticosterone levels in the rat. *J. Pharm Pharmacol,* 21:784-786, 1969.

Margolis, R.U. and Altszular, N.: Insulin in the cerebrospinal fluid. *Nature,* 215:1375-1376, 1967.

Marks, V., Greenwood, F.C., Howorth, P.J. and Samols, E.: Plasma growth hormone levels in spontaneous hypoglycaemia. *J Clin Endocrinol,* 27:523-528, 1967.

Martin, M.M., Mintz, D.H. and Tamagaki, H.: Effect of altered thyroid function upon steroid circadian rhythms in man. *J Clin Endocrinol,* 23:242-247, 1963.

Martini, L. and Ganong, W.F. (Eds.) : *Neuroendocrinology.* Academic Press, New York, 1966-1967.

Martini, L., Pecile, A., Saito, S. and Tani, F.: The effect of midbrain transection on ACTH release. *Endocrinology,* 66:501-507, 1960.

Mason, J.W.: A review of psychoendocrine research on the pituitary-adrenal cortical system. *Psychosom Med,* 30:576-607, 1968.

Mason, J.W., Sachar, E.J., Fishman, J.R., Hamburg, D.A. and Handlon, J.H.: Corticosteroid responses to hospital admission. *Arch Gen Psychiatry,* 13:1-8, 1965.

Mason, J.W., Tolson, W.W., Robinson, J.A., Brady, J.V., Toliver, G.A. and Johnson, T.A.: Urinary androsterone, etiocholanolone, and dehydroepiandrosterone responses to 72-hour avoidance sessions in the monkey. *Psychosom Med,* 30:710-720, 1968.

Mattingly, D.: A simple fluorimetric method for the estimation of free 11-hydroxycorticoids in human plasma. *J Clin Path,* 15:374-379, 1962.

Mattingly, D.: Plasma steroid levels as a measure of adrenocortical activity. *Proc Roy Soc Med,* 56:717-720, 1965.

Mattingly, D.: In discussion. *Mem Soc Endocrinol,* 17:157, 1967.

Mattingly, D. and Tyler, C.: Simple screening test for Cushing's syndrome. *Br Med J,* IV:394-397, 1967.

McCann, S.M. and Brobeck, J.R.: Evidence for a role of the supraoptico-hypophyseal system in regulation of adrenocorticotrophin secretion. *Proc Soc Exp Biol Med,* 87:318-324, 1954.

McClure, D.J.: The diurnal variation of plasma cortisol levels in depression. *J Psychosom Res,* 10:189-195, 1966.

McClure, D.J.: The effects of antidepressant medication on the diurnal plasma cortisol levels in depressed patients. *J Psychosom Res,* 10:198-202, 1966a.

McDonald, R.K. and Weise, V.K.: Effect of pitressin on adrenocortical activity in man. *Proc Soc Exp Biol Med,* 92:107-109, 1956.

McDonald, R.K., Weise, V.K. and Patrick, R.W.: Effect of synthetic lysine-vasopressin on plasma hydrocortisone levels in man. *Proc Soc Exp Biol Med,* 93:348-349, 1956.

McEwen, B.S., Weiss, J.M. and Schwartz, L.S.: Selective retention of corticosterone by limbic structures in rat brain. *Nature,* 220:911-912, 1968.

McEwen, B.S., Weiss, J.M. and Schwartz, L.S.: Retention of corticosterone by cell nuclei from brain regions of adrenalectomised rats. *Brain Res,* 17:471-482, 1970.

McHardy-Young, S., Harris, P.W.R., Lessoff, M.H. and Lyne, C.: Single-dose dexamethasone suppression test for Cushing's syndrome. *Br Med J*, 1:740-744, 1967.

McHugh, P.R. and Smith, G.P.: Negative feedback in the plasma 17-OH-corticosteroid response to amygdaloid stimulation in Macaca mulatta. Abstr II Int Cong Hormonal Steroid. Excerpta Medica International Congress Series No. 111, Ed. Romanoff, E.B. and Martini, L., p. 358, International Congress Series, Amsterdam, 1966.

Meikle, A.W., Takiguchi, H., Mizutani, S., Tyler, F.H. and West, C.D.: Urinary cortisol excretion determined by competitive protein-binding radioassay: A test of adrenal cortical function. *J Lab Clin Med*, 74:803-812, 1969.

Mendels, J.: Urinary 17-ketosteroid fractionation in depression: a preliminary report. *Br J Psychiatry*, 115:581-585, 1969.

Mess, B. and Martini, L.: The Central Nervous System and the Secretion of Anterior Pituitary-Trophic Hormones, in *Recent Advances in Endocrinology* (Ed. V.H.T. James). Churchill, London, pp. 1-49, 1968.

Metcalf, M.G. and Beaven, D.W.: The metopirone test of pituitary corticotrophin release. *Am J Med*, 45:176-186, 1968.

Michaux, M.H., Suziedelis, A., Garmize, K. and Rossi, J.A.: Depression factors in depressed and in heterogeneous inpatient samples. *J Neurol Neurosurg Psychiatry*, 32:609-613, 1969.

Migeon, C.J., Tyler, F.H., Mahoney, J.P., Florentin, A.A., Castle, H., Bliss, E.L. and Samuels, L.T.: The diurnal variation of plasma levels and urinary excretion of 17-hydroxycorticosteroids in normal subjects, night workers and blind subjects. *J Clin Endocrinol*, 16:622-633, 1956.

Miller, R.G., Rubin, R.T., Clark, B.R., Crawford, W.R. and Arthur, R.J.: The stress of aircraft carrier landings. 1. Corticosteroid responses in naval aviators. *Psychosom Med*, 32:581-588, 1970.

Mills, J.N.: Human circadian rhythms. *Physiol Rev*, 46:128-170, 1966.

Moll, J.: Localisation of brain stem lesions inhibiting compensatory adrenal hypertrophy following unilateral adrenalectomy, *Z Zellforsch Mikrosk Anat*, 49:515, 1959.

Moor, P. de, Osinski, P., Deckx, R. and Steeno, D.: The specificity of fluorometric corticoid determinations. *Clin Chim Acta*, 7:475-480, 1962.

Moor, P. de, Heirwegh, K., Heremans, J.F. and Declerck-Raskin, M.: Protein binding of corticoids studied by gel filtration. *J Clin Invest*, 41:816-827, 1962.

Morselli, P.L., Marc, V., Garattini, S. and Zaccala, M.: Metabolism of exogenous cortisol in humans. Influence of phenobarbital treatment on plasma cortisol disappearance rate. *Rev Eur Etudes Clin Biol*, 15:195-198, 1970.

Moses, A.M. and Miller, M.: Assessment of pituitary reserve in subjects pretreated with dexamethasone. *Metabolism*, 18:376-386, 1969.

M.R.C. Committee on Clinical Endocrinology: A standard method of estimating 17-oxosteroids and total 17-oxogenic steroids. *Lancet,* I:1415-1419, 1963.

M.R.C. Committee on Clinical Endocrinology: A critical appraisal of a method of estimating urinary 17-oxosteroids and total 17-oxogenic steroids. *Lancet,* I:124-127, 1969.

Mueller, P.S., Heninger, G.R. and McDonald, R.K.: Insulin tolerance test in depression. *Arch Gen Psychiatry,* 21:587-594, 1969.

Murphy, B.E.P.: Some studies of the protein-binding of steroids and their application to the routine micro and ultramicro measurement of various steroids in body fluids by competitive protein-binding radioassay. *J Clin Endocrinol,* 27:973-990, 1967.

Murphy, B.E.P.: Clinical evaluation of urinary cortisol determinations by competitive protein-binding radioassay. *J Clin Endocrinol,* 28:343-348, 1968.

Murphy, B.E.P., Cosgrove, J.B., McIlquham, M.C. and Pattee, C.J.: Adrenal corticoid levels in human cerebrospinal fluid. *Can Med Assoc J,* 97:13-17, 1967.

Murray, D.: Cortisol binding to plasma proteins in man in health, stress and at death. *J Endocrinol,* 39:571-591, 1967.

Naumenko, E.V.: Hypothalamic chemoreactive structures and the regulation of the pituitary-adrenal function. Effect of local injection of norepinephrine, carbachol and serotonin into the brain of guinea pigs with intact brain and after mesencephalic transection. *Brain Res,* 11:1-10, 1968.

Naumenko, E.V.: Effect of local injection of 5-hydroxytryptamine into rhinencephalic and mesencephalic structures on pituitary-adrenal function in guinea-pigs. *Neuroendocrinology,* 5:81-88, 1969.

Nauta, W.J.H.: Central nervous system organization and the endocrine motor system. In *Advances in Neuroendocrinology* (Ed.), Nalbandor, A.V., University of Illinois Press, Urbana, 1963, pp. 5-21.

adrenocortical activation during restraint stress. *Pharmacol Res Comm,*

Nelson, D. and Brodish, A.: Evidence for a diurnal rhythm of corticotrophin-releasing factor (CRF) in the hypothalamus. *Endocrinology,* 85:861-866, 1969.

Ney, R.L., Shimizu, N., Nicholson, W.E., Island, D.P. and Liddle, G.W.: Correlation of plasma ACTH concentration with adrenocortical response in normal human subjects, surgical patients and patients with Cushing's syndrome. *J Clin Invest,* 42:1669-1677, 1963.

Nichols, T., Nugent, C.A. and Tyler, F.H.: Diurnal variation in suppression of adrenal function by glucocorticoids. *J Clin Endocrinol,* 25:343-349, 1965.

Nielsen, E. and Asfeldt, V.H.: Studies on the specificity of fluorimetric determination of plasma corticosteroids ad modum de Moor and Steeno. *Scand J Clin Lab Invest,* 20:185-194, 1967.

Nistico, G. and Preziosi, P.: Brain and liver tryptophan pathways and adrenocortical activation during restraint stress. *Pharmacol, Res Comm,* 1:363-368, 1969.

Norymberski, J.K., Stubbs, R.D. and West, H.F.: Assessment of adrenocortical activity by assay of 17-ketogenic steroids in the urine. *Lancet,* I:1276-1281, 1953.

Nugent, C.A., Nichols, T. and Tyler, F.H.: Diagnosis of Cushing's syndrome. Single dose dexamethasone suppression test. *Arch Int Med,* 116:172-176, 1965.

Nyakas, C. and Endroczi, E.: Effect of hippocampal stimulation on the establishment of conditioned fear response in the rat. *Acta Physiol Acad Sci Hung,* 37:281-289.

Ojemann, G.A. and Henkin, R.I.: Steroid-dependent changes in human visual evoked potentials. *Life Sci,* 6:327-344, 1967.

Orth, D.N. and Island, D.P.: Light synchronisation of the circadian rhythm in plasma cortisol (17-OHCS) concentration in man. *J Clin Endocrinol,* 29:479-486, 1969.

Orth, D.N., Island, D.P. and Liddle, G.W.: Experimental alteration of the circadian rhythm in plasma cortisol (17-OHCS) concentration in man. *J Clin Endocrinol,* 27:549-555, 1967.

Pavlatos, F.C., Smilo, R.P. and Forsham, P.H.: A rapid screening test for Cushing's syndrome. *JAMA,* 193:720-723, 1965.

Perkoff, G.T., Eik-Nes, K., Nugent, C.A., Fred, H.L., Nimer, R.A., Rush, L., Samuels, L.T. and Tyler, F.H.: Studies of the diurnal variation of plasma 17-hydroxycorticosteroids in man. *J Clin Endocrinol,* 19:432-443, 1959.

Persky, H.: Adrenal cortical function in anxious human subjects: effect of corticotropin (ACTH) on plasma hydrocortisone level and urinary hydroxycorticosteroid excretion. *Arch Neurol Psychiatry,* 78:95-102, 1957.

Persky, H., Grinker, R.R., Hamburg, D.A., Sabshin, M.A., Korchin, S.J., Basowitz, H. and Chevalier, J.A.: Adrenal cortical function in anxious human subjects. Plasma level and urinary excretion of hydrocortisone. *Arch Neurol Psychiatry,* 76:549-558, 1956.

Persky, H., Grosz, H.J., Norton, J.A. and McMurtry, M.: Effect of hypnotically-induced anxiety on the plasma hydrocortisone level of normal subjects. *J Clin Endocrinol,* 19:700-710, 1959.

Peterson, R.E.: The miscible pool and turnover rate of adrenocortical steroids in man. *Recent Progr Horm Res,* 15:231-261, 1959.

Peterson, R.E., Wyngaarden, J.B., Guerra, S.L., Brodie, B.B. and Bunim, J.J.: The physiological disposition and metabolic fate of hydrocortisone in man. *J Clin Invest,* 34:1779-1794, 1955.

Pincus, G.: A diurnal rhythm in the excretion of urinary ketosteroids by young men. *J Clin Endocrinol,* 3:195-199, 1943.

Pinsker, P., Bultasova, H. and Svobodova, J.: Diagnostic value of the simultaneous determination of urinary free and conjugated cortisol in Cushing's syndrome. *Acta Endocrinol,* 58:183-190, 1968.

Platman, S.R. and Fieve, R.R.: Lithium carbonate and plasma cortisol response in the affective disorders. *Arch Gen Psychiatry,* 18:591-594, 1968.

Pohorecky, L.A. and Wurtman, R.J.: Induction of epinephrine-forming enzyme by glucocorticoids: steroid hydroxylation and inductive effect. *Nature,* 219:392-394, 1968.

Pohorecky, L.A., Zigmond, M.J., Karten, H.J. and Wurtman, R.J.: Phenyl-ethanolamine-N-methyl transferase activity (PNMT) in mammalian, avian and reptilian brain. *Fed Proc,* 27:239, 1968.

Popert, A.J., Grayzel, E., Longson, D. and Gowenlock, A.H.: Excretion of cortisol in patients with rheumatic and other diseases. *Ann Rheum Dis,* 23:246-247, 1964.

Purves, H.D. and Sirett, N.E.: The fluorimetric estimation of cortisol in human plasma. *Aust J Exp Biol Med Sci,* 47:589-599, 1969.

Rabhan, N.B.: Pituitary-adrenal suppression and Cushing's syndrome after intermittent dexamethasone therapy. *Ann Int Med,* 69:1141-1148, 1968.

Raisinghani, K.H., Dorfman, R.I., Forchielli, E. and Gyermek, L.: Uptake of intravenously administered progesterone, pregnanedione and preg-nanolone by the rat brain. *Acta Endocrinol,* 57:395-404, 1968.

Raisman, G.: Neural connexions of the hypothalamus. *Br Med Bull,* 22:197-201, 1966.

Ranson, S.W.: Somnolence caused by hypothalamic lesions in the monkey. *Arch Neurol Psychiatry,* 41:1-23, 1939.

Rayyis, S.A. and Bethune, J.E.: Radioimmunoassayable ACTH in dexameth-asone nonsuppressible Cushing's syndrome. *J Clin Endocrinol,* 29:1231-1237, 1969.

Reis, D.J. and Fuxe, K.: Depletion of noradrenaline in brainstem neurons during sham rage behaviour produced by acute brainstem transection in cat. *Brain Res,* 7:448-451, 1968.

Retiene, K., Espinoza, A., Marx, K.H. and Pfeiffer, E.F.: Uber das Verhalten von ACTH und Cortisol im Blut von Normalen und von Krankem mit primarer und Sekundarer Storung der NNR-Funktion. 1. Nachweis der vermehrten ACTH-Sekretion beim M. Cushing. *Klin Wschr,* 43:205-211, 1965.

Retiene, K. and Schulz, F.: Circadian rhythmicity of hypothalamic CRH and its central nervous regulation. *Horm Metab Res,* 2:221-224, 1970.

Robertis, E. de: Ultra structures and cytochemistry of the synaptic region. *Science,* 156:907-913, 1967.

Rose, L.I., Williams, G.H., Jagger, P.I., Lauler, D.P. and Thorn, G.W.: The paradoxical dexamethasone response phenomenon. *Metabolism,* 18:369-375, 1969.

Rose, S. and Nelson, J.: Hydrocortisone and ACTH release. *Aust J Exp Biol Med Sci,* 34:77-80, 1956.

Rosenthal, H.E., Slaunwhite, W.R. and Sandberg, A.A.: Transcortin: a cor-ticosteroid-binding protein of plasma. X. Cortisol and progesterone in-terplay and unbound levels of these steroids in pregnancy. *J Clin Endo-crinol,* 29:352-367, 1969.

Rosner, J.M., Cos, J.J., Biglieri, E.G., Hane, S. and Forsham, P.H.: Deter-mination of urinary unconjugated cortisol by glass fiber chromatography in the diagnosis of Cushing's syndrome. *J Clin Endocrinol,* 23:820-827, 1963.

Ross, E.J.: Urinary excretion of cortisol in Cushing's Syndrome: effect of corticotropin. *J Clin Endocrinol,* 20:1360-1365, 1960.

Ross, E.J., Marshall-Jones, P. and Friedman, M.: Cushing's Syndrome: diagnostic criteria. *Q J Med,* 35:149-192, 1966.

Ross, T.A.: *The Common Neuroses.* 2nd edition. Arnold, London, 1937.

Rubin, R.T. and Mandell, A.J.: Adrenal cortical activity in pathological emotional states: a review. *Am J Psychiatry,* 123:387-400, 1966.

Rubin, R.T., Mandell, A.J. and Crandall, P.H.: Corticosteroid responses to limbic stimulation in man: Localisation of stimulus sites. *Science,* 153:767-768, 1966.

Rubin, R.T., Miller, R.G., Clark, B.R., Poland, R.E. and Arthur, R.J.: The stress of aircraft carrier landings. II. 3-methoxy-4-hydroxyphenylglycol excretion in naval aviators. *Psychosom Med,* 32:589-597, 1970.

Rubin, R.T., Rahe, R.H., Arthur, R.J. and Clark, B.R.: Adrenal cortical activity changes during underwater demolition team training. *Psychosom Med,* 31:553-564, 1969.

Ruf, K. and Steiner, F.A.: Steroid-sensitive single neurone in rat hypothalamus and midbrain: identification by microelectrophoresis. *Science,* 156: 667-669, 1967.

Sachar, E.J.: Corticosteroids in depressive illness. A re-evaluation of control issues and the literature. *Arch Gen Psychiatry,* 17:544-553, 1967a.

Sachar, E.J.: Corticosteroids in depressive illness. A longitudinal psychoendocrine study. *Arch Gen Psychiatry,* 17:554-567, 1967b.

Sachar, E.J., Cobb, J.C. and Shor, R.E.: Plasma cortisol changes during hypnotic trance. *Arch Gen Psychiatry,* 14:482-490, 1966.

Sachar, E.J., Fishman, J.R. and Mason, J.W.: Influence of the hypnotic trance on plasma 17-hydroxycorticosteroid concentration. *Psychosom Med,* 27:330-341, 1965.

Sachar, E.J., Hellman, L., Fukushima, D.K. and Gallagher, T.F.: Cortisol production in depressive illness. A clinical and biochemical clarification. *Arch Gen Psychiatry,* 23:289-298, 1971.

Sachar, E.J., Kanter, S.S., Buie, D., Engle, R. and Mehlman, R.: Psychoendocrinology of ego disintegration. *Am J Psychiatry,* 126:1067-1078, 1970.

Sachar, E.J., Mackenzie, J.M., Binstock, W.A. and Mack, J.E.: Corticosteroid responses to psychotherapy of depressions. I. *Arch Gen Psychiatry,* 16:461-470, 1967.

Sachar, E.J., Mackenzie, J.M. Binstock, W.A. and Mack, J.E.: Corticosteroid responses to psychotherapy of reactive depressions. II. *Psychosom Med,* 30:23-44, 1968.

Sachar, E.J., Mason, J.W., Kolmer, H. and Artiss, K.: Psychoendocrine aspects of acute schizophrenic reactions. *Psychosom Med,* 25:510-537, 1963.

Salcman, M., Peck, L. and Egdahl, R.H.: Effect of acute and prolonged electrical stimulation of the amygdala of the dog upon peripheral plasma concentrations of corticosteroids. *Neuroendocrinology,* 6:361-367, 1970.

Sandberg, A.A., Eik-Nes, K., Nelson, D.H. and Tyler, F.H.: Levels of 17-hydroxycorticosteroids in body fluids. *J Lab Clin Med,* 43:874-879, 1954.

Sandberg, A.A., Slaunwhite, W.R. and Carter, A.C.: Transcortin: a corticosteroid binding protein of plasma. III. The effects of various steroids. *J Clin Invest,* 39:1914-1926, 1960.

Sassenrath, E.N.: Increased adrenal responsiveness related to social stress in Rhesus monkeys. *Hormones and Behaviour,* 1:283-298, 1970.

Scapagnini, U., van Loon, G.R., Moberg, G.P. and Ganong, W.F.: Effect of alpha-methyl-para-tyrosine on the circadian variation of plasma corticosterone in rats. *Eur J Pharmacol,* 11:266-268, 1970.

Schaepdryver, A. de, Preziosi, P. and Scapagnini, U.: Brain monoamines and adrenocortical activation. *Br J Pharmacol,* 35:460-467, 1969.

Schedl, H.P.: Absorption of steroid hormones from the human small intestine. *J Clin Endocrinol,* 25:1309-1316, 1965.

Schedl, H.P., Chen, P.S., Greene, G. and Redd, D.: The renal clearance of plasma cortisol. *J Clin Endocrinol,* 19:1223-1229, 1959.

Schon, J., Jansen, J. and Hvidberg, E.: Tissue-cortisol in man determined by a new micro-method. Evidence for decreased concentration in the menopause. *Nature,* 215:202-203, 1967.

Schteingart, D.E., Gregerman, R.I. and Conn, J.W.: A comparison of the characteristics of increased adrenocortical function in obesity and in Cushing's syndrome. *Metabolism,* 12:484-497, 1963.

Scurry, M.T. and Shear, L.: Stop-flow analysis of the reabsorption of cortisol. *Endocrinology,* 84:681-682, 1969.

Selye, H.: Stress and general adaptation syndrome (Heberden Oration). *Br Med J,* 1:1383-1392, 1950.

Shanfield, S., Tucker, G.J., Harrow, M. and Detre, T.: The schizophrenic patient and depressive symptomatology. *J Nerv Ment Dis,* 151:203-210, 1970.

Shopsin, B. and Gershon, S.: Plasma cortisol response to dexamethasone suppression in depressed and control subjects. *Arch Gen Psychiatry,* 24:320-326, 1971.

Shuster, S. and Williams, I.A.: Pituitary and adrenal function during administration of small doses of corticosteroids. *Lancet,* II:674-678, 1961.

Shute, C.C.D. and Lewis, P.R.: Cholinergic and monoaminergic pathways in the hypothalamus, *Br Med Bull,* 22:221-226, 1966.

Silverberg, A., Rizzo, F. and Krieger, D.T.: Nyctohemeral periodicity of plasma 17-OHCS levels in elderly subjects. *J Clin Endocrinol,* 28:1661-1663, 1968.

Slater, E. and Roth, M.: *Clinical Psychiatry.* 3rd edition. London. Bailliere, Tindall and Cassell. 1969.

Slaunwhite, W.R., Lockie, G.N., Back, N. and Sandberg, A.A.: Inactivity in vivo of transcortin-bound cortisol. *Science,* 135:1062-1063, 1962.

Slaunwhite, W.R. and Sandberg, A.A.: Transcortin: a corticosteroid-binding protein of plasma. *J Clin Invest,* 38:384-391, 1959.

Slusher, M.A.: Effects of cortisol implants in the brainstem and ventral hippocampus on diurnal corticosteroid levels. *Exp Brain Res*, 1:184-194, 1966.

Slusher, M.A. and Hyde, J.E.: Effect of limbic stimulation on release of corticosteroids into the adrenal venous effluent of the cat. *Endocrinology*, 69:1080-1084, 1961.

Smallberg, J.G.: The uptake of norepinephrine by synaptosomes: effect of steroids. M.D. Thesis (unpublished). Yale University. 1969.

Smookler, H.H. and Buckley, J.P.: Relationships between brain catecholamine synthesis, pituitary adrenal function and the production of hypertension during prolonged exposure to environmental stress. *Int J Neuropharmacol*, 8:33-41, 1969.

Sprunt, J.G., Browning, M.C.K. and Hannah, D.M.: Some aspects of the pharmacology of metyrapone. *Mem Soc Endocrinol*, 17:193-201, 1968.

Sprunt, J.G., Rutherford, E.R. and Nelson, D.H.: The impaired response to metyrapone in patients taking oestrogen. *Acta Endocrinol*, 59:447-453, 1968.

Staehelin, D., Labhart, A., Froesch, R. and Kagi, H.R.: The effect of muscular exercise and hypoglycaemia on the plasma level of 17-hydroxysteroids in normal adults and in patients with the adrenogenital syndrome. *Acta Endocrinol*, 18:521-529, 1955.

Stecher, P.G. (Ed.): *The Merck Index of Chemicals and Drugs*. 7th edition. Merck, Rahway, N.J., 1960.

Steinberg, M., Green, R. and Durell, J.: Depression occurring during the course of recovery from schizophrenia. *Am J Psychiat*, 124:699-702, 1967.

Steiner, F.A., Ruf, K. and Akert, K.: Steroid-sensitive neurones in rat brain: anatomical localisation and responses to neurohumours and ACTH. *Brain Res*, 12:74-85, 1969.

Stenback, A., Jakobson, T. and Rimon, R.: Depression and anxiety ratings in relation to the excretion of urinary total 17-OHCS in depressive subjects. *J Psychosom Res*, 9:355-362, 1966.

Stokes, P.E.: Pituitary suppression in psychiatric patients. The Endocrine Society (U.S.A.), 48th Meeting, 1966.

Stokes, P.E.: Alterations in hypothalamic-pituitary-adrenocortical (HPAC) function in man during depression. The Endocrine Society (U.S.A.). 52nd Meeting. St. Louis. June 10-12, 1970. (Abstract No. 337.)

Stokes, P.E.: Studies on the control of adrenocortical function in depression. In *Psychobiology of Depressive Illnesses* (Eds.), T. Williams and M. Katz. U.S. Government Printing Office. In Press. 1972.

Streeten, D.H.P., Stevenson, C.T., Dalakos, T.G., Nicholas, J.J., Dennick, L.G. and Fellerman, H.: The diagnosis of hypercortisolism. Biochemical criteria differentiating patients from lean and obese normal subjects and from females on oral contraceptives. *J Clin Endocrinol*, 29:1191-1211, 1969.

Superstine, E. and Sulman, F.G.: The mechanism of the push and pull principle. VII. Endocrine effects of chlordiazepoxide, diazepam and guanethidine. *Arch Int Pharmacodyn Ther,* 160:133-146, 1966.

Szentagothai, J.: Die Rolle diencephaler Mechanismen bei der Ruckwirkung von Schildrusen-Nebennierenrinden-und Sexual hormonen auf die Funktion des Hypophysenvorderlappens. In *Pathophysiologia Diencephalica,* Ed. Curri, S.B. and Martini, L., pp. 560-571, Wien, Springer, 1958.

Tait, J.F.: Review: the use of istopic steroids for the measurement of production rates *in vivo. J Clin Endocrinol,* 23:1285-1297, 1963.

Tait, J.F. and Burstein, S.: *In vivo* studies of steroid dynamics in man. In: "The Hormones," Ed. Pincus, G., Thimann, K.V. and Astwood, E.B., Vol. 5, Academic Press, London, pp. 441-557, 1964.

Takebe, K., Kuroshima, A., Yamamoto, M.: Effect of lysine vasopressin dimer on corticotropin release in man. *J Clin Endocrinol,* 28:73-78, 1968.

Takebe, K., Setaishi, C., Hirama, M., Yamamoto, M. and Horiuchi, Y.: Effects of a bacterial pyrogen on the pituitary-adrenal axis at various times in the 24 hours. *J Clin Endocrinol,* 26:437-442, 1966.

Tanaka, H., Manabe, H., Koshiyama, K., Hamanaka, Y., Matsumoto, K. and Uozimi, T.: Excretion patterns of 17-ketosteroids and 17-hydroxycorticosteroids in surgical stress. *Acta Endocrinol,* 65:1-10, 1970.

Taylor, A.N.: The role of the reticular activating system in the regulation of ACTH secretion. *Brain Res,* 13:234-246, 1969.

Taylor, Janet A.: A personality scale of manifest anxiety. *J. Abnorm Soc Psychol,* 487:285, 1953.

Thierry, A-M., Fekete, M. and Glowinski, J.: Effects of stress on the metabolism of noradrenaline, dopamine and serotonin (5HT) in the central nervous system of the rat. II. Modifications of serotonin metabolism. *Eur J Pharmacol,* 4:384-389, 1968.

Thierry, A-M., Javoy, F., Glowinski, J. and Kety, S.S.: Effects of stress on the metabolism of norepinephrine, dopamine and serotonin in the central nervous system of the rat. I. Modifications of norepinephrine turnover. *J Pharmacol Exp Ther,* 163:163-171, 1968.

Thies, R. and Kooyman, M.: Normal nerve conduction velocities in depressed and hypomanic patients. *Dis Nerv Syst,* 31:281-284, 1970.

Touchstone, J.G., Kasparow, M., Hughes, P.A. and Horwitz, M.R.: Corticosteroids in human brain. *Steroids,* 7:205-211, 1966.

Tucci, J.R., Espiner, E.A., Jagger, P.I., Lauler, D.P. and Thorn, G.W.: Vasopressin in the evaluation of pituitary-adrenal function. *Ann Int Med,* 69:191-202, 1968.

Tucci, J.R., Jagger, P.I., Lauler, D.P. and Thorn, G.W.: Rapid dexamethasone suppression test for Cushing's syndrome. *JAMA,* 199:379-382, 1967.

Uete, T., Nishimura, S., Ohya, H., Shimomura, T. and Tatebayashi, Y.: Corticosteroid levels in blood and cerebrospinal fluid in various diseases. *J Clin Endocrinol,* 30:208-214, 1970.

Vagnucci, A.I., Hesser, M.E., Kozak, G.P., Pank, G.L., Lauler, D.P. and

Thorn, G.W.: Circadian rhythm of urinary cortisol in healthy subjects and in Cushing's syndrome. *J Clin Endocrinol,* 25:1331-1339, 1965.

Vermeulen, A., Verdonck, G., van der Straeten, M. and Daneels, R.: Evaluation of the efficiency of 11- -hydroxylation of 11-deoxycortisol in human subjects. *J Clin Endocrinol,* 27:365-370, 1967.

Vingerhoeds, A.C.M., Kinderen, P.J. der, Thijssen, J.H.H. and Schwarz, F.: Steroid changes during starvation in Cushing's syndrome, Cushingoid obesity and simple obesity. *J Endocrinol,* 48:lxxviii, 1970.

Vogel, S.A., Janowsky, D.J. and Davis, J.M.: Effect of estradiol on stimulus-induced release of ^{3}H-norepinephrine and ^{3}H-serotonin from rat brain slices. *Res Comm Chem Path Pharmacol,* 1:451-457, 1970.

Vogt, M.: Cortical lipids of the normal and denervated suprarenal gland under conditions of stress. *J Physiol,* 106:394-404, 1947.

Vogt, M.: The role of hypoglycaemia and of adrenaline in the response of the adrenal cortex to insulin. *J Physiol,* 114:222-233, 1951.

Wada, J.A. and Asakura, T.: Circadian alteration of audiogenic seizure susceptibility in rats. *Exper Neurol,* 29:211-214, 1970.

Wasserman, M.J., Belton, N.R. and Millichap, J.G.: Effect of corticotropin (ACTH) on experimental seizures. *Neurology,* 15:1136-1141, 1965.

Weiss, J.M., McEwen, B.S., Silva, M.T. and Kalkut, M.: Pituitary-adrenal alterations and fear responding. *Am J Physiol,* 218:864-868, 1970.

Weitzman, E.D., Schaumberg, H. and Fishbein, W.: Plasma 17-hydroxycorticosteroid levels during sleep in man. *J Clin Endocrinol,* 26:121-127, 1966.

Werk, E.E., Choi, Y., Sholiton, L., Olinger, C. and Haque, N.: Interference in the effect of dexamethasone by diphenylhydantoin. *N Engl J Med,* 281:32-34, 1969.

West, H.F.: Corticosteroid metabolism and rheumatoid arthritis. *Ann Rheum Dis,* 16:173-182, 1957.

Wexler, B.C., Dolgin, A.E. and Trycyznski, E.W.: Effects of a bacterial polysaccharide on the pituitary-adrenal axis: further aspects of hypophyseal-mediated control of response. *Endocrinology,* 61:488-499, 1957.

Wied, D. de: The site of blocking action of dexamethasone on stress-induced pituitary ACTH release. *J Endocrinol,* 29:29-37, 1964.

Wied, D. de, Bohus, B., Ernst, A.M., Jong, W. de, Nieuwenhuizen, W., Pieper, E.E.M. and Yasumura, S.: Several aspects of the influence of vasopressin on pituitary-adrenal activity. *Mem Soc Endocrinol,* 17:159-172, 1968.

Wolff, C.T., Friedman, S.B., Hofer, M.A. and Mason, J.W.: Relationship between psychological defenses and mean urinary 17-hydroxycorticosteroid excretion rates. *Psychosom Med,* 26:576-609, 1964.

Woodbury, D.M. and Vernadakis, A.: Influence of hormones on brain activity. In *Neuroendocrinology* (Eds.), L. Martini and W.F. Garrong. New York. Academic Press. Vol. 2, 1967, pp. 335-375.

Woolley, D.E., Holinka, C.F. and Timiras, P.S.: Changes in ^{3}H-estradiol distribution with development in the rat. *Endocrinology,* 84:157-161, 1969.

Wynn, V.: The assessment of hypothalamic-pituitary-adrenocortical function in man. *Mem Soc Endocr,* 17:213-234, 1968.

Yates, F.E., Brennan, R.D. and Urquhart, J.: Adrenal glucocorticoid control system. *Fed Proc,* 28:71-83, 1969.

Yates, F.E. and Urquhart, J.: Control of plasma concentrations of adrenocortical hormones. *Physiol Rev,* 42:359-443, 1962.

Zarrow, M.X., Philpott, J.B., Denenberg, V.H. and O'Connor, W.B.: Localisation of ^{14}C-corticosterone in the 2 day old rat and a consideration of the mechanism involved in early handling. *Nature,* 218:1264-1265, 1968.

Zarrow, M.X., Philpott, J.E. and Denenberg, V.H.: Passage of ^{14}C-4-Corticosterone from the rat mother to the foetus and neonate. *Nature,* 226:1058-1059, 1970.

Zimmermann, H. and Critchlow, V.: Effects of intracerebral dexamethasone on pituitary-adrenal function in female rats. *Am J Physiol,* 217:392-396, 1969.

Zung, W.W.K.: A self-rating depression scale. *Arch Gen Psychiatry,* 12:63-70, 1965.

Chapter 7

POOR RESPONSE TO ANTIDEPRESSANTS AND DEXAMETHASONE NONSUPPRESSION

William R. McLeod

IN Chapter 5 it was shown that some severely depressed patients do not respond normally to a midnight dose of 2 mg dexamethasone phosphate. A group of "nonsuppressors" was defined in whom such midnight dexamethasone did not cause the morning plasma 11-OHCS to fall below $10\mu g/100$ ml. It was emphasized that this "nonsuppression" was dose dependent, since increasing the amount of dexamethasone given will cause suppression in all subjects.

A relationship between this evidence of hypothalamic dysfunction and poor short-term response to antidepressants was suggested in the course of a four-week comparison of a monoamine oxidase inhibitor tranylcypramine (Parnate® 10 mg t.d.s.) with a tricyclic antidepressant imipramine (Tofranil® 50 mg t.d.s.) This trial was conducted on consecutive patients with a primary depressive illness and whose symptoms were not judged severe enough to merit ECT after a period of observation of between seven and ten days. If at the end of four weeks' medication significant clinical improvement had occurred identical inert tablets were substituted for the active tablets and progress observed. The aims of this methodology were to define specific drug response (i.e. MAOI or tricyclic) and to contrast the clinical and rating scale assessments.

Before treatment was started the midnight dexamethasone test was conducted as described in Chapter 5. Ten patients suppressed 11-OHCS normally while six were nonsuppressors. The two groups of patients had similar mean scores of depression (Hamilton and Zung Self Rating Inventory); anxiety (Taylor), and neuroticism (Eysenck). They had the same age and sex distribution. These details are shown in Table 7-I.

202

TABLE 7-I

PLASMA 11-OHCS AND QUESTIONNAIRE RESULTS
(Means ± S.D.)

N	AM *Plasma* 11-OHCS (μg/100 ml)		*Zung Self- Rating Score*	*Hamilton Depression Score*	*Taylor Anxiety Score*	*N Score Eysenck Personality Inventory*
	Basal	*Post Dexa- methasone*				
10	21.4	4.4	54.3	21.3	32.6	17.3
	(6.9)	(1.4)	(9.0)	(3.9)	(7.8)	(4.0)
6	19.9	19.1	54.6	22.0	27.1	18.4
	(6.8)	(5.8)	(13.2)	(5.3)	(8.9)	(2.8)

At the end of one month the ten suppressors were well, all having responded to the particular antidepressant drug and not having relapsed, at that time, with placebo substitution. The six nonsuppressors, after one month's treatment with antidepressant alone had not improved and were all then treated with ECT with subsequent improvement.

This small study suggested that poor short-term response to antidepressants is related in some way to dysfunction of the hypothalamic-pituitary-adrenocortical axis. The results could not have been predicted from clinical or questionary data (McLeod *et al.*, 1970).

Since this study we have looked further at antidepressant responses, to see whether these findings could be confirmed.

SUBJECTS AND METHODS

Patients with primary depressive illnesses admitted as in-patients to the Professorial Psychiatric Unit were studied. They were all patients with agitation, psychomotor retardation, delusional and suicidal thoughts, as well as disturbances of sleep, appetite and bowel function. All received the same general nursing and medical care and were given a normal ward diet.

The dexamethasone test was done five to seven days after admission to hospital, at which time no other drug but amylobarbitone was being given. Blood for plasma 11-OHCS estimations was collected in tubes containing fifteen units of lithium heparin per 100 ml of blood. Samples were collected at 8:30 AM; dexamethasone phosphate 2 mg was given orally at midnight, and a further plasma 11-OHCS sample taken at 8:30 AM the next day. Plasma 11-OHCS determinations were measured by the fluorometric technique of Mattingly (1962) by means of a CGA spectrophotofluorometer (model DC/3000). The most severely ill patients were treated with ECT, and not considered further. The moderately depressed patients were treated with tricyclic antidepressants (usually imipramine or amitriptyline, in most cases, given in divided doses of 150 mg to 225 mg/day) for four weeks. If at the end of that period no marked clinical improvement had occurred, a course of ECT was commenced. It is emphasized that this initial treatment choice, and subsequent use of ECT was made on clinical grounds by the senior editor, unaware of the results of steroid tests. In this way a group of thirty-five "nonsuppressors" was found and these patients were matched with 35 "suppressors" on the basis of age and sex.

RESULTS AND DISCUSSION

The results are shown in Table 7-II. The severity of the illness on admission as judged by the Hamilton Depression Scale did not

TABLE 7-II

DEPRESSED PATIENTS TREATED WITH ANTIDEPRESSANTS
INITIALLY (Means and S.D.)

	Non-suppressors	Suppressors		
Men	15	16		
Women	20	19		
Mean Age	48.06 (13.89)	47.71 (11.52)		
Plasma 11-OHCS (AM) (μg/100 ml)	24.91 (7.15)	18.29 (6.13)	t = 4.17	p <0.001
Plasma 11-OHCS (AM) after 2 mg dexamethasone (μg/100 ml)	18.59 (5.92)	4.19 (2.02)	t = 13.64	p <0.001
Hamilton Depression Scale				
Total score	27.49 (6.67)	26.86 (4.49)	t = 0.49	N.S.
Subscore on psychomotor retardation	1.57 (1.12)	1.37 (1.00)	t = 0.79	N.S.
Subscore on agitation	1.34 (1.03)	1.31 (0.87)	t = 0.12	N.S.
Subscore on anxiety (psychological)	2.37 (1.19)	2.57 (1.09)	t = 0.73	N.S.
Subscore on anxiety (somatic)	1.63 (1.19)	1.86 (1.06)	t = 0.84	N.S.
Treated with ECT	26	13	X^2c = 9.78	p <0.005

differ between the groups, nor did any of the subscores. This contrasts to the finding of a previous study (Carroll and Davies 1970) when a group of "nonsuppressors," with a similar mean Hamilton score to a comparable group of "suppressors," had a significantly higher agitation subscore. In that study, however, subjects initially requiring ECT were included.

As expected the post-dexamethasone values are different but in addition significant differences were found in the pre-dexamethasone 11-OHCS values for the two groups, the nonsuppressors showing the higher pre-dexamethasone 11-OHCS level. At the end of the four weeks of treatment by antidepressants, significantly more of the nonsuppressors required treatment by ECT ($p < .005$).

This finding supports our earlier study and strengthens our suggestion that poor short-term response to antidepressants is related in some way to either:

1. The higher initial 11-OHCS levels which could influence the plasma levels of the tricyclic compounds used. Recent studies have suggested that clinical response to these antidepressants can be related to their plasma levels (Asberg *et al.*, 1970).

2. The abnormal dexamethasone response, as discussed in the previous chapter indicates some reversible abnormality of hypothalamic functioning which is not entirely dependent on initial plasma 11-OHCS levels, and is associated with a depressive syndrome that responds best to ECT.

CONCLUSIONS AND SUGGESTIONS FOR FURTHER STUDY

These two studies suggest that in depressed patients the 11-OHCS response to dexamethasone, as described, may indicate those who do not respond well to antidepressant medication at the usual dosage level. The patients studied had been selected as suitable for antidepressant treatment, other more severely ill patients having been treated with ECT as the treatment of choice. Possible reasons for the therapeutic failure of tricyclics are discussed.

These findings need replication in other centers, with more objective definition of "poor response to antidepressants," "the indications for ECT" and the relationship between hypothalamic-pituitary-adrenal function and tricyclic plasma levels and turn-over rates.

REFERENCES

Ashberg, M., Cronholm, B., Sjoquist, F. and Tuck, D.: Correlation of sub-jective side effects with plasma concentration of Nortriptyline. *Br Med J*, 4:18, 1970.

Carroll, B.J. and Davies, B.: Clinical Associations of 11-hydroxy-cortico-steroid suppression and nonsuppression in severe depressive illness. *Br Med J*, 1:789, 1970.

McLeod, W.R., Carroll, B. and Davies, B.: Hypothalamic dysfunction and antidepressant drugs. *Br Med J*, 2:480, 1970.

Mattingly, D.: A simple fluorometric method for the estimation of free 11-hydroxycorticoids in human plasma. *J Clin Pathol*, 15:373, 1962.

Section III

Indoleamines and Depression

Chapter 8

INDOLEAMINES AND THE CEREBROSPINAL FLUID

William R. McLeod and Margaret F. McLeod

LOW levels of 5 hydroxyindoleacetic acid (5 HIAA) were first reported in the cerebrospinal fluid (CSF) of depressed patients in 1960 (Ashcroft and Sharman). However, since this original observation, much conflicting evidence has accumulated:

1. 5 HIAA levels have been found by some workers to be reduced in severe depression, but not by others (Ashcroft *et al.*, 1966; Sjöstrom and Roos, 1970).
2. Low levels have been noted in other disorders (Dencker *et al.*, 1966; Gottfries *et al.*, 1968).
3. 5 HIAA levels may be affected by diet, age, medication and exercise (Bowers and Gerbode, 1968; Curzon and Green, 1968; Curzon, 1969).
4. It has been suggested that changes in concentration may be related to or follow alterations in cortisol, ACTH and cyclic AMP levels in brain (Lapin and Oxenkrug, 1969; Curzon and Green, 1968).
5. The findings may not be associated with the mood disorder per se, but caused by specific features of the illness such as sleep disturbance, agitation or psychomotor retardation (McLeod, 1970).

SEROTONIN AND ITS DERIVATIVES IN THE CNS

Serotonin, 5-hydroxytryptamine (5 HT) was discovered in the CNS by Twarog and Page in 1953. Page noted that 5 HT, and related compounds, functioned quite differently in brain compared to the rest of the body. Very little, if any, of the somatic 5 HT passes the blood brain barrier and 5 HT in the CNS is concentrated in areas concerned with autonomic and emotional activity (Page, 1968a, 1968b).

5 HT is important for the regulation of normal sleep (Caz-

zullo, 1967; Sheard, 1969); for temperature regulation (Van Praag, 1970); for the control of normal movement, and of some forms of behavior, particularly sexual behavior (Page, 1968a). Thus 5 HT with the other biogenic monoamines (norepinephrine and dopamine) appears to aid the organism in its adaptation to a changing environment (Page, 1968a).

5 HT is almost certainly a neurotransmitter, for it has been shown to possess the following properties:

1. The 5 HT is synthesized in the CNS from its precursor compound 5-hydroxytryptophan (5 HTP) (Green and Sawyer, 1964; Garattini and Valzelli, 1965; Weber and Horita, 1965; Bulat and Supek, 1967; Ichiyama *et al.*, 1968).

2. Once formed, the 5 HT is stored in the rhinencephalon and the midbrain, particularly in the latter, from whence the axones of the serotonergic neurones are distributed, usually in association with the medial forebrain bundle. The monoamine is localized in granular vesicles, ca. 500 Å in diameter, close to synaptic junctions (Aghajanian *et al.*, 1969; Fuxe *et al.*, 1969; Wooley and Shaw, 1954).

3. Release of 5 HT may be "internal," within the neurones, or "external" into the synaptic spaces, and occurs after the administration of many drugs (Carlsson, 1964, 1966; Carlsson *et al.*, 1969; Hagen and Cohen, 1966). The mechanism of normal release is poorly understood (Brodie and Reid, 1968; Carlsson *et al.*, 1969).

4. 5 HT applied directly to neurones produces profound changes in their firing patterns (Holmberg, 1963; Hinesley *et al.*, 1968).

5. Antagonists specific for 5 HT have been described. Behavioral changes consistent with those expected have been reported but not invariably, after the administration of 5 HT antagonists (Gaddum and Vogt, 1956; Gal *et al.*, 1968).

6. 5 HT is rapidly degraded to nonactive products. Although many alternate paths have been proposed (Garattini and Valzelli, 1965), 5 HT is metabolized principally by oxidative deamination with monoamine oxidase (MAO) to yield 5 HIAA (Blaschko and Levine, 1966).

THE EFFECTS OF DRUGS ON 5 HT AND 5 HIAA LEVELS

Pharmacological agents are known to interfere with the metabolism of 5 HT, 5 HIAA and the transport of 5 HIAA across the blood-brain barrier (Axelrod and Inscoe, 1963; Costa, 1969).

1. Experimental agents found to alter brain or CSF levels of these compounds include parachlorphenylalanine (PCPA) (Koe and Weissman, 1968; Sheard, 1969; Volicer, 1969); lysergide (Boakes *et al.*, 1969; Tonge and Leonard, 1969); alpha-methyltryptophan (Sourkes *et al.*, 1970); and parachloromethylamphetamine (CMA) (Verster and Van Praag, 1970).

2. Amino acids also change 5 HT and 5 HIAA CNS levels, e.g. tryptophan (Oates and Sjoerdsma, 1960; Coppen *et al.*, 1967), phenylalanine (Yuwiler and Geller, 1969) and leucine (Ramanamurthy and Srikantia, 1970); these changes may result from competition for transport mechanisms.

3. Therapeutic agents also affect CNS levels, e.g. morphine (Glassman, 1969), barbiturates (Pare *et al.*, 1969), allopurinol (Green and Curzon, 1968), alpha-methyl-dopa (Roos and Werdinus, 1963) and probenecid. The administration of probenecid results in increased CSF levels of 5 HIAA. This is probably due to an effect on the 5 HIAA CSF blood transport mechanism (Anderson and Roos, 1968; Van Praag *et al.*, 1970).

4. Psychotropic agents which are known to alter mood states also produce changes in the CNS levels of 5 HT and its metabolites. In the rat brain 5 HIAA levels decline exponentially after blockade with MAOI (di Carlo, 1964). Tricyclic antidepressants are also associated with higher CSF levels of CNS 5 HT, although in Ashcroft *et al.*, 1965, 1966, 5 HIAA levels were reduced after treatment with imipramine (see Table 8-I). Reserpine increases 5 HIAA in the CSF and the brain, at least temporarily, but decreases brain levels of 5 HT (Roos and Werdinus, 1962; Carney *et al.*, 1969). Phenothiazine and butyrophenone administration commonly produced slight increases in 5 HIAA (Persson *et al.*, 1968, 1969). However Chase *et al.*,

1970, showed that monoamine catabolites are raised only in those patients taking these drugs who remain free of extrapyramidal signs. The levels are lower in those patients who have these side effects.

5. Steroid administration in some patients may produce severe depression, e.g. oral contraceptives with large progestogen: estrogen ratios (Grant and Pryse-Davies, 1968; Rose, 1969; Winston, 1969); and cortisone and related compounds (Rose and McGinty, 1968). In addition severe depression may be associated with Cushing's syndrome. Plasma cortisol levels are often elevated in severe depression (see Chap. 4). 5 HT levels in the brain may be indirectly lowered by raised plasma cortisol via the activation of tryptophan pyrrolase (oxygenase) in the liver (Curzon and Green, 1968; Azmitia and McEwen, 1969) (a finding not confirmed by Benkert and Matussek, 1970).

It is readily apparent that major errors can be introduced in clinical research in evaluating levels of 5 HT and 5 HIAA unless medication is carefully controlled, and preferably avoided altogether.

REVIEW OF STUDIES OF THE 5 HIAA LEVELS IN THE CSF

Ashcroft and Sharman, 1960, 1962, and Sharman and Ashcroft, 1960, asserted that decreased CSF levels of 5 HIAA were a reflection of changes in the metabolism of brain 5 HT and much evidence has accumulated for this view (Ashcroft and Sharman, 1966; Van Praag, 1970). 5 HT levels were said to be reduced in depression, but returned to normal with ECT or antidepressant drugs (Garattini *et al.,* 1967).

Dencker *et al.* (1966) showed a decrease of CSF 5 HIAA in the acute phase of depression, with a fairly slow rise to normal values on recovery. A healthy group of volunteers had values of 20 to 60 ng/ml, a range which did not seem to vary with age. Depressed patients, on the other hand, showed values well below this, eleven out of fourteen having less than 30 ng/ml (see also Ashcroft *et al.,* 1965, 1966). Persson *et al.* (1969) found mean values of 29 ng/ml for normal persons (and for patients with schizophrenia, a mean of 26 ng/ml). These values are summa-

TABLE 8-1

5-HYDROXYINDOLES IN CSF (Expressed as 5 HIAA ng ml)
FROM VARIOUS AUTHORS AS SHOWN

Author	Depressive Illness	Other Psychiatric	Parkinson's Disease	Neurological	Healthy or Control
Ashcroft et al., 1966	11.1 (24) 8.8 (8) (after treatment)	Gp. 1 20 (8) 2 19.8 (6) 3 18.7 (4) 4 10.9 (7) 5 16.4 (7)		Gp. 1 33.3 (28) 2 17.4 (7)	
Bowers, 1969		19 (6)			
Bowers et al., 1968	31 (14)	31 (16)		36 (19)	
Bowers et al., 1969	34 (8)	26.8 (7)		43.5 (18)	
Bunney et al., 1971	25 (28)	31 (2)		37 (6)	
Chase et al., 1970		29.3 (6)		35.1 (7)	
Dencker et al., 1966	<10 (11) <30 (3)	<20 (4) <30 (2)			20-60 (40)
Eccleston et al., 1970 (a)					15.7 (3)
Gerbode et al., 1968		30 (33)		42 (16)	
Gottfries et al., 1968		Gp. 1 20 (10) 2 30 (18)	10 (24)		40 (25)
Johansson et al., 1967			<25 (24)		25-54 (34)
Olsson et al., 1968			30 (8)		40 (7)
Persson et al., 1968					26-47 (4)
Persson et al., 1969		26 (40)			29 (34)
Roos, et al., 1969		31 (17)	36 (19)		29 (26)
Sjöstrom and Roos, 1970	32 (37)	34 (42)			31 (29)
Van Praag et al., 1970	17 (14)				40 (11)

Average values (some approximately only) with number of cases shown in
brackets.

rized in Table 8-I. It will be seen that the levels vary greatly not only for the depressed patients, but also for all classes listed.

The 5 HIAA levels are also known to be decreased in the CSF of patients with Parkinson's disease (Johansson *et al.*, 1967; Gottfries *et al.*, 1968). Gerbode and Bowers (1968) show a significant difference between the CSF values obtained for neurological patients compared with those from "psychiatric" patients, i.e. 42 ng/ml versus 30 ng/ml. These values, it will be noted are much higher than those listed above. In another communication (Bowers and Gerbode, 1968), these same workers compared values in the CSF of persons with schizophrenia, manic depression, depression and neurological problems (the diagnostic categories are those used by the authors). Surprisingly all results were, when corrected for age, similar with minimum values (ca. 20 to 30 ng/ml 5 HIAA) obtained over the age range 40 to 50 years. This age range is that in which depressive illness is common.

PRESENT STUDY

The aim of this study is to examine the CSF 5 HIAA level in depressed patients.

The patients and methods were as described in Chapter 2.

Patients were excluded for the following reasons:
1. Doubt existed about the diagnosis.
2. Concomitant physical illness was present.
3. Any other drug had been taken in the previous week.
4. Technical difficulties at collection could not be overcome.

The CSF was taken from a standard site, as for a lumbar puncture, since a concentration gradient exists from the cerebral ventricles to the lower end of the vertebral canal (Gerbode and Bowers, 1969). It is known that exercise increases 5 HIAA levels (Gerbode and Bowers, 1968). Bowers (1969) also believes that the gradient is a reflection of an active transport system. An apathetic withdrawn person might show a lessening of mechanical mixing along this gradient (Glassman, 1969). This difficulty can be overcome by taking 5 HIAA from patients before rising in the morning, and indeed if the time of collection is standardized the diurnal variation noted by Quay (1968), will not produce great variations if the circadian rhythm approximates to a solar day.

Five ml of fluid was taken and estimated as quickly as possible (within two hours) or it was quick frozen, after the addition of L-cysteine, and estimated within a few days after collection. "Neurological specimens" were from patients undergoing investigations including lumbar punctures during pneumoencephalograms and myelograms.

The healthy or control group were those referred from a neurological clinic or a medical clinic for lumbar puncture but in whom no lesion was finally demonstrable.

BIOCHEMICAL METHODS

Ashcroft *et al.* (1962, 1966) (Sharman and Ashcroft, 1960) used a variation of the method of Udenfriend (1956). This method has the advantage of simplicity and rapidity but is said to be insensitive for amounts of 5 HIAA at levels of less than 30 ng/ml, although amounts as little as 10 ng/ml can be detected (Hanson, 1966). With the use of internal and external standards Roos found that the method could be made more sensitive, but failed to find any difference at all between his groups of patients (personal communication). We were also unable to demonstrate any difference using the Roos method (McLeod, 1970). The disadvantages of this method have been reviewed elsewhere (Bogdanski *et al.,* 1956; Garattini, 1965; Hanson, 1966).

A more sensitive and reliable method was developed by Maickel and Miller (1966), involving the use of an orthophthalaldehyde (OPT) fluorophore. A modification of this method was

TABLE 8-II

5 HIAA LEVELS IN THE CSF OF DIFFERENT PATIENT GROUPS

	Severe Depressive Illness	Other Psychiatric Disorders	Controls
CSF levels of 5 HIAA + S.D.			
(ng/ml)	20.2±12.1	28.1±12.1	32.6±11.4
Number of Patients			
Total	25	15	12
Males	7	10	7
Females	18	5	5
Age Range (Years)			
Total	28-77	17-62	22-78
Males	28-67	17-58	22-78
Females	42-77	47-62	37-46

used to obtain the results shown in Table 8-II (Korf and Valkenburgh-Sikkema, 1969).

RESULTS

The results are shown in Table 8-II. The evidence is of a significant difference between the 5 HIAA in the CSF of depressed
patients, compared with those of normal controls (p <0.01). A
difference between the CSF levels of depressed patients and other
psychiatric patients is also apparent, the difference is, however,
not statistically significant. No significant correlation was found,
in this small series, with the severity of the depressive illness as
indicated by the Hamilton Rating Scale, or with the subscore
items of the same scale, e.g. agitation, anxiety or psychomotor retardation. The values obtained here were similar to those reported in an earlier chapter (e.g. total score for the Hamilton Rating
Scale was 27.1 ± 6.4).

DISCUSSION

*Our findings show that, taken as a group, depressed patients do
have significantly lower levels of 5 HIAA in the CSF than do our
control patients.* What then is the reason for the confusion that
exists as reflected in Table 8-I?

Sjöstrom and Roos (1970), who found no significant differences
between depressed and other psychiatric patients, have suggested
a number of possible explanations as to why others might have
done so:

1. Ashcroft compared his depressives with neurological patients, and these latter have higher values than for the former group.

In Table 8-II it will be seen that neurological patients do have
higher CSF values for 5 HIAA compared with depressed patients,
but these values are still lower than those of the control groups.

2. Dencker (1966) compared male depressives with male and
   female controls. Sjöstrom and Roos found lower values for
   male than for female and argued that this might be a partial explanation for the discrepancy.

In our series there were seven male and eighteen female depressives, with no significant differences between the two groups.

Coppen believes that the preparation of the patients prior to the sampling is all important and that drugs should be avoided, exercise prohibited and that 5 ml of the initial CSF only should be used to avoid mixing lumbar CSF with that higher in the spinal canal which is known to have a higher concentration (Coppen, 1969).

Inadequate preparation of patients, insensitive chemical methods or poor controls may well be a partial explanation for the divergence of opinion that exists.

Perhaps the most important criticism, however, rests on the assumption of homogeneity within the group of severely depressed patients. This has possibly been overlooked because of the wide range of normal values which is known to exist (cf. Table 8-I). If different biochemical changes are found in subgroups of depressive patients then this may explain why some workers find differences between depressed and normal patients while others do not. Such differences have been described and three subgroups postulated, i.e. deficits in noradrenaline, dopamine and serotonin metabolism (Goodwin *et al.*, 1970; Bunney *et al.*, 1971), however in this chapter we are only concerned with indoleamines.

Dewhurst (1965, 1968) also regards the biogenic amines as important in the control of affect, but argues that molecular shape and spatial orientation are the most important factors.

Lapin and Oxenkrug (1969) have formulated a unifying hypothesis which attempts to link brain 5 HT deficits and raised blood corticosteroid levels which are elevated in depression as a consequence of excitement of the amygdaloid complex, on which 5 HT is normally an inhibitory influence. (See also Altman and Greengard, 1966; Curzon, 1969.)

Curzon and Green (1968) have shown that hydrocortisone in the rat does produce a lowering of brain 5 HT, but this change may not occur in the human brain (Benkert and Matussek, 1970).

We have shown (Table 8-III) that a direct correlation exists between 5 HIAA levels in the CSF and plasma 11-hydroxycorticosteroid levels both before and after dexamethasone. The significance of this finding is uncertain. The presence of a positive correlation is puzzling in view of the hypothesis of Lapin and Oxenkrug and suggests that the significance of lowered 5 HIAA

TABLE 8-III

COMPARISON OF 5 HIAA CSF LEVELS WITH 11-OHCS PLASMA LEVELS,
BOTH BEFORE AND AFTER A MIDNIGHT DOSE OF 2 mg OF
DEXAMETHASONE (All Samples Taken at 9:00 AM)

Sex	5 HIAA ng/ml	Plasma 11-OHCS ng/100 ml (Pre-dexamethasone)	Plasma 11-OHCS ng/100 ml (Post-dexamethasone)
M	26	19.6	27.4
F	22	31.5	13.1
F	13	29.0	12.2
F	39	48.8	11.5
F	54	31.5	34.3
F	6	11.0	5.8
F	33	25.0	23.6
F	5	21.6	3
F	7	21.8	1.9
M	21	24.5	3.7
M	7	22.7	5.6
F	8	16.9	4.2
F	35	36.6	21.3

Correlation coefficients: (i) 5 HIAA ng/ml and Pre-dexamethasone 11-OHCS, $r = 0.75$, (ii) 5 HIAA ng/ml and Post-dexamethasone 11-OHCS, $r = 0.71$.

levels in the CSF of depressed patients, when present, requires some other explanation.

SUMMARY

The original observations of Ashcroft and Sharman, that low concentrations of 5 HIAA are found in the CSF of depressed patients, have stimulated controversy and research; they are not yet finally accepted, but the observations reported here lend them further weight.

CONCLUSIONS AND SUGGESTIONS FOR FURTHER STUDIES

The studies here have shown the following:

1. Depressed patients have significantly lowered values of 5 HIAA in their CSF compared with those of a control group.
2. There is no significant difference berween the 5 HIAA values of patients with other psychiatric disorders when compared with either the control group or the depressive group.

3. A positive correlation exists between the CSF 5 HIAA values of depressed patients and the plasma 11-hydroxycorticosteroid levels both before and after a midnight dose of 2 mg of dexamethasone.

More studies are needed to delineate normal variations throughout the day (cf. Dixit and Buckley, 1967) and to determine whether there is any specific clinical picture which may be equated with the subgroups of severely depressed patients. The correlation of other such changes with other clinical and biochemical parameters of depression must be sought.

Specifically, more patients, completely free of drugs, with clear-cut psychiatric syndromes need to be studied, when ill and on recovery. This would be most easily accomplished through cooperative studies, with patients and controls drawn from many centers using standard assay methods and rating scales.

REFERENCES

Aghajanian, G.K., Bloom, F.G. and Sheard, M.H.: Electron microscopy of degeneration within the serotonin pathway of rat brain. *Brain Res,* 13:266, 1969.

Altman, K. and Greengard, O.: Correlation of kynurenine excretion with liver tryptophan pyrrolase levels in disease and after hydrocortisone induction. *J Clin Invest,* 45:1527, 1966.

Anderson, H. and Roos, B.E.: The effect of probenecid on the elimination from CSF of intraventricularly injected 5-hydroxyindoleacetic acid in normal and hydrocephalic dogs. *J Pharm Pharmacol,* 20:879, 1968.

Ashcroft, G.W., Crawford, T.B.B., Eccleston, D., Sharman, D.F., MacDougall, E.J., Stanton, J.B. and Binns, J.K.: 5-Hydroxyindole compounds in the cerebrospinal fluid of patients with psychiatric or neurological diseases. *Lancet,* II:1049, 1966.

Ashcroft, G.W., Eccleston, D., Knight, F., MacDougall, E.J. and Waddell, J.C.: Changes in amine metabolism produced by anti-depressant drugs. *J Psychosom Res,* 9:129, 1965.

Ashcroft, G.W. and Sharman, D.F.: 5-Hydroxyindoles in human cerebrospinal fluids. *Nature,* 186:1050, 1960.

Ashcroft, G.W. and Sharman, D.F.: Drug induced changes in the concentration of 5-OR indolyl compounds in cerebrospinal fluid and caudate nucleus. *Br J Pharmacol,* 19:153, 1962.

Axelrod, J. and Inscoe, J.K.: The uptake and binding of circulating serotonin and the effect of drugs. *J Pharmacol Exp Ther,* 141:161, 1963.

Azmitia, E.C. and McEwen, B.S.: Corticosterone regulation of TPN hydroxylase in mid-brain of the rat. *Science,* 166:1274, 1969.

Benkert, O. and Matussek, N.: Influence of hydrocortisone and glucagon on liver tyrosine transaminase and on brain tyrosine, norepinephrine and 5-hydroxytryptamine. *Nature*, 228:73, 1970.

Blashko, H. and Levine, W.G.: Metabolism of indolealkylamines. In Eichler, O. and Farah, A. (Eds.) : Handbuch der Experimentellen Pharmakologie, Berlin, Springer-Verlag., Vol. XIX, *5-Hydroxytryptamine and Related Indolealkylamines*, 1966.

Boakes, R.J., Bradley, P.B., Briggs, I. and Dray, A.: Antagonism by LSD to effects of 5-HT on single neurones. *Brain Res*, 15:529, 1969.

Bogdanski, D.F., Pletscher, A., Brodie, B.B. and Udenfriend, S.: Identification and assay of serotonin in brain. *J Pharmacol Exp Ther*, 117:82, 1956.

Bourne, H., Bunney, W.E., Colburn, R.W., Davis, J.M., Davis, J.N., Shaw, D.M. and Coppen, A.J.: Noradrenaline, 5-hydroxytryptamine and 5-hydroxyindoleacetic acid in hindbrains of suicidal patients. *Lancet*, II:805, 1968.

Bowers, M.B.: Deficient transport mechanism for the removal of the monoamine metabolites from CSF. *Brain Res*, 15:522, 1969.

Bowers, M.B. and Gerbode, F.A.: Relationship of monoamine metabolites in human cerebrospinal fluid to age. *Nature*, 219:1256, 1968.

Bowers, M.B., Heninger, G.R. and Gerbode, F.A.: Cerebrospinal fluid 5-hydroxyindoleacetic acid and homovanillic acid in psychiatric patients. *Int J Neuropharmacol*, 8:255, 1969.

Brodie, B.B. and Reid, W.D.: Serotonin in brain; functional considerations. In Garattini, S. and Shore, P.A. (Eds.) : *Recent Advances in Pharmacology*. New York, Academic Press, Vol. 6, 1968.

Bulat, M. and Supek, Z.: The penetration of 5-hydroxytryptamine through the blood-brain barrier. *J Neurochem*, 14:265, 1967.

Bunney, W.E. and Davis, J.M.: Norepinephrine in depressive disorders. *Arch Gen Psychiatry*, 13:483, 1965.

Bunney, W.E., Brodie, H.K., Murphy, D.L. and Goodwin, F.K.: Studies of alpha-methyl-para-tyrosine, 1-dopa and 1-tryptophan in depression and mania. *Am J Psychiatry*, 127:7, 1971.

Carlsson, A.: Functional changes of drug-induced changes in brain monoamine levels. In Himwich, W.E. and Himwich, W.A. (Eds.) : *Biogenic Amines*. Amsterdam, Elsevier. Vol. 8, *Prog Brain Res*, 1964.

Carlsson, A.: Drugs which block the storage of 5 HT and related amines. In Eichler, O. and Farah, A. (Eds.) : *Handbuch der Experimentellen Pharmakologie*. Berlin, Springer-Verlag., Vol. XIX, *5-Hydroxytryptamine and Related Indolealkylamines*. 1966.

Carlsson, A., Jonasson, J., Lindquist, M. and Fuxe, K.: Demonstration of extraneuronal 5 HT accumulation in brain following membrane and pump blockade by chlorimipramine. *Brain Res*, 12:456, 1969.

Carney, M.W.P., Thakurdas, H. and Sebastian, J.: Effects of imipramine and reserpine in depression. *Psychopharmacologia*, 14:349, 1969.

Cazzullo, C.L.: New trends in psychopharmacology. In *Excerpta Medica Foundation International Congress.* Series No. 150, Amsterdam, 1967, p. 308.

Chase, T.N., Schnur, J.A. and Gordon, E.K.: CSF Monomaine catabolites in drug induced extrapyramidal disorders. *Neuropharmacology,* 9:265, 1970.

Coppen, A.J.: Defects in monoamine metabolism and their possible importance in the pathogenesis of depressive syndromes. *Psychiat Neurol Neurochir,* 72:173, 1969.

Coppen, A.J., Shaw, D.M., Herzberg, B. and Maggs, R.: Tryptophan in the treatment of depression. *Lancet,* II:1178, 1967.

Costa, E.: Turnover of neuronal monoamines: Pharmacological implications. In *The Present Status of Psychotropic Drugs.* Cerletti, A. and Bove, F.J. (Eds.): Excerpta Medica Foundation, I.C.S., No. 180, Amsterdam, 1969.

Curzon, G.: Metabolic changes in depression. *Lancet,* 1:257, 1969.

Curzon, G. and Green, A.R.: Effect of hydrocortisone on rat brain 5-hydroxytryptamine. *Life Sciences, Part I,* 7:657, 1968.

Dencker, S.J., Malm, U., Roos, B.E. and Werdinius, B.: Acid monoamine metabolites of cerebrospinal fluid in mental depression and mania. *J Neurochem,* 13:1545, 1966.

Dewhurst, W.G.: On the chemical basis of mood. *J Psychosom Res,* 9:115, 1965.

Dewhurst, W.G.: New theory of central amine function and its clinical application. *Nature,* 218:1130, 1968.

di Carlo, V.: Action of serotonin, allied compounds and monoamine oxidase inhibitors on peripheral nerve fibres. In Himwich, E.W. and Himwich, W.A. (Eds.) : *Biogenic Amines.* Elsevier, Amsterdam. Vol. 8, *Progr Brain Res,* 1964.

Dixit, B.N. and Buckley, J.: Circadian changes in brain 5-hydroxytryptophan and plasma corticosterone in the rat. *Life Sciences, Part I,* 6:755, 1967.

Eccleston, D., Ashcroft, G.W., Crawford, B.B., Stanton, J.B., Wood, D. and McTurk, P.H.: Effect of tryptophan metabolism on 5 HIAA in cerebrospinal fluid in man. *J Neurol Neurosurg Psychiatry,* 33:269, 1970a.

Eccleston, D., Ritchie, I.M. and Roberts, M.H.: Long term effects of midbrain stimulation on 5-hydroxyindole synthesis in rat brain. *Nature,* 226:84, 1970b.

Fuxe, K., Hofelt, T. and Ungerstedt, U.: Distribution of monoamines in the mammalian central nervous system by histochemical studies. In Hooper, G. (Ed.) : *Metabolism of Amines in the Brain.* Macmillan, London, 1969.

Gaddum, J.H. and Vogt, M.: Some central actions of serotonin and various antagonists. *Br J Pharmacol,* 11:175, 1956.

Gal, E.M., Heater, R.D. and Millard, S.A.: Studies on the metabolism of 5-hydroxytryptamine. *Proc Soc Exp Biol Med,* 128:412, 1968.

Garattini, S. and Valzelli, L.: *Serotonin.* Elsevier, Amsterdam, 1965.

Gerbode, F.A. and Bowers, M.B.: Measurement of acid monoamine metabolites in human and animal cerebrospinal fluid. *J. Neurochem,* 15:1053, 1968.

Glassman, A.: Indoleamines and affective disorders. *Psychosom Med,* 31:107, 1969.

Goodwin, F.K., Brodie, H.K., Murphy, D.L. and Bunney, W.E.: Administration of a peripheral decarboxylase inhibitor with 1-dopa to depressed patients. *Lancet,* I:909, 1970.

Gottfries, C.G., Gottfries, I. and Roos, B.E.: HVA and 5 HIAA in the C.S.F. of patients with senile dementia, pre-senile dementia and Parkinsonism. *J Neurochem,* 16:1341, 1969.

Grant, E.C. and Pryse-Davies, J.: Effect of oral contraceptives on depressive mood changes and on endometrial monoamine oxidase and phosphatase. *Br Med J,* 3:777, 1968.

Green, A.R. and Curzon, G.: Decrease of 5-hydroxytryptamine in the brain provoked by hydrocortisone and its prevention by allopurinol. *Nature,* 220:1095, 1968.

Green, H. and Sawyer, J.L.: Biochemical-pharmacological studies with 5-hydroxytryptophan, precursor of 5-hydroxytryptamine. In Himwich, W.E. and Himwich, W.A. (Eds.): *Biogenic Amines, Progress in Brain Research,* 8:150, 1964.

Hagen, P.B. and Cohen, L.H.: Biosynthesis of indolealkylamines physiological release and transport of 5 HT. In Eichler, O. and Farah, A. (Eds.): *Handbuch der Experimentellen Pharmakologie.* Berlin, Springer-Verlag., Vol. XIX, 5-Hydroxytryptamine and related Indolealkylamines, 1966.

Hanson, A.: Chemical analysis of indolealkylamines and related compounds. In Eichler, O. and Farah, A. (Eds.) : *Handbuch der Experimentellen Pharmakologie.* Berlin, Springer-Verlag., Vol. XIX, 5-Hydroxytryptamine and related Indolealkylamines, 1966.

Hinesley, R.K., Norton, J.A. and Aprison, M.H.: Serotonin, norepinephrine and 3-4 dihydroxyphenylethylamine in rat brain parts following electroconvulsive shock. *J Psychiatr Res,* 6:142. 1968.

Holmberg, C.: Biological aspects of electroconvulsive therapy. *Int Rev Neurobiol,* 5:389, 1963.

Ichiyama, A., Hakamura, S., Nishizuka, Y. and Hayaishi, O.: Tryptophane 5-hydroxylase in mammalian brain. In Garattini, S. and Shore, P.A. (Eds.) : *Recent Advances in Pharmacology.* Academic Press, New York, Vol. 6A:5, 1968.

Johansson, B. and Roos, B.E.: 5-Hydroxyindoleacetic and homovanillic acid levels in the cerebrospinal fluid of healthy volunteers and patients with Parkinson's syndrome. *Life Sciences, Part I,* 6:1449, 1967.

Jonsson, J. and Lewander, T.: A method for the simultaneous determination of 5 HIAA and 5 HT in brain tissue and cerebrospinal fluid. *Acta Physiol Scand,* 78:43, 1970.

Korf, J. and Valkenburgh-Sikkema, T.: Fluorometric determination of 5 HIAA in human urine and C.S.F. *Clinica Chimica Acta,* 26:301, 1969.

Koe, B.W. and Weissman, A.: The pharmacology of p-chlorophenylanine. In Garattini, S. and Shore, P.A. (Eds.) : *Recent Advances in Pharmacology.* Academic Press, New York, Vol. 6B:29, 1968.

Lapin, I.P. and Oxenkrug, G.F.: The intensification of the central serotoninergic processes as a possible determinant of the thymoleptic effect. *Lancet,* I:132, 1969.

Maickel, R.P. and Miller, F.P.: Fluorescent products formed by reaction of indole derivatives and o-phthalaldehyde. *Analytical Chem,* 38:1937, 1966.

Maickel, R.P., Cox, R.H., Saillant, J. and Miller, F.P.: A method for the determination of serotonin and norepinephrine in discrete areas of rat brain. *Int J Neuropharm,* 7:275, 1968.

McLeod, W.R.: Indolealkylamines and severe depressive illness. Unpublished M.D. thesis, University of Melbourne, 1970.

Moir, A.T., Ashcroft, G.W., Crawford, T.B., Eccleston, D. and Guldberg, H.C.: Cerebral metabolites in cerebrospinal fluid as a biochemical approach to the brain. *Brain,* 93:357, 1970.

Oates, J.A. and Sjoerdsma, A.: Neurologic effects of tryptophan in patients receiving a monoamine oxidase inhibitor. *Neurology,* 10:1076, 1960.

Olsson, R. and Roos, B.E.: Concentrations of 5-hydroxyindole acetic acid and homovanillic acid in the cerebrospinal fluid after treatment with probenecid in patients with Parkinson's disease. *Nature,* 219:502, 1968.

Page, I.H.: *Serotonin.* U.S.A. Year Book Medical Publishers Inc., 1968a.

Page, I.H.: Advances in pharmacology. In Garattini, S. and Shore, P.A. (Eds.) : *Recent Advances in Pharmacology.* Academic Press, New York, Vol. 6A:281, 1968b.

Pare, C.M., Yeung, D.P., Price, K. and Stacey, R.S.: 5 HT, noradrenaline and dopamine in brainstem, hypothalamus and caudate nucleus of controls and of patients committing suicide by coal-gas poisoning. *Lancet,* 2:133, 1969.

Persson, T. and Roos, B.E.: Clinical and pharmacological effects of monoamine precursors of haloperidol in chronic schizophrenia. *Nature,* 217:854, 1968.

Persson, T. and Roos, B.E.: Acid metabolites from monoamines in the cerebrospinal fluid of chronic schizophrenics. *Br J Psychiatry,* 115:95, 1969.

Quay, W.B.: Differences in circadian rhythms in 5 HT according to brain region. *Am J Physiol,* 215:448, 1968.

Ramanamurthy, P.S. and Srikantia, S.G.: Effects of leucine on brain serotonin. *J Neurochem,* 17:27, 1970.

Roos, B.E.: On the occurrence and distribution of 5 HIAA in brain. *Life Sciences, Part I,* 1:25, 1962.

Roos, B.E. and Sjöstrom, R.: 5 HIAA (and HVA) levels in cerebrospinal fluid after probenecid application in patients with manic depressive psychosis. *Pharmacol Clin,* 1:1, 1969.

Roos, B.E. and Werdinius, B.: Effect of reserpine on the level of 5 HIAA in brain. *Life Sciences, Part I,* 3:105, 1962.

Roos, B.E. and Werdinus, B.: The effect of alpha-methyl-dopa on the metabolism of 5 HT in brain. *Life Sciences, Part I*, 2:92, 1963.

Rose, D.P.: Oral contraception and depression. *Lancet*, II:321, 1969.

Rose, D.P. and McGinty, F.: The influence of adrenocortical hormones and vitamins upon tryptophan metabolism in man. *Clin Sci*, 35:1, 1968.

Schildkraut, J.J.: Neuropharmacology and the affective disorders. *N Engl J Med*, 281:197, 281:248, 281:302, 1969.

Sharman, D.F. and Ashcroft, G.W.: 5-Hydroxyindoles in human cerebrospinal fluid. *Nature*, 186:1050, 1960.

Sheard, M.N.: The effect of PCP on behaviour in rats in relation to brain 5 HT, 5 HIAA. *Brain Res*, 15:524, 1969.

Sheard, M.N. and Aghajanian, G.K.: Stimulation of midbrain Raphe neurons: behavioural effects of serotonin release. *Life Sciences, Part I*, 7:24, 1968.

Sjöstrom, R. and Roos, B.E.: Measurement of acid monoamine metabolites in cerebrospinal fluid in manic-depressive psychosis. Paper presented at C.I.N.P., Prague, 1970.

Sourkes, T.L., Missala, K. and Oravec, M.: Decrease of cerebral 5 HT and 5 HIAA caused by (-)-alpha-methyltryptophan. *J Neurochem*, 17:111, 1970.

Tonge, S.R. and Leonard, B.G.: The effects of some hallucinogenic drugs upon the metabolism of 5 HT in the brain. *Life Sciences, Part I*, 8:805, 1969.

Twarog, B.M. and Page, I.H.: Serotonin content of some mammalian tissues and urine and method for its determination. *Am J Physiol*, 175:157, 1953.

Udenfriend, S., Bogdanski, D.F. and Weissbach, H.: Increase in tissue serotonin by administration of its precursor 5-hydroxytryptophan. *Fed Proc*, 15:493, 1956.

Udenfriend, S.: *Fluorescence Assay in Biology and Medicine*. New York, Academic Press, 1962.

Van Praag, H.M.: Indoleamines and the central nervous system. *Psychiat Neurol Neurochir*, 73:9, 1970.

Van Praag, H.M., Korf, J. and Puite, J.: 5 HIAA levels in the cerebrospinal fluid of depressive patients treated with probenecid. *Nature*, 225: 1259, 1970.

Verster, J. and Van Praag, H.M.: A comparative investigation of methylamphetamine and 4-chloro-N-methylamphetamine in healthy test subjects. *Pharmakopsychiatrie Neuropsychopharmakologie*, 3:239, 1970.

Volicer, L.: Correlation between behavioural and biochemical effects of PCP in mice and rats. *Int J Neuropharmacol*, 8:361, 1969.

Weber, L.J. and Horita, A.: A study of 5 HT formation from 5-hydroxytryptophan in the brain and other tissues. *Biochem Pharmacol*, 14:1141, 1965.

Weissbach, H.: Advances in pharmacology. In Garattini, S. and Shore, P.A.

(Eds.) : *Recent Advances in Pharmacology*. New York, Academic Press, 6A:131, 1968.

Winston, F.: Oral contraceptives and depression. *Lancet*, I:1209, 1969.

Wooley, D.W. and Shaw, E.: Some neurophysiological aspects of serotonin. *Br Med J*, 2:122, 1954.

Yuwiler, A. and Geller, E.: Brain serotonin changes in phenylalanine fed rats: synthesis storage and degradation. *Brain Res*, 16:999, 1969.

Chapter 9

AN EVALUATION OF L-TRYPTOPHAN AS AN ANTIDEPRESSANT AGENT: SEQUENTIAL COMPARISON WITH ELECTROSHOCK

BERNARD J. CARROLL

INTRODUCTION

OF increasing importance to research into the pathophysiology of mood disorders are hypothesis-oriented therapeutic trials to test the efficacy of precursors of the cerebral catechol and indoleamines in relieving depressive symptoms.

Such trials may not prove of practical importance in treating mood disorders, but their findings can be expected to clarify the role of cerebral amines in affective illness, and especially to help identify clinical features which are not mediated by amine dysfunction.

An example of this biochemical-pharmacological approach to both theory and disease patterns is seen in the carcinoid syndrome. As the clinical and biochemical findings had suggested, inhibition of serotonin synthesis with parachlorphenylalanine (PCPA) improved several of the features of this disease, but the incidence of flushing episodes was little affected. These were later shown to be related not to serotonin overproduction but to bradykinin release from tumor metastases. The therapeutic trials of PCPA confirmed the importance of excessive serotonin production but also provided fresh insight into the complexity of the disease mechanisms (Sjoerdsma et al., 1970).

It is likely that experience with amine precursors in depression will lead to a similar refinement of the simplistic monoamine deficit theories.

Our own interest in this area began with an attempt to confirm early reports that the indoleamine precursor, l-tryptophan, was an effective drug for the treatment of depressed patients.

INDOLEAMINE PRECURSORS: EARLY CLINICAL TRIALS

There are two precursors of 5-hydroxytryptamine (5 HT, serotonin) which can cross the blood-brain barrier—namely the amino acids l-tryptophan (TP) and 5-hydroxytryptophan (5 HTP). Figure 9-1 outlines the metabolic pathways of these compounds in the brain, and the subsequent degradation of serotonin to 5-hydroxyindoleacetic acid (5 HIAA).

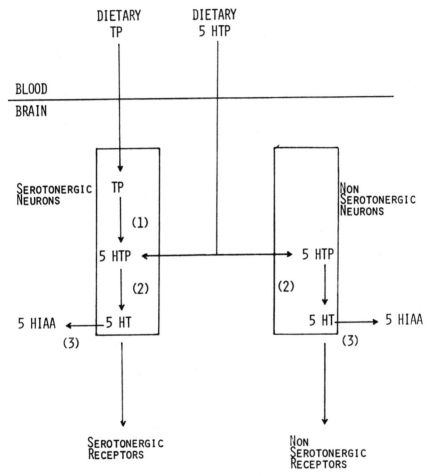

Figure 9-1. Metabolic pathways of large loading doses of indoleamine precursors in brain.

TP hydroxylation occurs only within serotonergic neurons, while 5 HTP enters both serotonergic and other neurons and is decarboxylated in both sites, causing 5 HT accumulation in neurons which normally contain no 5 HT (see Carroll, 1971, for detailed references).

In animals it has been shown that the levels of brain 5 HT are raised by both precursors, but the pattern of cerebral 5 HT metabolism differs from the normal when 5 HTP is used. This issue will be discussed more fully after the clinical studies have been described.

5-Hydroxytryptophan

In 1959 Pare and Sandler gave small intravenous doses (12.5 to 25 mg) of dl-5 HTP to three depressed patients. No beneficial effect was found, with or without the monoamine oxidase inhibitor (MAOI) iproniazid. A total dose of 150 mg of dl-5 HTP given intravenously over a forty-eight-hour period was also ineffective.

Four years later Kline and Sacks (1963) published a short note describing very good responses of depressed patients to intravenous 5 HTP, used in conjunction with various MAOIs. Of twenty "pure" depressives eighteen were said to have had a "definite" response. A smaller number (7) of thirty atypical cases responded. Kline's procedure involved the use of a single injection of 25 to 50 mg 5 HTP given usually a few hours after the first dose of the MAOI, and improvement was assessed twenty-four hours later.

Like the previous study this was an uncontrolled trial. When the same authors (1964) later attempted to repeat their findings in a double-blind study *no* evidence emerged to support a 5 HTP effect. Only five of thirty-seven patients receiving 50 mg and nine of forty-nine receiving 25 mg were considered to be "definite" responders. The injections in this trial were given at least three days after MAO inhibitors had been commenced.

A small study of fourteen patients by Glassman and Jaffe (1969) also failed to demonstrate any potentiation of an MAO inhibitor by either TP or 5 HTP.

Persson and Roos (1967) described one patient, refractory to both electroconvulsive therapy (ECT) and intravenous l-dopa who improved dramatically after five daily intravenous injections of 50 mg 5 HTP. The treatment was continued for two weeks at which time he was considered "cured." His additional drug treatment during both l-dopa and 5 HTP administration included a "small dose of opium." It is possible that the combination of 5 HTP with opium caused this patient's improvement; morphine has mood elevating properties and its behavioral exciting effect in animals is potentiated by 5 HTP (Carroll and Sharp, 1971).

The overall impression from these five studies is that 5 HTP does not have a powerful antidepressant action, nor does it potentiate monoamine oxidase inhibitors.

L-Tryptophan

L-tryptophan (TP) administration causes a rise in brain levels of 5 HT and a normal pattern of cerebral 5 HT metabolism. The 5-hydroxylation of TP to 5 HTP in brain is the rate limiting step in cerebral 5 HT production (Lovenberg *et al.*, 1968) and occurs only within serotonergic neurons.

The first trial of tryptophan as an antidepressant was reported in 1963 from Coppen's group, who claimed that the amino acid potentiated the action of a monoamine oxidase inhibitor (tranylcypromine). This was a double-blind controlled trial in which the patients, who were matched for age only, received tranylcypromine 30 to 50 mg per day for four weeks, together with pyridoxine hydrochloride 20 mg and vitamin B1 supplements daily. In the *second week only* of the four-week period they received either dl-tryptophan 214 mg/kg (10 to 17 gm) daily or a placebo suspension. The Hamilton rating scores of the tryptophan group were found to fall more rapidly in weeks 2, 3 and 4 than those of the placebo group. The authors concluded that TP potentiated the MAOI and that this effect was continued after TP was stopped.

In the same year Pare gave l-tryptophan together with either a tricyclic antidepressant or an MAOI. The patients had previously responded to the drug used and had later relapsed when the dose was reduced. This low dose was continued and TP was added, in a total daily amount of 7.5 or 15 gm. Only those who received TP and MAOI improved; six of fourteen patients were much improved within two or three days of commencing TP and relapsed when a placebo was substituted, but only one of nine patients receiving TP and a tricyclic antidepressant improved. Likewise, side effects were observed only in those receiving TP and MAOI.

Potentiation of an MAOI by tryptophan was also reported by Glassman and Platman (1969), in twenty patients who received phenelzine 30 mg b.d. with either placebo or 12 to 18 gm dl-tryptophan daily on a double-blind basis. Despite the small number of patients a definite TP effect was observed. Six of ten subjects receiving TP were discharged in three weeks, compared with two of those who received phenelzine alone.

Enthusiasm for tryptophan as a treatment for depression reached its peak with the claim, again from Coppen's group (1967) that the amino acid was as effective as electroconvulsive therapy (ECT) in the management of depressed patients. In this study a number of patients were treated with dl-tryptophan (5 to 6 gm daily). Some received tranylcypromine (30 mg daily), with (9 patients) or without (10 patients) potassium and carbohydrate supplements. A further twenty-two patients received tryptophan and the supplements but without the MAO inhibitor. Pyridoxine HCl 100 mg daily was also given to all patients. Improvement was assessed by self-rating scores on the Beck scale (1961) obtained over the treatment period of four weeks. The results were then compared with the Beck scores of another group of thirty-six patients who had received ECT in the same hospitals some time previously. No statistically significant differences were found between any of the three treatment regimens (ECT, TP + MAOI, TP alone). There was a trend for TP + MAOI to show a greater improvement than TP alone, and for ECT to be the most effective treatment. The authors concluded from these results that TP was as effective as ECT.

The study was carried out without acceptable controls: the patients in the three treatment groups had similar mean ages and admission Beck rating scores, but were not matched in any other way. The three groups were not treated over the same period of time and the allocation to treatments was not random. The use of a self-rating instrument as the sole criterion of severity and improvement is open to serious question (Carroll *et al.*, 1971). No apparent provision was made to exclude subjects with self-limiting depressive episodes from the "trial." From their score on the Beck scale the patients would appear to have been only mildly or moderately depressed. The responsiveness of such patients to a placebo regimen in combination with the nonspecific therapeutic elements of hospital care, especially a research unit, has been frequently documented. The paper suffers as well as from an attempt to demonstrate several contentions (about potassium and carbohydrate supplements; about TP + MAOI-v-TP alone, about TP-v-ECT) with the result that none of the issues is satisfactorily resolved.

Because of the theoretical and practical importance of the claim that tryptophan was as effective as ECT in the treatment of depression, we compared the two treatments in Melbourne, in severely depressed patients, using a more rigorous assessment (Carroll *et al.*, 1970).

SEQUENTIAL COMPARISON OF L-TRYPTOPHAN WITH ECT

A sequential trial was planned to compare directly the relative effects of ECT and TP on matched pairs of patients. A treatment period of three weeks was chosen since the data provided in the previous study indicated that a definite effect of TP could be detected at this time.

Patients

Consecutive admissions with primary depressive illnesses were considered for inclusion in the trial. After a week's observation and evaluation, if the patient was still significantly depressed, a clinical decision was made to treat the patient with either ECT or a tricyclic antidepressant. This is our usual practice.

The patients selected for ECT were those with more severe illnesses. They would be classified as endogenous depressives, manic depressives, or involutional depressives. They had been ill for one month to six months before admission and were neither acute situational reactions nor chronic unremitting depressions. None had evidence of schizoaffective or schizophrenic symptoms.

Their illness typically comprised lowering of mood and self-esteem, depressive ideation (pessimism and hopelessness), guilt feelings, suicidal ideas, sleep disturbance, weight loss, agitation, retardation, inability to work and loss of interest and energy which did not respond to environmental change. Somatic and psychological anxiety were often prominent, but depressive delusions were uncommon and paranoid delusions were not encountered. No patient had associated physical illness.

Only patients selected on clinical grounds as suitable for ECT were admitted to the trial and were then allocated by the research design to treatment with either ECT or tryptophan.

Measures of Severity and Change

The Hamilton rating scale for depression was used (see Chap. 12) to provide a global assessment of severity. Each patient was rated initially and after three weeks of treatment by a psychiatrist experienced in the use of the scale but not involved in the initial selection of patients and unaware of which patients were matched. At the second rating, however, he learned which patients had received ECT so that *this* rating was not blind.

Treatments

ECT was given through bitemporal electrodes after atropine premedication, thiopentone anesthesia and relexation with suxamethonium. As is our practice, three treatments were given each week for the three weeks except to three patients whose symptoms had completely remitted before this time.

A fixed dose of l-tryptophan (7 gm) was given each night as fourteen 0.5 gm tablets. This time was chosen to take advantage of the diurnal rhythm of liver tryptophan pyrrolase activity, which is lowest at night (Rapoport *et al.*, 1968). A total of 170 mg pyridoxine HCl was given together with the tryptophan. A nursing sister was present to supervise the taking of the TP dose.

Amylobarbitone sodium was given at night and as needed during the day to both ECT and TP groups. No other medication was prescribed.

Trial Design

A restricted sequential design using matched pairs of patients was chosen as it provides a more powerful statistical test although it has the disadvantage of increasing the potential number of tied pairs (Armitage, 1960). The dimensions of the chart were set to give an expected response-rate for ECT of 0.8 and for l-tryptophan of 0.4 with 0.95 power at the 0.05 level of significance. These dimensions require ECT to be twice as effective as tryptophan to emerge as clearly superior.

Patients entering the trial were matched for sex, age (tolerance ± 5 years), and initial Hamilton rating of severity (tolerance ± 5 points). Any patient who could not be matched immediately was allocated to treatment on a random basis and matched with the next patient admitted of the same sex and within the tolerance for age and rating of severity.

The order of allocation of patients to treatment in the trial was noted to test whether the matching procedure had led to a significant departure from randomness. Improvement was held to have occurred if a decrease of eight or more points in the Hamilton rating was reported. This single standard could be applied in the matched design as each pair of patients started from a similar point on the Hamilton scale, and the effects of a nonlinear scale were reduced.

The trial was terminated after twelve matched pairs had produced a significant finding on the sequential chart. The duration of the trial was five months and at the conclusion one male and three females had not been matched.

RESULTS

Clinical Findings

All twelve patients who received ECT improved greatly in three weeks. Three were symptom-free before this time; one man and three women needed further treatments beyond the trial period.

Only one of the twelve subjects treated with l-tryptophan was symptom-free at the end of the trial. Two others showed some improvement, while three were worse than they had been when the trial began. Eleven of the twelve subjects were considered to require ECT by a psychiatrist who had not been involved in the depression ratings. All then improved rapidly. The one patient who did improve on tryptophan later remained well when a placebo was substituted; thus his improvement may perhaps be regarded as coincidental.

Side effects with l-tryptophan were mild. Nausea was common

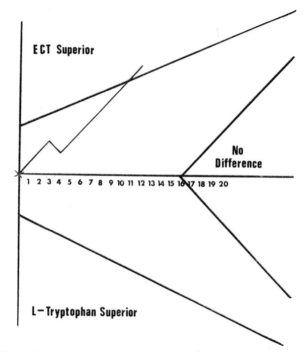

Figure 9-2. Sequential comparison of tryptophan and E.C.T.

in the first few days of treatment; "light-headedness" and visual blurring were also experienced but postural hypotension was not noted. No spontaneous remarks were made by the patients about improved sleep or increased dreaming.

Sequential Result

The upper boundary of the sequential graph was crossed in favor of ECT after twelve pairs of patients had been treated (six pairs male and six pairs female) (Fig. 9-2). ECT thus emerged at least twice as effective as tryptophan.

Group Mean Data

Table 9-I shows the means and standard deviations for ages, and initial and final Hamilton ratings, by treatment and by sex.

The standard deviation of the initial Hamilton score for the

TABLE 9-I

RESULTS (Means and Standard Deviations)

Treatment	No.	Age	(yr.)	Hamilton depression score Initial		Final	
E.C.T.:							
Males	6	57.3	(12.2)	24.6	(4.8)	8.1	(4.5)
Females	6	58.7	(11.4)	28.4	(5.9)	15.3	(5.6)
All	12	57.9	(11.7)	26.6	(5.6)	11.6	(6.1)
L-tryptophan:							
Males	6	58.1	(11.1)	23.3	(6.0)	16.5	(7.5)
Females	6	58.6	(11.3)	29.5	(3.2)	25.5	(3.3)
All	12	58.3	(11.1)	26.3	(5.7)	21.0	(7.3)
Whole group	24	58.1	(11.5)	26.4	(5.6)	16.4	(6.6)

group as a whole was found to be less than the standard of a change of eight points used in the trial to assess improvement.

A runs test (Sokal and Rohlf, 1969) carried out on the order of treatments allocated in the trial showed that no significant departure from randomness had been introduced by the matching procedure.

The contrast between initial and final Hamilton scores from Table 9-I was tested for significance by t-tests. The patients having ECT showed a significant decrease ($p < 0.001$) while no such decrease occurred in the ratings of the patients on tryptophan ($p < 0.2$).

The significant difference in response of the two treatments was confirmed ($p < 0.01$) when the nonparametric Wilcoxon matched pairs test (Siegal, 1956) was applied to the changes from initial to final Hamilton ratings for the two treatment groups.

ECT was thus found to be clearly superior to l-tryptophan clinically, in the sequential analysis, and on comparison of the group mean data, in this group of twenty-four severely ill patients.

DISCUSSION

L-tryptophan is clearly not as effective as ECT in the management of severely depressed patients. The deficiencies of the original study of Coppen's group have already been discussed. Our own rigorous evaluation of this issue, with careful selection and matching of patients produced an unequivocal result. At the present time this study provides the only definitive assessment of l-tryptophan's antidepressant properties. We found the amino acid *ineffective for severely ill subjects*. Since the patients in the original study of Coppen and associates were only mildly to moderately depressed the question of tryptophan's effectiveness in such subjects remains open. It could be resolved by a properly designed trial of a tricyclic antidepressant-v-l-tryptophan with a placebo introduced to control the nonspecific factors likely to influence the responses of such patients. Several preliminary notes have appeared which claim that tryptophan is as effective as imipramine but none appears to have contained placebo controls in an adequately designed trial (Coppen and Noguera, 1970; Broadhurst, 1970). Another brief note (Hertz and Sulman, 1968) refers to the prophylactic action of tryptophan in recurrent depression experienced by a single patient; this area might be worthy of systematic study. Several groups in the United States have now reported that l-tryptophan is ineffective in treating depression (Bowers, 1970; Bunney *et al.*, 1971; Mendels, 1970).

Potentiation of Monoamine Oxidase Inhibitors

Three studies give an affirmative answer to this question. The most convincing evidence is that of Pare and of Glassman and Platman. The methodology of the latter trial was the best controlled, although for unavoidable reasons a larger number of patients could not be studied and the trial was transferred between two centers during its progress. Further careful studies of this potentiation by tryptophan of MAO inhibitors would be valuable and of considerable research interest. However, the practical advantage of the combination is not clear and the incidence of side effects (Coppen *et al.*, 1963; Glassman and Platman, 1969; Pare, 1963) makes its regular use unlikely. The development of MAOIs with a selective action on 5 HT oxidation (Johnston, 1968) is a promising advance in this regard.

Biochemical Pharmacology of Tryptophan in Depression

Under normal conditions less than 3 per cent of dietary tryptophan enters the 5-hydroxylation pathway and only a minor fraction of this amount is destined for serotonin production in brain (White *et al.*, 1959). The major pathway of TP metabolism occurs in the liver where tryptophan pyrrolase splits the indole ring, forming kynurenine, from which a complex metabolic path leads to nicotinic acid (Fig. 9-3).

Serotonin production in brain is limited by a) tryptophan transport into brain, and b) activity of the rate-limiting enzyme tryptophan-5-hydroxylase (Lovenberg *et al.*, 1968). The decarboxylation of 5 HTP to 5 HT (serotonin) is a further step, which requires pyridoxal-5-phosphate as a cofactor. The decarboxylase enzyme is nonspecific and acts upon l-dopa, tyrosine and phenylalanine as well as 5 HTP (Yuwiler *et al.*, 1959).

A complex interrelationship exists between the two mentioned paths of tryptophan metabolism. Both tryptophan pyrrolase and tryptophan-5-hydroxylase are inducible by corticosteroids (Nistico and Preziosi, 1969) and by stress (Azmitia and McEwen, 1969; Knox and Auerbach, 1955). In addition, pyrrolase activity is increased by substrate loading with tryptophan (Knox 1951). An early suggestion was that competition for dietary TP occurred during stress or following corticosteroid administration and that brain 5 HT levels were decreased (Richter, 1967; Green and Curzon, 1968). This effect in animals could be blocked by the pyrrolase inhibitor, allopurinol. However, the functional significance of the observed *(in vitro)* increases of pyrrolase activity induced by cortisol appears to be doubtful (Kim and Miller, 1969) and it is clear that brain 5 HT turnover does really increase during stress, although steady state levels may be temporarily reduced (Bliss *et al.*, 1968; Thierry *et al.*, 1968; Nistico and Preziosi, 1969). On the other hand, pyrrolase induction by TP loading is associated with marked functional increases in substrate utilization along the kynurenine pathway (Kim and Miller, 1969). Further, several of the metabolites on this pathway (kynurenine, 3-hydroxykynurenine and 3-hydroxyanthranilic acid) are capable of inhibiting brain 5 HT synthesis by competitive interference with TP transport into the brain (Green and Curzon, 1970) (see Fig. 9-3). Elevated adrenocortical activity is common in depression and increased handling of tryptophan along the kynurenine pathway is also seen in this illness together with increased excretion of kynurenine and 3-hydroxykynurenine (Cazzullo *et al.*, 1966; Cur-

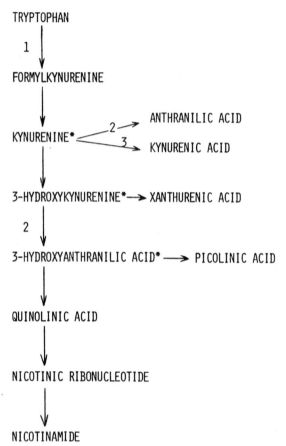

Figure 9-3. The kynurenine pathway of tryptophan metabolism. Enzymes: 1. Tryptophan pyrrolase, 2. kynureninase, 3. kynurenine aminotransferase. (* Metabolites which inhibit cerebral 5 HT production.)

zon and Bridges, 1970; Rubin, 1967). Thus when large doses of TP are given to depressed patients both substrate induction and enzyme induction of pyrrolase are to be expected. In normal patients TP loading increases brain 5 HT production, as reflected by 5 HIAA levels in cerebrospinal fluid (CSP) (Eccleston *et al.*, 1970). The limited evidence available suggests that TP may *not* increase 5 HIAA levels in the CSF of at least some depressives (Bowers, 1970).

This finding is in agreement with *in vivo* estimates of brain

5 HT turnover in depression, which reveal a significant impairment of the 5 HIAA increase in CSF when its clearance from CSF is blocked by probenecid (Korf and Praag, 1970; Praag *et al.*, 1970; Roos and Sjöstrom, 1969).

These lines of evidence point to the possibility that tryptophan-5-hydroxylase activity may be defective in some depressed patients. The defect may result in low brain 5 HT turnover and the appearance of depressive mood. More likely, the inducibility of brain tryptophan-5-hydroxylase by stress and by corticosteroids may be impaired, so that brain 5 HT turnover cannot increase under stress and behavioral adaptive mechanisms fail. *If such an enzyme defect does exist it will not be overcome by feeding tryptophan.* Van Praag and Korf (1970) have ventured that such a possibility might explain the divergent results of the clinical trials of tryptophan. This question could be resolved by a trial of TP during which adrenocortical activity and brain 5 HT turnover were estimated, so that these parameters might be correlated with clinical response.

Coppen (1970) has stated that the pyrrolase inhibitor allopurinol did not appear to potentiate the antidepressant action of tryptophan in patients he has studied.

5-Hydroxytryptophan

A deficiency of tryptophan-5-hydroxylase activity in depressed patients leads naturally to the suggestion that this block be circumvented by administering 5 HTP.

TP loading increases brain 5 HT and 5 HIAA levels in rats and dogs but 5 HTP does not appear in significant amounts. Loading with 5 HTP, however, is followed by an abnormally rapid production of 5 HIAA and the appearance of excessive amounts of 5 HT in brain regions which do not show such 5 HT increases after a tryptophan load (Moir and Eccleston, 1968). This study indicates that, after unphysiological loading, decarboxylation of 5 HTP probably occurs at sites which are not normally serotonergic. The 5 HT which is formed in the brain under these conditions, outside normal 5 HT containing neurons, is rapidly oxidized by MAO. In addition, the abnormally located 5 HT may enter catecholaminergic neurons, displace the endogenous dopamine or norepinephrine, and act as a "false transmitter" in these sites (Carlsson, 1964; Fuxe and Ungerstedt, 1967; Lichtensteiger *et al.*, 1967; Shaskan and Snyder, 1970). Thus the central amine alterations produced by 5 HTP may resemble those caused by dopa, i.e. displacement of nonhomologous amines in addition to increasing the tissue levels of 5 HT and catecholamines respectively.

Despite these metabolic studies, however, there is ample evidence that 5 HTP can produce behavioral changes in animals and that it modifies the effects of centrally acting drugs in man (Wyatt *et al.*, 1970) and in animals (Carroll and Sharp, 1971; Eidelberg and Schwartz, 1970; Hoyland *et al.*, 1970).

Clinically 5 HTP has been reported useful in the treatment of one depressed patient (Persson and Roos, 1967); it has improved symptoms in one case of manganese poisoning (Mena *et al.*, 1970) and has reversed the hypotonia of children with trisomy-21-Down's syndrome (Bazelon *et al.*, 1967). The amount of 5 HTP needed to obtain substantial modification of extrapyramidal symptoms in adults (Mena *et al.*, 1970) is of the same order as the dose of l-dopa effective in Parkinson's disease, i.e. above 3 gm per day.

A trial of such large doses of 5 HTP in depressed patients, possibly with a peripheral decarboxylase inhibitor as well, is obviously needed. Preliminary studies in this direction are already in progress (Brodie and Barchas, 1971).

Pyridoxine Supplements

In Coppen's study of tryptophan-v-ECT pyridoxine supplements (100 mg per day) were given for the reason that 5 HTP decarboxylase requires pyridoxal-5-phosphate as a coenzyme. In fact, no evidence of pyridoxine deficiency was present in the patients and these large vitamin supplements appear not to have been justified. In our own trial a similar large pyridoxine supplement was given, relative to the l-tryptophan dosage.

The presence of these supplements might well be ignored but for the fact that pyridoxine is now known to antagonize, by an uncertain mechanism, the clinical response to l-dopa in Parkinsonism (Duvoisin *et al.*, 1969; Fellman and Roth, 1971). Thus the possibility must be considered that pyridoxine given in the clinical trials of tryptophan prevented the emergence of an antidepressant effect. Certainly, the doses of pyridoxine used were very large, in comparison with those required to reverse clinical B_6 deficiency or even sideroblastic anaemia where amounts as little as 10 mg will suffice (Davidson, 1964).

In the metabolism of tryptophan, pyridoxal-5-phosphate is a cofactor, not only of 5 HTP decarboxylase, but also of kynureninase and of kynurenine aminotransferase (Fig. 9-3). Thus the net effect of pyridoxine supplements may be to promote tryptophan metabolism beyond 3-hydroxyanthranilic acid, rather than favor 5 HT production in brain (Rose, 1969). For example, Bowers (1970), using 2 to 8 gm TP plus 100 mg pyridoxine daily recorded generally minor increases in CSF 5 HIAA levels, not only in depressives but also in some schizophrenic patients at the end of eight to twelve days of treatment.

A recent study of this question in rats (Carroll and Dodge, 1971) has shown that pyridoxine did not diminish the rise in brain 5 HT or 5 HIAA following a tryptophan load; in addition pyridoxine did not alter the basal turnover rate of 5 HT in rat brain. A direct assessment of the interaction between TP and pyridoxine in humans is still needed, however. Pare (1963) mentioned that 20 mg of pyridoxine did not alter the side effects experienced by one patient receiving TP with an MAO inhibitor.

Toxicity of Tryptophan Loads

Adverse effects of unphysiological loading with amino acids have been well documented. A recent major review details the toxicity of TP (Harper *et al.*, 1970).

Tryptophan has been shown to produce growth depression, renal tubular damage and high mortality in animals on low-protein diets. L-tryptophan is somewhat better tolerated than the D form. Products of ruminal metabolism of TP in cows have been associated with the rapid development of interstitial pulmonary emphysema.

Metabolic effects of TP include suppression of gluconeogenesis in rats, and the induction of other enzymes besides tryptophan pyrrolase, e.g. tyrosine transaminase and phenylalanine hydroxylase. The long-term consequences of these and other metabolic changes have not been followed in chronic feeding studies.

The clinically observed side effects of TP (Bowers, 1970; Car-

roll *et al.*, 1970; Coppen *et al.*, 1967; Smith and Prockop, 1962)
include drowsiness, euphoria, nystagmus, "light-headedness," nausea and visual blurring. In combination with MAO inhibitors
toxic symptoms are more troublesome, and include nystagmus, behavior resembling alcohol intoxication, tremor, hyperreflexia,
clonus, flushing, sweating, paresthesiae and orthostatic hypotension
(Coppen *et al.*, 1963; Glassman and Platman, 1969; Hodge *et al.*,
1964; Oates and Sjoerdsma, 1960; Pare, 1963).

SUMMARY

The importance of hypothesis-oriented therapeutic trials in depression is outlined. The major benefit of such trials may be to
clarify which clinical features of depression can be accounted
for in terms of monoamine dysfunction, and to identify elements of the depressive syndromes for which another explanation must be sought.

The clinical trials of the indoleamine precursors in the treatment of depression are reviewed. 5-Hydroxytryptophan has not
proved generally useful but further studies with high dosage are
warranted. Tryptophan appears to potentiate the actions of
MAO inhibitors; however, the regular clinical use of this combination is not practical, because of side effects. The early claim
that tryptophan was effective by itself is critically examined. The
methodological defects of the original study are discussed. A rigorous evaluation of this claim is described in detail. It is concluded that tryptophan does not possess significant antidepressant
properties in severely ill patients.

The clinical trials of tryptophan are discussed with reference
to the biochemical pharmacology of tryptophan in depression.
Recent evidence suggests that the hypothesis of Curzon and
Green, which assigned an etiological role to liver tryptophan
pyrrolase in depression, cannot be accepted in its original form.

The possibility of an enzyme defect at the level of brain tryp-
tophan-5-hydroxylase in depression is discussed. The available
clinical evidence is consistent with this possibility.

The potential antitherapeutic action of large pyridoxine supplements in the clinical trials of tryptophan is considered, in the
light of recent evidence, that pyridoxine antagonizes the central
actions of l-dopa.

SUGGESTIONS FOR FURTHER STUDIES

1. A direct assessment of the interaction between pyridoxine and the central effects of l-tryptophan in man.
2. An evaluation of the antidepressant actions of l-tryptophan in mildly and moderately ill patients. For a convincing answer, the study should compare tryptophan with a known antidepressant, such as imipramine, with a placebo control group being included also.
3. A study of the antidepressant effects of large doses of 5-hydroxytryptophan (>3 gm per day), preferably with a peripheral decarboxylase inhibitor as well.

REFERENCES

Armitage, P.: *Sequential Medical Trials.* Oxford, O.U.P., 1960.

Azmitia, E.C. and McEwen, B.S.: Corticosterone regulation of tryptophan hydroxylase in midbrain of the rat. *Science,* 166:1274-1276, 1969.

Barbeau, A.: L-dopa therapy in Parkinson's disease: A critical review of nine years' experience. *Can Med Assoc J,* 101:791-800, 1969.

Bazelon, M., Paine, R.S., Cowie, V.A., Hunt, P., Honck, J.C. and Mahanand, D.: Reversal of hypotonia in infants with Down's syndrome by administration of 5-hydroxytryptophan. *Lancet,* I:1130-1133, 1967.

Beck, A.T., Ward, C.H., Mendelson, M., Mock, J. and Erbaugh, J.: An inventory for measuring depression. *Arch Gen Psychiatry,* 4:561-571, 1961.

Bliss, E.L., Aclion, J. and Zwanziger, J.: Metabolism of norepinephrine, serotonin and dopamine in rat brain with stress. *J Pharmacol Exp Ther,* 164:122-134, 1968.

Bowers, M.B.: Cerebrospinal fluid 5-hydroxyindoles and behaviour after l-tryptophan and pyridoxine administration to psychiatric patients. *Neuropharmacology,* 9:599-604, 1970.

Broadhurst, A.D.: L-tryptophan versus E.C.T. *Lancet,* 1:1392-1393, 1970.

Brodie, H.K.H. and Barchas, J.: Personal communication, 1971.

Bunney, W.E., Brodie, H.K.H., Murphy, D.L. and Goodwin, F.K.: Studies of alpha methyl-para-tyrosine, l-dopa and l-tryptophan in depression and mania. *Am J Psychiatry,* 127:872-881, 1971.

Calne, D.B.: L-dopa in the treatment of Parkinsonism. *Clin Pharmacol Ther,* 11:789-801, 1970.

Carlsson, A.: Functional significance of drug-induced changes in brain monoamine levels. *Progr Brain Res,* 8:9-27, *Biogenic Amines.* Ed. H.E. Himwich and W.A. Himwich, Elsevier, Amsterdam, 1964.

Carroll, B.J., Fielding, J.F. and Blashki, T.G.: Ratings of Depression: A Comparison of the Zung and Hamilton Scales. In press.

Carroll, B.J. and Dodge, J.: Unpublished observations.

Carroll, B.J., Mowbray, R.M. and Davies, B.M.: Sequential comparison of l-tryptophan with E.C.T. in severe depression. *Lancet,* I:967-969, 1970.

Carroll, B.J. and Sharp, P.T.: Rubidium and Lithium: Opposite Effects on Amine-Mediated Excitement. In press.

Cazzullo, C.L., Mangoni, A. and Masherpa, A.: Tryptophan Metabolism in Affective Psychoses. *Br J Psychiatry,* 112:157-162, 1966.

Coppen, A. and Noguera, R.: L-tryptophan in depression. *Lancet,* I:111, 1970.

Coppen, A., Shaw, D.M. and Farrell, J.P.: Potentiation of the antidepressive effect of a monoamine oxidase inhibitor by tryptophan. *Lancet,* I:79-81, 1963.

Coppen, A., Shaw, D.M., Herzberg, B. and Maggs, R.: Tryptophan in the treatment of depression. *Lancet,* II:1178-1180, 1967.

Copper, A.: Personal communication. 1970.

Curzon, G. and Bridges, P.K.: Tryptophan Metabolism in Depression. *J Neurol Neurosurg Psychiatry,* 33:698-704, 1970.

Davidson, S.: In *Principles and Practice of Medicine.* Livingstone, London, 1964, p.502.

Duvoisin, R.C., Yahr, M.D. and Cote, L.D.: Pyridoxine reversal of l-dopa effects in Parkinsonism. *Trans Amer Neurol Assoc,* 94:81-84, 1969.

Eccleston, D., Ashcroft, G.W., Crawford, T.B.B., Stanton, J.B., Wood, D. and McTurk, P.H.: Effect of tryptophan administration on 5-HIAA in cerebrospinal fluid in man. *J Neurol Neurosurg Psychiatry,* 33:269-272, 1970.

Eidelberg, E. and Schwartz, A.S.: Possible mechanism of action of morphine on brain. *Nature,* 225:1152-1153, 1970.

Fellman, J.H. and Roth, E.S.: Inhibition of tyrosine aminotransferase activity by L-3,4-dihydroxyphenylalanine. *Biochemistry,* 10:408-414, 1971.

Fuxe, K. and Ungerstedt, U.: Localisation of 5-hydroxytryptamine uptake in rat brain after intraventricular injection. *J Pharm Pharmacol,* 19:335-337, 1967.

Glassman, A. and Jaffe, F.: Cited in Glassman, A.: Indoleamines and affective disorders. *Psychosom Med,* 31:107-114, 1969.

Glassman, A.H. and Platman, S.R.: Potentiation of a monoamine oxidase inhibitor by tryptophan. *J Psychiatry Res,* 7:83-88, 1969.

Green, A.R. and Curzon, G.: Decrease of 5-hydroxytryptamine in the brain provoked by hydrocortisone and its prevention by allopurinol. *Nature,* 220:1095-1097, 1968.

Green, A.R. and Curzon, G.: The effect of tryptophan metabolites on brain 5-hydroxytryptamine metabolism. *Biochem Pharmacol,* 19:2061-2068, 1970.

Harper, A.E., Benevenga, N.J. and Wohlhueter, R.M.: Effects of ingestion of disproportionate amounts of amino acids. *Physiol Rev,* 50:428-558, 1970.

Hertz, D. and Sulman, F.G.: Preventing depression with tryptophan. *Lancet,* 1:531-532, 1968.

Hodge, J.V., Oates, J.A. and Sjoerdsma, A.: Reduction of the central effects of tryptophan by a decarboxylase inhibitor. *Clin Pharmacol Ther,* 5:149-155, 1964.

Hoyland, V.J., Shillito, E.E. and Vogt, M.: The effect of parachlorophenylalanine on the behaviour of cats. *Br J Pharmacol,* 40:659-667, 1970.

Johnston, J.P.: Some observations upon a new inhibitor of monoamine oxidase in brain tissue. *Biochem Pharmacol,* 17:1285-1297, 1968.

Kim, J.H. and Mills, L.L.: The functional significance of changes in activity of the enzymes, tryptophan pyrrolase and tyrosine transaminase, after induction in intact rats and in the isolated, perfused rat liver. *J Biol Chem,* 244:1410-1416, 1969.

Kline, N.S. and Sacks, W.: Relief of depression within one day using an MAO inhibitor and intravenous 5-HTP. *Am J Psychiatry,* 120:274-275, 1963.

Kline, N.S., Sacks, W. and Simpson, G.M.: Further studies on one-day treatment of depression with 5-HTP. *Am J Psychiatry,* 121:379-381, 1964.

Knox, W.E.: Two mechanisms which increase *in vivo* the liver tryptophan peroxidase activity: Specific enzyme adaptation and stimulation of the pituitary-adrenal system. *Br J Exp Pathol,* 32:462-469, 1951.

Knox, W.E. and Auerbach, V.H.: The hormonal control of tryptophan peroxidase in the rat. *J Biol Chem,* 214:307-313, 1955.

Korf, J. and Praag, H.M. van: The intravenous probenecid test: A possible aid in evaluation of the serotonin hypothesis on the pathogenesis of depressions. *Psychopharmacologia,* 18:129-132, 1970.

Lichtensteiger, W., Mutzner, U. and Langemann, H.: Uptake of 5-hydroxytryptamine and 5-hydroxytryptophan by neurons of the central nervous system normally containing catecholamines. *J Neurochem,* 14:489-497, 1967.

Lovenberg, W., Jéquier, E. and Sjoerdsma, A.: Tryptophan hydroxylation in mammalian systems. *Adv Pharmacol Chemother,* 6A:21-36, 1968.

Mena, I., Court, J., Fuenzalida, S., Papavasiliou, P.S. and Cotzias, G.C.: Modification of chronic manganese poisoning. Treatment with l-dopa or 5-OH tryptophane. *N Engl J Med,* 282:5-10, 1970.

Mendels, J.: Personal communication, 1970.

Moir, A.T.B. and Eccleston, D.: The effects of precursor loading in the cerebral metabolism of 5-hydroxyindoles. *J Neurochem,* 15:1093-1108, 1968.

Nistico, G. and Preziosi, P.: Brain and liver tryptophan pathways and adrenocortical activation during Restraint Stress. *Pharmacol Res Comm,* 1:363-368, 1969.

Oates, J.A. and Sjoerdsma, A.: Neurologic effects of tryptophan in patients receiving a monoamine oxidase inhibitor. *Neurology,* 10:1076-1078, 1960.

Pare, C.M.B.: Potentiation of monoamine oxidase inhibitors by tryptophan. *Lancet,* II:527-528, 1963.

Pare, C.M.B. and Sandler, M.: A clinical and biochemical study of a trial of iproniazid in the treatment of depression. *J Neurol Neurosurg Psychiatry*, 22:247-251, 1959.

Persson, T. and Roos, B.E.: 5-Hydroxytryptophan for depression. *Lancet*, II:987-988, 1967.

Persson, T. and Waldeck, B.: Effect of protriptyline on the formation of (3_H) noradrenaline from (3_H) dopa. *J Pharm Pharmacol*, 20:966-968, 1968.

Praag, H.M. van, Korf, J. and Puite, J.: 5-Hydroxyindoleacetic acid levels in the cerebrospinal fluid of depressive patients treated with probenecid. *Nature*, 225:1259-1260, 1970.

Praag, H.M. van and Korf, J.: L-tryptophan in depression. *Lancet*, II:612, 1970.

Rapoport, M.I., Beisel, W.R. and Dinterman, R.E.: Circardian periodicity of tryptophan metabolism. *J Clin Invest*, 47:934, 1968.

Richter, D.: Tryptophan metabolism in mental illness. In Himwich, H.E., Kety, S.S. and Smythies, J.R. (Eds.) : *Amines and Schizophrenia*, Oxford, O.U.P., 1967.

Roos, B.E. and Sjöstrom, R.: 5-Hydroxyindoleacetic acid (and homovanillic acid) levels in the cerebrospinal fluid after probenecid application in patients with manic depressive psychosis. *Pharmacologia Clinica*, 1:153-155, 1969.

Rose, D.P.: Oral contraceptives and depression. *Lancet*, II:321, 1969.

Rubin, R.T.: Adrenal cortical activity changes in manic depressive illness. Influence on intermediary metabolism of tryptophan. *Arch Gen Psychiatry*, 17:671-679, 1967.

Shaskan, E.G. and Snyder, S.H.: Kinetics of serotonin accumulation into slices from rat brain: Relationship to catecholamine uptake. *J Pharmacol Exp Ther*, 175:404-418, 1970.

Siegal, S.: *Nonparametric Statistics for the Behavioural Sciences*. New York, 1956.

Sjoerdsma, A. (Moderator), Lovenberg, W., Engelman, K., Carpenter, W.T., Wyatt, R. J. and Gessa, G.L.: Serotonin Now: Clinical implications of inhibiting its synthesis with parachlorophenylalanine. *Ann Intern Med*, 73:607-629, 1970.

Smith, B. and Prockop, D.J.: Central nervous system effects of ingestion of L-tryptophan by normal subjects. *N Engl J Med*, 267:1338-1341, 1962.

Sokal, R.R. and Rohlf, J.: *Biometry*. San Francisco, 1969; White, A., Handler, P., Smith, E.L. and Stettin, de W.: *Principles of Biochemistry*. New York, 1959.

Wyatt, R.J., Engelman, K., Kupfer, D.J., Fram, D.H., Sjoerdsma, A. and Snyder, F.: Effects of L-tryptophan (a natural sedative) on human sleep. *Lancet*, II:842-846, 1970.

Yuwiler, A., Geller, E. and Eiduson, S.: Studies on 5-hydroxytryptophan decarboxylase. 1. *In vitro* inhibition and substrate interaction. *Arch Biochem*, 80:162-173, 1959.

Chapter 10

SODIUM AND POTASSIUM TRANSFER TO CEREBROSPINAL FLUID IN SEVERE DEPRESSION

BERNARD J. CARROLL

INTRODUCTION

DISTURBANCES of water and electrolyte metabolism in depressive illness have often been suggested, and a number of established findings have been demonstrated, as well as some for which the evidence is still in doubt (see Coppen, 1967; Baer *et al.,* 1970 for detailed reviews).

One such disputed finding is that of Coppen (1960) who measured the rate of entry of radioactive sodium-24 (^{24}Na) from plasma to the lumbar cerebrospinal fluid (CSF). He found that depressed patients had low transfer rates, compared with control subjects and recovered depressives.

The precise significance of the transfer rate (as it is measured) is not clear. The ^{24}Na which appears within one hour in the lumbar CSF following intravenous injection of the isotope does not come from the ventricles (Selverstone, 1958) but by diffusion from the pia mater and from the cord parenchyma (Davson, 1967). The rate of sodium entry is thus considered to reflect the retention and rate of turnover of sodium by the nervous system. A low transfer rate might be seen as consistent with the postulated increase of intracellular sodium and also with the retention of whole-body sodium in depression (Coppen, 1967; Baer *et al.,* 1969; 1970).

During 1967-68 we carried out a study of the transfer rate of ^{24}Na in severely depressed patients, in an attempt to confirm Coppen's (1960) report. Estimates of adrenocortical function were obtained at the same time because of the known effects of cortisol and of adrenocorticotropic hormone (ACTH) on sodium metabolism (Wasserman *et al.,* 1965). To provide complementary

247

data the transfer rate of radioactive potassium (^{42}K) into CSF was measured as well. Aspects of this study have been reported previously (Carroll *et al.*, 1969).

SUBJECTS AND METHODS

Eleven patients had transfer rates measured before and after treatment. All were severely ill, diagnosed as psychotic endogenous depressives, who required admission to hospital and whose clinical features were as described in Chapter 2. Their mean age was sixty-three years and they had been ill for an average time of six weeks before admission. Their treatments are detailed in Table 10-I. The first test was carried out in the second week after admission and retesting was delayed until at least one week after the last ECT.

Six other depressed patients were studied only before treatment, as were two manic patients and five control subjects (Tables 10-II and 10-III). Except as indicated in Table 10-I no patient received any drugs other than amylobarbitone or aspirin.

THE TEST PROCEDURE

All patients rested in bed and received 2 microcuries of ^{24}Na and 150 microcuries of ^{42}K in isotonic sodium chloride intravenously after 20 ml of blood had been taken for background counting and for plasma cortisol estimation. Premedication was not given. Lumbar puncture was performed with the patient in the lateral position and was timed so that the CSF was being collected between fifty-five and sixty-five minutes after the injection of ^{24}Na. Ten ml of CSF were taken in one tube and a small amount was removed after mixing for cytological examination to confirm the absence of contamination by blood. Immediately after the lumbar puncture another 20 ml of blood was collected from the opposite arm.

COUNTING PROCEDURE

Differential counting of ^{24}Na and ^{42}K in 4 ml aliquots of CSF and plasma was planned, with the use of a well scintillation detector (Nuclear, Chicago). Resolution of gamma emission by ^{24}Na from that due to ^{42}K by pulse-height analysis presented no difficulty, since the high energy 2.75 MeV radiation of ^{24}Na could be measured. However, the estimation of ^{42}K in the presence of ^{24}Na was subject to considerable error, since the low energy gamma ray of ^{24}Na (1.37 MeV) is not easily resolved from the 1.52 MeV radiation of ^{42}K and their scintillation spectra overlap to a large extent. Values given for ^{42}K transfer rates have an error of ±50 per cent; the systematic error of the ^{24}Na estimations was ±10 per cent.

The rate of entry of the isotopes from plasma to CSF was expressed as the following ratio:

$$\frac{\text{CSF concentration}}{\text{Plasma concentration}} \times 100 \text{ per cent at 1 hour}$$

RADIATION DOSAGE

The whole body radiation received from $100\mu Ci$ of ^{24}Na and $150\mu Ci$ of ^{42}K amounts to 0.3 rads. This compares with an exposure of 1.5 rads during a barium meal or enema and 1.0 rads during intravenous pyelography.

MEASURES OF ADRENOCORTICAL FUNCTION

Plasma cortisol was measured as 11-hydroxycorticosteroids by the fluorometric method of Mattingly (1962). Satisfactory estimation of the very low levels present in CSF was not possible by this method. The midnight 2 mg dexamethasone suppression test was performed as described in Chapter 5, using the plasma 11-OHCS level the following morning as the index of suppression.

RESULTS

Sodium

In eleven patients before treatment the mean transfer rate was 2.7 and this value rose to 3.2 after treatment. The rate increased in seven and decreased in four individuals; the mean values did not differ significantly and a wide range of results was found on both occasions (Table 10-I).

When the three subjects who had begun treatment before the first test are omitted the mean values are 2.5 and 3.3 (paired $t = 1.50$, $p < 0.10$).

In the six depressives studied only on admission the mean transfer rate was 3.2 (Table 10-II) and for the five control sub-

Depressive Illness

TABLE 10-I

^{24}Na TRANSFER ON ADMISSION AND RECOVERY*

Patient	Sex	Age	^{24}Na Transfer Rate(%) On Admission	On Recovery	Interval (Days) Between Testing	Treatment
1	M	57	2.3	2.6	21	ECT
2	F	72	2.5	2.8	64	ECT
3	M	52	3.0	3.7	35	ECT
4	M	62	2.9	1.8	41	ECT
5	F	74	2.8†	3.1	41	ECT
6	F	75	4.3‡	3.4	20	ECT
7	M	59	4.0	3.9	64	ECT and
8	F	61	1.9	2.1	28	imipramine
9	M	62	2.4	5.7	56	ECT and
10	F	72	2.7§	2.3	74	imipramine
11	F	51	1.3	3.7	81	ECT and
Mean		63	2.7	3.2	48	amitriptyline
S.D.		—	4.7	1.0	—	Imipramine

* t = 1.09, not significant (paired t).
† After four ECT.
‡ After three ECT.
§ After two weeks on imipramine.

jects the mean value was 2.1 (Table 10-III). The two manic patients had transfer rates of 1.5 and 2.9.

The mean plasma cortisol (11-OHCS) levels at the time of isotope injection in the eleven patients tested twice were 18.8 (S.D. 6.4) μg/100 ml on admission and 14.2 (S.D. 5.0) μg/100 ml after treatment. There was no significant correlation between the plasma cortisol levels and the ^{24}Na transfer rates. Ten of these

TABLE 10-II

^{24}Na TRANSFER IN DEPRESSED PATIENTS ON ADMISSION ONLY

Patient	Sex	Age	^{24}Na Transfer Rate(%)
a	F	62	3.8
b	F	50	2.6
c	F	80	2.9
d	F	42	3.4
e	M	42	2.7
f	M	55	3.9
Mean		55	3.2
S.D.		—	0.56

TABLE 10-III

^{24}Na TRANSFER IN CONTROL PATIENTS

Patient	Diagnosis	Sex	Age	^{24}Na Transfer Rate(%)
v	Anxiety state	F	30	1.8
w	Schizophrenia	M	17	1.6
x	Hysteria	F	68	2.8
y	Adolescent reaction	M	19	2.5
z	Prostatic hypertrophy	M	66	1.8
Mean			40	2.1
S.D.			—	0.5

TABLE 10-IV

^{42}K TRANSFER RATES (%)

Patient	On Admission	On Recovery
1	—	10
2	5.0	3.6
3	9.0	4.2
4	2.8	—
5	—	66.0
6	—	12.2
7	21.0	29.0
8	11.0	16.0
9	27.6	37.0
10	14.0	20.0
11	22.0	8.0
a	46.0	
b	15.0	
c	16.0	
d	33.0	
e	16.0	
f	33.0	
v	8.0	
w	*	
x	—	
y	—	
z	*	

— = Result not reliable.
* ^{42}K not given.

patients had an abnormal response to the midnight 2 mg dexamethasone suppression test before treatment while all suppressed normally after recovery. No correlation was found between the ^{24}Na transfer rate and response to dexamethasone.

Potassium

The results for ^{42}K transfer rates which were considered acceptable are given in Table 10-IV. The rates are considerably higher than those of ^{24}Na and a large variation is apparent.

Of the seven patients for whom data are available before and after treatment the ^{42}K transfer rate rose in five and decreased in two.

The mean value on admission (n = 14) was 19.6 and on recovery (n = 10) was 19.7. These results do not differ significantly.

DISCUSSION

Sodium Transfer

In the patients we studied no significant difference could be demonstrated between the ^{24}Na transfer rates of depressed, recovered and control patients. To this extent our results do not seem to agree with those of Coppen (1960). Since the values were distributed over a wide range, small sample numbers are not really adequate for the purpose of showing differences between groups of patients. Under these circumstances the most appropriate strategy is to repeat observations in individual subjects.

In the eleven patients whom we have retested the mean transfer rate moved in the same direction as Coppen had suggested (2.7 ± 0.7 before treatment compared with 3.2 ± 1.0 after recovery). When the three subjects pretreated before the first test are omitted the mean values become 2.5 and 3.3 in eight subjects. The corresponding data of Coppen were 2.4 and 3.6 in three patients. With these small numbers the differences are not significant but the trend is certainly suggestive.

Two other groups have reported ^{24}Na transfer rates in depressed patients. Fotherby *et al.* (1963) found no difference between the transfer rates of eleven depressed and eleven schizophrenic subjects. A subgroup of four severely depressed patients had a mean transfer rate of 2.4, compared with a mean of 3.5

TABLE 10-V

COMPARISON OF PUBLISHED ^{24}Na TRANSFER RESULTS IN
DEPRESSION (Means and S.D.)

| Author | Patients Tested Twice | | | Patients Tested Once | | |
	Depression on Admission	Recovered Depression	Depression	Recovered Depression	Depression Not Responding to ECT
Coppen, 1960	2.4	3.6	2.7 ± 0.67	3.8 ± 1.55	2.4 ± 0.54
No.	3	3	20	10	11
Fotherby *et al.*, 1963 .			3.48 ± 1.9		
No.			11		
Present series	2.7 ± 0.7	3.2 ± 1.0	3.2 ± 0.56		
No.	11	11	6		
Baker, 1971	2.0	4.4	2.8 ± 1.27		1.9
No.	1	1	12*		1

* Eight psychotic depressed, and four manic depressed.

for the original group of eleven. Baker (1971) studied forty-six
patients in six diagnostic groups and found that the transfer
rates of ^{22}Na in eighteen manic, manic depressed and psychotic
depressed subjects were *significantly lower* than those in twenty-
eight neurotic depressed, schizophrenic and miscellaneous patients (mean 2.7-v-3.6). In a small number a trend was noted for
increasing transfer rate with recovery.

The results of the four studies are summarized in Tables 10-V
and 10-VI.

To overcome the possible bias in small samples which may account for some of the discrepancies seen in Tables 10-V and
10-VI the results from all four series have been pooled and mean
transfer rates calculated on the larger samples—Table 10-VII. A

TABLE 10-VI

^{24}Na TRANSFER RATES IN CONTROL PATIENTS

Author	No.	Transfer Rate	Patients
Coppen, 1960	12	3.9 ± 0.98	Normal Ss.
	19	4.0 ± 1.3	Schizophrenic
Fotherby *et al.*, 1963	11	3.16 ± 0.70	Schizophrenic
Carroll *et al.*, 1969	5	2.1 ± 0.5	Miscellaneous
Baker, 1971	12	4.3 ± 1.5	Miscellaneous
	4	3.5 ± 1.2	Schizophrenic

TABLE 10-VII

SODIUM TRANSFER RATES: POOLED DATA

Patients	Number	Transfer Rate (Mean ± S.D.)
Manic	8	2.35 ± 0.67
Depressed	60	2.91 ± 1.12
Recovered depressed	21	3.49 ± 1.29
Control	63	3.71 ± 1.57
Manic-v-Depressed		$t = -1.38$, not significant
Manic-v-Recovered		$t = -2.36$, $p < 0.02$ (one-tail)
Manic-v-Control		$t = -2.41$, $p < 0.01$ (one-tail)
Depressed-v-Recovered		$t = -1.94$, $p < 0.05$ (one-tail)
Depressed-v-Control		$t = -3.24$, $p < 0.001$ (one-tail)
Recovered-v-Control		$t = -0.59$, not significant

progressive rise in the mean values is seen, with the results in manic and depressed patients being significantly below those of recovered depressed and control subjects.

These results do support the original conclusion of Coppen (1960). They also illustrate the difficulties inherent in the use of small samples of patients and the need for replication of studies so that adequate data can be accumulated.

MANIC PATIENTS

The sodium transfer values found in the two manic patients were 1.5 and 2.9. Baker (1971) found a mean rate of 2.4 (S.D. 0.59) in six manic subjects. From Table 10-VII the mean transfer rate in mania is lower than in depression but the available data is not sufficient to yield a significant difference ($p > 0.10$). These findings tend to support the proposal of Coppen *et al.* (1966) that residual sodium is increased in mania to a greater extent than it is in depression.

Potassium Transfer

No significant change in potassium transfer between our depressed and recovered patients was found. This finding may be considered consistent with the reports that there is no change in whole-body or exchangeable potassium in depression (Gibbons, 1960; Coppen and Shaw, 1963; Platman *et al.*, 1970). Our control data are not adequate to allow comment on the claim of Shaw and Coppen (1966) that whole-body potassium is low in depression and fails to increase with clinical recovery. This claim could not be confirmed by Platman *et al.* (1970) using whole-body counting rather than isotope dilution techniques.

The higher transfer rate of ^{42}K into CSF than that of ^{24}Na is of interest in view of the studies of Bradbury and Kleeman (1967) who found that brain and CSF potassium levels remain remarkably stable in the face of severe alterations in whole-body potassium. An active transport mechanism for ^{42}K into CSF was found by these workers whereas sodium transfer is a slower process and in the lumbar theca may depend on passive diffusion. The results of Bradbury and Kleeman cast serious doubt on the proposal of Shaw and Coppen (1966) that the reduction in whole-body potassium which they observed would cause a reduction in neuronal membrane potentials; even if the whole-body data are accepted as reliable, the brain does not appear to be involved, but is protected from the general ionic disturbance.

CONCLUSIONS AND SUGGESTIONS FOR FURTHER STUDIES

Our earlier conclusion (Carroll *et al.,* 1969) that the transfer rate of ^{24}Na was not significantly affected in depression must now be reconsidered: the necessity for cautious negative conclusions from small samples is apparent. The results of Baker (1971) and the pooled results from the four series indicate that sodium transfer is reduced in both depressed and manic patients. The abnormality seems also to be reversible with clinical recovery. Coppen's original conclusions (1960) would appear to be confirmed.

The potassium transfer rates which we have obtained (accepting the error of the estimations) did not differ between depression and recovery and no trend was apparent.

Further studies of the sodium transfer rate are indicated to examine the factors responsible for the abnormality in depressed and manic patients. Since sodium retention and urinary 17-hydroxycorticosteroid excretion are positively related (Baer *et al.,* 1969) a detailed study of hypothalamic-pituitary-adrenal function together with transfer rate estimations may be suggested, including the study of CSF cortisol levels.

The reported finding of a low sodium content in the CSF of

depressed patients (Ueno *et al.*, 1961) also requires confirmation, in conjunction with studies of the sodium transfer rate.

Since the abnormality of sodium transfer now appears to be established, further experimental strategies are required to determine what is the functional significance of this finding and to relate it to measures of whole-body sodium turnover, as well as to clinical features in depressed patients.

REFERENCES

Baer, L., Durell, J., Bunney, W.E., Levy, B.S. and Cardon, P.V.: Sodium-22 retention and 17-hydroxycorticosteroid excretion in affective disorders. *J Psychiatry Res*, 6:289-297, 1969.

Baer, L., Platman, S.R. and Fieve, R.R.: The role of electrolytes in affective disorders. *Arch Gen Psychiatry*, 22:108-113, 1970.

Baker, E.F.W.: Sodium transfer to cerebrospinal fluid in functional psychiatric illness. *Can Psychiatry Assoc J*, 16:167-170, 1971.

Bradbury, M.W.B. and Kleeman, C.R.: Stability of the potassium content of cerebrospinal fluid and brain. *Am J Physiol*, 213:519-528, 1967.

Carroll, B.J., Steven, L., Pope, R.A. and Davies, B.: Sodium transfer from plasma to CSF in severe depressive illness. *Arch Gen Psychiatry*, 21:77-81, 1969.

Coppen, A.: Abnormality of the blood-cerebrospinal fluid barrier of patients suffering from a depressive illness. *J Neurol Neurosurg Psychiatry*, 23:156-161, 1960.

Coppen, A.J. and Shaw, D.M.: Mineral metabolism in melancholia. *Br Med J*, 2:1439-1444, 1963.

Coppen, A., Shaw, D.M., Farrell, J.P. and Costain, R.: Mineral metabolism in mania. *Br Med J*, i:71-75, 1966.

Coppen, A.: The Biochemistry of affective disorders. *Br J Psychiatry*, 113:1237-1264, 1967.

Davson, H.: *Physiology of the Cerebrospinal Fluid*. Churchill, London, 1967.

Fotherby, K., Ashcroft, G.W., Affleck, J.W. and Forrest, A.D.: Studies on sodium transfer and 5-hydroxyindoles in depressive illness. *J Neurol Neurosurg Psychiatry*, 26:71-73, 1962.

Gibbons, J.L.: Total body sodium and potassium in depressive illness. *Clin Sci*, 19:133-138, 1960.

Mattingly, D.: A simple fluorimetric method for the estimation of free 11-hydroxycorticoids in human plasma. *J Clin Pathol*, 15:369-374, 1962.

Platman, S.R., Fieve, R.R. and Pierson, R.N.: Effect of mood and lithium carbonate on total body potassium. *Arch Gen Psychiatry*, 22:297-300, 1970.

Shaw, D.M. and Coppen, A.: Potassium and water distribution in depression. *Br J Psychiatry*, 112:269-276, 1966.

Selverstone, B.: In Wolstenholme, G. and O'Connor, C.M. (Eds.). *Ciba Foundation Symposium on Cerebrospinal Fluid.* Churchill, London, p. 147, 1958.

Ueno, Y.: Electrolyte metabolism in blood and cerebrospinal fluid in psychoses. *Folia Psychiat Neurol Jap,* 15:304-326, 1961.

Wasserman, M.J., Belton, N.R. and Millichap, J.G.: Effect of corticotropin (ACTH) on experimental seizures. *Neurology,* 15:1136-1141, 1965.

Section IV

The Measurement of Depression

Chapter 11

THE CLASSIFICATION OF DEPRESSION

Robert M. Mowbray

THE term "depression" applies to a state of lowered affect, a mood of prevailing sadness which, when encountered clinically, may be incidental to illness or pathognomic of illness. It can mean symptom or syndrome, and as either, can be regarded as a psychological reaction or as a manifest end-point of some physiological or physiochemical process. The condition can be acute or chronic, can present over a wide range of severity and has been variously labeled as primary, secondary, psychotic, manic depressive, neurotic, endogenous, reactive, constitutional, agitated, anaclitic or periodic. It may be overt or masked. It occurs in grief and in reaction to significant life events, or it may be independent of situational factors. Our knowledge of the illness has grown to a point at which the original single term has become too imprecise for definition.

Certain themes have persisted in the literature about depressive illness. Kraepelin's (1921) idea of an *endogenous disorder* was developed against the background of Morel's concept of degeneration of germ plasm, and his assertion that manic depressive psychosis was independent of external influences was later to be confirmed in the claims that a familio-genetic basis for the disorder could be displayed.

The idea of *reactive depression* was stimulated by claims that external influences were significant and that a specific psychopathology of depression could be demonstrated (e.g. Ross, 1926). The dichotomy between endogenous and reactive forms of depression was denied by Mapother (1926) on the grounds of clinical experience and was not found by Lewis (1934) in his classical detailed study of sixty-one cases. However, the dichotomy has persisted in the literature with the added nomenclature of psychotic versus psychoneurotic forms of depression. It is not clear at which point in the history of psychiatry the dichotomous

261

view arose. There is evidence that it predated the Kraepelinian classification, and Altschule (1967) interprets some words of St. Paul as referring to psychotic and nonpsychotic types of depression.

Kraepelin's account of depressive psychosis has survived as classical even though it was written at a time when the psychiatrist's role was confined to meticulous description of the phenomena shown by his depressed patients in asylums. In effect, a condition which is now capable of being treated successfully by a number of methods, is still conceived and classified on the basis of features of the illness shown by patients for whom no treatment was available.

Response to treatment has been proposed as an alternative to the phenomenologically based classification. However, the fact that some forms of depression respond better to ECT and others to drugs or to psychotherapeutic regimes has tended to reinforce the previous dichotomies rather than provide a new basis for classification. As yet, the more conventional basis for classification, etiology, has not proved feasible in spite of widely based and persistent research efforts in studying affective disorders.

The controversy about the nature of depression can be reduced to the question of whether it is to be regarded as a single illness with differing manifestations or as a number of illnesses with at least one common symptom, depression of affect. Rumke (1960) has proposed thirteen types of depression, but the usual alternative to the single-illness view is the dichotomy, variously described as endogenous/reactive, psychotic/neurotic, vital/personal (Van Praag, 1965), physiological/psychological (Pollitt, 1965).

In these dichotomies the distinction is drawn between depression as a basic biological disorder and as a pattern of personal reaction to environmental stress. Other distinctions have been proposed, e.g. by Leonhard (1959) who, in the wider context of affective disorders, distinguished between the *bipolar* form in which the patient shows both manic and depressive features, and the *unipolar* form characterized either by depression alone or by mania alone.

These various ways of conceiving depression have been held by different clinicians as opposing "schools of thought" and clinical observation alone has not provided an adequate basis on which to resolve the conceptual differences.

An alternative approach has been favored. A wide range of observational data is collected from depressed patients and submitted to statistical analysis and in particular to procedures which have been evolved to handle large numbers of variables simultaneously. These multivariate techniques have been applied in order to test the validity of an existing classification or to reveal patterns in the wide variety of phenomena of depression. Over thirty of these studies have appeared in the past twelve years and most of these have already been reviewed by Mendels and Cochrane (1968) and by Costello (1970). In this chapter reference will be made to some of the key studies in order to illustrate the methods, compare the findings and to assess the extent to which the use of factor analysis and discriminant function analysis have successfully contributed to an understanding of depression. A short account of the techniques of multivariate analysis is presented in Appendix A.

FACTOR ANALYSIS

The factor analytic solution to the problem of one or two forms of depression rests on the manner in which the original observations are resolved. If the major factor is general, all the observations have been affected by a single common underlying characteristic, and this is consistent with the one depression viewpoint. If, on the other hand, the major factor is bipolar, i.e. splits the observations into positive and negative loadings, in such a way that the positive features characterize one type of depression and the negative features characterize the other, then this argues in favor of the "two depressions" viewpoint.

Hamilton and White (1959) offered this type of reasoning in their original study. From their factor analysis of ratings made on depressed patients they identified a bipolar factor in which retardation and agitation were contrasted. In the overall pattern of this factor certain other features were associated with retardation and others with agitation. When these constellations of features were examined in patients, it was found that patients with retarded depression constituted a different population from those with agitated depression. The emergence of a factor containing two distinct patterns of signs and symptoms on the basis of which depressed patients could be differentiated in a clinically realistic manner was taken to be sufficient evidence for the two-way view of depression.

In a double-blind controlled trial of imipramine carried out at Newcastle, Kiloh and Ball (1961) found that patients diagnosed as suffering from endogenous depression made a significantly better response to the drug than patients assessed as showing neurotic depression. Further, their clinical observations confirmed the distinction between endogenous and neurotic forms of depression. Kiloh and Garside (1963) subsequently carried out a factor analysis on the data of this trial, which comprised a list of thirty-five clinically observed features noted as present or absent in each of the 143 cases treated. Their factor analysis yielded a general factor and a bipolar factor which was of greater magnitude. In ninety-two cases the diagnosis of endogenous or neurotic depression had been made with reasonable certainty. In these cases the pattern of the bipolar factor gave a high correspondence with the endogenous or neurotic diagnosis. Again, a clear-cut distinction between two forms of depression had been demonstrated although the terms used were different from the retarded versus agitated distinction made by Hamilton and White.

This study made the question of classifying depression into endogenous and neurotic more than an academic or theoretical issue. It became a matter of some practical clinical concern in view of the originally reported different responses of patients suffering from the two kinds of depression to what at that time was a new form of treatment, antidepressant medication. Other workers were stimulated to use factor analysis, to examine both the classification of the illness itself and the significance of particular features of depression.

Kiloh and Garside, for example, had found that early morning wakening was related to the endogenous end of the bipolar factor and initial insomnia to the reactive end, a finding in line with the current thinking about the sleep disturbance in depression. However, in the same issue of the journal in which the Kiloh and Garside findings appeared, Costello and Smith (1963) reported a preliminary study which eventually led to their claim that nurses' observations had not revealed any differences in sleep patterns between a group of patients with endogenous and another with reactive depression. Thus, the confirmation of one part of the clinical "lore" of depression was countermanded by another study. Coincidences of claim and counterclaim appear in the subsequent published reports of factor-analytic studies.

McConaghy and his colleagues (1967) in Melbourne replicated the Kiloh and Garside study. They observed one hundred depressive outpatients on forty clinical features, thirty-two of which were the same as in the Newcastle study. None of the factors which emerged from their analysis of this data differentiated endogenous from neurotic depression. As a further test, they carried out a factor analysis on eight selected features, four of which were considered most likely to be associated with endogenous depression (age over forty; depression worse in morning; weight loss of 7 lb or more; early wakening), and four most likely to be associated with neurotic depression (responsive to environmental change; presence of significant precipitating factors; self-pity; initial insomnia). Even on these restricted items, a factor differentiating between endogenous and neurotic depression did not appear. They found that the presence of the features of one type of depression did not exclude the presence of features of the other. None of the one hundred patients showed all four endogenous features with none of the reactive features, and only one showed the four features of neurotic, with none of the features of endogenous depression.

The Australian workers could not confirm the Newcastle findings. However, in the same journal issue, some support to Kiloh and Garside was offered from Harvard. Rosenthal and Gudeman (1967), in the paper immediately following that of McConaghy and his colleagues, reported a factor analysis of forty-eight signs and symptoms shown by one hundred depressed women. This yielded two factors—the first being consistent with the endogenous pattern found by Kiloh and Garside. The second factor was described as "the self-pitying constellation" and included features such as hypochondriasis, self pity, blaming the environment, demanding and complaining behavior, reactivity to the environment, hostility and irritability. Although they confirmed Kiloh and Garside's picture of endogenous depression, their second type of depression did not emerge as a polar opposite, but from a separate factor. Accordingly they chose to interpret their two factors as representing common clinical pictures rather than two separate disease entities or clear-cut patient groups.

Kendell (1968), at the Maudsley Hospital, factor-analyzed data recorded from a series of seven hundred depressed patients and extracted twelve first-order factors, which he claimed were meaningful in that they were logically or psychologically related. However, none of these corresponded to a diagnostic entity. Continuing the analysis, he reduced these factors to four second-order factors, the first of which was identified with neurotic depression, and the second with psychotic depression. The third factor could not be interpreted and the fourth seemed to be related to neuroticism, or instability of personality. These four factors were then in their turn reduced to two third-order factors, the first providing "an almost uncontaminated profile of neurotic depression and the second a similarly clear profile of psychotic depression." However, these emerged as distinct factors and not, as in Kiloh and Garside's study as a bipolar factor. A bipolar factor, similar to the Newcastle factor, emerged from Kendell's data at the fourth order of analysis and only at a very minor level of significance.

On the balance of evidence, the original clear-cut distinction between endogenous and neurotic depression reported by Kiloh and Garside had, at best, been blurred and sometimes contradicted by subsequent work.

In the meantime, Carney, Roth and Garside (1965), from Newcastle again, had reported a detailed study of 129 depressed inpatients from whom ECT had been prescribed. Their sample of patients differed from that in Kiloh and Garside's investigation which had been conducted on outpatients being treated by an antidepressant drug. In particular it would be surmised that inpatients being treated with ECT would be more severely depressed than the outpatient group. Carney, Roth and Garside also used a more sophisticated technique of factor analysis than was employed in the Kiloh and Garside study.

In spite of these differences in patients and method, a bipolar and general factor were again isolated. As before, the bipolar factor was highly correlated with the assessment of either endogenous or neurotic depression. Further, the cluster of features associated with endogenous depression agreed with that reported by Kiloh and Garside. Once again it was concluded that the pattern yielded by the data "broadly corresponded with the classical descriptions of endogenous and neurotic depression."

However, although the general pattern was in agreement, differences appeared between the two Newcastle studies about the significance of certain features. As Costello (1970) points out, the significantly high relationship between type of sleep disturbance and type of depression found originally by Kiloh and Garside did not appear in the Carney, Roth and Garside study. The second study also found a significantly high negative correlation between anxiety and endogenous depression compared to the original study in which the correlation was negative but not significant; a discrepancy which could be attributed to the difficulty in making a reliable clinical distinction between anxiety and agitation. Carney, Roth and Garside also drew attention to two other findings which were at variance with accepted clinical beliefs, viz. that "neither family history nor morning aggravation of the symptoms had appreciable correlations with diagnosis."

As before, the "type" of depression was found to be related to response to treatment. At follow-up of the patients at three and six months after ECT approximately 80 per cent of the endogenous but only 17 per cent of the neurotic depressives were considered to have responded well. A predictive index of response to ECT was constructed by calculating weights for ten clinical features. Features such as weight loss, pyknic habitus, early waking, somatic and paranoid delusions were weighted toward a good response, and among others, anxiety symptoms worse in the evening, self-pity, hypochondriacal and hysterical features toward a poor response to ECT. This index was found to be capable of giving correct forecasts of response to ECT at six months in 87 per cent of patients.

Carney, Roth and Garside's prognostic features confirmed these previously isolated by Hobson (1953) and were, in their turn, immediately confirmed independently in the same journal issue by Mendels (1965, a,b,c) who reported that from such features he was able to predict correctly the response to ECT in 90 per cent of his cases. Mendels similarly found that response to ECT could be differentiated in terms of the broad categories endogenous and reactive. However, he did not agree on the major issue of classification, as there was so much overlap of symptoms that he did not differentiate his patients on this basis and referred to the majority as being "endoreactive." Again, the clear-cut distinction between the two forms of depression made by Carney, Roth and Garside was immediately blurred in the simultaneous publications by Mendels.

An example can also be quoted of divergent findings from workers in the same locale. Hamilton and White (1959) in Leeds classified sixty-four male patients into four groups—endogenous, doubtful endogenous, doubtful reactive and reactive. They found that the main difference between these groups lay in their total scores on the Hamilton rating scale, the endogenous being highest, the reactive lowest. Hamilton and White concluded that the distinction between endogenous and reactive was quantitative only, in terms of severity of illness. Rose (1963), again from Leeds, repeated Hamilton and White's study on twenty male and twenty female patients classified into the same four groups, but found no differences between these groups in their Hamilton scores, indicating that all patients were showing depression of equal severity. However, as patients with endogenous depression responded more favorably to ECT, Rose rejected the hypothesis of a quantitative difference and argued in favor of a qualitative distinction between the reactive and endogenous forms of depression.

DISCRIMINANT FUNCTION ANALYSIS

In the second Newcastle study Carney, Roth and Garside went a stage further than Kiloh and Garside in order to demonstrate the dichotomy between endogenous and neurotic depression. They used the loadings of items on the bipolar factor to produce weights which would increase the discrimination between the two categories of depression.

Ten clinical features were selected and weighted from their factor loadings to produce a diagnosis score. For example, nihilistic delusions (+2.49), depressive psychomotor activity (+1.8) and weight loss (+1.61) were loaded toward a diagnosis of endogenous depression and anxiety (−14.), blames others (−1.24) were loaded toward neurotic depression. These weightings were applied whenever one of these items was scored as present in an individual case and the sum of the weights was used as the patient's diagnosis score. When the frequency distribution of these diagnosis scores in the whole group of patients was plotted and tested, a clearly bimodal distribution was found supporting the hypothesis that endogenous and neurotic forms of depression are distinct clinical entities.

Kendell (1968) used weights derived from discriminant function analysis (see Appendix A) of item sheet data from the records of over six hundred depressed patients at the Maudsley Hospital. In the first place, his items showed similar weights to those found by the Newcastle workers. For example, delusions of guilt and retardation were weighted to the psychotic (endogenous) diagnosis, and previous hysterical symptoms and precipitating causes to the neurotic diagnosis. As before these weights were used to provide a diagnosis score. However, in Kendell's group of patients the frequency distribution of these scores was unimodal, without any hint of bimodality. From this Kendell rejected the idea of two distinct clinical entities and suggested that psychotic and neurotic were simply end-points on a single continuum of depression. His use of the term "psychotic" rather than "endogenous" does not indicate a change of emphasis, for in subsequent discussion of the differences between his own "one depression" and the Newcastle "two-depression" viewpoints he treats these terms as synonyms.

The basic question of whether depression is a single or a two-form illness remained as open as when it had been discussed on the basis of clinical judgment alone. However, the question was now posed in such a manner that it could be put to an apparently direct test. If the features which discriminated between psychotic (endogenous) and neurotic depression were weighted, a bimodal distribution of the resultant scores in the group of patients would support the two-illness view, and a unimodal distribution the one-illness view.

A Replication of Kendell's Study

Information on the same items used by Kendell (see Chap. 13) was available for seventy-three depressed patients admitted to our unit in 1967. The records showed that twenty of these patients had been diagnosed as suffering from psychotic and fifty-three from neurotic depression. Granted this smaller population, a replication of Kendell's study was carried out using the same method of discriminant function analysis (Mowbray, 1969).

For each item, proportions were calculated of patients in the psychotic and neurotic categories who showed the feature. The critical ratio (see Appendix A) of the difference between these two proportions was computed and used as the discriminant weight for the item.

This procedure yielded weights of smaller magnitude than Kendell's. When these were applied to produce diagnostic scores for patients, the mean diagnostic scores for the psychotic group (9.5; SD 2.9) was significantly different (p <0.001) from that of the neurotic group (1.2; SD 3.9).

These first steps appeared to confirm Kendell in that they had successfully discriminated between the psychotic and neurotic diagnosis. However, the frequency distribution of the diagnosis scores for the whole group of patients was composed of two approximately normally distributed curves on the continuum, a position more consistent with bimodality of the distribution, and at variance with Kendell.

The weights obtained from the 1967 group were subsequently used to calculate diagnostic scores in eighty-five patients admitted with depression in the following year. On this occasion, no significant difference was found between the mean diagnostic scores for psychotic and neurotic depressives. The failure of weights determined on one occasion to discriminate observations made on a similar sample on a subsequent occasion indicates that these weights were unreliable. The original weights discriminate maximally between the observations made in two groups which have already been differentiated. Thus, errors, random or otherwise, in the original observations will not appear in the original weights, but will operate when the weights are applied to new data.

At Kendell's suggestion, his weights were applied to our combined 1967 and 1968 groups of patients. This led to a significant difference between the mean diagnostic scores for neurotic and psychotic patients. Further, the frequency distribution of the scores was unimodal. This was an interesting finding and might appear to be confirmatory evidence of the reliability of Kendell's weights and of his conclusion that a continuum existed rather than two discrete diagnostic entities. However, it is in part fortuitous, as Kendell's weights tended to exaggerate the discrimination as they had been derived from a much larger sample and were, in consequence, greater than the weights from our sample.

When the Melbourne and Maudsley weights were compared, a correlation was found between their relative magnitude $(r = +0.52; p = 0.01)$, and a 65 per cent agreement occurred in the direction of the weightings—either toward endogenous or neurotic depression. These levels of agreement were greater than chance, but are not strikingly high. Examination of the differences between the two sets of weights showed that in the Melbourne group, social withdrawal and rapid changes of mood were loaded to psychotic depression, whereas in the Maudsley study they were weighted toward the neurotic diagnosis. On the other hand, neurotic illness in a sibling, previous obsessional symptoms, preoccupation with bodily functions, duration of illness before admission of under one month and severe insomnia (unspecified) were loaded to neurotic depression in the Melbourne patients, but to psychotic depression in the Maudsley patients.

As with factor analysis, it would seem that in using discriminant function analysis, apparently similar methods of analyzing apparently similar data have produced different answers about the nature of depression.

The simple logic of this discriminant function approach may be deceptive. The test rests on whether two sets of values placed on one single continuum produce separate clusters or are intermingled. Unimodality favors the one-illness and bimodality the two-illness viewpoint. However, the basic question is the nature of the characteristic which defines the continuum. If, as is likely, it were severity of illness, the bimodal distribution could reflect a distinction between a group of mildly depressed and another of severely depressed patients, suffering from one and the same illness. Similarly, the unimodal distribution could contain patients suffering from two different illnesses but at similar levels of severity.

COMMENT

The application of techniques of multivariate analysis to settle the question of one or two forms of depression resulted in an impasse as insoluble as that which had previously been reached when the argument was based on clinical impression alone.

The argument appeared to have been resolved in favor of the one illness viewpoint when Mendels and Cochrane (1968) reviewed the factor analytic studies of depression and concluded that the endogenous factor represented the core of depressive symptomatology. They claimed that the reactive factor was composed of manifestations of psychiatric disorders other than depression, e.g. anxiety, chronic neurotic personality patterns or tendencies to react to stress with neurotic symptoms. This conclusion was based on their demonstration that for endogenous depression there was an "impressive" amount of agreement between the factor analytic studies. Seven studies agreed that retardation, intensity of depression, loss of interest, visceral symptoms and middle insomnia were all positively weighted to endogenous depression, and that negative weights should be assigned to response to environmental change, precipitating factors and to self-pity. However, as Costello (1970) points out, this optimistic conclusion was based on selected items only, and when the agreement between the studies was estimated on the full range of items examined, it was reduced to the less impressive figure of 15 per cent.

The studies cited so far have been mainly concerned with establishing whether or not the endogenous/reactive (or psychotic/neurotic) forms of depression exist and they reflect a concern with this problem which has existed for some time in British psychiatry. Perhaps the indirect contribution of multivariate techniques has been to cast doubts on the feasibility of answering this question. The endogenous versus reactive issue is so ubiquitous in biology as to have reached the status of a cliché—"Nature versus Nurture."

In general, American workers in this field have been less concerned to test the validity of a classification, and have tended to use multivariate techniques more profitably to seek patterns in the phenomena of depression. Grinker and his colleagues (1961) in a study of ninety-six depressed patients, resolved their data into fifteen possible factors. Five of these factors, i.e. hopelessness, concern about loss, guilt, "free anxiety" and envy were related to the patient's feelings. The remaining ten factors were characteristic of behavioral manifestations and included features such as withdrawal, retardation and somatic complaints. They stressed that these factors were not mutually exclusive and any one patient could show a number of these features.

Friedman *et al.* (1963), in studying the psychodynamic themes presented by a group of 170 psychotic depressed patients (all over thirty-seven years of age) confirmed the findings of the Grinker study and postulated four subtypes of depression: a) retarded, withdrawn and apathetic, b) "classical" with guilt and loss of self-esteem, c) "biological" with appetite loss, sleep disturbance and constipation and d) agitated, clinging or demanding hypochondriacal depression. This latter group of depressed patients had not been described previously and was found to contain a greater than expected number of patients who were Jewish, who were less likely to be treated by ECT, and who showed less improvement when given ECT. The existence of this subtype was attributed to the greater likelihood of psychotherapy being used as a treatment in patients who expected, and made demands for a relationship with the doctor.

Used in this manner, the multivariate analysis of patient data is capable of throwing light on groups of depressed patients who show common characteristics. Rosenthal and Gudemann (1967) drew attention to the "self-pitying constellation in depression" and Hamilton and White (1959) found a group of patients whose depression occurred in the setting of abnormal personality and who differed in sufficient ways from other depressives to be identified as "psychopathic depression."

ERROR IN MULTIVARIATE ANALYSIS

It is still too early to dismiss multivariate analysis as an approach to studying depression, even though the existing studies have failed to yield agreed findings. They have failed because they have been wrongly applied and because they have not yet been able to deal with two sources or error; the *technical* and the *observational*.

In the first place, factor analysis and discriminant function analysis have both been used in attempting to examine the classification of depression. There are logical errors in applying two different kinds of statistical procedure to the same question. Eysenck (1970) pointed out that the method of factor analysis was relevant in examining the question of whether depression was unitary or binary in nature, and concluded that, on the balance of evidence, it had demonstrated in favor of the binary view. On the other hand, the test of the distribution of diagnostic scores, as applied by Kendell, is not relevant to the unitary or binary question but only to the question of the dimensional nature of depression.

Eysenck's characteristic solution to the problem of classification is to offer *two dimensions* of depression; endogenous and reactive. Kendell's single continuum from psychotic to neurotic is "severely limited and inferior to a proper two-dimensional representation of the patient's position in a two-dimensional surface generated by the main factors of endogenous and reactive depression." The most economical position, and, as Eysenck avows, the only proper solution, is that each patient has to be portrayed by two scores, one on the endogenous dimension, and the other on the reactive dimension. This is plausible, but reopens the issue of which characteristics adequately define the endogenous and which the reactive dimensions.

Error in its *technical* sense is the main problem of statistical analysis of any kind. It is usually reduced by ensuring adequate numbers of observations, and for factor-analysis, sample sizes of

100 or so, which are clinically large, are generally too small to bring error into reliable control. The danger is that errors or "impurities" in the data may be refined to give spurious factors which the experimenter interprets as genuine clusters or constellations.

The basic patterns which emerge from the factor analysis can be predetermined by the nature of the data. Thus, a primary psychological factor may result from a wide range of psychological observations in the original data and show little agreement with the factor emerging from a relatively small number of physiological observations. If the researcher is concerned to detect patterns of relationship between psychological and physiological variables, he must originally achieve some balance between the two kinds of observations.

Factors can also be influenced by less obvious characteristics of the input data. As Hamilton (1967) points out, a general factor of severity of depression only emerges clearly if data is collected from patients showing a wide range of severity of illness. If the range of severity is limited, the first and general factor can be obliterated and a second factor can emerge as primary. This would explain Kiloh and Garside's (1963) finding of a bipolar factor of greater magnitude than the general factor, as their data was taken from outpatients with a narrow range of severity of illness.

The fact that some of the studies quoted have yielded 15 and others only 1 or 2 factors may be interpreted by the cynic as evidence of inconsistency in the method. However factor-analysis is a tool which can be used in different ways by different investigators. One investigator may stop the analysis when he has achieved clusters of symptoms which are not necessarily mutually exclusive features of the illness. Another may continue until he has resolved all the original observations to one or two factors. Differences in intention are more likely to give rise to different findings than the technique itself.

It is also possible that the researcher's own individual style of thinking can affect what he takes from a factor analysis. Bruner's experiments on the relationship between cognition and personality (Bruner, Goodnow and Austin, 1956) have led to a number of studies (e.g. Kogan and Wallach, 1964) which indicate that individual differences occur between subjects in their methods of categorizing data. Thus, one investigator may characteristically be a "lumper" of data and another a "splitter."

Observer error operates even though the investigator sets out to remain open-minded. The multivariate analyses, in this contest, were applied to observations made in a clinical setting and the observer's judgments still operate even though they are accorded a numerical value. General clinical impressions are usually avoided, and separate observations of each of a number of features are preferred. However, this procedure is still open to the dangers of the "halo effect" in which the rating of each single separate item is unwittingly colored by the rater's overall opinion of the patient's condition. This unknown loading from the halo effect on each rating could lead to the emergence of factors or groupings of features determined more by the rater's attitudes than by the phenomena shown by the patients.

Kendell (1968) has gone to commendable lengths to demonstrate the extent to which observer error can operate. For example, the clinician's belief, derived from his experience and training, that depression is a single illness, or two, or several kinds of illness was shown to influence the manner in which the presence or absence of signs and symptoms were recorded on a standard list of features.

CONCLUSIONS AND SUGGESTIONS FOR FURTHER STUDY

Multivariate analysis of data has shown some success in isolating further subgroups of patients suffering from depression. However, its use in the problem of classifying depression has produced as little agreement as previous attempts based on clinical observations alone.

The failure lies, not in the methods, but in the data to which they are applied. Factor analysis is still the ideal approach to classification, but its economy and elegance are vitiated by data which have been rendered untrustworthy because of observer error. Until the basic data can be made firm, the applications of factor analysis must be judged as premature.

Control of observer error can be achieved from examining the relevant factors in studies of the processes involved in clinical judgment and in reaching diagnoses. This has been done, and even if the implications are not widely accepted, there has already been sufficient demonstration of the inconsistencies and disagreements in the clinical situation. This is a necessary but negative first step. The positive approach is to find ways of overcoming the deficiencies likely to be shown by the clinical observer and ultimately to train him in new techniques.

This can only occur in the long-term. The current WHO programs of Research in Psychiatric Epidemiology and Social Psychiatry include studies, in an international context, on diagnostic variation between psychiatrists in order to clarify diagnostic procedures and were planned for a period of ten years, ending with a revision of the classification of Mental Disorders Section of the International Classification of Diseases in 1975. However the original aims also stated that . . . "it can be expected that systematic recording of symptoms and behavioral disturbance can lead to the recognition of objectively identifiable syndromes." Such systematic recording has begun to be used in the rating scales for depression discussed in the next chapter.

Granted that systematic, objective recording of clinical data will be achieved, the problem of adequate sample size will arise. It is unlikely that any single investigator will be able to amass data on a sufficient number of patients to meet the number of observations required for an error-free factor analysis. The approach requires pooling of observations from a variety of sources: local, national or even international—with the attendant difficulties of establishing agreed criteria for diagnosis and common bases for observing and reporting relevant features.

Chapter 12

RATING SCALES FOR DEPRESSION

Robert M. Mowbray

THE value of any clinical research into depressive illness depends ultimately on how far it can be demonstrated that the subjects were in fact suffering from depression, and on how reliably the findings from these subjects can be generalized to other groups of depressed patients. This means that agreement about diagnosis, severity of illness and criteria of recovery must be achieved between members of the research group and further that the basis for their agreement must be capable of being made public to other workers.

There is ample evidence to suggest that for psychiatric diagnosis in general such agreement is not readily achieved. In his review of this question Zubin (1967) indicates that the percentage agreement reported between psychiatrists for the general category of affective psychoses ranges from 35 per cent to 65 per cent; for involutional psychosis from 26 per cent to 57 per cent; and for manic depressive psychosis (depressed) from 36 per cent to 82 per cent. The ordinary methods of clinical diagnosis result in disagreement between observers (and to some extent within observers) because of differing conventions regarding what is to be observed, how it should be observed and what significance should be attached to an observation. Shepherd *et al.* (1968) have begun to elucidate some of the issues in the experimental setting of a diagnostic exercise and have demonstrated that in addition to the variables of observation, the inferences drawn from observations and the different systems of classification employed by observers contribute to disagreements and difficulties in communication.

Rating-scales were introduced to remove some of the inconsistencies in clinical observation by specifying what features are to be observed and how the observations are to be made. For example the characteristic "aggressiveness" might be specified as referring only to overt instance of aggressive behavior and not to

278

instances in which behavior might be interpreted as indicating latent or unconscious aggression. The amount of the rating can be specified by providing cues or standards for judgment against which to rate the observed behavior. For example a rating of *mild* for social withdrawal could be exemplified as applying if the patient can still respond to invitations to participate in social activities; *moderate* if he only does so about half the time; *marked* if he participates infrequently in spite of urging, and *severe* if he never responds.

The methods of devising and constructing such rating scales resemble those employed in the development of other standardized psychological tests and include checks for reliability and validity. However, the scales are not alternative procedures to the clinical interview, but are basically methods of recording data which has been observed or reported at interview. In general they have produced high levels of agreement between observers, but this agreement is reached on the basis of the items contained in the scale and not on overall diagnosis. Most authors state that their scales are not intended as methods of reaching a diagnosis, but only for use once the diagnosis of depression has been made.

In the past ten years a number of rating scales for depression have been devised and published. Some illustrative examples are:

HAMILTON RATING FOR DEPRESSION
(Hamilton, 1960, 1967)

The scale was devised as a means of recording objectively the signs and symptoms of depression. On the basis of his clinical interview and from data available from other sources, the clinician rates seventeen items on either a 3- or 5-point scale. For each item, cues or guidelines are provided to illustrate the behavior to which each rating applies. The clinician takes into account the patient's condition over the previous week or so and attaches due weight to frequency and intensity of each symptom.

The items covered are as follows:
1. Depressed mood.
2. Guilt.
3. Suicide.
4. Initial insomnia.
5. Middle insomnia.

6. Delayed insomnia.
7. Work and interests.
8. Retardation.
9. Agitation.
10. Psychic anxiety.
11. Somatic anxiety.
12. Gastrointestinal symptoms.
13. General somatic symptoms.
14. Loss of libido.
15. Hypochondriasis.
16. Loss of insight.
17. Loss of weight.

Diurnal variation, derealization/depressionalization, obsessive-compulsive features and paranoid symptoms were not covered in the original 1960 version but their inclusion was suggested in 1967.

In its usual form, the patient's score is the sum of all the ratings and provides a measure of severity of depression. It is simple to use and the practicing clinician can produce reliable results with some experience and training. The reliability of the ratings should not be assumed without establishing that inter-rater reliability is being achieved in the particular study. For two raters at the same interview the correlation coefficient for the two sets of ratings has reached 0.9 and as a practical check the total scores given by raters should agree to within 2 points. In our own experience this level of agreement can be achieved and any disagreement beyond this can be resolved when the two observers discuss their ratings item by item.

ZUNG SELF-RATING DEPRESSION SCALE

(Zung, 1965)

The scale was designed to measure the subjective intensity of depression regardless of whether it occurs as an illness in itself or as a symptom of another illness, emotional or physical. Thus it is not intended for use in diagnosis.

The patient rates himself on twenty statements in one of four categories: "None or a little of the time"; "some of the time"; "a good part of the time"; "most or all of the time." The use of four categories reduces the tendency for patients to bias the answers in favor of a middle or "average" category.

To prevent the patient from establishing a bias in his answers, half the statements are worded positively, e.g. "I still enjoy sex," and the other half negatively, e.g. "I feel downhearted and blue."

Each category is graded from 1 to 4 in the direction of the greatest degree of disturbance. The sum of all the categories used (maximum 80) is converted to a self-rating depression (SD) index (a percentage), and in a group of clinically ascertained depressive patients the mean SD index is of the order of 75 per cent, while normal controls can yield a mean SD index of 33 per cent.

The scale is short and statements are couched in terms that the patient can be expected to understand. However, patients may require guidance in completing items such as "I still enjoy sex" for virgins or elderly widows, and in using the prescribed four categories to answer "I notice that I am losing weight." Suicidal feelings are indicated indirectly by "I feel that others would be better off if I were dead." Guilt feelings, retardation, hypochondriasis and loss of insight are not covered.

The scale has been used in a number of studies and the scores have been reported as showing good correlation with clinical and psychometric assessments of depression (Zung, 1967).

INDIVIDUAL MOOD CHECKLIST

(Bunney and Hamburg, 1963)

The scale was developed at the National Institute of Mental Health (NIMH) to record behavioral data on hospitalized patients on a continuous day-to-day basis. By using frequent ratings, changes in the patient's clinical state could be correlated with biochemical measurements and the natural history of depressive illness could be followed. Because nurses are in a position to make the required frequent observations of patients, the checklist was designed to be used mainly by nursing personnel, specially trained in the technique of rating.

The main areas of depression, anger, anxiety, psychotic behavior and speech are covered by twenty-four items, each rated on a 15-point scale, the highest value representing the "worst ever seen or heard," the lowest representing normal. The items include general impressions of depression, anger and anxiety and the rater's attention is drawn to the patient's verbalizations, facial expressions and overt behavior in the published guides to each item.

In the early stages of development of the checklist, intra-class correlation coefficients between observers on each item were calculated in order to demonstrate which items required more specific instructions. It was found that the degree of agreement between observers fell off as the intensity of anxiety and depression increased, and it was suggested that because extremes of this type of behavior were less often observed by staff, they were more difficult to rate accurately on the scale. Satisfactory agreements with psychiatrists' ratings and with patients' own ratings were also established in these preliminary studies.

In its present form the scale has a detailed set of directions for the staff, each item is defined and cues are provided on how to rate the item. This scale has been in use for over seven years at NIMH and has consistently shown high interrater reliability. Its main value lies in its local use in the hands of trained and experienced raters but it does not appear to have been used by other investigators. Reports of its use generally quote scores and changes on single items rather than total scores (Goodwin *et al.*, 1970).

AN INVENTORY FOR MEASURING DEPRESSION

(Beck *et al.*, 1961)

This inventory was constructed to provide a quantitative assessment of the intensity of depression as evaluated by the patient.

From observations of depressed patients undergoing psychoanalytic psychotherapy, Beck selected twenty-one categories of symptoms and attitudes which characterized the overt behavioral manifestations of depression.

At interview the patient is presented with the inventory of these twenty-one items. The interviewer reads each item to him, and on the basis of the patient's response the item is evaluated and rated by the interviewer on a 4- or 5-point scale. The procedure is simple and is a self-assessment in which the patient's difficulties in scaling his responses are overcome by having the observer rate for him, and in which his difficulties in understanding are overcome by having the items elaborated or explained to him.

Ninety-seven per cent agreement between psychiatrist's rating to within one point on the four-point scale was found. The inventory showed high reliability and each item showed a significant relationship to total score. When its validity was assessed against clinical assessment of depth of depression, significant correlation coefficients were found between the inventory score and this clinical criterion. Patients in this validity study were not restricted to the diagnostic category of depression, and a number of schizophrenics were included. However, the purpose of the inventory is to discriminate intensity of depression, and not to differentiate diagnostic categories.

Hamilton (1969) points out that the Beck inventory is limited to the patient's evaluation of himself at the time of the interview and cannot take into account fluctuations in the patient's condition. Retardation, agitation, and loss of insight are not covered, and anxiety is represented only by "irritability." The rating procedure is also open to observer bias and is not a self-rating in the usual sense.

THE DEPRESSION RATING SCALE
(Wechsler *et al.*, 1963)

The Wechsler scale was constructed to reveal changes in the various components that make up the different syndromes of depression. It combines self-ratings and observer ratings and is completed on the basis of the patient's own statements and the physician's observations.

It contains a total of twenty-eight items scored variously on a 6, 5, 4 or 3-point scale. The first fourteen items deal with the patient's own attitudes and feelings and a further five with his comments about his physiological functions. The remaining nine are observed by the interviewer and cover aspects of activity, speech, appearance and ideation. The score is the sum of all the ratings, with a maximum of 131 points and a minimum of 28 points.

The scale was constructed from an initial selection of thirty-four items to cover the following:

1. Physical functioning.
2. Motor activity.
3. Motivation and drive.
4. Mood and affect.
5. Intellectual functioning.
6. Self-devaluation and guilt.

The final twenty-eight items were chosen after these original items had been pretested by a group of thirty-seven psychiatrists.

In a series of studies involving over two hundred depressed patients the correlation coefficient between ratings made at the same interview was 0.88 and on ratings made one week apart was 0.78. Somewhat surprisingly, the correlation between ratings of the same patients made independently by two raters on the same day was only 0.52. This would suggest that the ratings are dependent on the patient's state at interview, rather than over a broader period and that they are affected by diurnal variations in the patient's condition.

Diurnal variation in symptoms is not included in the rating scale, nor is loss of libido. Agitated and retarded motor activity are not differentiated as both are scored in the same item in the same direction, simply as deviation from normal. The initial studies showed satisfactory agreements between the rating scale scores and clinically assessed severity of depression and degree of improvement.

Other scales have been devised by particular authors for specific purposes in studying depression. Among these are the Massachusetts Mental Health Center Depression Rating Scale (Greenblatt *et al.*, 1962), the Psychiatric Judgment Depression Scale (Overall *et al.*, 1962), the Clinical Quantification of Depressive Reactions (Cutler and Kurland, 1961), the Phenomena of Depressions (Grinker *et al.*, 1961) a Questionnaire Indicating Anxiety and Depression during Pregnancy and the Puerperium (Pitt, 1968) and the Depression Questionnaire (Pilowsky *et al.*, 1969). In addition, scales for measuring depression appear in multidimensional psychiatric inventories, e.g. the Wittenborn Psychiatric Rating Scale (Wittenborn, 1955); the Inpatient Multidimensional Psychiatric Scale (Lorr *et al.*, 1962); its derivative, the Brief Psychiatric Rating Scale (Overall and Gorham, 1962); the 16 PF (Cattell, 1964); the MMPI (Gilberstadt and Duker, 1965); and the Symptom-Sign Inventory (Foulds and Hope, 1968).

The above list is by no means exhaustive, and it indicates the wide range of measures currently available for studying depression and its symptomatology.

SELECTION OF A SCALE

The choice of a scale for use in clinical research will be governed by the investigator's personal preference, the aims of the investigation and the severity of illness shown by the subjects. Some guidelines can be offered:

Type of Patient

If severely depressed patients are involved, subjective ratings are less acceptable than objective. It is almost axiomatic that such patients will be unable to complete even the most simple rating form. Very retarded, anxious or agitated subjects need close supervision while they assess themselves. Denial of illness, which characterizes some forms of depression, may further invalidate subjective measures.

Design of the Study

In general, studies which involve *between* patient comparisons call for a scale which samples a wide range of signs and symptoms of depression (e.g. the Hamilton Scale). On the other hand, a longitudinal study intended to bring out changes within patients will require a more sensitive scale capable of reflecting day-to-day, diurnal changes in the patients (e.g. the Bunney-Hamburg scale).

The contrast between the two kinds of investigation demanding different kinds of scale may be drawn by instancing the therapeutic trial requiring a rating of severity at admission and after a period of several weeks treatment. At the other extreme a study of the correlations between biochemical and behavioral changes may require ratings to be performed several times per day, for example, in studying rapid cycling manic depressive patients. In this case, nonspecific or chance behavioral fluctuations may obscure the pattern of influences. Frequent ratings also carry the risk of increasing the error from the "halo effect," as general impressions from one rating are readily transferred to the next.

Popularity

A scale may become popular because of its initial use in a particular area of research. Subsequent investigators who replicate the study feel compelled to include the same measuring technique as the original investigator. A scale that is well known may be selected because findings based on it may be more readily communicated to other workers. Because of its popularity, the Hamilton scale is still used in its original seventeen-item form (1960) although the 1967 version includes a further four items and yields slightly different component factors.

Ease of Administration

Most of these scales are short and do not demand much time for completion or for scoring. In general the brevity of the scale may not be consistent with accuracy as the fewer the items the greater the risk of error. Thus if accuracy of measurement is desired a longer, more time-consuming scale might be preferred.

In large scale studies scoring by computer might be required and the ease with which the ratings can be transferred to date cards may have to be considered.

Type of Rater

Psychiatrist, psychologist, social worker, nurse or other professional worker may rate the patients, or the patient may rate himself. As the scales are methods of recording judgments, the degree of sophistication, experience and orientation of the rater can be significant factors. In general, self-assessment by patients would appear to be more likely to produce errors than assessment by professional personnel because of their difficulties in comprehension, diversity of interpreting items and inexperience with rating methods.

If several raters are to be employed, the degree to which the scale has been shown to yield inter-observer agreement should be considered. In the investigation itself the extent to which inter-observer agreement has actually been reached should be checked. If one observer only is to be used, the consistency of his ratings should be considered.

Nurses' observations are of advantage for studies of hospital-ized patients as they cover a wider range and longer timespan of contact with patients. However, the use of nurses' ratings only as indicators of clinical state may not be acceptable. Goodwin *et al.* (1970) reported that l-dopa with MK 485 produces improvement in depressed patients as measured by reductions in the ratings made by nurses on the Bunney and Hamburg Individual Mood Checklist. In commenting on this, Abrams (1970) asserted that nurses' ratings may lack the validity of observations made by clinical psychiatrists.

The use of several observers, e.g. psychiatrist, nurse and pa-tient, and of several scales in a study may appear to be the best way of ensuring that the relevant changes are not missed. How-ever, this may lead to practical difficulties in interpreting the find-ings because of differing bases for judgment and different char-acteristics of the scales.

Linearity of Ratings

The convention of transferring degrees of judgment to nu-merical values for computational purposes is convenient, but may involve error. For example, a change from a total rating of 40 points to 30 points on the Hamilton scale represents a change of the same numerical order as from 15 to 5 points but the de-gree of clinical change reflected by these various values is mark-edly different. The use of proportional change does not neces-sarily reduce this error. Short of devising an equal interval scale for recording judgments, which is technically difficult, it is best to assume that the current scales are not linear, and to recognize that changes occurring from different initial values may not be comparable.

Sensitivity of the Scales

The nonlinearity of the scales means in effect that their sensi-tivity to change may differ at various levels. The overall sensitivi-ty of the scale should also be taken into account as an insensitive scale may mask a genuine treatment effect. If the scale contains personality traits as well as symptoms, the weighting of the long-standing traits may render the scale insensitive to symptom change.

Design and Construction

Account should be taken of the original uses for which a scale was devised, the manner in which the items were selected, any efforts made to establish its reliability (the consistency with which it yields scores) and its validity (the extent to which the scores reflect the phenomenon to be measured). Even if the scale has originally been validated against clinical diagnoses it may be biased to reflect local diagnostic conventions which need not apply to practice in other centers. The original tests of agreement between observers, and of reliability and validity offer some guides in choosing a rating scale but it should not be assumed that the scale will automatically produce the same findings in other settings.

COMPARISONS BETWEEN SCALES

So far, only a few attempts have been made to evaluate the available scales against each other. Schwab *et al.* (1967) compared the results of ratings made on the Hamilton and Beck scales on 163 medical inpatients. In general, a significant degree of correlation (0.75) was found between the two scores. However, when the differences were examined, it was found that the Hamilton scale tended to emphasize the somatic symptoms of depression and the Beck to focus on features such as pessimism, failure and self-punishment. The two scales are biased to measure different components of depression.

Carroll *et al.* (1971) compared the scores on the Hamilton scale with those on the Zung scale in a group of sixty-seven depressed patients in three clinical settings, inpatient, day hospital and general practice. On clinical grounds inpatients were assessed as having moderate to severe depression, day hospital patients mild to moderate and general practice patients mild depressive symptoms.

Table 12-I summarizes the findings. The Hamilton scores for the groups paralleled the clinically assessed severity of illness in

TABLE 12-I

HAMILTON AND ZUNG SCORES OF PATIENT GROUPS

Setting	N	Hamilton Total Score Mean (S.D.)	Zung S.D. Index Mean (S.D.)
Inpatient	24	29.5 (7.8)	64.9 (15.0)
Day hospital	18	23.7 (4.2)	70.4 (12.5)
General practice	25	14.7 (5.8)	61.2 (10.5)

that inpatients showed the highest mean, significantly higher than the mean for day hospital patients which in its turn was significantly higher than the mean for the general practice group. The SDS Index from the subjectively rated Zung scale, by contrast, did not accord with the levels of severity. The highest mean index occurred in the day hospital group and was significantly different from the lowest in the general practice group. The inpatients were in a midway position and their mean index was not statistically different from either of the other two groups.

From these findings the sensitivity of the Zung scale was questioned. When corresponding items in the two scales were examined it was found that the highest correlations between the ratings occurred for insomnia (0.67) and weight loss (0.59). Items such as somatic anxiety, general somatic symptoms and agitation showed no significant correlation. It was pointed out that some agreement between the scales could be reached but only on the most restricted and straightforward items.

FACTOR SCORES

In most of these scales the ratings on each item are summed to give a single overall measure of severity of depression. However, it is possible to obtain further information from the ratings in the form of *component* or *factor scores*. Briefly the procedure involves a factor analysis (see Appendix A) of the ratings on a sufficiently large group of patients and then using the factor-saturations to derive weightings for each item. Each patient's rating on any item is then multiplied by this weight and his score on each factor can be obtained by summing the products.

This procedure means that several scores can result from the original ratings and these derived scores are potentially useful in examining the characteristics of a subgroup of depressed patients to test whether they show features which distinguish them from other patient groups. In view of the comments made in the previous chapter, it should be pointed out that the factor analysis in this case is not being used to test the validity of any classification of depression, but simply to demonstrate whether patient groups can be isolated on the basis of component factors originally extracted from the intercorrelations of items. Hamilton (1960) in his original analysis of ratings on his scale for depression carried out on forty-nine patients found four factors:

1. Retarded depression.
2. Gastrointestinal symptoms.
3. Psychic anxiety/agitation.
4. General somatic symptoms.

In a subsequent paper (Hamilton, 1967) ratings on a further 103 male patients and 120 female patients were added. The four factors yielded from this data were the following:

1. General factor of depressive illness (severity).
2. Retarded versus agitated depression.
3. Insomnia, fatigue and loss of appetite, contrasted with guilt, suicide and loss of insight.
4. Hypochondriasis and general instability of personality.

Separate factor analyses were done for male and female patients, and while sex differences in the factor saturations were found, there was sufficient correspondence to justify describing a common pattern of factors. The use of factor scores was illustrated by Hamilton's finding that high scores on factor 4 appeared in a group of patients whose depression occurred in a setting of instability of personality and social history.

A FACTOR ANALYSIS OF HAMILTON RATINGS
Aims

In the studies reported in this monograph the Hamilton scale was consistently used as a measure of severity of depression. It was decided to use this data in a factor analysis (Mowbray, 1971): a) to isolate the underlying components of the scale and to compare these with Hamilton's factors, b) to investigate the possibility of using factor scores to discriminate between samples of depressed patients.

Material

The basic data was chosen from our records. Ratings on one occasion per patient were used, usually at admission, and follow-up ratings were discarded. Cases in which the diagnosis of depression was in doubt were excluded and the ratings were confined to those made by four senior clinicians, all experienced in using the Hamilton scale, and each of whom had checked his ratings with other members of the group.

To avoid biasing the factors the widest available range of severity of depression (i.e. total Hamilton scores) was incorporated. This acted as a safeguard for the emergence of a general factor (see Appendix A). It was also established that the original frequency distribution of the Hamilton scores was not significantly different from normal, in order to ensure that any bipolar factor was not likely to be simply an artifact of bimodality in the input data.

Ratings on a group of 347 depressed patients were used, composed of 134 male and 213 female patients. The sex ratio is more in accord with the usual sex incidence in depression than in Hamilton's group and it was further established that both sexes covered a similar wide range of severity scores and their separate frequency distributions did not depart from normal.

Method

The factor analysis was carried out on the IBM 7044 computer at the University of Melbourne, using the standard FACTOR programme of the University of Miami Biometrics Laboratory. This yields mean and standard deviations for each variable, the matrix of intercorrelations, principal components and varimax rotation. The findings from the principal components analysis are discussed here, and only factors with mean square values greater than unity are considered (Harman, 1968).

Results

Table 12-II shows that the means and standard deviations of the total Hamilton score for males and females were almost

TABLE 12-II

HAMILTON SCALE
Total Score and Item Score by Sex Means and Standard Deviations

	Males (N = 134) Mean (S.D.)	Females (N = 213) Mean (S.D.)	Sig.
Total Hamilton	19.2 (8.6)	19.6 (8.6)	N.S.
Items			
Somatic anxiety	1.14 (1.0)	1.69 (1.1)	0.001
Psychic anxiety	2.26 (0.9)	1.93 (1.2)	0.05
General somatic symptoms	1.43 (0.7)	1.07 (0.8)	0.01
Hypochondriasis	0.89 (0.9)	0.65 (0.9)	0.02
Loss of insight	0.69 (0.8)	0.45 (0.7)	0.01

identical. When the mean scores for each of the items in the scale were examined, it was found that statistically significant sex differences appeared in five of the seventeen. These items are also listed in Table 12-II.

Females showed higher ratings than males on *anxiety* (both somatic and psychic) and on *general somatic symptoms,* a finding which agreed with Hamilton (1967). Males, on the other hand, had significantly higher ratings on *hypochondriasis* and on *loss of insight,* whereas in Hamilton's study, males were higher on *reduced work and interests, early insomnia and retardation.*

These sex differences in item scores are reflected in the different patterns found from the factor analysis. The factor saturations for males and females are presented in Tables 12-III and 12-IV with the corresponding values found by Hamilton (1967).

The first factor was unequivocally general for both sexes. All seventeen items were included with positive saturations, and as there was an almost complete correlation with total score on the Hamilton scale (0.9) it was readily identifiable as Hamilton's general factor of depression, measuring severity of illness. Figures 12-1 to 12-4 plot the main items only in each of the subsequent factors against the vertical scale of their saturations, in order to portray the factor patterns.

The second factor (Fig. 12-1) was bipolar for both sexes. The items with the strongest positive saturation were *somatic and psychic anxiety* and *general somatic* complaints for both sexes.

TABLE 12-III
PRINCIPAL COMPONENTS
Factor Saturations per Item
Males

Item	Present Study (N = 134)						Hamilton (1967) (N = 152)					
	FI	FII	FIII	FIV	FV	FVI	F1	F2	F3	F4	F5	F6
1. Depression	0.752	-0.070	0.157	-0.280	0.204	-0.084	0.675	-0.128	0.222	0.295	-0.186	-0.117
2. Guilt	0.375	0.133	0.088	-0.256	0.040	0.432	0.474	-0.083	0.497	0.096	0.005	0.181
3. Suicide	0.381	-0.177	-0.249	-0.730	0.053	-0.162	0.480	-0.228	0.344	0.119	-0.000	-0.473
4. Insomnia (early)	0.481	0.129	-0.605	-0.173	-0.165	-0.081	0.313	0.175	-0.411	-0.168	-0.078	-0.577
5. Insomnia (middle)	0.561	-0.155	-0.426	0.156	0.029	0.219	0.346	0.021	-0.583	0.107	-0.021	-0.136
6. Insomnia (late)	0.499	-0.212	-0.313	0.070	0.436	0.346	0.505	-0.055	-0.198	-0.112	-0.422	0.326
7. Work/interests	0.593	-0.277	0.306	-0.215	0.119	-0.298	0.561	0.244	-0.095	0.120	0.117	0.190
8. Retardation	0.470	-0.638	0.179	0.210	0.089	-0.052	0.605	-0.409	-0.050	0.277	0.062	0.223
9. Agitation	0.569	0.059	-0.031	0.369	0.277	-0.336	0.187	0.644	0.281	-0.036	-0.222	-0.348
10. Anxiety (psychic)	0.547	0.523	0.180	0.151	0.367	-0.165	-0.063	0.753	0.159	0.171	-0.021	0.082
11. Anxiety (somatic)	0.549	0.538	0.059	0.328	0.052	-0.006	-0.085	0.751	0.051	0.277	0.083	0.131
12. Gastrointestinal	0.574	-0.055	0.302	0.018	-0.482	0.208	0.632	0.096	-0.425	0.014	-0.097	0.053
13. General somatic	0.522	0.356	0.439	-0.217	-0.057	0.147	0.168	0.161	-0.273	0.285	0.732	-0.017
14. Loss of libido	0.538	0.139	-0.277	0.189	-0.229	0.355	0.500	0.177	0.105	0.263	0.036	0.051
15. Hypochondriasis	0.280	0.458	-0.242	-0.064	-0.416	-0.452	0.352	0.184	0.084	-0.683	0.402	0.104
16. Loss of insight	0.418	-0.548	-0.044	0.299	-0.290	-0.291	0.622	-0.123	0.297	-0.354	0.299	-0.086
17. Loss of weight	0.582	-0.147	0.241	0.076	-0.322	0.156	0.376	0.366	-0.074	-0.402	-0.252	0.222
Eigenvalues	5.621	1.872	1.387	1.277	1.149	1.133	3.441	2.132	1.448	1.265	1.154	1.032

TABLE 12-IV

PRINCIPAL COMPONENTS

Factor Saturations per Item

Females

Item	Present Study (N = 213)						Hamilton (1967) (N = 120)					
	FI	FII	FIII	FIV	FV	FVI	F1	F2	F3	F4	F5	F6
1. Depression	0.794	0.279	-0.102	0.036	-0.170	0.011	0.701	0.174	0.234	-0.248	-0.024	-0.029
2. Guilt	0.582	0.211	-0.202	0.178	-0.151	0.444	0.539	0.044	0.180	-0.573	0.020	0.026
3. Suicide	0.474	0.077	-0.422	-0.138	-0.535	0.080	0.676	0.294	0.176	-0.321	-0.034	-0.040
4. Insomnia (early)	0.607	-0.203	-0.008	-0.180	0.071	0.086	0.067	0.382	-0.433	-0.096	0.038	0.468
5. Insomnia (middle)	0.533	-0.001	-0.179	0.354	0.266	-0.176	0.238	0.295	-0.470	-0.076	0.542	-0.162
6. Insomnia (late)	0.610	-0.280	-0.115	0.116	0.211	-0.278	0.530	-0.035	-0.266	0.243	0.184	-0.220
7. Work/interests	0.664	0.232	-0.190	0.144	-0.098	-0.116	0.748	0.066	-0.077	0.222	-0.009	-0.088
8. Retardation	0.694	-0.098	-0.056	0.144	0.033	0.248	0.603	-0.514	0.102	0.143	0.008	0.040
9. Agitation	0.598	-0.237	0.237	0.422	0.101	-0.088	0.393	0.489	-0.290	-0.129	-0.224	-0.149
10. Anxiety (psychic)	0.483	0.501	0.313	0.319	0.165	-0.091	0.031	0.662	-0.052	0.128	-0.143	-0.226
11. Anxiety (somatic)	-0.297	0.398	0.518	-0.301	0.019	0.267	-0.309	0.727	0.152	0.208	-0.124	-0.034
12. Gastrointestinal	0.647	-0.187	-0.018	-0.442	0.128	-0.233	0.530	-0.086	-0.059	0.451	0.297	0.242
13. General somatic	0.528	0.437	0.191	-0.154	-0.196	-0.391	0.336	0.263	0.534	0.478	0.164	-0.164
14. Loss of libido	0.198	0.375	-0.298	-0.335	0.625	0.294	0.070	0.274	0.601	0.012	-0.032	0.353
15. Hypochondriasis	0.487	-0.272	0.569	-0.174	-0.126	0.096	0.120	-0.062	-0.228	0.253	-0.720	-0.163
16. Loss of insight	0.439	-0.620	0.116	0.136	-0.009	0.360	0.647	-0.379	-0.051	-0.054	-0.308	-0.067
17. Loss of weight	0.603	-0.379	-0.137	-0.392	0.030	-0.187	0.335	0.126	-0.206	0.174	-0.206	0.656
Eigenvalues	6.338	1.749	1.218	1.169	0.969	0.951	3.698	2.141	1.473	1.242	1.188	1.052

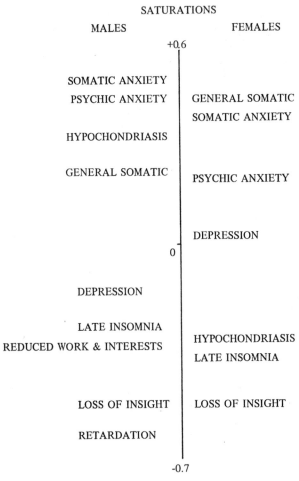

Figure 12-1. Factor II.

In males, *hypochondriasis* was also associated with the anxiety features, while in females it appeared at the negative end of the factor. *Loss of insight* and *late insomnia* occurred at the negative pole for males and females, and in males were accompanied by *retardation and reduced work and interests.* For females *loss of weight* and *hypochondriasis* also had negative values. This bipolar factor did not distinguish *agitation and retardation* as Hamilton's factor 2 had done. In neither sex did *agitation* emerge with significant positive values, and only in males was *re-*

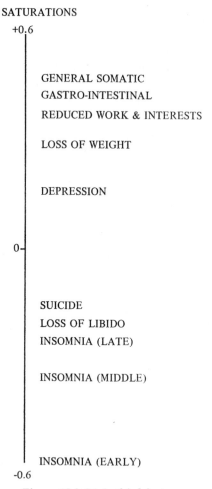

MALE THIRD FACTOR

SATURATIONS
+0.6

GENERAL SOMATIC
GASTRO-INTESTINAL
REDUCED WORK & INTERESTS

LOSS OF WEIGHT

DEPRESSION

0—

SUICIDE
LOSS OF LIBIDO
INSOMNIA (LATE)

INSOMNIA (MIDDLE)

INSOMNIA (EARLY)
-0.6

Figure 12-2. Male third factor.

tardation significantly loaded at the negative end. The factor appears to isolate *anxiety* features from *depression,* which does not emerge significantly in the factor.

The third factor for the males (Fig. 12-2) had no counterpart in the factor pattern for females. It polarized the somatic aspects of the depressive syndrome, but not in any immediately clinically obvious fashion.

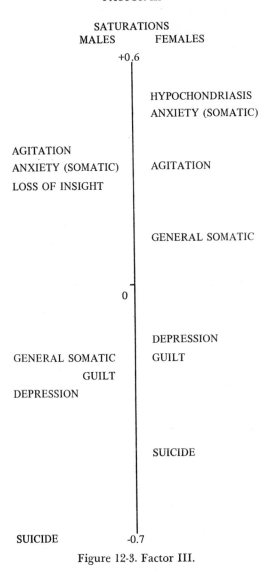

Figure 12-3. Factor III.

There was, however, correspondence between the fourth factor for males and the third factor for females (shown as Factor III in Fig. 12-3), the negative end bringing out a suicidal component, and the positive end highlighting *agitation* undifferentiated from *somatic anxiety*. The negative components of this factor, i.e. *depression, guilt and suicide* correspond to the negative pole

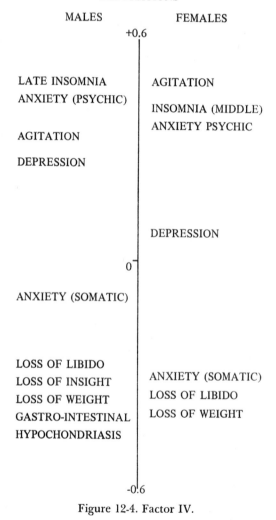

FACTOR IV

SATURATIONS

MALES   FEMALES
+0.6

LATE INSOMNIA   AGITATION
ANXIETY (PSYCHIC)
                         INSOMNIA (MIDDLE)
                         ANXIETY PSYCHIC
AGITATION

DEPRESSION

                         DEPRESSION

0

ANXIETY (SOMATIC)

LOSS OF LIBIDO
LOSS OF INSIGHT   ANXIETY (SOMATIC)
LOSS OF WEIGHT   LOSS OF LIBIDO
GASTRO-INTESTINAL   LOSS OF WEIGHT
HYPOCHONDRIASIS

-0.6

Figure 12-4. Factor IV.

of Hamilton's second factor and the correspondence is further strengthened by the emergence of *agitation* with positive loadings. However, the polarity between *agitation and retardation* found by Hamilton still does not appear.

Factor IV (Fig. 12-4) is the male fifth factor and the female fourth factor. Once again it brings out *agitation,* this time in association with *psychic anxiety* and differentiates this from *somatic anxiety. Loss of libido and loss of weight* occur at the negative end on both male and female factor patterns.

One further factor with latent roots above unity emerged for males. This sixth factor is not portrayed here but it had a positive constellation of *guilt, loss of libido, late and middle insomnia,* with negative loadings for *hypochondriasis, agitation, reduced work and interests and loss of insight.* It split up the accompaniments of depressive illness, but not in any clinically obvious fashion, and bore some resemblance to a sixth factor found by Hamilton for males, but which he did not interpret.

Comment

The above four factors correspond in general for males and females, and differences in the loadings for *hypochondriasis* could have occurred because of the initial differences between the sexes on the rating for this item (Table 12-II). However, in other items, sex differences occurred in the loadings which cannot be explained from the initial comparisons in this table.

On clinical grounds sex differences are recognized in incidence, and in response to treatment, but differences between males and females in the features and form of presentation of depressive illness have not, as yet, been fully documented.

APPLYING FACTOR SCORES

The factors are new ways of classifying the original data, and they can be given some significance by inspection of their patterns. However, a more practical test can be applied. As was described in the previous chapter the factor loadings can be converted to give weightings for each item. These weights when applied to the ratings made on any patient will produce his score on each factor. These factor scores can potentially extend the information contained in the original ratings.

Method

In brief the computation of factor scores (Hamilton, 1968; Mowbray, 1971) involves converting both the original factor loadings and the patient's rating on each item to standard scores. These standard scores are multiplied and summed to give the factor score for each patient. As a further refinement the factor scores can be transformed into a T-score with a mean of 49.5 and a standard deviation of 10. The T-score is a useful way of comparing factor scores on one factor between two groups of patients, or of examining differences in one group of patients between scores on a number of factors.

Of the four factors described above, the first general factor was so obvious a measure of severity of illness that factor scores would contribute little information beyond that already given by the total Hamilton scores. However, the remaining three were considered worthy of further examination and a computer program was written to calculate their factor scores using the appropriate male and female weighting per item, and to produce means and standard deviations for factor scores (T-form) in specified groups of patients.

Material

Patients could be split up on the basis of treatment setting:

1. In both male and female *inpatient groups,* the diagnosis of depression had been established with care and they were considered to be showing illness of moderate to severe intensity. This group included patients described in Chapters 2, 4 and 9.
2. Groups of *day hospital* patients of both sexes were also selected. These patients were attending a day hospital for antidepressant medication, and also participated in a psychotherapeutic and recreational program. These patients presented with depressive symptoms, often with associated neurotic features.
3. The female patients who presented with depression in *general practice* (Chap. 13) constituted a group in whom the diagnosis of depression had been established with care. No

counterpart of this group was available for males and the third group of males was selected from inpatients in a general hospital psychiatric ward, all with mild depressive symptoms but with associated psychiatric disturbances. These patients are referred to as *mixed patients*.

Results

The findings are presented in Table 12-V.

Age: Within each sex, inpatients are significantly older (p = 0.001) than the other two groups, but for each group the between sex differences in age are not significant.

Severity: From their Hamilton scores the inpatients are the most severely depressed for each sex, significantly higher (p = 0.001) than the other two groups. For females the difference between the mean Hamilton scores for the general practice and day hospital groups is also significant (p = 0.01) but the difference in means between the mixed and day hospital male groups does not reach significance.

Factor II: The scores on Factor II for females show an opposite trend from severity. Inpatients have significantly lower scores than day hospital patients (p = 0.01) who in their turn are significantly lower than general practice patients (p = 0.01). In the male patients the mixed inpatients are lower, but not significantly so on this factor than the inpatients, but both are significantly lower than the day-hospital patients (p = 0.01).

This factor gave high loading to anxiety features and a high anxiety component is reflected in the high scores of the female general practice group. For males the highest score occurring in the day hospital patients could be expected from the composition of this group. However, female day-hospital patients only score at the mean value for this factor. The explanation may be the differential weighting accorded to hypochondriasis which on this factor was positively saturated for males and negatively for females.

The third factor for males is not depicted here. As described above, it polarized the somatic aspects of depression but scores on this factor did not discriminate between the three subgroups of males.

TABLE 12-V

AGE, TOTAL HAMILTON AND FACTOR SCORES (T-form) BY GROUP
MEANS AND STANDARD DEVIATION

	N	Age Mean	Age (S.D.)	Total Hamilton Mean	Total Hamilton (S.D.)	Factor II Mean	Factor II (S.D.)	Factor III Mean	Factor III (S.D.)	Factor IV Mean	Factor IV (S.D.)
A. Males											
Inpatient	48	55.1	(11.7)	24.3	(8.2)	45.4	(11.9)	49.7	(10.5)	48.8	(11.1)
Day hospital	49	41.1	(12.9)	18.6	(4.8)	56.0	(10.1)	52.1	(10.4)	51.0	(10.1)
Mixed inpatient	24	43.9	(15.9)	17.1	(9.7)	42.9	(13.1)	42.8	(8.1)	47.2	(10.3)
B. Females											
Inpatient	69	55.6	(13.7)	25.7	(8.6)	43.5	(12.8)	48.1	(13.9)	44.1	(11.8)
Day hospital	30	40.6	(10.2)	20.9	(4.8)	49.8	(9.9)	54.7	(8.9)	56.9	(10.2)
General practice	82	37.3	(14.2)	16.9	(4.9)	55.8	(7.3)	50.2	(8.4)	48.3	(7.5)

Factor III: The female third, and male fourth factor brought out the highest scores for both male and female day-hospital patients, but only scores at the mean for both male and female in-patients. The saturation of the items on this factor approximated those found by Hamilton (1967) in his fourth factor, which he had used to isolate a group of patients whose depression was associated with personality and social problems (see Chap. 12) and it is likely that such patients would appear in a day-hospital setting. The lowest values on this factor appear in the male mixed group, and could be attributed to the high negative weights accorded to suicide on this factor. These patients came from a general hospital ward where a considerable part of the activities was devoted to management of cases admitted following suicidal attempts or gestures.

Factor IV: Factor IV showed the day-hospital patients to have the highest scores. None of the differences between the male groups was statistically significant. For the females, inpatients showed scores significantly below the mean and the day-hospital patients significantly above the mean. These findings are consistent with the interpretation of the factor as polarizing psychological aspects of depression at the positive end and somatic aspects at the negative end.

DISCUSSION

This use of factor scores was reported mainly to illustrate the application of the method in examining samples of depressed patients, selecting treatment setting as the basis for discrimination.

Generalization of these findings is limited, as the groups were selected more on opportunist grounds than on the basis of strict sampling procedure. However it is worthwhile observing that both sex and treatment setting effects operated. In Factor II male day-hospital patients showed high scores which did not appear in female day-hospital patients. This, as was suggested, could be due to sex-differences in this particular factor pattern. More simply it could have arisen because males and females are admitted to day-hospital care on different criteria.

In a comparable study based on treatment setting but using a wider range of data than the present Hamilton scale, Paykel *et al.* (1970) found that severity of illness was the single factor on which differences were shown between four groups of depressed patients: a) hospitalized, b) outpatients, c) day patients and d) patients treated in an Emergency Treatment Service. Factor scores derived in a similar fashion to the present also permitted further distinctions to be drawn between the samples.

Detailed comparisons between this and the present study are not appropriate because of differences in the data used, and because Paykel *et al.* did not take account of sex differences. However, if the pattern of depression is dependent upon the setting in which it is presented and treated, as Paykel *et al.* conclude, the clinical investigator must exercise caution in generalizing from limited research samples of patients. The present study would suggest that the sex composition of the research sample is a further variable to be taken into account.

CONCLUSIONS AND SUGGESTIONS FOR FURTHER STUDY

In general the development of rating scales for depression represents a beginning and not an achievement. They provide an opportunity for comparing populations of patients, but their use is still suspect by the clinician. He can argue,

1. That they only sample interview information and are less informative than a clinical interview.
2. That they concentrate too much on single items rather than the picture of "the patient as a whole."
3. That they are of necessity concerned only with features of illness that are common to patients rather than with features that are unique to an individual patient.
4. That the objectivity of these scales may be spurious as they may cloak influences such as the observer's personal or theoretical bias, or the amount and quality of his experience.

Some of these objections are well founded and will disappear as more sophisticated methods of devising rating scales are used and as the realization grows that the demonstrated errors in clinical judgment are matters for scientific concern rather than for personal or professional affront.

The rating scale method draws attention to which clinical observations can, and which cannot be made on a sufficiently rigorous basis to be valid and reliable. In this it could be predicted that they will eventually provide sufficiently "hard" clinical data for the appropriate application of multivariate techniques (Chap. 11) in studying the nature of depression.

Their current use in allowing clinical investigators to communicate the characteristics of the patients studied can be extended to epidemiological research concerned with demographic variables. The sex difference discussed in this chapter would suggest that a fruitful line of inquiry could be conducted into the whole question of how male and female patients differ in the form of presentation of their depressive illness.

REFERENCES

Abrams, R.: Correspondence. *Lancet,* I:7661, 1394, 1970.

Altschule, M.D.: The two kinds of depression according to St. Paul. *Br J Psychiatry,* 113:779, 1967.

Beck, A.T., Ward, C.H., Mendelson, M., Mock, J. and Erbaugh, J.: An inventory for measuring depression. *Arch Gen Psychiatry,* 4:561, 1961.

Blashki, T.G., Mowbray, R.M. and Davies, B.M.: Controlled trial of amitriptyline in general practice. *Br Med J,* 1:133, 1971.

Bruner, J.S., Goodnow, J.J. and Austin, G.A.: *A Study of Thinking.* Wiley, New York, 1956.

Bunney, W.E., Jr. and Hamburg, D.A.: Methods for reliable longitudinal observation of behaviour. *Arch Gen Psychiatry,* 9:280, 1963.

Carney, M.W.P., Roth, M. and Garside, R.F.: The diagnosis of depressive syndromes and the prediction of E.C.T. response. *Br J Psychiatry,* 111:659, 1965.

Carroll, B.J., Fielding, J.M. and Blashki, T.G.: Ratings of depression—a comparison of the Zung and Hamilton scales. In press, 1971.

Cattell, R.B.: *IPAT Handbook for the Sixteen Personality Factor Questionnaire.* Illinois, Champaign, 1964.

Costello, C.G. (Ed.) : *Symptoms of Psychopathology: a Handbook.* Wiley, New York, 1970.

Costello, C.G. and Selby, M.M.: Sleep patterns and reactive and endogenous depressions. *Br J Psychiatry,* 111:497, 1965.

Cutler, R.P. and Kurland, H.D.: Clinical quantification of depressive reactions. *Arch Gen Psychiatry,* 5:280, 1961.

Foulds, G.A. and Hope, K.: *Manual of the Symptom-Sign Inventory.* University of London Press, London, 1968.

Friedman, A.S., Cowitz, B., Cohen, H.W. and Granick, S.: Syndromes and themes of psychotic depression. *Arch Gen Psychiatry,* 9:504, 1963.

Gilberstadt, H. and Duker, J.: *A Handbook for Clinical and Actuarial MMPI Interpretation.* W.B. Saunders, Philadelphia, 1965.

Goodwin, F.K., Brodie, H.K.H., Murphy, D.L. and Bunney, W.E., Jr.: Administration of a peripheral decarboxylase inhibitor with l-dopa to depressed patients. *Lancet, I*:7653, 908, 1970.

Greenblatt, M., Grosser, G.H. and Wechsler, H.: A comparative study of selected anti-depressant medication and EST. *Am J Psychiatry,* 119:144, 1962.

Grinker, R.R., Sr., Miller, J., Sabshin, M., Nunn, R. and Nunnally, J.C.: *The Phenomena of Depressions.* Hoeber, New York, 1961.

Hamilton, M.: A rating scale for depression. *J Neurol Neurosurg Psychiatry,* 23:56, 1960.

Hamilton, M.: Development of a rating scale for primary depressive illness. *Br J Soc Clin Psychol,* 6:278, 1967.

Hamilton, M.: Some notes on rating scales. *The Statistician,* 18:1, 11, 1968.

Hamilton, M.: Standardised assessment and recording of depressive symptoms. *Psychiat Neurol Neurochir,* 72:201, 1969.

Hamilton, M. and White, J.M.: Clinical syndromes in depressive states. *J Ment Sci,* 105:985, 1959.

Harman, H.H.: *Modern Factor Analysis.* University of Chicago Press, Chicago, 1968.

Hobson, R.F.: Prognostic factors in electric convulsive therapy. *J Neurol Neurosurg Psychiatry,* 16:275, 1953.

Kaiser, H.F.: Formulas for component scores. *Psychometrika,* 27:83, 1962.

Kendell, R.E.: *The Classification of Depressive Illness.* Maudsley Monograph No. 18. Oxford University Press, London, 1968 (a) .

Kendell, R.E.: The problem of classification in recent developments in affective disorders. Coppen, A. and Walk, A. (Eds.) . *Br J Psychiatry, Special Publication No. 2,* 1968 (b) .

Kendell, R.E.: The classification of depressive illness: The uses and limitations of multivariate analysis. *Psychiatry Neurol Neurochir,* 72:207, 1969.

Kiloh, L.G. and Ball, J.R.B.: Depression treated with imipramine. *Br Med J,* 1:168, 1961.

Kiloh, L.G. and Garside, R.F.: The independence of neurotic depression and endogenous depression. *Br J Psychiatry,* 109:451, 1963.

Kogan, N. and Wallach, M.A.: *Risk-taking: A Study in Cognition and Personality.* New York, Holt, Rinehart and Winston, 1964.

Kraepelin, E.: *Manic-Depressive Insanity and Paranoia.* Robertson, G.M. (Eds.) . Edinburgh, E. and S. Livingstone, 1921.

Leonhard, K.: *Aufteilung der Endogenen Psychosen.* Akademie Verlag, Berlin, 1959.

Lewis, A.J.: Melancholia: A clinical survey of depressive states. *J Ment Sci,* 80:277, 1934.

Lorr, M., Klett, C.J., McNair, D.M. and Lasky, J.J.: *Inpatient Multidimensional Psychiatric Scale.* Consulting Psychologists Press, Palo Alto, 1963.

McConaghy, N., Jaffe, A.D. and Murphy, B.: The independence of neurotic and endogenous depression. *Br J Psychiatry*, 113:479, 1967.

Mapother, E.: Discussion on manic-depressive psychosis. *Br Med J*, 2:872, 1926.

Mendels, J.: Electro-convulsive therapy and depression: I. The prognostic significance of clinical factors. *Br J Psychiatry*, 111:675, 1965.

Mendels, J.: Electro-convulsive therapy and depression: II. Significance of endogenous and reactive syndromes. *Br J Psychiatry*, 111:682, 1965.

Mendels, J.: Electro-convulsive therapy and depression: III. A method for prognosis. *Br J Psychiatry*, 111:687, 1965.

Mendels, J. and Cochrane, C.: The nosology of depression: the endogenous-reactive concepts. *Am J Psychiatry* (Supp.), 124:1, 1968.

Moran, P.A.P.: The establishment of a psychiatric syndrome. *Br J Psychiatry*, 112:1165, 1966.

Mowbray, R.M.: Classification of depressive illness. Correspondence. *Br J Psychiatry*, 115:1344, 1969.

Mowbray, R.M.: The Hamilton scale for depression: A factor analysis. In press. *Psychological Medicine*.

Overall, J.E. and Gorham, D.R.: The brief psychiatric rating scale. *Psychol Rep*, 10:799, 1962.

Overall, J.E., Hollister, L.E., Pokorny, A.D., Casey, J.F. and Katz, G.: Drug therapy in depression. *Clin Pharmacol Ther*, 3:16, 1962.

Paykel, E.S., Klerman, G.L. and Prusoff, B.A.: Treatment setting and clinical depression. *Arch Gen Psychiatry*, 22:11, 1970.

Pilowsky, I., Levine, S. and Boulton, D.M.: The classification of depression by numerical taxonomy. *Br J Psychiatry*, 115:937, 1969.

Pitt, B.: "Atypical depression" following childbirth. *Br J Psychiatry*, 144:1325, 1968.

Pollitt, J.D.: Suggestions for a physiological classification of depression. *Br J Psychiatry*, 111:489, 1965.

Praag, H.M. van, Uleman, A.M. and Spitz, J.C.: The vital syndrome interview. *Psychiatry Neurol Neurochir*, 68:329, 1965.

Rose, T.J.: Reactive and endogenous depressions-response to E.C.T. *Br J Psychiatry*, 109:213, 1963.

Rosenthal, S.H. and Gudeman, J.E.: The self-pitying constellation in depression. *Br J Psychiatry*, 113:485, 1967.

Rosenthal, S.H. and Gudeman, J.E.: The endogenous depressive pattern: an empirical investigation. *Arch Gen Psychiatry*, 16:241, 1967.

Ross, T.A.: Discussion on manic-depressive psychosis. *Br Med J*, 2:877, 1926.

Rümke, H.C.: *Psychiatrie*. Amsterdam, Scheltoma, 1960.

Schwab, J.J., Bialow, M.R. and Holzer, C.E.: A comparison of two rating scales for depression. *J Clin Psychol*, 23:94, 1967.

Shepherd, M., Brooke, E.M., Cooper, J.E. and Lin, T.: An experimental approach to psychiatric diagnosis. *Acta Psychiatry Scand (Supplement 201)*, Copenhagen, Munksgaard, 1968.

Wechsler, H., Grosser, G.H. and Busfield, B.L., Jr.: The depression rating scale. *Arch Gen Psychiatry,* 9:334, 1963.

Winokur, G., Clayton, P.J. and Reich, T.: *Manic-Depressive Illness.* C.V. Mosby, St. Louis, 1969.

Wittenborn, J.R.: *Manual: Wittenborn Psychiatric Rating Scales.* Psychological Corporation, New York, 1955.

Zubin, J.: Classification of the behaviour disorders. *Ann Rev Psychol,* 18:373, 1967.

Section V

Depression in General Practice

Chapter 13

DEPRESSIVE DISORDERS IN HOSPITAL AND GENERAL PRACTICE

Timothy G. Blashki

INTRODUCTION

STUDIES in general practice have shown that depressive symptoms are a frequent and important problem. Watts (1956) in a survey of his general practice found depressive disorders amounted to 36 per cent of all new psychiatric cases seen over a ten-year period. Shepherd *et al.* (1966) administered the Cornell Medical Health Questionnaire to a large sample of surgery attenders and reported that "3.5 per cent of men and 6.5 per cent of the women at risk usually felt unhappy and depressed, and that 1 per cent of the men and 3 per cent of the women 'often wished they were dead and away from it all.'" Porter (1970) found in his general practice that one in thirteen women presented at least once over a thirty-two-month period on account of a depressive illness.

Few of the patients who present to their general practitioner with psychiatric illness are referred to psychiatric outpatient clinics and fewer still are admitted to the hospital. Watts (1956) in a survey conducted in his general practice treated 75 per cent of his cases of endogenous depression and referred only 25 per cent to consultants. Other studies in general practice (Shepherd *et al.*, 1959; Kessel, 1962) have found a referral rate of one in ten for diagnosed psychiatric disorder. Here differences in referral rate most likely reflect differing attitudes of practitioners to psychiatric referral and this has been reviewed fully by Rawnsley and Loudon (1962).

Thus, there are likely to be differences in depressive illness encountered in general practice and psychiatric hospitals. Yet, much of the current thinking on depression has been derived exclusive-

311

ly from the study of hospital patients, who constitute only a small proportion of depressed patients in the community as a whole.

The purpose of this study was to examine a group of depressed patients in the setting of general practice using a number of demographic and clinical criteria. To ensure that the group of patients was representative, attention was paid to sampling procedures. An operational definition of depression was established and a reliable means of patient assessment was chosen. Having established the characteristics of the general practice group, comparisons were then made with a similar group of depressed patients in a psychiatric hospital.

METHODOLOGY

General Practice Population

Twenty-one general practitioners were selected from the Melbourne metropolitan area so as to cover eight economic areas which had previously been delineated (Jones, 1967). Over a six-month period consecutive female patients presenting in these practices with a depressive illness were investigated.

Criteria for inclusion in the study were established beforehand. These were as follows: complaints of persistent lowering of mood with depressive symptoms, i.e. sleep and appetite disturbance, loss of interest and inability to concentrate. The depressed mood had to be apparent on mental state examination. Patients were excluded if they showed evidence of underlying psychiatric syndromes such as organic brain syndrome, schizophrenia, alcoholism, epilepsy or mental retardation, and if they had been treated by ECT in the previous three months or by antidepressants in the preceding four weeks.

The depressed patients were selected by the general practitioner and seen by the author in the practitioner's surgery the next day. A full psychiatric examination was undertaken and recorded on an item sheet based on the Institute of Psychiatry Item Sheet 4, in use at the Maudsley Hospital (Kendell, 1968). Patients were also rated on the Hamilton Scale and completed the Zung self-rating scale (see Chap. 12).

Hospital Population

The hospital population comprised the depressed female patients admitted to the University of Melbourne Professorial Psychiatric Unit over a two-year period (1967/1968). These patients had been assessed on admission on the same item sheet by a group of psychiatrically trained medical officers. A number had also been rated for severity of depression on the Hamilton and Zung self-rating scales.

RESULTS

Comparison of Socioeconomic and Demographic Variables

The hospital inpatients and general practice patients did not differ significantly with regard to the socioeconomic status of the Melbourne suburbs in which they lived (Table 13-I). However, four of the hospital patients came from country areas, whereas the general practice patients were drawn only from the metropolitan area. Only two of the eight-three general practice patients were subsequently referred to hospital.

Demographic data (Table 13-II) was available on all eight-three general practice patients and on ninety-two of the hospital patients. There was no significant difference between the two groups with regard to age, marital status, country of birth, level of education, patient's occupation or the occupation of the head of the household. However, significantly more Catholic patients were in the general practice group and significantly more Protestants in the hospital group. In both populations the majority of

TABLE 13-I

NUMBER OF PATIENTS FROM SUBURBAN AREA ACCORDING TO
SOCIOECONOMIC STATUS OF SUBURB

Socioeconomic Status of Suburb	General Practice	Hospital	P
(Jones)	n = 83	n = 92	
High[1, 2, 3]	30	29	
Middle[4, 5]	18	25	N.S.
Low[6, 7, 8]	35	36	
Country	0	4	

TABLE 13-II

POPULATION COMPARISONS ON DEMOGRAPHIC VARIABLES

Demographic Factors	General Practice n = 83	Hospital n = 92	P
Age	36.77 (S.D. 14.06)	38.35 (S.D. 16.40)	N.S.
Marital Status:			
Single	12	22	
Married	57	47	N.S.
Separated	8	7	
Divorced	1	2	
Widowed	5	14	
Country of birth:			
Australia	61	72	N.S.
Europe	14	7	
Britain	4	10	
Other	4	3	
Religion:			
Catholic	36	25	Sig.
Protestant	43	55	p .05
Other	4	12	
Education:			
Primary	10	9	
Secondary	66	73	N.S.
Tertiary	4	8	
Unknown	3	2	
Occupation of patient:			
Professional, semi-professional or managerial	3	9	N.S.
Commercial, clerical	15	9	
Trades and skilled	7	4	
Semi- and unskilled	8	9	
Home duties	47	50	
Other	3	9	
Unknown	—	2	
Occupation of head of house:			
Professional, semi-professional or managerial	12	13	N.S.
Commercial, clerical	12	10	
Trades and skilled	23	25	
Semi- and unskilled	21	25	
Other	1	2	
Unknown	14	17	

patients were married housewives of Australian extraction, who had reached a secondary level of education. The occupation of heads of the household showed some preponderance in the skilled and semiskilled tradesmen classes over the professional, managerial and clerical classes.

Comparison on Clinical Variables

Severity of Depression

Hamilton and Zung scores were available for only forty-two of the one hundred hospital inpatients. As there were no grounds for considering these cases to be unrepresentative as regards to severity of the hospital population, this data was used for comparison with the general practice group, all of whom had scores on these scales. Comparison showed the hospital group to be significantly more depressed on the Hamilton scale (p = 0.001). A similar trend was evident on the Zung self-rating scale, but did not reach statistical significance (Table 13-III).

Comparison by Discriminant Analysis

The fifty-two items relating to depression selected from the Institute of Psychiatry Item Sheet covered family history, previous personal history, history of present illness, etiology, mental state and severity of depression and are listed in Table 13-IV. However, this method had the disadvantage of not dealing sufficiently with minor disturbances of appetite, weight and sleep; while paranoid ideation and feelings of guilt were not recorded unless of delusional proportions.

Comparison between the general practice and inpatient groups was made by discriminant function analysis (see Tables 13-V, 13-VI, 13-VII and 13-VIII. The proportion of patients in each group possessing each of the fifty-seven items is given at the end of the chapter and the significance of the difference between the proportions was determined from the critical ratio. A negative critical ratio indicates that the item is shown by more of the gen-

TABLE 13-III

SEVERITY OF DEPRESSION, HAMILTON AND ZUNG RATINGS

	General Practice Population	Hospital Population	Significance
Hamilton	17.41 (5.63)	24.97 (5.88)	P 0.001
Zung	50.61 (11.1)	53.14 (9.63)	N.S.

TABLE 13-IV

CLINICAL FEATURES DISCRIMINATING GENERAL PRACTICE
FROM HOSPITAL PATIENTS

  (1) Neurotic illness in parent.
  (2) Neurotic illness in sibling.
  (3) Childhood neurotic traits.
  (4) Previous illness similar to present.
  (5) Previous hysterical symptoms.
  (6) Previous anxiety symptoms.
  (7) Previous preoccupation with bodily symptoms.
  (8) Always ailing.
As part of presenting episode:
  (9) Apathy.
  (10) Social withdrawal.
  (11) Irritability.
  (12) Anxiety.

CLINICAL FEATURES DISCRIMINATING HOSPITAL PATIENTS
FROM GENERAL PRACTICE PATIENTS

  (1) Previous (cyclical) mood variation.
  (2) Previous suicidal attempt.
  (3) Suicidal attempt before admission.
  (4) Important sexual precipitating cause.
  (5) Important occupational precipitating cause.
As part of presenting episode:
  (6) Agitation.
  (7) Delusions of guilt, self-reproach or unworthiness.
  (8) Suicidal feelings or intent.

eral practice patients and the positive sign favors the hospital group. A critical ratio of more than two is significant at the 5 per cent level for these sample sizes.

The two groups differed significantly on twenty of these items. From their histories the general practice patients had a significantly greater frequency of occurrence of neurotic illness in parents and in siblings, of a personal history of childhood neurotic traits and of anxiety and hysterical symptoms. Previous similar illness to the present, previous preoccupation with bodily symptoms and a history of always having been ailing also occurred more frequently in the general practice group. The features of the present episode which emerged more often in the general practice patients were anxiety, irritability, social withdrawal and apathy. On the other hand, the items which showed significantly more in the hospital patients were the occurrence of cyclical mood variation prior to the presenting episode, previous suicidal attempts, a suicidal attempt just prior to admission and the presence of important sexual and occupational precipitating factors. In their present episodes agitation, delusions of guilt or unworthiness, and suicidal feelings or intent appeared more frequently in the hospital patients.

For both groups of patients, the most frequent items were the following:

1. Previous illness similar to present.

TABLE 13-V

CLINICAL FACTORS SELECTED FOR COMPARISON OF POPULATION

Clinical Factors	General Practice % n = 83	Hospital % n = 100	Critical Ratio	Signif- icance
Family History:				
Affective psychoses in parent	1	3	0.86	N.S.
Neurotic illness in parent	37	13	−3.87	S.
Affective psychosis in sibling	4	0	−1.76	N.S.
Neurotic illness in sibling	27	5	−4.05	S.
Previous Personal History:				
Childhood neurotic traits	37	18	−2.95	S.
Previous illness similar to present	53	35	−2.48	S.
Previous hysterical symptoms	49	7	−5.19	S.
Previous obsessional symptoms	12	7	1.14	N.S.
Previous anxiety symptoms	69	19	−2.25	S.
Previous mood variations	20	10	3.77	S.
Previous preoccupation with bodily function	23	4	−2.80	S.
Previous suicidal attempts	11	1	2.37	S.
Always ailing	30	2	−5.38	S.
History of present illness				
Duration of symptoms				
7 days	6	2	−1.36	N.S.
7-30 days	19	12	−1.34	N.S.
1-6 months	35	28	−1.01	N.S.
6-12 months	17	15	−0.34	N.S.
12 months and over	18	30	1.91	N.S.
Onset gradual	35	34	−0.13	N.S.
Onset gradual with sudden exacerbation	40	30	−1.38	N.S.
Onset sudden	19	10	−1.76	N.S.
Suicidal attempt before present admission	1	12	3.12	S.
Etiology of present illness:				
Precipitating causes unimportant	7	4	−0.87	N.S.
Precipitating causes important				
Marital	30	36	0.85	N.S.
Occupational	2	12	2.62	N.S.
Physical handicap or illness	6	24	−0.62	N.S.
Sexual	6	21	3.10	S.
Social	31	34	0.38	N.S.

TABLE 13-V *(cont.)*

Clinical Factors	General Practice % n = 83	Hospital % n = 100	Critical Ratio	Significance P = .05
Disturbance of behavior or activity:				
Stupor/semi-stupor	0	1	0.99	N.S.
Retarded activity	17	21	0.71	N.S.
Agitated	11	36	4.27	S.
Apathetic	58	18	−6.00	S.
Social withdrawal	78	30	−7.50	S.
Compulsive acts or rituals	5	1	−1.50	N.S.
Disturbance of mood:				
Depressed	98	91	−1.98	N.S.
Manic/hypomanic	0	0	0.00	N.S.
Anxious	70	53	−2.38	S.
Rapid changes of mood	5	9	1.13	N.S.
Suspicious	12	3	−2.29	S.
Irritable	70	10	−9.99	S.
Perplexed	6	2	−1.36	N.S.
Suicidal feelings or intent	22	41	2.89	S.
Abnormality of speech:				
Mute or garrulous	2	2	−0.19	N.S.
Speech unduly rapid/slow	8	3	−1.55	N.S.
Impaired intellectual functioning psychogenic	1	2	0.43	N.S.
Obsessional fears and thoughts	4	6	0.76	N.S.
Delusions and misinterpretations:				
Delusions of guilt, self reproach unworthiness	1	16	3.84	S.
Delusions of bodily change or disorder	5	1	−1.50	N.S.
Ideas of reference	4	4	0.14	N.S.
Nihilistic delusions	1	0	−0.99	N.S.
Persecutory delusions	0	2	1.42	N.S.
Perceptual disturbances:				
Auditory hallucinations	1	0	−0.99	N.S.
Subjective sensory abnormalities (aches/pains)	4	3	−0.23	N.S.
Depersonalization, derealization	6	7	0.27	N.S.
Miscellaneous:				
Severe insomnia	22	20	−0.33	N.S.
Gross disturbance of food intake	9	8	−0.24	N.S.
Gross disturbance of weight	7	6	−0.27	N.S.

2. Duration of illness 1 to 6 months.

3. Gradual onset of illness with or without sudden exacerbation just prior to presentation.

4. Marital and social factors as important precipitants.

5. Social withdrawal.

6. Depressed mood.
7. Anxiety.
8. Suicidal feelings or intent.
9. Insomnia as part of presenting episode.

DISCUSSION

These results confirm that the picture of depressive disorder as seen in general practice differs in many aspects from that seen in hospital practice. At the outset differences on demographic variables were small. There were more Catholic patients in the general practice group and more Protestants in the hospital group. These differences may have been due to chance sampling of a disproportionate number of Catholic practices. However, it is possible that this could have arisen from differences in patient's attitudes to hospital admission. The finding that the two populations did not differ on any of the other demographic variables contrasts with that of Rickels and his co-workers (1970), who found major differences between general practice and hospital clinic populations with regard to marital state, occupation of patient, educational level and social class. The present finding that 34 of the total of 175 depressed females were single, does not substantiate Porter's comment that "single women are almost entirely spared from depressive illness and married ones are particularly at risk."

Because the groups were in effect matched on socioeconomic and demographic variables, greater weight can be placed on the major differences between them which was found in the clinical variables. The hospital patients were more severely depressed than the general practice patients. The *general practice* patients more commonly had a family and personal history of neurotic illness, a preoccupation with bodily symptoms and a history of chronic attendance of their general practitioner. Their depressive episodes were distinguished from those of the hospital group by the occurrence of apathy, anxiety, irritability and social withdrawal. On the other hand, hospital patients more commonly had a history of cyclical mood variation, previous suicidal attempt and attempted suicide just prior to their presentation. Sexual and occupational causes as precipitating factors were also more important in this group. The presenting episode was differentiated from the general practice group by the presence of agitation, delusions of guilt, self-reproach or unworthiness and suicidal intent.

Many of the above features shown by the hospital inpatients were those of severe depression, and differences between the two groups may reflect the greater likelihood of referral of more severely depressed patients to the hospital. For example, suicidal attempt or suicidal intent (items which appeared in a significantly higher proportion of hospital patients) are likely to lead to admission because of the anxiety they cause in the doctor and the need for hospital care.

There was a tendency for the two groups to conform to the traditional concepts of "neurotic" and "psychotic" depression. Thus, the general practice group was characterized by the occurrence of childhood neurotic traits, hysterical symptoms and hypochondriasis, features which have been associated with neurotic depression. The hospital group showed a previous history of cyclical mood change, delusions of guilt, self-reproach or unworthiness and suicidal intent, characteristic of "psychotic" depression. However, against this, the groups could not be distinguished on features such as family history of severe affective disorder, appetite and weight disturbance, or on the occurrence of important precipitating factors. Any further study of the question of "neurotic" versus "psychotic" depression should therefore include a general practice population to reduce bias introduced by the use of hospital patients alone.

There have been no detailed comparative studies of general practice and hospital patients with which to compare the present study. In the last twenty years a number of epidemiological studies of psychiatric disorders in general practice have been published and these have been summarized by Kessel and Shepherd 1962 but only a few have been concerned specifically with depressive disorder. Watts (1956) described depressed general practice patients seen in a solo general practice over a period of ten years and focused particularly on the occurrence of "endogenous" depression in this group. The findings of this study have been discussed earlier. Porter (1970) compared depressed patients with nondepressed patients in the one general practice and noted the high relapse rate in depression, the absence of any age group in depression being at particular risk from this disorder and the increased likelihood of depressed patients becoming dissatisfied and changing their doctor.

Rickels and his co-workers (1970) have found differences on demographic and clinical variables in depressed hospital clinic and general practice populations. In addition to the differences already mentioned between this study and the present, they found that the general practice patients were significantly more severely ill on several measures of depression, while the clinic patients were worse with regard to somatic symptomatology. This conflicts directly with the present findings. However, detailed comparison between the few studies in this area is virtually impossible, because of differing criteria used for selection of patients in the study, differences in means of patient assessment in administrative attitudes in Australia, United States and Britain to hospitalization and in resources available out of hospital for patient management.

The major criticism of the present study relates to the different methods of collecting data for the two groups. Item sheets on the hospital patients were filled in as a routine task by a rotating group of medical officers. This tended to increase error due to observer variation while decreasing individual bias. On the other hand data on the general practice patients was collected by the one observer which allowed individual bias but decreased error arising through loss in constancy.

CONCLUSION AND SUGGESTIONS FOR FURTHER STUDY

There is sufficient evidence from this study to conclude that depressive illness as seen in the hospital is not representative of depressive illness in the general population.

Many of the current notions on subclassification of depressive illness, phenomenology and natural history which have been based on hospital studies do not give a true picture of the disorder.

Only two of the eighty-three patients seen in this general practice study were admitted to hospital. Hospital populations are influenced by factors such as referring habits of doctors, administrative attitudes to hospital admission and community resources for patient management outside the hospital. This leads to a highly selected patient group being admitted to hospital, the characteristics of which reflect social factors determining admission as much as the disorder itself.

There is a need for further epidemiological research into depressive disorder as it is diagnosed and treated in general practice. Similar methods of collecting data should be used and more studies done on criteria for hospital admission in different countries.

REFERENCES

Jones, F.L.: A social ranking of Melbourne suburbs. *Aust NZ J Sociol,* 3:93, 1967.

Kendell, R.E.: *The Classification of Depressive Illness.* Oxford University Press, London, 1968.

Kessel, W.I.N.: Psychiatric morbidity in a London general practice. *Br J Soc Prev Med,* 14:16, 1960.

Kessel, W.I.N. and Shepherd, M.: Neurosis in hospital and general practice. *J Ment Sci,* 108:159, 1962.

Porter, A.M.W.: Depressive illness in a general practice. A demographic study and a controlled trial of imipramine. *Br Med J,* 1:773, 1970.

Rawnsley, K. and Loudon, J.B.: Factors influencing the referral of patients to psychiatrists by general practitioners. *Br J Prev Soc Med,* 16:174, 1962.

Rickels, K., Gordon, P.E., Jenkins, B.W., Perloff, M., Sachs, T. and Stepansky, W.: Drug treatment in depressive illness (amitriptyline and chlordiazpoxide in two neurotic populations). *Dis Nerv Syst,* 31:30, 1970.

Shepherd, M., Fisher, M., Stein, L. and Kessel, W.I.N.: Psychiatric morbidity in an urban group practice. *Proc Roy Soc Med,* 52:269, 1959.

Shepherd, M., Cooper, B., Brown, A.C. and Kalton, G.W.: *Psychiatric Illness in General Practice.* Oxford University Press, 1966.

Watts, C.A.H.: The incidence and prognosis of endogenous depression. *Br Med J,* 1:1392, 1956.

Chapter 14

A CONTROLLED TRIAL OF AN ANTIDEPRESSANT (AMITRIPTYLINE) IN GENERAL PRACTICE

TIMOTHY G. BLASHKI

INTRODUCTION

IN the previous chapter the problem of depressive symptoms in general practice was reviewed and discussed. To the individual general practitioner today the important practical questions are concerned with the benefit such patients may receive from antidepressant medication. While most antidepressants are used outside of hospital practice, only a few controlled trials in this area have been reported (Blashki *et al.*, 1971; Porter, 1970; and Rickels *et al.*, 1970).

Trials of antidepressants have been reported from hospitals and, in general, they have yielded conflicting results (Leyburn, 1967).

In a review of the conflicting reports about the efficacy of antidepressants (Davies, 1968) it was pointed out that psychiatric opinions about the value of these drugs range from the optimistic view that "antidepressants have revolutionized the treatment of depressed patients" to the cynical view that "antidepressants are only complex placebos for doctors."

Four placebo controlled trials of amitriptyline (Browne *et al.*, 1963; Garry and Leonard, 1963; Master, 1963; and Skarbeck, 1963) showed amitriptyline to be superior to an inert substance, while one study (Hollister *et al.*, 1964) comparing amitriptyline, imipramine and atropine (as a control) failed to demonstrate any advantage for the two antidepressants in reducing eight of nine measures of depression. Two comparative studies of amitriptyline (Hoenig and Visram, 1964; and Horden *et al.*, 1964) and imipramine show the former as being more effective while another such study (Hutchinson and Smedberg, 1963) favored the latter drug.

In a series of general practitioner drug trials, a number of antidepressants, minor tranquilizers and sedatives have been compared for their effectiveness in anxiety and depression in populations of depressed neurotic patients (General Practitioner Research Group, Reports 51, 53, 72, 99, 115, 127; and Wheatley, D., 1970).

Important studies from Rickels and his co-workers (Desilverio *et al.,* 1970, and Rickels *et al.,* 1968) have studied the effects of amitriptyline with fluphenazine and perphenazine together and separately. Marked differences in treatment responses were found in hospital and general practice patients, irrespective of treatment given. Hence the importance of properly conducted therapeutic trials in general practice.

There are certain practical problems in studies in this field. The general practitioner is reluctant to allow the investigator access to his patients, and the patients, usually expect only to see their private doctor. Only a good relationship between the practitioner and the main investigator can overcome these problems. Other difficulties relate to the operational definition of depression, the use of reliable measures of change, and ensuring that patients included in the final sample have taken their tablets. All these last problems are present in conventional hospital trials. The effects of patients' expectations and physician's enthusiasm can be reduced by the usual double-blind conditions.

Bias due to socioeconomic factors can be overcome by selecting patients from a number of practices. However, in one important respect the general practice trial *is* considered to differ from the hospital trial. Most hospital trials do not select patients until they have been in the hospital for a period of seven to ten days, and any patient who improves in this time is usually excluded from the trial. Such a waiting period would be clinically unreal in general practice, and it was decided that a practical trial had to start from the patient's first presentation.

PATIENTS AND METHODS

The patients studied were attending twenty-one general practitioners in Melbourne over a six-month period. The practices were deliberately selected to conform to eight socioeconomic areas of the city that have been described (Jones, F. L., 1967). In view of the reported sex differences in incidence of depression and in response to antidepressants (Hamilton, 1967) only females over fifteen years were studied (mean age 37.7).

Rigorous clinical criteria for admission to the trial were established beforehand and were discussed in detail with each of the general practitioners involved. It was agreed that a patient should have a persistent lowered mood with depressive symptoms—sleep and appetite disturbances, loss of interest and inability to concentrate and that her mental state should show depression. Other psychiatric syndromes (i.e. organic brain disorders, schizophrenia, epilepsy, alcoholism and mental retardation) had to be absent. Further, no patient was admitted to the trial if she had had electroconvulsive treatment in the previous three months or had received any antidepressant medication in the previous month. This group is largely but not completely the same group discussed in the previous chapter.

Patients were selected by the general practitioner and were asked to return to the surgery on the following day to be seen for one hour by the author, a qualified psychiatrist. The capsules were then given to the patient by her family doctor. Every effort was made to avoid biasing the circumstances of the trial away from those that would normally occur in the management of depressive illnesses in a general practice setting.

Measures of Depression and Anxiety

In addition to the clinical examination, a number of objective and subjective assessments were undertaken of depressive and anxiety symptoms.

The Hamilton Rating Scale (Hamilton, 1960) for depression was completed by the psychiatrist. This scale covers seventeen symptom groups, each of which is rated by the clinician from zero to two, or from zero to four. The sum of these ratings was used as a score for global severity of the illness.

The Zung Rating Scale (Zung, 1965)—the patient is asked to rate himself on a number of symptoms of depression. The total score gives a measure of the severity of subjective depression, and was used here to complement the objective ratings.

A Clinical Rating of the severity of the depression was made by the psychiatrist on a zero to four scale.

The Taylor Manifest Anxiety Scale (Taylor, 1953) is a true false questionnaire, completed by the patient, containing a number of symptoms of anxiety, and is a well-established measure of the degree of anxiety experienced by the patient.

A Clinical Rating of the severity of the anxiety symptoms was made by the psychiatrist on a zero to four scale.

A twenty-three-item list of side-effects was presented to the patient and she was asked to indicate any which she experienced.

These six measures were completed at the start of the trial (day 1) and after seven and twenty-eight days. At these times patients were seen in the general practitioner's surgery by the psychiatrist who also made a full clinical psychiatric assessment on each occasion. To maintain the conditions as close as possible to those of general practice, the general practitioner continued to see the patient during the trial at his usual rate, about once a week.

TREATMENTS

Amitriptyline (Laroxyl®) (25 and 50 mg), amylobarbitone (50 mg) and an inert substance were all prepared in identical orange capsules. Riboflavin (2.5 mg) was added to each capsule so that at 7 and 28 days, urine samples could be tested for riboflavin fluorescence (Jones, I., 1967) in order to detect patients who were not taking their capsules.

Every general practitioner was given a number of coded bottles each containing a four-week supply of capsules. When he admitted a patient to the trial he noted the patient's name against the code on the label and instructed her to take one capsule three times a day. The code was kept separately so that both the general practitioner and the psychiatrist were blind as regards the contents of the capsules received by any patient. When the general practitioner thought a hypnotic was needed, nitrazepan (Mogadon®) was supplied (5 to 10 mg nocte). No other drugs were prescribed during the period of the trial. General practitioners were provided with an "escape clause" so that any patient who, in their opinion, became worse, or complained of severe side-effects could be removed from the trial.

RESULTS

During the six months, eighty-two patients were admitted to the trial but two were excluded by the psychiatrist (on day 1) as being too ill for general practitioner treatment, and two failed to attend for the psychiatric interview. A further seventeen failed to complete the trial (noncompleters) and will be discussed later. Of the sixty-one patients who completed the trial, it was found that:

Eighteen had received the inert capsules.

Sixteen had received amylobarbitone (50 mg t.d.s.).

Thirteen had received amitriptyline (25 mg t.d.s.).

Fourteen had received amitriptyline (50 mg t.d.s.).

Analysis of data from the patients' records showed that no differences in composition occurred between any of the four treatment groups and the "noncompleters" with regard to marital status, number of children, education, socioeconomic background, religion and country of birth.

The differences in number in the treatment groups would ap-

TABLE 14-I

SCORES (Means and Standard Deviation) AT INITIAL AND
FOLLOW-UP ASSESSMENTS BY TREATMENT GROUP

		Initial	7 Days	28 Days
Inert Tablets	Hamilton	18.9 (4.8)	14.2 (6.2)	11.4 (9.6)
N = 18	Depression Rating ...	2.5 (0.6)	1.7 (0.9)	1.4 (1.3)
Mean Age 37.3	Zung	54.3 (9.9)	46.6 (13.3)	43.2 (15.6)
(SD) (14.0)	Taylor	30.3 (10.2)	28.7 (11.4)	25.4 (10.6)
	Anxiety Rating	1.9 (0.6)	1.6 (0.7)	1.3 (1.1)
Amylobarbitone	Hamilton	15.4 (9.9)	9.0 (6.7)	8.3 (6.0)
150 mg/day	Depression Rating ...	2.2 (0.6)	1.3 (0.9)	1.1 (0.9)
N = 16	Zung	49.9 (9.4)	44.6 (12.3)	44.3 (13.1)
Mean Age 37.1	Taylor	27.1 (10.1)	22.4 (12.1)	23.6 (13.4)
(SD) (13.3)	Anxiety Rating	1.8 (0.8)	1.0 (0.9)	0.8 (0.7)
Amitriptyline	Hamilton	17.5 (5.2)	11.2 (3.9)	6.4 (5.4)
75 mg/day	Depression Rating ...	2.3 (0.5)	1.4 (0.9)	1.1 (0.9)
N = 13	Zung	51.4 (8.4)	42.8 (12.8)	38.8 (11.4)
Mean Age 37.2	Taylor	30.3 (10.4)	27.1 (12.7)	22.6 (11.9)
(SD) (12.6)	Anxiety Rating	1.8 (0.7)	1.0 (0.9)	1.1 (0.9)
Amitriptyline	Hamilton	17.6 (4.5)	7.1 (4.7)	5.1 (4.9)
150 mg/day	Depression Rating ...	2.6 (0.5)	0.9 (0.9)	0.5 (0.7)
N = 14	Zung	50.4 (8.3)	41.9 (8.9)	34.5 (7.3)
Mean Age 35.4	Taylor	30.5 (7.9)	27.1 (12.9)	22.6 (11.9)
(SD) (12.7)	Anxiety Rating	1.9 (0.8)	1.1 (0.8)	0.3 (0.6)

pear to have arisen by chance, as no relationship was found between treatment allocated and failing to complete the trial. Of the seventeen "noncompleters" five were in fact in the inert group of four in each of the other treatment groups.

Table 14-I shows the mean scores and their standard deviations for each treatment group at the three assessments.

INITIAL RATINGS

When student's t tests were applied to the initial scores, no significant differences were found between mean ages and between mean scores on all measures for the four treatment groups, except for the patients on amylobarbitone who were rated as significantly lower on the Hamilton Scale than the group on inert treatment ($\gamma = 2.1$; $p = 0.05$). With this exception the groups were considered to be matched for age, severity of depression and anxiety at the beginning of the trial.

The initial mean Hamilton Score for the group of sixty-one patients was 17.4 (S.D. 4.9), indicating that these patients were less depressed than a group of hospital patients (mean 26.4, S.D. 5.6) selected for electroconvulsive treatment for the study described in Chapter 9. Their initial levels of anxiety (mean Taylor score of 29.5, S.D. 9.7) can be contrasted with a group of hospital patients diagnosed as suffering from primary anxiety (mean 34.8, S.D. 3.3) (Carroll *et al.*, 1970).

CHANGES IN EACH TREATMENT GROUP

Changes in the measures during the course of the trial were examined for each treatment group. The significance levels of these changes from the initial values for seven and twenty-eight days were ascertained by Student's t test and are given in Table 14-II.

Over the twenty-eight days of the trial all treatment groups showed a significant reduction in objective ratings of depression (Hamilton and depression ratings) and this change was marked in the first seven days. Subjective ratings of depression (Zung) were in the same direction and at the end of the trial significant reductions had occurred in the groups on inert medication and on the two dosage levels of amitriptyline, but not on the group receiving amylobarbitone 150 mg/day.

TABLE 14-II

SIGNIFICANCE LEVELS*

	Hamilton		Depression Rating		Zung		Anxiety Rating		Taylor	
	7	28	7	28	7	28	7	28	7	28
Inert Medication	.02	.01	.01	.01	NS	.05	NS	NS	NS	NS
Amylobarbitone 150 mg/day	.01	.001	.01	.001	NS	NS	.02	.01	NS	NS
Amitriptyline 75 mg/day	.01	.001	.01	.001	NS	.01	NS	.05	NS	NS
Amitriptyline 150 mg/day	.001	.001	.001	.001	.02	.001	.05	.001	NS	.01

Note: Significance levels (by Student's t test) of differences between initial scores and scores at 7 and 28 days by treatment groups.

TABLE 14-III

SIGNIFICANCE LEVELS (T TEST) OF DIFFERENCES BETWEEN PREPARATIONS AT SEVEN AND TWENTY-EIGHT DAYS

	Hamilton		Depression Rating		Zung		Anxiety Rating		Taylor	
	7	28	7	28	7	28	7	28	7	28
Inert versus amylobarbitone	.05	NS	NS	NS	NS	NS	.05	NS	NS	NS
Inert versus amitriptyline 75 mg/day	NS	NS	NS	NS	NS	NS	NS	NS	NS	NS
Inert versus amitriptyline 150 mg/day	.01	.05	.05	.05	NS	NS	NS	.05	NS	NS
Amylobarbitone versus amitriptyline 75 mg/day	NS	NS	NS	NS	NS	NS	NS	NS	NS	NS
Amylobarbitone versus amitriptyline 150 mg/day	NS	NS	NS	NS	NS	.05	NS	.05	NS	NS
Amitriptyline 75 mg/day versus amitriptyline 150 mg/day	.05	NS	NS	NS	NS	NS	NS	.02	NS	NS

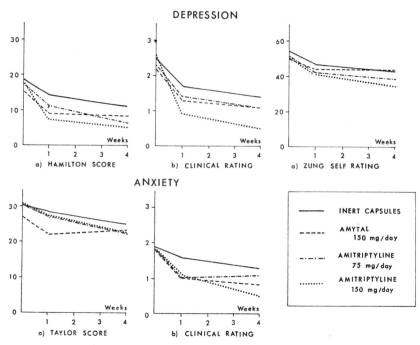

Figure 14-1. Changes in depression and anxiety scores.

Significant reductions in objective ratings occurred over the trial for all treatments except the inert. Amylobarbitone 150 mg/day and amitriptyline 150 mg/day produced significant reductions at 7 days. A significant reduction in subjectively rated anxiety (Taylor Scale) occurred only in the amitriptyline 150 mg/day group. Figure 14-1 shows changes in scores graphically. changes in scores graphically.

COMPARISONS BETWEEN TREATMENTS

Table 14-III shows the levels of statistical significance for the comparisons between treatment at seven and twenty-eight days.

At seven days on objective (Hamilton and clinical rating) the group taking amitriptyline 150 mg/day was significantly less depressed than the inert group and (on the Hamilton scale only) the amitriptyline 75 mg/day treatment group. A significant difference in Hamilton scores between the amylobarbitone and placebo groups before starting treatment was still present at seven days. There were no significant differences between treatment on the subjective (Zung) ratings of depression.

Clinical ratings of anxiety showed the amylobarbitone 150 mg/day group to be less anxious than the group on inert capsules, but this difference did not show on the subjective (Taylor) scale.

At *twenty-eight days* the amitriptyline 150 mg/day group remained significantly less depressed than the inert group on both objective ratings of depression, but not on the Zung subjective ratings. However, the amitriptyline 150 mg/day group was significantly less depressed on this scale when compared to the amylobarbitone 150 mg/day group.

Clinical objective ratings of anxiety showed the amitriptyline 150 mg/day group to be significantly less anxious than the other three treatment groups, although this difference was not significant on the Taylor's subjective rating of anxiety.

The Effect of Situational Factors

In this group of patients some considerable influence on the course of the symptoms could have been exerted by nonspecific factors such as personal or domestic problems, and treatment effects could have been obscured by the patients' reaction to changes in such problems. At the initial interview the presence of such situational problems was noted and assessed clinically as "relevant" or "not relevant" to the clinical picture. At seven and twenty-eight days subsequent changes in the situation were noted. At the end of the trial, forty-eight of the sixty-one patients were considered to have been subject to relevant situational factors. Testing by X^2 showed that no significant differences occurred between the four treatment groups in the number of cases in whom the situational factors were considered to be relevant or not, and in the numbers of cases in which the relevant situational factors were considered to have improved, remained the same or worsened.

Table 14-IV relates the presence of relevant situational factors to the assessed outcome for the group as a whole at the end of the trial. No significant differences were found by X^2 between the numbers "improved" or "not improved" showing "relevant" or

TABLE 14-IV

RELATIONSHIPS BETWEEN SITUATIONAL FACTORS AND OUTCOME

| | Situational Factors | | | |
| | Not Rele- vant | Relevant | | |
		Better	Same	Worse
Improved	7	3	27	7
Not improved	6	1	7	3
	13	4	34	10

"not relevant" situational factors, nor in the numbers in whom the situational factors improved, remained the same or worsened.

SIDE-EFFECTS

Patients recorded their experiences of side-effects on the prepared list of twenty-three items, with space provided for any other symptoms. This method was more convenient than simply noting any spontaneously reported complaints, but it involved the risk of suggesting side-effects to the patients. As all patients used these lists, no bias toward any treatment group could operate. This recording was done at the beginning of the trial as well as at the two follow-up interviews. Table 14-V summarizes the findings in terms of the average number of side-effects reported at the beginning of the trial (a), from this it is seen that a considerable number of "symptoms" were already present before the trial began. Some of these initial symptoms persisted during the course of the trial (b). "True" side-effects were taken to be those which only emerged in the course of treatment and their average numbers are given in (c). No significant differences between the treatment groups were noted in the average numbers of side-ef-

TABLE 14-V

AVERAGE NUMBERS OF SIDE-EFFECTS REPORTED

	Inert Capsules	Amylobarbitone 150 mg/day	Amitriptyline 75 mg/day	Amitriptyline 150 mg/day
(a) Present initially	5.5	6.1	6.9	6.9
(b) Persisting during trial	1.3	2.1	2.5	2.2
(c) Emerging during trial	2.6	1.8	2.6	2.6

TABLE 14-VI

FREQUENCY OF SIDE-EFFECTS BY TREATMENT

Side-Effects	Inert Capsules N=18	Amylobarbitone 150 mg/day N=16	Amitriptyline 75 mg/day N=13	Amitriptyline 150 mg/day N=14	Whole Group N=61
Shakiness of legs or arms	4	2	3	4	13
Dry mouth	—	2	5	6	13
Blurred vision	3	2	3	4	12
Fuzziness in head	4	3	—	5	12
Drowsiness	5	—	3	5	10
Restlessness	3	—	3	—	6
Headache	—	5	—	—	5
Pains in stomach	—	—	2	2	4

TABLE 14-VII

CHARACTERISTICS OF SEVENTEEN PATIENTS WHO DID NOT COMPLETE THE TRIAL

Treatment Allocated	N	Initial Ratings Hamilton	Initial Ratings Taylor	Reasons for Not Completing Side-Effects	Reasons for Not Completing Depression Worse	Reasons for Not Completing Failed to Attend
Placebo	5	17.2 (7.1)	27.0 (9.9)	4	0	1
Amylobarbitone 150 mg/day	4	19.25 (6.9)	28.5 (8.3)	0	3	1
Amitriptyline 75 mg/day	4	13.5 (1.7)	36.3 (4.2)	4	0	0
Amitriptyline 150 mg/day	4	17.0 (4.9)	34.2 (5.2)	3	0	1
Whole group	17	16.9 (5.8)	31.2 (7.7)	11	3	3

fects occurring during the trial. This analysis provides perspective and indicates the difficulty of identifying side-effects of any drug.

The eight side-effects which appeared most frequently (i.e. in more than four out of the total group) are listed in Table 14-VI in the manner in which they were presented to the patients. "Shakiness of legs or arms" and "blurred vision" were reported in all treatment groups. "Dry mouth" was more common with amitriptyline but was also reported by two patients on amylobarbitone. "Fuzziness or unclearness in the head" was reported by all groups, except for amitriptyline 75 mg/day. "Pains in the stomach" appeared to be related to amitriptyline alone. Of the less frequent side-effects (not listed) which could be attributed to amitriptyline "swelling of legs" was reported by three of the amitriptyline 75 mg/day group only; "incoordination of legs or arms" by two of the amitriptyline 150 mg/day group only; and "chest pain" by two of the amitriptyline 75 mg/day only. In fact no obvious differences were observed between the number and nature of side-effects at the two dosage levels of amitriptyline. Somewhat unexpectedly, "constipation" was not reported with either of the two levels of amitriptyline—the two patients in the whole group who reported this were taking amylobarbitone.

NONCOMPLETERS

Because they contributed a group comparable in size to the treatment groups it is important to consider in detail the seventeen patients who failed to complete the trial. As mentioned previously, failure to complete was not related to the allocated treatment, and Table 14-VII further shows that there were no significant differences between the initial scores on the Hamilton and Taylor scales on this group and the sixty-one who completed the trial.

The eleven patients who failed to complete treatment because of side-effects were distributed equally between the inert capsules and the two dosage levels of amitriptyline. For those taking amitriptyline the two major reasons given were excessive drowsiness and a general slowing down of all activities. Nausea, drowsiness, dry mouth and fuzziness of the head were reported by the patients on inert capsules. While none reported side-effects, three patients taking amylobarbitone stopped the capsules because they felt they had become more depressed.

All of these fourteen patients stopped taking the tablets within the first week of the trial. Twelve admitted spontaneously that they had stopped taking the capsules. The other two did not admit to having stopped, but urine testing showed no evidence of riboflavin fluorescence. These were the only cases in which failure to take the capsules was detected. All the sixty-one patients who completed the trial had positive riboflavin in their urine at days seven and twenty-eight.

DISCUSSION

Multiple measures of change in the patients provided a wide coverage of both observer rating and self-assessment of depression and anxiety features. There was an overall agreement in the trends yielded by these measures (see Fig. 14-1) but there were obvious differences (see Tables 14-II and 14-III) in the degree to which the changes reached statistical significance. In general the observer ratings tended to be more likely to yield significance than the self-assessments. The problem then arises of whether to place more weight on the doctor's ratings and judgments or the patient's own assessment.

The rating scale method is relatively new and so far no specific information is available on the intercorrelations between these measures and their relative sensitivity to change. On general grounds, Hamilton (1960) argues that because the patient is inexperienced or unsophisticated in filling in inventories of this kind, the reliability of assessment methods is likely to be lower than the ratings of the experienced clinician. Rickels *et al.,* 1970 emphasized the sensitivity of the Zung self-rating scale to population effects and its lack of sensitivity to drug effects when compared to objective ratings of depression. On these grounds the greater weight was placed on the objective measures.

As a group, the patients who completed the trial all showed some improvement in their depression irrespective of which treatment was allocated. It is of interest to note that after seven days, 55 per cent and at twenty-eight days 61 per cent of the patients on the inert substance were considered to have improved on clinical grounds. This represents a higher rate of improvement than occurs with inert tablets in psychiatric outpatients and inpatients.

Against this placebo response, only amitriptyline 150 mg/day is capable of reflecting a consistent advantage on the objective measures and assessments of depression. This superiority appears at one week and four weeks after treatment.

The effects of amitriptyline 25 mg t.d.s., amytal and inert capsules did not appear to be capable of being differentiated with any degree of consistency. Thus the effectiveness of amitriptyline would appear to be at the higher dosage levels preferred in hospital patients. Many general practitioners use tricyclic antidepressants at dosage levels of 75 mg/day because they are concerned about possible side-effects. This blind study indicates that there is no evidence that the effective dosage of 150 mg of amitriptyline/day either produced more side-effects or caused more patients to stop their treatment because of side-effects than 75 mg/day.

In Porter's (1970) placebo controlled study of imipramine in general practice, the dosage of imipramine was changed from 75 to 150 mg/day in the course of a three-week trial. No differences between imipramine and placebo were demonstrated leading to the conclusion that depression in general practice may be effectively treated with support and a placebo. The findings of the present study would suggest that at the level of 150 mg/day, amitriptyline has effects over and above the placebo effect. Rickels *et al.*, 1970 found that amitriptyline at a dosage of 100 mg/day was superior to placebo over a four-week period.

Comparative trials of imipramine and amitriptyline have produced conflicting results. The different results which have been reported are most likely due to differences in the patients selected for the trials, to lack of uniformity in the dosage and length of administration of the antidepressants as well as to differences in the methods used to assess changes in the patient's condition.

The effects of the medications on anxiety symptoms are of interest. All treatments, except the inert substance, produced a significant reduction in anxiety scores, which paralleled the reduction in depressive scores. After twenty-eight days, amitriptyline 150 mg/day was significantly better than the other treatments. Amylobarbitone was superior to the inert tablets at seven days in reducing anxiety scores, but this did not persist to twenty-eight days, when amylobarbitone, inert treatment and amitriptyline 75 mg/day could not be separated. The advantages of amitriptyline 150 mg over amylobarbitone 150 mg/day could not be demonstrated to a statistically significant degree. This raises the question of whether "sedative" or "antidepressant properties" are being measured. In general the tendency was for amylobarbitone 150 mg/day to achieve its improvement, in the first seven days only, whereas improvement with amitriptyline 150 mg/day continued over the period of the trial. This continued improvement may be consistent with so called antidepressant effects. However analysis of the Hamilton ratings in terms of Hamilton's depression and anxiety factors showed that while both amylobarbitone 150 mg/day and amitriptyline 150 mg/day produced improvement on these two factors, the improvement with amitriptyline was significantly greater. A more specific study would be required to test whether antidepressant and sedative effects could be separated and would require variation in the dosage of amylobarbitone administered.

The group of patients who did not complete the trial could not be identified on the basis of their background data or on the measures made at the beginning of the trial. The proportion of "noncompleters" to those admitted to the trial agrees with that found in Porter's study (19/93). However, this finding that fourteen of these nineteen were on the active drug, imipramine, was not confirmed in the present study as neither the active treatment nor its dosage level affected the members who stopped taking their capsules. The size of this group is sufficient to justify further intensive study of these patients.

CONCLUSIONS AND SUGGESTIONS FOR FURTHER STUDY

The practical conclusions from this trial of the effects of amitriptyline in a group of depressed women being treated in general practice are the following:

1. A considerable placebo effect occurs.
2. No improvement over placebo was found with 75 mg amitriptyline or 150 mg amylobarbitone/day.
3. 150 mg. of amitriptyline/day was superior to placebo in relieving anxiety and depressive symptoms.

4. Depressed patients who stop medication complaining of side-effects do not necessarily do so because these are pharmacologically induced; these patients need further study.
5. Finally, further trials in the general practice field need to be carried out.

ACKNOWLEDGMENTS

I would like to thank the Research Committee of the Victorian Branch of the Australian College of General Practitioners for their cooperation and help. I would especially like to thank the individual general practitioners: Drs. D. Brodie, D. Buchanan, T. Connors, J. Downes, J. Egan, C. Gutch, L. Hartman, D. Kaplan, G. Miles, M. Nissen, K. Owen, E. Phillips, J. Riddell, J. Sanders, T. Springer, J. Starr, D. Stewart, H. Sutcliffe, E. Thurin, T. Wawryke and R. Williams.

REFERENCES

Blashki, T.G., Mowbray, R. and Davies, B.: A controlled trial of an anti-depressant (amitriptyline) in general practice. *Br Med J*, 1:133, 1971.

Browne, M.W., Kreiger, L.C. and Kazamia, N.G.: A clinical trial of amitriptyline in depressive patients. *Br J Psychiatry*, 109:692, 1963.

Carroll, B.J., Mowbray, R.M. and Davies, B.: Sequential comparison of l-tryptophan with E.C.T. in severe depression. *Lancet*, 1:967, 1970.

Davies, B.: Problems in the evaluation of anti-depressant drugs. *Aust NZ J Psychiatry*, 2:194, 1968.

Desilverio, R.V., Rickels, L., Weise, C., Clark, E.L. and Hutchinson, J.: Perphenazine-amitriptyline in neurotic depressed outpatients. A controlled collaborative study. *Am J Psychiatry*, 127:3, 1970.

Garry, J.W. and Leonard, T.J.: Trial of amitriptyline in chronic depression. *Br J Psychiatry*, 109:54, 1963.

General Practitioners Research Group—Report No. 51: Dexamphetamine compared with an inactive placebo in depression. *The Practitioner*, 192:151, 1964.

General Practitioners Research Group—Report No. 53: A dexamphetamine-barbiturate combination in anxiety-depressive states. *The Practitioner*, 192:275, 1964.

General Practitioners Research Group—Report No. 72: A new anti-depressant drug. *The Practitioner*, 194:546, 1965.

General Practitioners Research Group—Report No. 99: Two new psychotropic drugs. *The Practitioner*, 198:135, 1967.

General Practitioners Research Group—Report No. 115: Combined therapy in neurotic depression. *The Practitioner*, 199:814, 1967.

General Practitioners Research Group—Report No. 127: Protriptyline in depression. *The Practitioner*, 201:506, 1968.

Hamilton, M.: A rating scale for depression. *J Neurol Neurosurg Psychiatry*, 23:56, 1960.

Hamilton, M.: Matching the drugs with the patients in depression. *Drugs and the Mind*. Univ. of Otago, 80, 1967.

Hoenig, J., Visram, S.: Amitriptyline versus imipramine in depressive psychosis. *Br J Psychiatry*, 110:840, 1964.

Hollister, L.E., Overall, J.E., Johnson, M., Pennington, V.V., Katz, G. and Shelton, J.: Controlled comparison of amitriptyline, imipramine and placebo in hospitalized depressed patients. *J Nerv Ment Dis*, 139:370, 1964.

Hordern, A., Burt, C.G., Gordon, W.F. and Holt, N.F.: Amitriptyline in depressive states—six months treatment results. *Br J Psychiatry*, 110:641, 1964.

Hutchinson, J.R. and Smedberg, D.: Treatment of depression: A comparative study of E.C.T. and 6 drugs. *Br J Psychiatry*, 109:536, 1963.

Jones, I.: Riboflavine as an indication of drug taking behaviour. *Med J Aust*, 1:202, 1967.

Jones, F.L.: A social ranking of Melbourne suburbs. *Aust NZ J Sociol*, 3:93, 1967.

Leyburn, P.: A critical look at anti-depressant drug trials. *Lancet*, 2:1135, 1967.

Master, R.S.: Amitriptyline in depressive states—a controlled trial in India. *Br J Psychiatry*, 109:826, 1963.

Porter, A.M.W.: Depressive illness in general practice: A demographic study and a controlled trial of imipramine. *Br Med J*, 1:773, 1970.

Rickels, K., Jenkins, B.W. and Zomostein, B.: Pharmacotherapy in neurotic depression: Differential population responses. *J Nerv Ment Dis*, 145:475, 1968.

Rickels, K., Gordon, P., Jenkins, B.W., Perloff, M., Sachs, T. and Stepansky, W.: Drug treatment in depressive illness: Amitriptyline and chlordiazepoxide in two neurotic populations. *Dis Nerv Syst*, 31:30, 1970.

Skarbek, A.: A trial of amitriptyline in chronic depression. *Dis Nerv Syst*, 24:115, 1963.

Taylor, J.A.: A personality scale of manifest anxiety. *J Abnorm Soc Psychol*, 48:2-285, 1953.

Wheatley, D.: Comparative trial of new monoamine-oxidase inhibitor in depression. *Br J Psychiatry*, 117:573, 1970.

Wheatley, D.: Amphetamines in general practice: Their use in depression and anxiety. *Seminars in Psychiatry*, 1:163, 1969.

Wheatley, D.: A comparative trial of imipramine and phenobarbital in depressed patients seen in general practice. *J Nerv Ment Dis*, 145:542, 1967.

Zung, W.W.K.: A self-rating depression scale. *Arch Gen Psychiatry*, 12:63, 1965.

Appendix

NOTES ON MULTIVARIATE ANALYSIS

Robert M. Mowbray

THESE notes are intended to provide the general reader with a simple account of the relatively sophisticated statistical techniques of multivariate analysis which have been used in studying the phenomena of depression (see Chap. 12).

Multivariate analysis is a general term which refers to statistical methods whereby the effects of several variables in a collection of data can be analyzed simultaneously. The techniques have been known for some time, but as they require a considerable amount of computation their applications were restricted until computer facilities became readily available. They have been used in biological and psychological research and are beginning to be applied in medical research. In these notes particular reference is made to the techniques which have been used in psychiatric studies of depression:

    1. Factor analysis.

    2. Discriminant function analysis.

In general, these methods have different uses and applications to the problem of diagnostic classification. Factor analysis is capable of revealing a *new* basis for classification in a collection of data. Discriminant function analysis starts with a *given* basis for classification and tests how successfully a series of observations can discriminate between the categories established from this classification.

They can be regarded as complementary approaches but, because of the difficulties described in Chapter 12 when they were used as alternative methods, it is best to consider them as separate approaches.

FACTOR ANALYSIS

Factor analysis was designed to deal with a large number of observations or measures made on a given population of subjects. It simplifies the information contained in the data by examining

340

all the possible relationships that can exist between the original measures and then resolves these relationships into patterns or factors. For example, the complex interrelationships between some twenty to thirty measures undertaken on hundreds of subjects may be reduced to four or five or even to one single explanatory factor.

From the original data (in numerical form) the relationships between the measures are expressed as correlation coefficients. Correlation coefficients are calculated for each measure with every other measure to produce a *table of intercorrelations*. Factor-patterns are detected and displayed from this table.

As the technique of correlation is basic to factor analysis an explanation of the nature of the correlation coefficient will assist in understanding the method.

Correlation Coefficient

The correlation coefficient is a numerical expression of a mutual relationship which exists between two sets of measures (say A and B) which have been obtained from the same group of subjects. It is expressed in the notation rAB and can have a value ranging from $+1$ to -1, including zero.

The value $rAB = +1$ indicates perfect positive correlation and would arise when a complete and direct relationship existed between the two measures. It would indicate that the subject with the highest score on measure A also had the highest score on measure B, and the subject with the lowest score on A would have the lowest score on B. For all the other subjects the order of their scores from high to low on A would correspond exactly to the order of their scores on B.

The value $rAB = -1$ indicates also a perfect but negative correlation and would arise when a complete inverse relationship existed between the two measures. The subject with the highest score on A would have the lowest score on B. The lowest score on A would be given by the subject with the highest score on B. The order of scores for the other subjects on A would be the inverse of the order on B.

The value $rAB = 0$ indicates that absolutely no relationship occurs between the order of scores on A and B.

These particular values are unlikely to be found in practice, but they illustrate the extremes of the situations portrayed by the correlation coefficient. The correlation coefficient can be regarded as indicating the extent to which any individual subject's score on measure B can be predicted from his score on measure A. Given $rAB = +1$, the perfect positive relationship means that a completely accurate prediction can be made from a high score on A to a high score on B and from a low score on A to a low score on B. The value $rAB = -1$ again allows completely accurate prediction, but in an inverse manner from a high score on A to a low score on B and vice versa. When $rAB = 0$, no prediction at all can be made from one set of scores to the other.

A more realistic value for the correlation coefficient between two sets of measures used in clinical research would be $rAB = +0.6$. The correlation is positive but less than absolute, so the prediction between the two measures will be less than perfect. Further, the relationship between the two measures may simply have occurred by chance. The statistical significance of the correlation coefficient depends upon the number of subjects used and in this instance $rAB = +0.6$ obtained from measures undertaken on ten subjects would not reach statistical significance. If one hundred subjects had been used it would be statistically significant and could be interpreted as a trend for scores on measure A to be of a similar order as scores on B. A value of $rAB = -0.6$, derived from sufficient observations to be statistically significant, would indicate a trend to an inverse relationship.

The correlation coefficient portrays a relationship that exists between two variables, *but it in no way indicates that the relationship is causal.* For example, a positive and significant correlation could arise between measures of shoe size and scores on a reading test taken on all children attending a particular school. The causal relationship is patently absurd and the correlation between these two measures arises because both are dependent upon a *common factor,* age of the child.

This idea of mutual dependence upon a common factor can be used to illustrate the more complex situation contained in the intercorrelations between several variables, for which factor analysis is appropriate.

Intercorrelation

Three scores, on measures P, Q, and R taken from the same group of subjects have been correlated, each with the other, to give the values as shown in Table A-I.

This table gives the correlation coefficients calculated from the three possible combinations of P with Q, P with R, and Q with R. The diagonal values of +1.00 are the ideal values which would arise if the scores on P, Q and R were correlated with themselves.

Some inferences can be drawn from inspection of this table. The correlation coefficients all have positive values and each is expressing a trend towards direct relationship. As above, the correlation coefficient between P and Q arises because both measures are dependent upon a common factor. P and R are similarly dependent upon a common factor and Q and R are dependent upon a common factor. If the interrelationships between the three measures are each determined by a mutual factor, this factor must be common to all three measures. Thus, reasoning from the table of intercorrelations has provided some new information about the measures, i.e. that their relationships are determined by some factor which they all have in common. They are all measures of the same thing.

It may be possible to guess what factor underlies the three measures, but if its nature is not obvious further reasoning is required to identify it. The intercorrelation table shows the highest correlation between P and Q and the lowest between Q and R. It can then be argued that P must be measuring more of this unknown factor than R because of the differences which occur when both are related to Q. By similar reasoning Q must be mea-

TABLE A-1

INTERCORRELATIONS

	P	Q	R
P	+1.00	+0.56	+0.48
Q		+1.00	+0.42
R			+1.00

suring more of this factor than R, but less than P. The different amounts to which each measure reflects the common factor may be helpful in identifying its nature.

Principles of Factor Analysis

Reasoning by inspection is difficult even from a small number of variables. With large numbers of variables the table of inter-correlations will extend beyond the limits of reasoning, particularly if it contains some negative coefficients and some approximating zero.

Factor analysis involves the same kind of approach to the table of intercorrelations but uses statistical inference. It first of all detects the existence of the factor, calculates how much of the factor is being measured by all the intercorrelations, i.e. the total *loading*, and then apportions to each individual measure the amount to which it measures the factor, i.e. the loading or *factor saturation* of the variable. The table of loadings for the three variables considered above could appear as follows.

TABLE A-II

Variable	Factor Saturation
P	0.8
Q	0.7
R	0.6

The relative order of magnitude of the factor saturations of these variables agrees with that inferred from their intercorrelations—P, the highest saturation, measuring the factor to the greatest extent and R, the lowest saturation, to the least extent.

The values of these particular factor saturations illustrate the basic manner in which the original correlation coefficients provide information about their common factor. The correlation cofficient between two variables contains the product of their separate loadings on their common factor. Thus, $rPQ = +0.56$ is the product of the loading of $+0.8$ on P and $+0.7$ on Q. The loading of $+0.6$ on R multiplied by the loading of $+0.7$ on Q produces $rRQ = +0.42$. Factor analysis determines the loadings of a variable on a given factor by taking into account all the correlations of this variable with every other variable.

The issues so far are simple and have covered the situation in which one common factor is sufficient to explain the intercorrelations. The products of the factor saturations given above are exactly equal to the values of the correlation coefficients. This means that the relationships between the variables is fully accounted for simply on the basis of their saturation with one factor and no other factor need be postulated.

A more likely situation rises when more than one factor operates. In this case the products of the saturations on the first factor are not sufficient to account fully for the values in the table of intercorrelations. Factor analysis goes on to seek out the further factor necessary to explain the correlations.

Suppose the following table of intercorrelations had appeared

TABLE A-III
INTERCORRELATIONS

	P	Q	R
P	+1.00	+0.75	+0.84
Q		+1.00	+0.65
R			+1.00

(Table A-III) and further, suppose that, as before, the saturations on the first factor had been calculated (Table A-IV).

TABLE A-IV

Variable	Saturation (Factor I)
P	0.8
Q	0.7
R	0.6

The amount of correlation between the variables determined by their dependence on this particular factor can be calculated by multiplying the loadings (Table A-V).

TABLE A-V
INTERCORRELATIONS ACCOUNTED FOR BY FIRST FACTOR

	P	Q	R
P		+0.56	+0.48
Q			+0.42

These can be removed by subtracting from the observed values to yield a *table of residuals* (Table A-VI).

TABLE A-VI

TABLE OF RESIDUALS

	P	Q	R
P		+0.19	+0.36
Q			+0.23

The original procedure can be repeated by determining the total loading on a second factor in the table of residuals and then apportioning the loadings to each variable. This is displayed as factor saturations of the variables on the second factor and will yield a different order of magnitude for the variables than the first factor, e.g. R may now appear to have the highest saturation. If the second factor does not account for the values in the table of residuals, a further set of residuals can be derived and a third factor analyzed. This process can be repeated until the residual values are too small to yield reliable information. As each factor is calculated, an estimate is made of the amount of the total variance for which it accounts. This indicates the relative strengths of the factors and can be used to fix the point at which to stop further analysis.

The factor saturations of variables may be positive or negative. If the pattern is such that all the variables are positively saturated the factor is termed *general* and indicates that there is one underlying characteristic that is being measured by all the variables. If some variables have positive and some negative saturations the factor is *bipolar* and suggests that the variables can be grouped in clusters.

A number of refinements of the technique may be required to bring out the factors clearly. For example, to correct for negative values in the table of intercorrelations the technique of *rotating the axes* may be applied. The most negative correlation coefficient is given the value of zero, and all other values are corrected proportionally. The term arises because the axes of a graph of the distribution of the intercorrelations can be rotated until the most negative value reaches zero. The amount of rotation needed to reach this point is the correction applied to all other values.

Factor analysis can be conceived as a process of refining the original data. The relationships between the variables are resolved into components or factors, and the extent to which each variable is a measure of each factor is revealed. The investigator is thus informed of new relationships within his data. However, factor analysis does not yield this new information automatically. In using the technique some skill is required in identifying the factors and in interpreting their significance.

A factor may be discarded by an investigator because it does not conform to any known manner of classification. Another investigator might feel that such a factor is valuable enough to warrant further investigation in order to determine its significance as a possible new method of classification. The danger to be avoided is that a factor may be spurious as it arose from errors or tolerances in the original data. In general, the more unreliable the data, the more likely is the danger of extracting false factors.

The usual source of unreliability is individual variation in the measures and the convention is to dissipate this unreliability by using large numbers of subjects. Large sample sizes to the statistician are of the order of several hundreds. However, it is difficult to achieve these numbers in clinical research and the clinician's large sample is usually less than one hundred. Many of the published factor analytic studies of depression appear to fall short of the statistician's requirements for numbers.

DISCRIMINANT FUNCTION ANALYSIS

A test of a given classification can be made by undertaking a series of observations on subjects or patients already allocated in appropriate categories. The degree to which each observation discriminates between the categories can then be ascertained. Knowing the discriminatory powers of these observations, either individually or collectively, will permit an assessment of whether the original categories can be validly maintained.

The discriminatory powers of the observations are tested directly, and the validity of the classification only indirectly. A lack of discriminatory power in the observations may arise because the observations themselves were invalid and not the classification. In general this error is overcome by ensuring that a wide range of observations is undertaken.

Example

Assume that one hundred patients have been assigned in such a way that there are fifty in each of two categories R and E (say *Reactive* or *Endogenous Depression* in this context). For each patient five characteristics are observed (e.g. positive family history of depression, responsiveness to environmental change, diurnal variation in mood, early waking, delusions of guilt) and simply recorded as present or absent.*

Table A-VII gives some illustrative findings for the number of patients in each group in whom the characteristics I-V were recorded as present. The significance of the first three characteristics in this table is obvious from inspection. Characteristic 1 appears in all the R patients and in none of the E patients. The position is reversed for characteristic 2. In these cases, simply knowing whether or not any one of the one hundred patients showed the characteristic would be sufficient to classify him accurately in R or in E. These items have each the maximum power of discrimination between R and E.

Characteristic 3 appears in half of the R patients and half of the E patients. In this case the knowledge that a patient has this characteristic is of no help at all in allocating him to a category. This item has no discriminatory power at all.

The data for the remaining two characteristics are more difficult to interpret by inspection. More patients in R (30/50) show characteristic 4 than patients in E (22/50). Fewer in R (18/50) show characteristic 5 than those in category E (35/50). In these cases all that can be said is that a patient showing the characteristic is more likely to be in one group than another.

---

* The simple *present/absent*, or *yes/no* method is a convenient way of recording clinical observations, but it has drawbacks. The observer may find it difficult to be unequivocal and, in practice, care must be taken to ensure that a *no* response means that the characteristic was definitely not present, and *not* that the information was not sought or was not available.

TABLE A-VII

Characteristic	Category R N = 50	Category E N = 50
1	50	0
2	0	50
3	25	25
4	30	22
5	18	35

Statistical procedures can provide a more precise estimate of this degree of likelihood. The convention is that the numbers which actually appear in each group are compared with the numbers that would be expected simply on the basis of chance. In this case a chi-squared test of association could be applied to the data for characteristics 4 and 5 and would show that the figures for characteristic 4 were not significantly different from those that would appear on the basis of chance. For characteristic 5 the figures are significantly different from chance expectation.

For discriminant function analysis there are advantages in using an alternative statistical procedure, *viz.* a test of the significance of the difference between two proportions. This is similar to the well-known "student's t test" of the significance a difference between means and produces a critical ratio (C.R.) for which levels of statistical significance can be ascertained. The ratio includes the actual difference between the proportions and if all the tests are done in the same manner, the positive or negative sign will provide an indication of which category has the greater frequency. Thus if the proportion in category R is subtracted from that in E, characteristic 4 will have a positive sign and characteristic 5 will have a negative sign.

The value of the critical ratio, independent of its sign, indicates whether or not the difference between the two portions reaches a required level of statistical significance, and in Chapter 13 it was used in this manner to indicate which clinical features discriminated between depressed patients in hospital and in general practice. However, the value of the critical ratio itself can be used as a weight and when used with its positive sign it can indicate by how much and in what direction an item is loaded.

TABLE A-VIII

Characteristic	Weight
1	+10
2	−10
3	0
4	+ 1.7
5	− 3.8

Using this method, and keying the positive sign to R, the original data, in Table A-VIII can be transformed to the following weights, using 10 as the maximum value.

This table confirms the interpretation of the original data that items 1 and 2 show maximum discrimination, item 3 has no discriminatory power at all. Item 4 shows some discrimination, but not as much as item 5.

By selecting items which discriminate significantly between the categories, a battery of observations can be built up to provide an overall diagnostic index for a patient. Each time the observation is recorded its weight is applied and the final index can be the simple sum of all the weights. The method of discriminant function analysis was used in this way in Chapter 11 to produce diagnostic scores for patients. These scores were applied erroneously as a means of detecting differences between neurotic and endogenous forms of depression.

REFERENCES

Adcock, C.J.: *Factor Analysis for Non-Mathematicians.* University of Melbourne Press, Melbourne, 1948.

Harman, H.H.: *Modern Factor Analysis.* University of Chicago Press, Chicago, 1968.

INDEX